Sweet Charlie, Dike, Cazzie, and Bobby Joe

High School Basketball in Illinois

Taylor H. A. Bell

University of Illinois Press

Urbana and Chicago

Library of Congress Cataloging-in-Publication Data
Bell, Taylor H. A., 1940–
Sweet Charlie, Dike, Cazzie, and Bobby Joe :
high school basketball in Illinois / Taylor H.A. Bell.
p. cm.
Includes bibliographical references and index.
ISBN 0-252-02948-8 (cl. : alk. paper)
ISBN 0-252-07199-9 (pbk. : alk. paper)
1. Basketball—Illinois—History. 2. School sports—
Illinois—History. 3. Basketball players—Illinois.
4. Racism in sports—Illinois—History. I. Title.
GV885.72.I3B45   2004
796.323'09773—dc22   2004002535

Contents

Chapter 5: The 1980s

Chapter 6: The 1990s

Photos follow pages 64, 124, and 180

The Bench

My wife Gail would rather pass up a shopping trip to Sak's than miss our annual four-day safari to the Elite Eight finals of the boys Class AA basketball tournament in March. In fact, she was the inspiration for this book.

"You've spent so many years [more than forty] covering high school sports," she said. "Why not write a book recalling your fondest memories, the people you met, the great games, the teams, the coaches, the players? Has it ever been done before?"

The longtime Chicago sportswriter Jim Enright authored *March Madness* in 1977. But it was a year-by-year compilation of state tournament records and box scores, interviews with a handful of former players and coaches, and stories about some of the greatest teams in state history.

Bob Williams, a longtime sportswriter for the *Indianapolis Star*, wrote *Hoosier Hysteria* in 1982, a thoroughly compelling, comprehensive, and well-researched overview of the most celebrated players, teams, and coaches in the glorious history of high school basketball in Indiana.

Illinois, I felt, deserved no less. As in Indiana, basketball is king in Illinois. Football boasts a proud tradition, especially in the old Chicago Catholic League, but the sport doesn't trigger emotions as basketball has in Downstate communities since the 1930s.

After all, before there was Milan, the small Indiana hamlet that won the 1954 state championship and was the impetus for the motion picture *Hoosiers,* there was Hebron, which in 1952 became the smallest school ever to win a state title in Illinois. And before there was Oscar Robertson, there was Dike Eddleman, as legendary a figure as there ever was.

Unfortunately, Eddleman died a few months before I began my research. I also regret not having an opportunity to interview Nate Middleton, Dolph Stanley, Ernie Kivisto, Jake Fendley, Paxton Lumpkin, Dawson Hawkins, John Thiel, Wes Mason, Tom Millikin, Glenn Whittenberg, and Frank Lollino.

What a wonderful history they helped to write. I hope I've done them justice.

Sweet Charlie, Dike, Cazzie, and Bobby Joe

Pregame Warm-Up

Shelby Foote, the distinguished author and historian who made the Civil War must-reading for a generation that didn't know Grant from Lee, once said: "you don't know where you are going until you know where you have been." He was referring to how the conflict of 1861–65 defined the American character and set the tone for life as we know it.

The former basketball coach Larry Hawkins, an educator who founded the Institute for Athletics and Education at the University of Chicago, once said: "It is important to have a black history to be sure that kids realize they are standing on the shoulders of some people who stood on the shoulders of others, that they didn't start by themselves." According to Hawkins, very few kids understand the historical significance of the people who built the game of basketball. "They need to know the ghosts," he said.

Hawkins was referring to the evolution of the game from the 1940s and 1950s to the twenty-first century, from an era when African Americans weren't permitted to participate in the state championship series and were treated with as much disrespect and hatred in Johnston City and Pekin as they were in Birmingham and Oxford, to a time when they dominate the game.

While researching this book, traveling from Cairo to Moline and Quincy to Champaign and interviewing hundreds of former coaches and players who wrote unforgettable chapters in the history of high school basketball in Illinois from the 1940s through the 1990s, one topic continued to surface that had an impact on one and all: race.

I wasn't looking for a controversial issue at the outset. Oh, I knew it was there. I had planned to do a story on the segregated schools in southern Illinois in the 1940s, the old conference of black schools that paved the way for a fully integrated state tournament in the 1950s. But the more I traveled, the more people I talked to, and the more stories I heard. Race was an issue everywhere, from Mounds City to Rockford, from Centralia to Lawndale, from Mount Vernon to Woodlawn, from Champaign to La Grange.

Some people shrugged it off, like a foul in the first quarter. Others preferred to talk about X's and O's rather than black and white. But the subject can't be ignored. Even today, a restaurant in a prominent southern Illinois community refuses to serve African Americans. The issue is treated as "accepted segregation" by people in the community, as it was in the 1940s and 1950s.

While blacks acknowledged that there were places they couldn't go, they understood that they were welcome on the basketball court. The game brought everyone together. It was a common denominator that took them off the streets and into the gyms. For a few exciting hours, they were cheered and booed as they sweated and competed, all for the love of a game.

A history of high school basketball in Illinois cannot be written without reference to race. That the black man has played a significant role in the evolution of the game is obvious, but how he came to play a part is no less fascinating.

In many towns, ignorance and arrogance fueled racism. On the basketball floor, however, it didn't seem to matter. If you were good enough, black or white, rich or poor, you had an opportunity to play. Coaches, pressured to win, understood that their best players had to be on the court, regardless of color or religion, or they'd risk losing their jobs.

Today we are familiar with Cazzie Russell, Mo Cheeks, Isiah Thomas, Doc Rivers, Rickey Green, Kevin Garnett, Eddie Johnson, Mark Aguirre, Michael Finley, Hersey Hawkins, Tim Hardaway, Quentin Richardson, Eddy Curry, Darius Miles, and other African Americans from Illinois who became headliners in the NBA. But where would they be without the pioneers who came before them, the ones who broke down racial barriers in the 1940s and 1950s, such as Gene Cross, Sweetwater Clifton, Art Hicks, Nate Middleton, Robert Owens, Chico Vaughn, Preacher McBride, Jim Stokes, Willis Powell, Jesse Clements, Walt Moore, Al Avant, Bobby Joe Mason, Sweet Charlie Brown, and Ivan Jefferson?

This book is about them as much as it is about the great teams, coaches, and players who have made Friday and Saturday nights in Illinois a social happening for decades.

In the 1950s, when high school basketball in Illinois was forever changed, Bobby Joe Mason and Sweet Charlie Brown emerged as legendary figures who made an enormous impact and left big footprints for generations to follow. They met when Mason went to Chicago to visit a mutual friend. They played against each other in college. Mason said that Brown was the first player who ever stole the ball from him. In an era before ESPN's SportsCenter, *USA Today*, recruiting web sites, Nike, and Adidas, they built sterling reputations in their communities.

"Charlie Brown was the first person I ever saw who could shoot from half-court," Mason said. "When he made the first one, I said it was luck. When he made the second one, I said maybe he might know what he is doing. When he made the third one, I knew he knew what he was doing."

Brown had great respect for Mason, too. They played against each other in college when Mason was at Bradley and Brown was at Seattle. "Bobby Joe was the man," Brown said. "He taught me and everyone at Seattle [including Elgin Baylor] a move. He'd get a rebound, put the ball behind his back and lay it up. His body language said he was going one way and he went the other way. We would say: 'We are going to put a Bobby Joe on you.' He was as talented as anyone I ever saw."

Mason was an icon in Centralia and southern Illinois in the 1950s, as Dike Eddleman had been in the 1940s. Pinckneyville coach Duster Thomas said that Mason was the best player he ever saw. Herb Williams, a Centralia star in the 1960s, said that Mason "was the best player I ever saw, before I saw Earl Monroe and Magic Johnson."

Brown and Paxton Lumpkin starred at Chicago Du Sable, which changed the face of the game with its fast-breaking, pressing, and hot-dogging style in 1953–54. Sweet Charlie astounded opponents and spectators with his pinpoint shooting from the twilight zone, Lumpkin with his flashy ballhandling.

In the 1940s and 1950s, racism was a way of life. In Centralia, no one made an issue of it. Everyone stayed in their place. Roland Burris, Mason's classmate and later the attorney general of Illinois, protested when blacks weren't permitted to swim in the community pool. Town officials finally relented and opened it up. "There was an accepted rule—they didn't say it—but you knew you couldn't go to certain places or you wouldn't be treated well," Mason said. "Being black, you could feel things. You could look at someone's face and see a friendly or unfriendly atmosphere."

Mason attended an all-black elementary school that was located eight blocks from his home on Centralia's South Side; he couldn't attend an all-white elementary school that was three blocks from his home. He recalls his classmate Billy Norwood, who later became the first black pilot for United Airlines, being expelled from school for one year for dating a white girl. Later, he was allowed to return to school and graduate.

Brown discovered racism in 1953, when Chicago Du Sable became the first all-black team to qualify for the state finals. Charlie and some teammates went to a pool hall in Champaign. "Nobody would let us have a cue stick," he recalled.

That wasn't all. If it hadn't been for Du Sable's white principal, Evelyn Carlson, the team wouldn't have been given rooms at a local motel. At restaurants, she had to go in, get the food, and bring it back to the bus for the players to eat.

"I looked at it as, if guys around me accepted it, I did," Brown said. "I didn't want to deal with it. If I went somewhere they didn't want me to eat, I didn't want to be there if I heard they didn't seat black people.

"The experience taught me how to deal with what life is all about, to deal with realities in our society, and to learn how to accept it. Whatever someone tells you does or does not have to be what they say it is. You must learn how to analyze what is put before you, how to put it all in perspective, so if it happens again you will know how to deal with it."

1
The 1940s

Centralia: Winningest Team in History

The Green Grill is to Centralia what Fritzel's was to Chicago, what Toots Shor's was to New York, and what the Brown Derby was to Hollywood. After a basketball game, everybody who was anybody showed up for a beer and burger.

It opened in 1934 on North Poplar before moving to its current location on Route 161 at Route 51 in downtown Centralia in 1936. In the 1940s and 1950s, however, Centralia's great basketball stars, Ken "Preacher" McBride and Bobby Joe Mason, couldn't go there.

"There were about a thousand blacks in the community, 120 in the high school," Mason recalled. "We became aware of racial things that were going on when we went out of town, when we went to eat at restaurants. We had to go in the back door for blacks in Centralia. I couldn't go into certain places, like the Green Grill. At the movie theater, I had to sit upstairs."

Mason, whose retired number 14 jersey hangs in Trout Gym with Dike Eddleman's number 40 and Lowell Spurgeon's number 13, doesn't live in Centralia. He once worked for his former Centralia classmate Roland Burris when Burris was comptroller and attorney general of Illinois. Now he lives in Springfield and is employed by the Springfield Housing Authority's Community Center.

McBride, a three-sport athlete and an All-State basketball player in 1947, settled in Centralia in 1987 after playing with the Harlem Magicians and then working for a YMCA in Chicago for sixteen years and for the State of Illinois for ten years.

"There was a lot of prejudice in the 1940s when I was growing up," said McBride, who started on Centralia's 1946 state runner-up. "When the city built a new swimming pool in Fairview Park, we couldn't swim in it. Segregation was accepted in those days. Now I ask why it was like that. Why did we accept it? What could we have done about it? We had no power."

A sign at one restaurant read: "Colored served to go." But McBride claimed that he found no prejudice at the high school. He credited the coach, Arthur Trout. When some townspeople complained that two blacks were on the 1945 team, Trout said that he would play his best players, no matter what color. "That set the tone," McBride said.

So there was McBride, sitting in the dining room of the Green Grill, enjoying a lunch with Lowell Spurgeon, Bill Castleman, Bob Jones, Bill Niepoetter, Butch Border, and Bill "Pops" Taylor, swapping stories and reliving memories of Trout, Eddleman, Mason, the Wonder Five, 1942, 1946, and 1963.

Spurgeon, looking fit at age eighty-seven, graduated in 1934 with twelve varsity letters. He was a three-time All-Stater in football and a two-time All-Stater in basketball. He held the state high jump record of 6 ft., 5 ⅛ in., for twenty-seven years.

McBride's heroes were Spurgeon and Jesse Owens. He built a jumping pit in his backyard. He started to play basketball after his father reminded him that he couldn't play major league baseball because he was black.

Castleman played on the Wonder Five in 1941 but never went to college. He wanted to work on the railroad, like his father. After five years, he joined a private company, then worked for the City of Centralia. He retired in 1985. He has attended games at Trout Gym for five decades.

Jones was born in Ashley, a few miles south of Centralia. He coached at McLeansboro, Norris City, and Metropolis before succeeding Bill Davies as head coach at Centralia in 1962. He coached until 1972 and served as athletic director until 1983.

Niepoetter, a 1946 Centralia graduate, left college when his father was killed in a coal mine disaster. He joined the *Centralia Sentinel* as a sportswriter in 1957 and retired in 1979. He cofounded the Centralia Sports Hall of Fame with Bob Jenkins.

Border, a 1961 Centralia graduate, has served as president of Centralia's all-sports booster club since 1994. He is also a former president of the Centralia Sports Hall of Fame, which was founded in 1980.

Taylor, a 1962 Centralia graduate, describes himself as "the biggest fan the school has ever had." He also is very active in the booster club and the Centralia Hall of Fame.

They have a lot to be proud of. Few schools in Illinois can match Centralia's winning tradition. A state sign on the outskirts of the Marion County community proclaims that Centralia is home to "the winningest high school basketball team in the United States."

Until recent years, Arthur Trout was the winningest coach in Illinois history with 809 career victories. He also won three state championships (1918, 1922, 1942). Dike Eddleman is generally acknowledged as the greatest male athlete in state history.

Centralia was a thriving community in the 1940s. It owed its prosperity to the railroad, coal mining, and oil. At one time, the Centralia oil field was the largest in the world. Now the population has dipped from eighteen thousand to 14,500. Marion County has the second-highest unemployment rate in Illinois.

Trout was the most revered man in Centralia. Jones was in heaven when Trout and the Wonder Five showed up at his eighth-grade basketball banquet. "That's why I became a coach," he said.

Every year, Spurgeon makes a trip to Bruceville, Indiana, Trout's hometown, to place flowers on his former coach's grave. "He did more things for this community that people didn't know about," Spurgeon said.

Trout claimed that he invented his famed "kiss shot" because high school players have small hands and can't shoot one-handed. He said that he could tell that the shot was executed correctly if he saw dust on a player's lip. The higher the trajectory of the shot, he said, the better chance it would go in the basket.

"He was a legend, and you don't talk back to legends," McBride said.

Trout's 1941 team, dubbed the "Wonder Five," with Eddleman, Castleman, Jack Klosterman, Harold Wesner, and Bob Michael, was heavily favored to win the state title. But they lost to Morton of Cicero 30–29 in the semifinals and settled for third place with a 44–2 record.

"It was a terrible feeling. I am going on eighty, and I haven't forgotten it yet," Castleman said. "You never forget the game, the guys, the town. Trout said every team has one bad game a year regardless of how good it is. That was our bad game."

In 1942, Castleman was gone, and Eddleman was the only returning starter. Mount Vernon with Junior Kirk was the preseason favorite, but Centralia upset the Rams in the sectional final. Eddleman fouled out midway through the fourth quarter, but Farrell Robinson keyed the victory.

In the state finals, Eddleman, Robinson, Fred Pearson, and Jim Seyler carried the team. They rallied from a thirteen-point deficit in the last five minutes to stun unbeaten Paris 35–33 for the crown. Eddleman was the tournament's leading scorer with seventy-two points in four games.

In 1946 McBride was a junior. After experiencing a 6–24 season in 1943–44, the worst in Trout's career, which included a 60–20 loss to Pinckneyville, Trout promised seniors Colin Anderson and Don Schnake that they would play in Huff Gym in March. Anderson missed twelve games with a bad back, and Centralia lost eight of them. But they finished with a 24–13 record and reached the state final, finishing second to Champaign.

"There has never been another Trout," said Schnake, who published a book on his former coach, *Trout: The Old Man and the Orphans,* in 1992. "They were junior high school coaches compared to him. He was bigger than the game. Other coaches were about strategy and fundamentals. He went beyond that. He hit an area that others didn't."

After Trout retired in 1950, Jimmy Evers produced some outstanding teams in the 1950s (he was 105–22 from 1951 to 1955), and Bill Davies coached 29–2 and 29–3 teams in 1961 and 1962. Rich Rapp, an All-Stater on the 1961 team, said that old-timers still insist that the best game ever played was Collinsville's 66–64 victory over Centralia in the 1961 supersectional at Salem.

But as long as the game is played in Centralia, they will remember Jones's 1963 team, the 32–2 powerhouse that was top-ranked in the state but lost in the state final to Chicago Carver 53–52 on Anthony Smedley's dramatic last-second steal and game-winning shot. "That loss still haunts the community more than any other game in school history, even more than 1941," Castleman said.

No one thinks about it more than Herb Williams, the two-time All-Stater who had the ball stripped from his hands in the closing seconds, setting the stage for Smedley's winning shot. "To me, the game was the summation of a career," Williams said. "I wasn't only playing for myself but for my big brothers . . . Rich Rapp, Russell Coleman, Chuck Garrett, Mel Blackwell, Wendell Meeks, the guys on the 1961 and 1962 teams who had worked so hard. I was totally crushed. It is one of those things you never get over. But you accept it. My disappointment wasn't so much for myself but that I felt I let so many people down. You realize you did the best you could, but it wasn't meant to be."

Dike Eddleman: The Greatest Athlete of All

It is a love story that Hollywood missed: the peppy cheerleader and the star athlete. They were married for nearly fifty-six years. He achieved success in three sports and won the hearts of many during his years as an athlete and business executive, and his wife was with him every step of the way.

Thomas Dwight "Dike" Eddleman lived on the West Side of Centralia. He was an outstanding athlete in a sports-crazy town who had a marvelous two-handed shot but absolutely no ego. In fact, he was downright embarrassed by most adulation.

"No one ever said anything bad about him," said Bill Castleman, a teammate on Centralia's famed Wonder Five of 1941.

"He handled his fame at a young age like no other," said Bill Niepoetter, a 1946 Centralia graduate who was a sports reporter for the *Centralia Sentinel* from 1957 to 1979.

Teddy Georgia Townsley lived with her grandparents on the East Side of Centralia. Her grandfather was a Chicago Cubs fan and listened to their games on the radio. Teddy wasn't much of a sports fan. Cheerleading, she said, was her only claim to fame.

As a sophomore, she was walking through the gym with a friend, Marge Hoyt, when Eddleman, a year older, asked her to go to a movie. Teddy said no. "I wasn't that impressed," she said. Two weeks later he asked again, and she accepted.

They sat on the swing on her front porch or went to a movie at the Illinois Theatre. They'd sit in the front row so Dike could dangle his long legs on the railing. Jitterbugging was the rage, but Dike preferred the two-step. They began going steady during Dike's senior year. Although he was very private and unpretentious, he also had a jealous streak. He got mad whenever Teddy got calls from gentleman admirers.

While Dike made a reputation that attracted sportswriters from Chicago and national magazine writers from New York to the tiny Marion County town, Teddy recalls that her most memorable moment came when coach Arthur Trout, who was admired and respected but feared by one and all, asked someone to tell her during a game: "Don't turn flips in front of the bench."

Eddleman became the most celebrated athlete in Illinois high school history. He became a cult hero. Fan mail was addressed to Eddlemanville, Illinois, but the post office always delivered the letters to Dike. Tom Siler of *Sport* magazine said that Eddleman was "the most sought-after athlete in America." *Look* magazine published a seven-page spread with pictures.

"I believe my father's story forever will be unique," said Diana Eddleman Lenzi, who published the book *Dike Eddleman: Illinois' Greatest Athlete* in 1997, "because of the diversity of his accomplishments, the humility he maintained, and the fact that it all happened in a magical era gone by."

After Eddleman scored an unprecedented 969 points as a junior, Paramount Pictures approached his coach about making a movie about the seventeen-year-old. The proposal was rejected. After he graduated from the University of Illinois with eleven varsity letters, he was offered the leading role in a Tarzan movie.

"He was a good-looking guy, and I wanted to go out with him," Teddy recalled. "His three sisters didn't like me. They didn't want him to be tied down. Dike didn't talk about it. We were just two young people falling in love."

There wasn't much time, however. Trout didn't permit his athletes to attend dances, and Teddy loved to dance. Dike was so busy training for football, basketball, and the high jump that he scheduled only one date each weekend with Teddy.

"I only have about ten years for basketball and other athletic competitions," he told the sportswriter Donald H. Drees of the *St. Louis Star-Times* in 1942. "I have the rest of my life for girls. I limit my dating to one night each weekend. Just so I won't go stale."

In football, he joined Trout's team as a senior and was named to the All-State team. Later, he was a record-setting punter on Illinois's 1947 Rose Bowl championship team.

In basketball, he was a three-time All-Stater who became the first player in state history to score more than two thousand points in his career. He led Centralia to the 1942 state championship after finishing third in 1941. Later, he was named the Big Ten's most valuable player on an Illinois team that finished third in the NCAA tournament in 1949. He also played five years of professional basketball.

In the high jump, he won three state championships in a row. Later, he was a standout on Illinois's 1947 NCAA outdoor championship team and qualified for the 1948 Olympics.

"I covered a golden age of sports that featured championship teams from Centralia High School and the University of Illinois," said the former *Champaign News-Gazette* sports editor Pat Harmon. "Dike Eddleman was a central part of my stories about those teams, and I have never forgotten his achievements. He followed his athletic career with a record of service to his school. He is the greatest."

Curiously, Eddleman had an idol, someone he admired more than any other athlete. Lowell Spurgeon, a 1934 Centralia graduate, was the town's most admired athlete before Eddleman. He won twelve varsity letters, was a three-time All-Stater in football, a two-time All-Stater in basketball, and set a state high jump record of 6 ft., 5⅛ in., that stood for twenty-seven years. Later, he was a three-sport star at the University of Illinois.

"Much of my success as a high jumper can be attributed to Lowell Spurgeon," Eddleman said. "I tried to emulate him as a youngster."

Eddleman left big footprints. Don Schnake, who played on Centralia's 1946 state runner-up, saw Eddleman play for four years and was in awe.

"He was a god," Schnake said. "Everyone wanted to be like him. You couldn't believe you were playing on the same floor as he did."

Eddleman's athletic feats were extraordinary and legendary, especially in basketball. After the famed Wonder Five of Eddleman, Castleman, Jack Klosterman, Harold Wesner, and Bob Michael had to settle for third place in 1941 after losing to Morton of Cicero 30–29 in the semifinals, Eddleman was devastated. He was determined to come back in 1942 even though he was the only returning starter.

In his book *Trout: The Old Man and the Orphans*, Schnake details the closing seconds of the 1942 state championship game as Eddleman rallied his Centralia teammates from a thirteen-point deficit in the last six minutes to upset Paris 35–33, snapping the Tigers' thirty-nine-game winning streak: "Eddleman, with a fury-filled drive through the Paris team, brought the Orphans within two. [Jim] Seyler, fouled by Nate Middleton, hit two free throws to tie.

"Dave Humerickhouse, fouled by [Bernard] Schifferdecker, dropped two through and Paris regained the lead.

"As the clock turned red and seven thousand fans turned insane, Eddleman exploded down the side and attacked the basket with all-out determination. [Max] Norman fouled him to prevent the score. The clock stopped—along with many hearts—at fifty-five seconds as Dike approached the line. He made two clean shots and it was tied again.

"An overanxious Warren Collier missed everything. [Bob] Wham recovered the errant shot. Centralia had the ball and thirty seconds to break the tie. Wham to Seyler to Eddleman. But he missed.

"Humerickhouse rebounded—but couldn't hold on.

"Eddleman pounced on the loose ball and dropped it in at the buzzer. Champions! Champions! Champions!"

Even after playing in the Rose Bowl, the Final Four, the Olympics, and the NBA, Eddleman considered the victory over Paris to be his greatest thrill in sports.

"He never talked about what he did unless he was asked," Teddy said. He was proud of his achievement in 1942, but he never forgot the disappointment of 1941. He died of a heart ailment in 2001. He was seventy-eight.

He always remembered his roots. In 1963, after another favored Centralia team had lost a heartbreaking last-second decision to Chicago Carver for the state championship, he entered the locker room and asked Centralia coach Bob Jones if he could speak to the team.

"The kids were crying and hanging their heads," Jones recalled. "Eddleman said: 'The same thing happened to us. But I'll make you one promise. The sun will come up tomorrow. My old coach said the same thing to us in 1941.' He said beans and mashed potatoes will taste the same. All we did was lose a game."

Then Eddleman sought out Centralia star Herb Williams, who was distraught after having the ball stripped from him to set up Carver's winning shot. He attempted to console him.

"When I was growing up, Eddleman and Bobby Joe Mason were the biggest icons in town," Williams said. "He put his arm around me and said: 'You'll forget about this because you've got better things coming.' It still hurt, but somehow he made it feel a little better."

Taylorville: 45–0 in 1943–44

Old-timers in Taylorville made a big fuss a few years ago when high school officials voted to retire the jersey of Allison Curtin, who led the girls basketball team to second place in the 1997 Class AA tournament and a two-year record of 64–3.

Hadn't they forgotten somebody?

"Allison was deserving," said Harold "Slick" Parrish, who has been taking film and pictures of Taylorville's football and basketball teams since 1948. "But what about Johnny Orr and Ron Bontemps? They put Taylorville on the map."

Parrish and other community leaders soon corrected the oversight. Orr, Bontemps, and coach Dolph Stanley led Taylorville to a 45–0 record in 1943–44. The Tornadoes were the first unbeaten champion in the history of the state tournament.

When the retirement ceremony was conducted, Bontemps's number 34 and Orr's number 43 were included. "We chose those numbers because we said: 'Let's confuse 'em,'" Bontemps said.

Basketball in Taylorville in the 1940s and early 1950s wasn't confusing; it was overwhelming and exciting, a must-ticket on Friday and Saturday night. The gym, which was built in 1938, was always filled to capacity.

"Years later, I look back and realize we were the first unbeaten state champion," said Orr, who later coached at Michigan and Iowa State. "How the hell did we ever do it? You don't realize it until much later, what a helluva thing it was."

It began in 1939–40, when James Willis Powell, the town's great African American athlete, took Dolph Stanley's first team to the Sweet Sixteen. Many townspeople listened to radio reports of Taylorville's 36–35 overtime loss to Paris in the first round.

Powell missed a free throw at the end of the game. Earlier, he threw a floor-length pass to an open teammate who missed a layup. Powell also was an outstanding fullback on the football team. He later played for the Harlem Globetrotters.

"Powell was my idol growing up," Ron Bontemps said. "He was flashy. He had big hands. He would wave the ball over his head."

"He was the first guy I saw palm a ball," said Billy Ridley, who was Powell's guardian for the last three years of his life. "I once saw him throw a football fifty yards from behind his back."

There were no black/white issues, at least none that were made public. Nobody talked about segregation, not in Centralia or Mount Vernon or Paris or Taylorville.

"Segregation is dead wrong, but nobody got pushy in those days. Nobody made an issue of it, not like in the 1960s," Ron Bontemps said. "There were no militant blacks. Everyone had their place. The general feeling was if they stay in their place, it is all right. Now I wish I could have asked my parents a lot of questions about things I know about now, about Willis Powell and Taylorville in the 1940s."

Powell was gone, but the enthusiasm for basketball continued in 1942–43 when

Taylorville was ranked number one in the state at the end of the regular season. But they finished 29–2, losing to Decatur, with Eddie Root and Glenn Jackson, 39–36 in the sectional.

"It was a bitter disappointment to lose, the first time I ever felt sick about losing," Orr said. "We had a great team. Our 1943 team was better than our 1944 team. That was a building thing for Dolph. He never mentioned the game again."

The tradition turned into legend in 1943–44 when Taylorville went 45–0. The top-ranked Tornadoes beat third-rated Champaign four times, the last time 40–36 in the state semifinals. Stanley scheduled several state powers. They beat Pinckneyville by eleven when both teams were unbeaten. They also beat second-ranked Canton, Paris, Centralia, and Mount Vernon.

The team didn't lose its luster after Orr and Bontemps graduated and Stanley left in 1946. In 1950 and 1952, Taylorville reached the state quarterfinals with 5' 7" guard Billy Ridley.

"The tradition carried over," Ridley said. "We lived and died basketball in those days."

But the 1943–44 team established the tradition. As a fourth grader, Ridley practiced in his driveway, imitating the shots of Orr, Bontemps, and their teammates Schultte Bishop and Dave Jones.

"There was nothing before or since that brought more notoriety to the town and brought the town together," said Ridley, who later played at the University of Illinois. "They were a great influence on my life."

Stanley's Tornadoes were the biggest thing ever to hit Taylorville, an old coal-mining, farming, and railroad town southeast of Springfield. In the 1920s and 1930s, the coal miners challenged Notre Dame's football team.

There is a square and a courthouse downtown. The Capitol and Ritz Theaters are gone. Teens went to Springfield for fun, Manners Park to swim, and Green Gables for a jukebox and hamburgers. Rene's Drive-In, Rene Mazzotti's drugstore, and George's Candy Shoppe also were popular. There were band concerts on the square on Wednesday nights. The high school gym was open all summer so kids could shoot hoops. All the athletes got their crewcuts at Pete and Bob's barbershop.

"We didn't do spectacular things," Ron Bontemps said. "You were satisfied with what you did until you saw other things."

Dolph Stanley changed everybody's perspective. Jim Frisina, who owned the theaters and was one of the state's leading amateur golfers, is credited with persuading Stanley to move from Mount Pulaski to Taylorville.

"I was in awe of him. He was right under God, on the same pedestal," Billy Ridley said.

Stanley organized the basketball program. He called for a 9 P.M. curfew. His teams practiced on Saturday and Sunday or whenever they weren't playing. He was big on nutrition—raisins, dates, vitamins, and teaspoons of honey. He also emphasized conditioning, fundamentals, and hygiene. He routinely checked to see if players showered after practice and games.

He introduced the original "four corners" offense: he referred to it as his "open court" offense. He didn't allow his players to sit down or drink water during time-outs. If you weren't on the bus at five o'clock for away trips, you stayed home. He smoked a pipe, but never around the players, and wore red socks to all games.

He instructed Frisina and Boyd Dappert, the scorekeeper who had a key to the gym, to pick up about forty kids every Tuesday and Thursday night and take them to the gym, where they would choose up sides and play basketball games until they were exhausted.

"He had the town under control," Orr said. "He demanded perfection. We worked on fundamentals of passing, dribbling, and shooting and did it over and over until we did it right. His philosophy was to outwork everybody. He convinced us that we could win the state title. There was never a doubt in his mind that we [could] win every game."

"He was a learn-all-you-can, play-as-hard-as-you-can, and work-your-butt-off-or-you're-out type of guy," Carl Bontemps said. "That was his philosophy. He taught that you had to live basketball, that it was the most important part of your life. If you didn't live up to his standards, you were out."

After the disappointment of 1943–44, Johnny Orr and Ron Bontemps concentrated on getting better. Orr lived on the East Side and hung out with Jack Richards, Joe McAdam, Max Siegrist, and Chuck Reister. Bontemps lived on the West Side. He played one-on-one with student manager Franny Stahr over the summer.

They ran a pick-and-roll that opponents never seemed to pick up. It was Stanley's primary play on offense. "If we execute it right, even if they know it is coming, we should score," Stanley said. He also introduced what he described as his "tipping offense." After a missed free throw, the ball was tipped to one side and the player on the opposite side of the floor would break to the basket.

"We never scouted anybody," Orr said. "We played our way, and that's the way we played no matter what the opponent did. Our style was up-tempo, pick-and-roll, get the ball down court in a hurry and put it up, man-to-man defense all over the floor."

Bontemps was 6' 3" and Orr 6' 2", big for that time. Both were named to the All-State team. Bontemps's eyesight was so poor that he couldn't see the basket beyond five feet, but he always knew where it was. Orr had a smooth shot from the right corner. Both were good passers, ball handlers, and rebounders.

But the team's strength was teamwork. Stanley made sure that everyone was involved. He didn't allow a team picture to be taken until after thirty-one games. He didn't want his players to read newspapers, even the *Taylorville Breeze-Courier.*

In the state finals, they trounced East St. Louis 52–34 and Kewanee 51–30, got past Champaign by four, then smashed Elgin 56–33 for the championship. Orr scored sixty-four points in four games; Bontemps had forty-nine. Both were named to the all-tournament team.

"Huff Gym was a big thing in those days, with the big map on the wall with the lights designating the sixteen schools that had qualified for the Sweet Sixteen," said Ron Bontemps, who later played on the gold-medal-winning Olympic team in 1952.

"It was a dream world to us. It was tough to play on Thursday, Friday, and twice on Saturday. But it was where all the kids wanted to go, to play in front of six thousand people. We couldn't visualize anything better . . . until we went to Chicago Stadium and Madison Square Garden."

Paris: The Ernie Eveland Era

From the moment he was hired as Paris's basketball coach in 1935, Ernie Eveland understood that he was in a no-win situation. He was informed that one group wanted to run the town and the basketball program, and another group "will get you if you don't watch out."

Eveland never blinked. He did things his way, and he became one of the most successful coaches in state history. In the next twelve years, he won two state championships, two second places, and a third place. He won thirty or more games for six seasons in a row. In twenty-nine years, he won 779 games.

Because of his enormous success, he polarized the town. You were either for or against Eveland. People wanted to win, but some felt that there was too much emphasis on basketball. Some resented his strict rules. School board members complained about his coaching tactics. A mother complained that her son had to get up too early to practice.

"I understand Bob Knight because I played for Eveland," said Dick Foley, an All-Stater on the 1943 state championship team. "He hated to lose more than anyone I ever knew."

"He was a strong disciplinarian," said Warren Collier, a starter on the 1942 state runner-up. "He was way ahead of his time in basketball knowledge. He knew how important it was to be physically fit and sound. We practiced all the time."

Even today, Eveland's players recall the torturous schedule that produced winning teams in the late 1930s and 1940s. Practice at 6:30 in the morning. Shoot a hundred free throws underhanded. Scrimmage until the first bell rings. Ten minutes to shower and get to class. Shootaround at noon. Run cross-country in the afternoon, eight laps around the track. Practice for two hours after school.

"You had to run cross-country or you couldn't make the team. We went seven straight years without losing a cross-country meet," said Dave Humerickhouse, another All-Stater on the 1943 state championship team. "He wasn't emotional, but he took his basketball very seriously. 'There is only one winner,' he said. 'Losing is for the other person.'"

Until his knee gave out, Eveland participated in morning scrimmages with his players. It was a free-for-all, no-fouls-called, take-no-prisoners type of game. Players learned to protect themselves. He loved to throw his elbows around.

"I'm looking for guys who will do what I say," Eveland told his players. "It may be wrong, but we'll win."

Foley, Collier, Humerickhouse, Max Norman, and Nate Middleton understood and accepted his philosophy. They formed the guts of the 1941, 1942, and 1943 teams that put Paris on equal footing with Centralia, Taylorville, Champaign, and Decatur as the preeminent programs in the state.

"At the time, there were about six good coaches in the state. They dominated the game: Arthur Trout at Centralia, Gay Kintner at Decatur, Harry Combes at Champaign, Dolph Stanley at Taylorville," Norman said. "Eveland was one of them, and he had a demanding personality. 'Do it my way,' he said. And you did it."

Eveland was color-blind in a town with few blacks. Middleton was the only African American on the 1942 team. In fact, he was one of only three blacks on the sixteen teams in the 1942 state finals.

Robert Owens was the only African American on the 1947 state championship team. On one occasion, the team stopped at a diner to eat during a road trip. The owner said that Owens would have to eat in the kitchen, so Eveland said that the entire team would eat in the kitchen.

Paris, the seat of Edgar County, had only two classes—rich and poor, not black and white. The rich owned farmland. Many poor people were on welfare. The teen pregnancy rate was the highest in the state for many years. Papadakos, or Pap's, was a popular teen hangout on the West Side of the square.

"If you lived on the right side of the tracks, you played," Collier said. "I was from a poor family. Had I tried to play basketball before Eveland came, I never would have made the team. Neither would Nate Middleton."

In 1942, Rodney Bell, a member of the school board that had hired Eveland seven years earlier, told Eveland that he couldn't have an African American represent the team as captain. Eveland said that the players had elected Middleton. Bell told him to choose a co-captain. Eveland said that they wouldn't choose a co-captain, and that was the end of the debate.

He didn't outlaw dating, but "he made it so uncomfortable that you didn't want to mess with it," Collier said. Eveland was a health freak. He took vitamin pills and distributed them to his players. Before morning workouts, players ate oranges and had doses of cod liver oil. They didn't eat before games. At halftime, they were given spoonfuls of honey.

Eveland was 5' 6". The media called him "Shorty," but family and friends called him "Coach" or "Ernie." He was very frugal, tight with a nickel. He had come from nothing. As a student at Bradley University, he washed dishes at a restaurant to pay for room and board. He always wore a suit and bow tie to games.

In 1941–42, Paris was coming off of a 31–4 season in which three sophomores—Foley, Norman, and Humerickhouse—had started. They lost to Centralia and Dike Eddleman 45–24 in the quarterfinal round at Centralia. Because of World War II, only four teams were brought to Champaign for the last two games.

Middleton became a starter as a senior. As a junior, he had been the last man on the roster. His mother said that he had been running in the streets. He was undisciplined, and she couldn't control him. Eveland assigned Collier, Foley, and Norman to look out for him.

"We lived together," Norman said. "We called ourselves 'the Four Musketeers.' We went to church together, played cards, played touch football, ate together. Nate was one of us. There were no problems, no issues. Our parents' attitude was Nate was part of the team."

Middleton got motivated as a senior. He made the honor roll for one quarter. He also was the number two runner on the cross-country team behind Norman. Unknown as a junior, he was named as a senior to the 1942 All-State team with Eddleman, Junior Kirk of Mount Vernon, Bill Berberian of Thornton, Chuck Tourek of Morton (Cicero), and Gerald Dirksen of Freeport.

"Nate was ahead of his time," Collier said. "He could do a lot of things that kids do today. He was very athletic, all arms and legs. You threw a bad pass, and he made you look good."

Paris won its first thirty-nine games in 1941–42, including a 47–35 victory over Centralia. In the state final, Paris led Centralia by thirteen points with six minutes to play and by ten with three minutes remaining. Farrell Robinson, Centralia's second-best player, fouled out, but Bernie Schifferdecker came off the bench and made a kiss shot from the far corner to ignite the Orphans. Down the stretch, Jim Seyler scored eight points, and Eddleman made two baskets and two free throws, and Centralia won 35–33.

"That was devastating. We thought we would be the first unbeaten state champion," Norman said. "It broke us up. You don't forget things like that, even fifty years later. I recall 1942 for losing almost as much as I recall 1943 for winning. To this day, I think 1942 was a better team than 1943."

Paris didn't blow the lead in 1943. Foley, Norman, and Humerickhouse were back. The other starters were the juniors Gordon Taylor and Delbert "Babe" Glover and Paul Pederson, who split time.

The key was beating Salem, with the All-Stater Roy Gatewood and the 6' 7", 230-pound Dean White, 53–50 in the semifinals. Gatewood, who scored twenty-two against Paris, was the leading scorer in the state finals with ninety-six points in four games. He was the first jump shooter that the Paris team had ever seen.

In the final, Paris beat Moline 46–37; Taylor scored twelve points, and Glover scored ten. Halfway through the fourth quarter, Moline star Cal Anders, who shot three of fifteen and was limited to eight points, asked Moline coach Roger Potter to take him out of the game because he was exhausted. "We always felt we could outrun any opponent," Foley said.

Paris was ranked among the state's top teams in 1945 and 1946 but didn't return to the state finals until 1947, when Robert Owens, Glen Vietor, Don Glover, Dow Morris, and John Wilson led what Eveland insisted was his best team to a 40–2 record and a 58–37 rout of defending champion Champaign for the state title.

Owens scored twenty-two points and hounded Champaign star Rod Fletcher to four-of-nineteen shooting. "We couldn't stop Owens. We'd get the ball to Fletcher, and he couldn't make it happen. Owens was very agile and guarded very close," Champaign's Fred Major said.

"Owens wasn't tall [6' 2"], but he had the longest arms I ever saw. They were in better condition. They ran us to death," Champaign's John McDermott said.

"I never saw the town so enthusiastic as it was in the 1940s," said Linda Shirar,

Eveland's daughter who was a cheerleader in 1955. "People stood in line for tickets. The town celebrated spring vacation during the state tournament in March, not during Easter in April."

"Those days taught me how to get along with people and how to be a winner, to feel on top of the world," said Humerickhouse, who later was an All-American at Bradley. "It sticks with you. Once a winner, always a winner."

Decatur: End of an Era

Like people who will never forget where they were or what they were doing when President Kennedy was assassinated, Bob Fallstrom recalls the day Gay Kintner died.

Kintner was the legendary basketball coach at Decatur High School. He won 649 games, including state championships in 1931, 1936, and 1945. And he laid the framework for another state title in 1962 before he collapsed on the bench and died of a heart attack at halftime during a game in 1960.

Fallstrom was a sportswriter for the *Decatur Herald and Review*. Later he served as sports editor from 1964 to 1986. At seventy-five, he still works fifty to sixty hours a week. Since 1991 he has been the newspaper's community news editor.

"I had assigned a part-time reporter to cover the game at Decatur MacArthur," said Fallstrom, who covered sports for thirty-six years. "All of the full-time members of the sports staff went to see the Illinois/Ohio State basketball game in Champaign. At halftime, I got a call from the office, informing me that Kintner had died. We all rushed back to Decatur. It was one of the biggest stories our paper has had. It was the biggest funeral ever in Decatur. It was held in Kintner Gym."

Now Kintner Gym is gone. So is Decatur High. So are the Runnin' Reds, the name attached to the fast-breaking teams of the 1960s. The gym was torn down in the 1970s to provide space for the Civic Center. The old school was demolished, too.

"Decatur was a thriving town in the 1950s with a downtown high school, theater, and shops," Fallstrom said. "People dressed up and lined up to go to Kintner Gym on Friday nights. It sat forty-two hundred. It was like going to Madison Square Garden. It was the best gym between Chicago and St. Louis."

As a freshman basketball player, Jerry Hill was sitting behind the varsity bench when Kintner died. "Before the game, he put his hand on my shoulder and said, 'How you doing?' I didn't know he knew I existed. Maybe he thinks I can play, I thought to myself. That was the highlight of my freshman year," he said.

Later, Hill was a starting guard on the 1962 state championship team. Today, he drives into the downtown area and can't believe that Kintner Gym isn't there.

"I don't see how it is possible to have basketball without Decatur High School," he said. "The Runnin' Reds are gone. In the 1960s, we knew we'd win. There were forty-two hundred screaming people at every game. Now everything is gone except the memories."

In the 1930s, 1940s, and 1950s, Kintner was to Decatur what Dolph Stanley was to Taylorville, Arthur Trout to Centralia, Duster Thomas to Pinckneyville, Ernie Eveland to Paris, and Harry Combes to Champaign. "He was like Bear Bryant, so revered," Fallstrom said.

Kintner was strict. Players knew they were in trouble if they heard him whistling. They had to be in bed by nine o'clock on the night before a game. He would personally come around to check. He would toss his coat during games and often couldn't find it. He once left his players at Huff Gym after a state tournament game and had to go back to get them.

He played a switching man-to-man defense, but even his assistant coaches couldn't figure how what his offense was. His plan was to run and go get the ball and shoot. There were no set plays. He didn't keep statistics. He was the beginning of zero tolerance.

"We had a great coach, and we owed it to ourselves and the town to do as well as we could," said Bob "Chick" Doster, an All-Stater on the 1945 state championship team. "Decatur took great pride in its basketball team. If you were on the team, you were known. There was no place for anything but the team."

When Kintner wanted to make a point to his players, he subbed the whole team. He never chewed out his players in front of the crowd. Instead, he'd get red in the face and lead a Patton-like march out of the gym to the hallway. He wanted to correct a mistake right away, in a teamlike atmosphere.

After losing to West Frankfort in the first round of the 1943 state tournament and to Paris in the sectional in 1944, Decatur expected to field an outstanding team in 1944–45. Doster, Ralph Rutherford, and John Malerich were back, and 6' 7" center George Riley emerged as a dominant big man in an era when 6' 3" was considered tall.

Champaign and Decatur were ranked first and second in the state after splitting a pair of conference games.

In the quarterfinals, Decatur fell behind Galesburg 22–11 and trailed by three with eight seconds to play when Riley intercepted a pass, was fouled, and made a free throw. Doster made a ten-footer at the buzzer to force overtime. Trailing by one with fourteen seconds to play, Doster made a game-winning basket.

Decatur beat Champaign 62–54 for the state championship; Doster scored eighteen, Riley sixteen.

After Kintner died in 1960, his assistants, John Schneiter and Jack Kenny, were named co-coaches. They took the team, led by Tom Sidney, Gather Warnsley, Al Risby, and a promising sophomore named Ken Barnes, to fourth place in the state tournament. With no one taller than 6' 2", they made up for their lack of size by playing a pressing defense and running. They became the Runnin' Reds.

Later, Schneiter was appointed head coach. The team finished 13–12 in 1961. From 1960 to 1966, it was the only Decatur team that didn't qualify for the state finals. Schneiter was hung in effigy after losing a pair of one-pointers to Bloomington and Springfield, even though the team was 11–2 at the time. "That told me how competitive the people in Decatur were," he said.

Nobody expected Decatur to contend for the 1962 state title, not Schneiter or Kenny or any of their players. James "Bulldog" Johnson, an All-State football player, didn't think he would play at all. The team was small—Barnes was the tallest at 6' 3"—and lacked depth. No one talked about going to state.

"Schneiter was experimenting," Johnson said. "He had a starting lineup which I wasn't on, then a big team which I was on. Two kids who were starting earlier transferred when they were benched. But we started to work things out."

The Reds, with Johnson, Barnes, Prentis Jones, and a pair of outstanding guards in Hill and Jim Hallihan, got on a roll at the end of the regular season, finishing 22–4 and being ranked thirteenth in the state. They believed that if they were good enough to win the Big Twelve Conference (Springfield, Champaign, Bloomington, Lincoln, and Danville), they could beat anyone.

In the sectional, they beat Bloomington (they had split two earlier games). In the supersectional, however, they barely got past conference rival Urbana 41–40 after beating them by twenty-five in two earlier matchups. Barnes stole the ball in the closing seconds, drove the length of the floor, and scored. Then Urbana's Jim Booth missed the last shot.

Decatur ousted Rock Island by five in the quarterfinals and Quincy 47–44 in the semifinals, setting up a duel with Chicago Carver and Cazzie Russell for the title. Decatur prevailed 49–48 in one of the most bizarre finishes in state history.

Carver broke out to a 13–2 lead as Russell dunked the ball. Schneiter called timeout. "They are pressing us, let's press them," he told his players. The momentum of the game changed as Carver's 6' 6" Joe Allen suffered a knee injury and was forced to sit down. Decatur rallied for a 39–34 lead after three quarters.

Carver regained the lead as Russell, who led all scorers with twenty-four points, demonstrated why he was the premier player in the state. Johnson made two free throws with fifty seconds left to tie at forty-eight. Then Carver opted to hold the ball for a last shot.

Inexplicably, with a minute to play, Carver guard Bruce Raickett threw the ball to an official but managed to retrieve it. Then Raickett threw the ball to Hill, who was guarding him.

"I had no time to think. I was shocked," Hill said. "I dribbled down and called timeout." The ball went to Barnes, who was fouled with four seconds left. He made the first free throw but missed the second. Russell's half-court shot failed.

"I don't remember a thing that happened to me two weeks ago, but I remember that game like it was yesterday," Hill said. "I remember that play. You don't forget an experience like that."

Hill and Hallihan returned in 1962–63, and expectations were higher than ever. The team finished 25–6 but lost to Peoria Central in the quarterfinals. Afterward, Schneiter accepted an offer to coach at New Trier in Winnetka. His 1973 team finished second in the state.

Kenny replaced Schneiter. The cupboard wasn't bare: Jack Sunderlik and Dave Scholz took the Reds to third in the state in 1964, and Scholz took them to the quarterfinals in 1965. Terry Johnson and Rich Smith led the Reds to fourth in 1966.

"Today, it is an eerie feeling driving by the Civic Center, where Kintner Gym was, where Decatur High was. It was my school, where I sweated a lot of hours and had a lot of memories," said Scholz, who later was an All–Big Ten player at the University of Illinois.

"What was at Decatur was more than Decatur High. The community was drawn to Kintner Gym and supported the Reds. There was a positive feeling about everything associated with the program. It was something good for the community, and then it died. It was like losing a family member."

Champaign: Combes to Cabutti

Harry Combes was twenty-two years old when he succeeded Les Moyer as head basketball coach at Champaign High School. Born in nearby Monticello, he had been an All–Big Ten guard at the University of Illinois. Everyone called him Harry, not "coach" or "Mr. Combes."

Combes inherited a thriving program. Moyer, who finished second in the state in 1925 and 1929, established a feeder program at eight grade schools in the 1930s. He persuaded physical education students at the university to serve as coaches. The kids practiced once a week and played games on Saturday mornings in Champaign's gym.

"It gave us an early taste of team basketball before a crowd with officials and prepared us for junior high and high school competition," Ted Beach recalled.

Few players enjoyed the remarkable success that Beach did. He was a two-time All-Stater who started on three straight state finalists with Fred Major and John McDermott, a rarity. At Illinois, he played on Combes's teams that won two Big Ten championships and qualified for the NCAA's Final Four on two occasions.

Combes's success was no less mind-boggling. In nine years at Champaign, his teams won 85 percent (254–46) of their games. They were 106–7 in his final three seasons when they finished second, first, and second in the state tournament. During that time, they never lost a home game. When he succeeded Doug Mills as head coach at the University of Illinois in 1946, his teams won Big Ten titles and advanced to the Final Four in three of his first five seasons.

But Combes wasn't the winningest coach in Champaign history. Lee Cabutti won 446 games from 1956 to 1985. His 1968–69 team, led by All-Stater Clyde Turner, finished third in the state.

It wasn't the same as the 1940s, however. The battles between Combes and Decatur's Gay Kintner were the stuff of legend. They were fierce rivals. They didn't like each other, and they didn't care if anyone noticed.

Downstate teams dominated Illinois basketball in those days: Centralia, Champaign, Decatur, Taylorville, Paris, Pinckneyville, Mount Vernon. From 1942 through 1950, they accounted for every state championship.

Beach, Major, McDermott, Jesse Clements, Jim Cottrell, and Rod Fletcher, the guts of the Champaign teams from 1944 to 1947, attended all the state tournaments at Huff Gym. They were impressed by Dundee's 1938 state champions and awed by Centralia's Dike Eddleman in 1941 and 1942.

Then Combes arrived. On the first day of practice in 1944, he told his players: "We were fourth last year. We're going to do better this year, and here's how."

He proceeded to teach a switching man-to-man pressing defense. Opponents had no clue how to combat it. The team won thirty-four of thirty-six games and finished second in the state.

"You would run through a wall for him," Beach said. "He was tough but fair. He was volatile, like [Purdue coach] Gene Keady. He was a players' coach, friendly but not a back slapper. On road trips, he would play cards with the players. He was one of the boys. But he was the boss."

Combes didn't allow dating after the state tournament began. Players climbed rope at six in the morning to strengthen themselves. Combes told Beach to go out for track as a sophomore to improve his speed. He was young enough to go one-on-one with his players.

He was big on defensive rebounding: he would shoot and have two players battle for the rebound. It was a knock-down, no-holds-barred, take-no-prisoners, barroom brawl in sneakers.

"Cut lips were commonplace," said Major, who later played football at the University of Illinois and often teamed with Earl Harrison in the rebounding hijinks. "By the time we got done fighting each other, playing the other teams was easy."

In 1944–45, Champaign lost to Decatur, Bob Doster, and 6' 7" George Riley 62–54 for the state championship. The Maroons were limited to seven players after team leader Jim Cottrell got pneumonia before the first game, McDermott broke his leg in the first game, and Del Cantrell tore up his knee.

Everything came together in 1945–46. Beach, Cottrell, Major, McDermott, and Harrison were joined by Fletcher, a strong rebounder. Champaign was 38–1 and ranked number one in the state. The Maroons lost to second-rated West Frankfort in the Centralia tournament but beat Centralia 54–48 for the state title.

Perhaps their toughest game was against Danville in the sectional semifinal. Danville, behind 6' 6" Bob Murrin and 6' 4" Bill Gross, led by one after three quarters, but Champaign rallied to win by four. It was the fourth time Champaign had beaten Danville.

In the state final, Combes designated Major to defend against Colin Anderson, Centralia's All-Stater. Major limited him to seven-of-twenty-four shooting and fourteen points. Beach led Champaign with twenty-two. McDermott's three-point play with three minutes left in the game sealed the victory.

In 1946–47, four of the top six players returned, and Champaign was a near-unanimous choice to repeat. Combes said that it was his best team, but the Maroons were missing their floor leader, Cottrell. Ray Walters tried to pick up the slack.

After losing three games in the regular season, Champaign upset top-ranked Dundee 47–45 in the quarterfinals. "After that, we felt we had won the state title," Beach said. But the Maroons were stomped by Paris and Robert Owens 58–37 in the final.

"It was the most disappointing loss of my life," said Beach, who shot five of twenty and was limited to eleven points. "We really expected to win a second straight state title. We were 106–7 in my high school career. It was a terrible way to go out. I felt we had lost the world. The town didn't believe it."

Cabutti rekindled the winning tradition, but he always had some regrets that he left Herrin in 1956. His last team had won twenty-eight games and lost three by a total of four points.

But Cabutti wanted a pay raise; he was offered a hundred dollars. He and the principal never got along very well, so Cabutti decided to take the job in Champaign. "I hated to leave, but it was a new start," he said. In 1957, Herrin's new coach Earl Lee took John Tidwell, Ivan Jefferson, and Richard Box to the state championship.

Cabutti left a volatile racial situation in Herrin. "There was considerable prejudice in the town. There was an antiforeign and anti-Catholic element. And there were southern Baptists and rednecks who ran the town," he said.

Cabutti discovered that the racial climate in Champaign was just as heated. After three years, he said that he was going to return to Herrin. He had to disconnect his telephone. He was called "nigger lover" by townspeople who didn't want to see more than one African American on the basketball team.

"It was okay for black ladies to clean the homes of wealthy white ladies while they played golf," Cabutti said, "but it wasn't okay for their sons to play ahead of a white kid on the basketball team. I started two blacks in my first season. You have to play the best kids. That was the only negative thing about the program."

Beach saw the way it was in the Cabutti years. He worked the clock and scoreboard for Illinois basketball games for thirty-eight years and handled the same duties for the state high school tournament for thirty years. He insisted that there was no racial strife at Champaign in the 1940s.

He said that Jesse Clements, an All-Stater on the 1944 and 1945 teams, was a hero at Champaign High. "We looked up to him. He wasn't black as far as we were concerned," Beach said. And he said that Bobby Clark, another great black athlete at Champaign, was treated in the same manner. "Everybody loved him and respected him."

Integration was slow to come to the University of Illinois's basketball program, too. In 1956, Combes finally changed the complexion of the roster when he recruited Mannie Jackson and Govoner Vaughn from Edwardsville's state runner-up.

"I got along with black kids because I went through prejudice when I was growing up in Johnston City," Cabutti said. "A lot of old barriers are breaking down, but some never will change. As long as you raise kids to believe that blacks are inferior, we'll have problems."

In 1968–69, Cabutti's best player was black. Clyde Turner, who later played at Minnesota, was 6' 6" and the leading scorer in the state tournament. Champaign had high expectations. The Maroons were 30–4 and came within a sprained ankle of winning the state title.

Cabutti knew that his team had to beat Normal Community to get to the state finals. He personally scouted them on ten occasions. To combat Normal's noted press, he assigned his tallest players, Turner and Dave White, to handle the ball. Champaign won the supersectional thriller 55–53 in triple overtime.

In the semifinal, Champaign was in a position to upset top-ranked Proviso East and 6' 6" Jim Brewer, who played despite a severely sprained ankle. The Maroons had the ball with twenty seconds to play, trailing by one. Turner missed a short shot, and Brewer rebounded and was fouled. Brewer converted two free throws to win 37–36. "I felt we belonged in the state final," Cabutti said.

South Shore: Gaining Respect

Chicago Public League basketball was the Rodney Dangerfield of Illinois in the 1940s: it got no respect. The Kelly Bowl (now Prep Bowl) football game was the biggest event in town. Bill DeCorrevont and Babe Baranowski were football legends.

City schools had a "bladder rule." Athletes could participate in football or basketball but not both. Most chose football. There was no tradition, no feeder programs, and no community support. Schools hired physical education teachers, not coaches.

Nobody took Public League teams seriously. They were considered "pushovers" by perennial state powers in Centralia, Paris, Decatur, Champaign, and Mount Vernon. City kids never heard of Dike Eddleman or Arthur Trout or Ernie Eveland or Gay Kintner.

Players couldn't play basketball in spring or summer leagues. They played sixteen-inch softball. Coaches didn't attend clinics. It was a slow game that didn't excite players or fans. The jump shot was in its infancy, as foreign to a South Sider as a ruble.

Tony Maffia showed up at South Shore in 1941, a year after the school opened. He came from Marshall, where he played second fiddle to Lou Weintraub's great junior teams. He was looking for an identity of his own, and he found it on 76th Street, in an upper-middle-class neighborhood near Lake Michigan.

Maffia had an immediate impact. He introduced a fast break and a full-court press. He scheduled preseason games in Downstate communities. At a time when city kids didn't care about the state tournament, he reminded his players that no Chicago team had placed in the event since 1931 and challenged them to do better.

His 1943–44 team was unranked at the end of the regular season. But the Tars, led by All-State forward Paul Schnackenberg, guard Dan Trahey, and 6' 5" center Jack Harr, beat Harper 51–37 for the Public League championship, crushed Quincy 62–38 in the first round of the Sweet Sixteen, and ousted West Rockford 39–33 in the quarterfinals before losing to Elgin 48–47 in the semifinals. They trounced Champaign 52–34 for third place, completing a 23–6 season.

South Shore built a 31–19 halftime lead against Elgin. But Harr fouled out, and Schnackenberg and Trahey were in foul trouble. Elgin's Jim Rager scored the winning basket with a minute to play. Schnackenberg was the tournament's leading scorer with sixty-six points in four games, two more than Taylorville's Johnny Orr.

"I really think our kids did a great thing for Chicago basketball," Maffia said after

South Shore finished third in the 1944 state tournament. "In the past, it's been a general opinion outside of Chicago that our teams are no good. Now they'll respect any school that comes out of our league."

"We were nothing when the state tournament opened, a sure first-round loss, but we were famous by the third game and the crowd was really for us," Jack Harr said. "We woke up Downstaters and made them realize there is basketball in Chicago. Our pressing defense and fast break caught everyone's attention."

In 1946–47, South Shore returned to the state finals. Led by All-Stater Jake Fendley, who had seen little playing time as a freshman on the 1943–44 squad, the Tars were 24–3. They reached the state quarterfinals before losing to the eventual state champion, Paris, 49–37. A week later, they won the city championship by beating the Catholic League champion, Leo, 37–28 before eighteen thousand in Chicago Stadium.

"After 1944 and 1947, more kids were motivated to play basketball in the city," said Bob Joor, a starter on the 1947 team who later coached at Waukegan. "It was a historic transition that was ready to happen. For years, kids dwelled in their own neighborhoods. But after World War II, people left their neighborhoods for jobs elsewhere. Kids had a hungry attitude. South Shore proved they were ready to be motivated and show that Chicago can play with anyone."

Shelly Stark, a 1954 South Shore graduate, said that Du Sable changed the game forever with its fast-breaking, pressing, jump-shooting, colorful style in the 1950s. "But without Maffia," Stark said, "the Public League never would have been on the map. He doesn't get the credit he deserves. He was way ahead of his time."

Harr, Trahey, Howie Erzinger, and Bud Wineburgh attended Bradwell Elementary School; Schnackenberg attended Parkside. Carmie Esposito, who transferred from Chicago Vocational for his senior year, joined Trahey in the backcourt.

They improvised. Unlike the Lawndale neighborhood on the West Side, where Marshall players had four Boys' Clubs to choose from, South Shore had no indoor facilities. They played on a dirt court at Rainbow Beach. They constructed their own court on an empty lot at 77th and Colfax. They played all summer long, three against three, from ten in the morning until three in the afternoon.

Under Maffia's stern hand, they learned to play the game. He was a no-nonsense guy. Downstaters didn't give Chicago coaches much respect, but city players knew that Maffia, Parker's Eddie O'Farrell, Tilden's Bill Postl, Hyde Park's Ellie Hasan, and Vocational's Paul Erickson knew their X's from their O's.

Maffia coached junior and senior teams. The school had two gyms, one for boys and one for girls. While he drilled one team in one gym, the other team was polishing its shooting skills in the other gym. He drove his team to Catholic League schools for preseason scrimmages. Sometimes the workouts would last ten to twelve quarters.

"We couldn't understand why he made us run for twenty minutes without stopping," Esposito said. "We couldn't figure out what he was doing. We had only one guy over six feet tall, but we were in great shape and played great defense."

Trahey said that the team clicked because of its man-to-man defense, Harr's rebounding, and the scoring of Schnackenberg and Trahey. "We were very quick. We would get teams in foul trouble, and that changed the atmosphere late in the game," he said.

They were aware they were making a statement. Even Marie Voy Brewster, South Shore's principal, became a fan. When the 1943–44 season began, she had never attended a game. After the team won ten games, she was seen popping into the gym to observe a few games. When the Tars got to the city playoff, she was a regular. She sat in a chair at one end of the gym because she refused to sit in the bleachers.

"She once called me into her office," said Trahey, who later was a principal at two Chicago high schools, then served as a district superintendent from 1975 until his retirement in 1993. "She wondered if I was eating well. I weighed only 140 pounds. She gave me a bottle of vitamin pills and said to take one a day. She took an interest in us."

When the team went Downstate, Brewster learned that the Illinois High School Association (IHSA) had reserved a "second-rate hotel" for her team's overnight accommodations. She told tournament officials, "If you don't move them to a good hotel, I'm taking them home." After beating Quincy in the first round, South Shore took their rooms.

Schnackenberg was the star of the team. He later played at Miami (Ohio) with Ara Parseghian and was drafted by the New York Knickerbockers. His father was speaker of the House of Representatives in Illinois and an Illinois Supreme Court judge.

"He was an All-Stater," Bud Wineburgh said. "But Maffia wouldn't hesitate to take him or anyone else out of a game if they weren't doing it right. The players liked him because he was fair. If you wanted to play, you did what he wanted you to do."

Harr said that the only mistake he thinks Maffia ever made was not playing Jake Fendley more as a freshman. "I never could understand why he never coached in college or the pros. He was a leader in innovating systems. He was a pioneer. He had new ideas that other coaches didn't have at the time," Harr said.

Fendley and Joor attended Bryn Mawr Elementary School, one of four schools that fed into South Shore. The players on the 1944 team were their heroes. "They motivated us to play basketball," Joor said.

Fendley was born in Danville, Illinois, but came to Chicago as a seventh grader. He was only 6' 1", but he could jump like he was 6' 6". The two-time All-Stater was recruited by Adolph Rupp, Kentucky's legendary coach, and later played for the Fort Wayne Zollner Pistons in the NBA.

In a city playoff game against Tuley and 6' 8" Joe Graboski, who later was an all-star in the NBA, Maffia ordered Fendley to drive on Graboski, who had been controlling the game. Fendley forced Graboski to foul out, and South Shore went on to win.

"He was very mature, well developed, a talented athlete at an early age," Bob Joor said. "He was worlds ahead of the rest of us. In softball, he could hit a ball out of sight. If he had been a football player, he probably would have been an All-Stater. He was in a class by himself."

In 1946–47, Fendley, Joor, Norm Berglund, Don Freeburn, Peter Giannapolous, and

Stu Weissman beat Lane Tech 58–38 for the Public League title, then eliminated Galesburg 43–37 before being ousted by Paris in the quarterfinals.

"We didn't play a team that we didn't think we could beat," Joor said. "Maffia had high expectations. Jake was the motivator. Before the playoff, he talked to each guy. He had been there and he wanted to go back. We were in the game against Paris until Jake fouled out early in the fourth quarter."

Pinckneyville: Two Legendary Coaches

Shane Hawkins met one legendary coach and played for another. He learned what the tradition of Pinckneyville basketball was all about, from Duster Thomas to Dick Corn, and he became the best player the school ever produced.

He met Thomas when he was four. The coach lived next-door to his grandparents. When he was six he walked into Thomas Gymnasium and was awed when he saw Thomas's picture and the 1948 state championship trophy in the hallway. In 1994, he added another.

Hawkins's father, Tom, had played on Duster's last team. Thomas had put Pinckneyville, a coal-mining town of thirty-one hundred, on the map. Pinckneyville annually battled two other celebrated programs, Centralia and Mount Vernon, for bragging rights in southern Illinois.

"When you see a town that size, only one class, only thirty-one hundred people, competing and beating the gods of high school basketball, that was special," Shane Hawkins said.

The state tournament has changed, and so has Pinckneyville. The population was thirty-one hundred in 1932, and it still is. But officials count two thousand prisoners at a nearby correctional facility to boost the figure to fifty-one hundred for tax purposes.

Perry County once produced more coal than any other county in the United States, but it now has the highest unemployment rate of any county in Illinois. Founded in the early 1800s, Pinckneyville was named after Gen. Charles Cotesworth Pinckney, a Revolutionary War hero and statesman.

The town once had five automobile dealerships and a movie theater; now they are gone. So is Olin Luke's, a popular restaurant located on the square, which was the focus of a *Sports Illustrated* article on Pinckneyville basketball in the 1950s. Now it is Carnes's Pizza.

Merrill Thomas arrived in Pinckneyville in 1935. More people called him "Doc" than "Duster." After serving as an assistant for three years, he became head coach in 1938. He wasn't an instant success. His background was in softball. He didn't know anything about basketball; he'd never played the game.

He took suggestions from everyone, even teachers and boosters. He went to clinics and read books. He tried anything if he thought it would help him win. He prac-

ticed on Sundays and holidays and all summer long. He arranged the class sched-
ules of his players so they could practice for two hours before lunch. After school,
they practiced for as long as he wanted.

He was big on fundamentals, discipline, and meetings. He constantly tested his
players on the rules of the game: he wanted them to know the rules better than the
officials. He didn't permit his players to date from October to March. A math teacher,
he kept statistics, especially possessions. He never used profanity, encouraged his
players to attend church, and was always proud of those who went to college.

Matt Sheley, a sportswriter for the *Pinckneyville Democrat,* is credited with embel-
lishing the Thomas legend. He coached "fire-wagon basketball," a crowd-pleasing, fast-
breaking, full-court-pressing style copied from Marion coach Cuss Wilson.

But Thomas deserted that style as his reputation was beginning to take off. His
1943–44 team, led by Gene Stotlar, won seventeen games in a row and played
Taylorville's unbeaten state championship team to a standstill before losing 40–29.

To win a state title, Thomas felt that he had to switch to a more deliberate offense,
which he did in 1946–47. He didn't want to fast break and risk committing too many
turnovers. In tournaments, he felt that his up-tempo teams wore themselves out in
the first game and were physically exhausted in the second.

"He always hated to see a kid's name spelled wrong in the newspaper," said Jim
Lazenby, who starred on Thomas's three 33–3 teams that finished third in the state
in 1953–55. "He'd read newspaper clippings before practice to inform the kids what
people were saying about them."

The 1946–47 team was 32–7 and finished third in the state. With starters Frank
Gladson, Bob Johnson, and Dave Davis returning, there were high expectations for
1947–48. They were joined by seniors Tom Millikin, who didn't play as a junior, and
Percy Clippard.

Pinckneyville won thirty-three of thirty-four games. The Panthers lost to Edwardsville
in the final of the Mount Vernon Holiday Tournament. In the sectional final, they beat
Centralia by one.

But their toughest matchup was in the state semifinal against Pekin, whom they
had beaten in the 1947 consolation game. Pekin was ranked number one in the state.
Pinckneyville beat them 36–31. In the final, they overwhelmed Rockford East 65–39;
Gladson and Johnson each scored twenty-one points.

Afterward, townspeople bought Thomas a new car, a 1949 Packard. Later they
named the new gym after him. Built in 1952 with seating for about twenty-five hundred, it remains one of the best high school facilities in the state. After it opened, the
team won fifty-eight games in a row at home.

Thomas retired in 1957 after winning 495 games. He always talked about the state
championships he should have won, especially with the 33–3 teams of 1953–55 with
Lazenby, Ron and Gene Purcell, Arlen Hill, and Don Margenthaler, and the 1956–57
powerhouse of John Daffron, Alex Singer, and Tom Decker that lost to state champion Herrin 75–47 in the sectional.

"He felt he should have won in 1954 if Ron Purcell hadn't transferred to Litchfield,"
said Don Stanton, who succeeded Thomas and coached for five years. "He was

shocked by the defeat to Herrin. He didn't see much material ahead. He thought he'd win state and retire, go out on a high note."

Even though Stanton produced a 30–2 team in 1959–60 that was ranked number one in the state before losing to Granite City in the sectional final, he wasn't popular in Pinckneyville. He and Thomas didn't see eye to eye. Stanton preferred an up-tempo style. The community didn't believe in what he was doing because it conflicted with Duster.

After Stanton left, Pinckneyville went through five coaches and a lot of mediocrity. One lasted for only one season. "No one could follow Duster," Tom Hawkins said. How bad was the program? "We were horrible," said Wade Grasewicz, a 1981 graduate who was the school's all-time leading scorer before Shane Hawkins.

Dick Corn was hired in 1975. He and Duster Thomas had something in common: both were Sunday school teachers and teetotalers. But Corn had played basketball at Benton, the seventh man on Rich Herrin's 1967 supersectional team. Herrin personally recommended him for the job.

At twenty-five, Corn applied for every opening in southern Illinois. He interviewed at Newton, Sparta, and Nashville. If Pinckneyville had opened up in the spring, they would have hired an established coach. But it opened late, and Corn was available.

Townspeople were patient. His first two teams got to the sectional, his third struggled to .500, but his fourth won twenty games and reached the sectional final. "That was the turning point," Corn said. In 1980–81, his team was 29–4, won its first conference title in fifteen years, and lost in the supersectional. "It was like winning the state title," Wade Grasewicz said.

For thirteen seasons in a row, from 1983 to 1996, Corn's teams won twenty or more games. He has won more than six hundred games, including state championships in 1994 and 2001 and a second in 1988. He admits that when the state title "slipped through [his] hands in 1988," it drove him harder. He wondered if he would get another chance.

The 1987–88 team, led by Barry Grasewicz, was 32–3. They beat Watseka by nineteen in the quarterfinals and Walther Lutheran by twenty-two in the semifinals. But center Kevin Bird suffered a knee injury against Watseka and was sidelined for the last two games. In the final against Pana, they were tired, turned the ball over on four of their last five possessions, and lost 62–58.

In 1993–94, Pinckneyville played up to expectations. Shane Hawkins was returning from a 29–2 sectional finalist. The Panthers lost only twice in thirty-five games, both to Carbondale, which was second in the Class AA tournament. They beat top-ranked and unbeaten Teutopolis 55–54 in the quarterfinals as Jarritt Sommer made a three-point play with twelve seconds remaining. In the final, Pinckneyville edged Eureka 67–65 as Hawkins passed to Ryan Bruns, who scored the game-winning basket at the buzzer.

"I don't know if I've ever seen a coach who could be as calm and collected in the last two minutes of a game," Shane Hawkins said. "Even at state, when we won two of three games with last-second shots, he would call time-out and not panic. He gathers you and tells you what we will do and we go out and believe in him. And it happens exactly as he drew it up."

In 2000–2001, Corn didn't expect to win the Class A title. Tim Bauersachs was the team's best player. "He was one of the best leaders I've ever been around," Corn said. But his mother was dying of cancer. The adversity drew the players closer together.

Pinckneyville, behind Bauersachs, Cody Majewski, and Haven Hicks, beat Westmont and the all-time tournament scoring leader Pierre Pierce in the semifinals, then clipped Pana 77–50 in the final to close out a 31–4 campaign.

"I don't have any great strength as a coach," Corn said. "I treat my kids as I want to be treated, establish a sound work ethic, and do things simple. I want the game to be fun for kids. I don't subscribe to the star theory. I want all of my players to get their hands dirty and share the workload."

Mount Vernon: Three Titles in Six Years

In 1950, as top-ranked and unbeaten Mount Vernon was relentlessly and unerringly moving toward its second state championship in a row, the Rams were pitted against their South Seven Conference rival Benton in the regional.

Benton had lost two previous meetings with Mount Vernon, so the Rangers decided to employ a different strategy. They held the ball. At halftime, Mount Vernon led 4–2.

In the locker room, Max Hooper, John Riley, Eddie King, Walt Moore, and the Mount Vernon players were moaning and groaning. They were the defending state champions, and they had been limited to only four points in the first sixteen minutes.

"What's wrong?" coach Stan Changnon asked. "We have doubled the score on them."

"That's the kind of pyschology he had. He kept everything in perspective," King said. "In the fourth quarter, we held the ball as Hooper [who was 6' 5"] held the ball over his head. We were going to show them that it works both ways."

Mount Vernon won 12–7.

It wasn't the first time Changnon had used a psychological ploy to motivate or calm his team, and it wouldn't be the last.

After the 1949 season, Changnon invited the celebrated *Chicago Daily News* sports editor and columnist John P. Carmichael to speak at the team's banquet.

"A real champion is not a champion unless they repeat," Carmichael told the players. "That is the test of a real champion, if you can come back and win again."

"We knew the coach had put him up to it," King recalled. "In the summer, we worked out in the gym voluntarily after American Legion baseball. We never had done it before. If we were going to win again, we had to work extra hard. Anything less than the state title would have been a huge disappointment."

Changnon came from West Frankfort with an impressive resume. He coached a 28–

6 Sweet Sixteen qualifier in 1942 and a 28–5 state quarterfinalist in 1943. Mount Vernon won a title in 1920 but hadn't qualified for the state finals since 1931. Changnon, it was hoped, could rebuild the program and make the Rams competitive with their bitter rival, Centralia.

Centralia was the winningest high school program in the nation. Coach Arthur Trout and three-time All-Stater Dike Eddleman were legendary figures in southern Illinois. But within ten years, Changnon had escaped from Centralia's shadow by achieving a milestone that Centralia has never surpassed. Mount Vernon has four state titles, Centralia only three.

The towns are only twenty-two miles apart, and the rivalry was intense and emotional, always the biggest game of the year. Changnon wanted to put his stamp on his program, and he didn't want to copy Trout. Instead of teaching Trout's famed kiss shot, he taught a one-handed jump shot, and he taught the taller Hooper to execute a two-handed, over-the-head shot that was virtually impossible to block.

Changnon was 5' 11" and weighed 215 pounds with very broad shoulders. He was mild-mannered and even-tempered, never profane. If he got perturbed, he shouted, "Hell's bells!" It was enough to get his players' undivided attention.

He picked up his players at six in the morning so they could shoot free throws before class. Practice consisted of learning how and where to shoot a jump shot. He even taught the fundamentals of hand position on the ball. He wanted them to close their eyes, catch the ball, and get the proper grip.

His players had certain positions to play, and they learned how to play them. Hooper was the scorer, Moore the ballhandler, Riley the rebounder, and King the outside shooter. They didn't date during the season. Before road trips, they ate dinner at Hunt's restaurant on the square. No mashed potatoes, no milk shakes.

In 1949, Mount Vernon was ranked number four in the state but lost its last regular-season game to Johnston City by one. After winning the sectional to earn a trip to the Sweet Sixteen, Changnon said: "We can go up to Champaign to win or have a good time." They beat Johnston City in the first round by two, then swept Decatur, West Aurora, and Hillsboro to win the state title.

With Hooper, Moore, Riley, and King returning in 1949–50, the Rams were a popular choice to repeat. To prepare, they practiced all summer. It was a very hot summer, so Changnon installed big fans at the main doors to the gym to prevent his players from suffering too badly from the heat.

"We have always been called one of the top teams in state history," Riley said. "We felt the pressure, but we probably put more pressure on ourselves because we knew we were undefeated and we were determined that we wouldn't let anyone upset us."

Mount Vernon was dominant. Perhaps its closest game was a 57–48 victory over Elgin in the state semifinals. In the final, the Rams crushed second-ranked Danville 85–61 as Hooper scored thirty-six points, setting a state tournament record. They outscored Danville 45–28 in the second half to pull away.

"We were the Tiger Woods of that era," King said. "We knew people would wonder if we were for real. It was one of the best defensive games we played all year. We didn't want it to be close. We wanted to make a statement."

How good were they? "I saw some teams that were just as good," Moore said. "But we had to rank among the top two or three teams in state history."

Moore and Riley returned in 1950–51, and Mount Vernon was ranked sixth in the state. But the Rams' forty-six-game winning streak was snapped by Centralia, and they lost to Pinckneyville in the sectional. Pinckneyville coach Duster Thomas devised a brilliant plan to upset Mose Stokes, who fouled out early in the game.

In 1951–52, Mark Mannen, Joe Johnson, Don McCann, and Mose and Jim Stokes led Mount Vernon to third place in the state tournament. The Rams were 32–4, losing to Quincy 54–51 in the semifinals, then beating Rock Island 71–70 in the consolation game. It was Changnon's last season.

In 1953, Mount Vernon lost a one-pointer to Harrisburg in the sectional final as Al Avant missed the last shot. He never forgot the experience. The Rams led until the last thirty seconds. "It was a long season when you didn't go to state," Avant said.

With four starters returning, there were high expectations for 1953–54. Changnon had retired to become athletic director. Harold Hutchins, a pupil of Changnon's, was in his second season, but Changnon ran the program, sometimes coming onto the floor to direct practice. Hutchins did what Changnon told him to do.

They were 20–3 and ranked fourth in the state after the regular season. They split a pair of games with Don Ohl and Edwardsville, which finished fourth in the state. They were very well balanced, with all five starters averaging in double figures—Avant (sixteen points per game), Goff Thompson (thirteen), Don Richards (fourteen), 6' 5" center Larry Whitlock (fifteen), and Fred Deichman (ten).

In the sectional, Avant converted two free throws after time had expired to beat Mount Carmel and Archie Dees by one. Afterward, a booster named Tater Hill, who had gone to Chicago to scout Du Sable, told them that Charlie Brown, Paxton Lumpkin, and the city team was as good as people said they were.

Du Sable was unbeaten but unranked, an indication that city schools got no respect from Downstaters. After the Panthers smashed Bowen, Quincy, and Edwardsville in the first three games, however, everyone outside of Mount Vernon predicted a rout in the championship game.

"We thought we could beat Du Sable because we were a team, and they weren't," Thompson said. "They had great talent but played as individuals. Charlie Brown was a great player, as good a player as I had ever seen. But they didn't play together."

The game was tied after the third quarter. Then Mount Vernon, with Avant scoring twenty-three points and Richards twenty-five, pulled away to win 76–70. There was considerable controversy over the officiating, especially a charging foul that sent Lumpkin out of the game and two walking calls against Brown in the closing minutes.

"They didn't play hard defense. That's what beat them," Avant said. "We played good defense and had good shooters. If they had played tough defense, they might have won."

"They couldn't stop Avant, who was as athletic as they were," Thompson said. "Afterward, they wanted to play us in Chicago in an extra game, to show us they could beat us. If they had played as a team, I don't think we could have beaten them."

Later, coaches Gene Haile, Bob Arnold, Lee Emery, and Doug Creel took teams to the state finals. And there were more good players, including Coleman Carrodine, Terry Gamber, Nate Hawthorne, Jamar Sanders, and Kent Williams. But nobody could duplicate the glory of the 1950s.

In fact, Mount Vernon didn't send a team to the Elite Eight from 1969 to 1997, when Williams and company lost to West Aurora in the quarterfinals. In his three seasons, the Rams were 25–5, 25–4, and 28–1. He finished as the school's all-time leading scorer with 2,185 points. But the 1999 supersectional loss to East St. Louis and Darius Miles was hardest of all to swallow.

"The whole team had played together since fifth grade," Williams said. "It was our last chance. We were 28–0. We were ranked number two in the state and in the top twenty-five in *USA Today*. It was a heartbreaker. We felt we let the town down. We wanted to bring back a state title."

Max Hooper: The Captain

Even today, his former teammates refer to Max Hooper as "the Captain." Hooper led the 1949 and 1950 Mount Vernon teams to 30–3 and 33–0 seasons, triggered a forty-six-game winning streak, and won two consecutive state championships.

"Hooper was to Mount Vernon what Dike Eddleman was to Centralia," said Terry Gamber, an All-Stater on Mount Vernon's 1965 state quarterfinalist who now is a circuit court judge. "To get young kids to understand, I say Hooper was to Mount Vernon what Arnold Palmer was to the PGA tour. He is the first one everybody thinks about when they talk about Mount Vernon basketball, the guy who got the tradition going."

Now retired and living in Birmingham, Alabama, Hooper hasn't forgotten his roots. He established a database of names, addresses, and telephone numbers of everyone in his graduating class. He e-mails classmates about birthdays so they can send cards. He still returns to Mount Vernon several times a year to visit friends, attend games, and talk to coaches and athletes.

Walt Moore, a two-time All-Stater who teamed with Hooper on the 1949 and 1950 state champions, said that Hooper "always was a guy who looked at everything, the leader who kept everyone in line."

"When you mention Hooper, you mention Mount Vernon, and vice-versa," said ninety-one-year-old Noble Thomas, who coached basketball and football at Mount Vernon in the 1950s.

"The newspaper was always Hooper, Hooper, Hooper. He was a big star. Everyone looked up to him," said Al Avant, who starred on Mount Vernon's 1954 state championship team and now is the athletic director at Chicago State University.

"We watched Hooper and Moore and the 1949 and 1950 teams. When they won the state title, we felt we would be state champions. The kids who played basketball were put on a pedestal. People knew who they were. Our dream was to play basketball for Mount Vernon and be a state champion."

Eddie King, a starter on the 1949 and 1950 state champions, referred to Hooper as "the peacemaker." Whether it was touch football or baseball in John Riley's yard or basketball on cinders in the alley, Hooper tried to make sure that everyone was treated fairly, that everyone got a chance to play.

Hooper, King, and Riley, an All-Stater on the 1950 powerhouse, grew up together on Logan Avenue and attended an all-white elementary school. Walt Moore, an African American, grew up on the South Side of town and attended an all-black elementary school. In the 1940s and 1950s, in an era that Hooper and Moore referred to as "accepted segregation," there were no racial issues.

"Kids mixed, but the town didn't," Hooper recalled. "We didn't know the difference. No one told me that blacks were different than I was. In the sandlot, we sweated and played ball with them. We practiced, ate, and traveled together. I never gave any thought of what his life was like when he went home."

As he looks back, however, Hooper realizes that the lives of Walt Moore, Wiley Mays, Jim and Mose Stokes, and Al Avant were different. At Mount Vernon's three movie theaters, a section in the back was roped off for African Americans. They couldn't eat in restaurants on the square. All of the town's officials were white. In the school yearbook, black students were listed at the end, while whites were listed in alphabetical order.

"I was naïve," Hooper said. "I thought that was the way it was. Today, when I go back to Mount Vernon, it is the same as it was. Blacks still live on the South Side of town. Whites still give occasional inferences that blacks aren't of the same caliber.

"Segregation is alive and well in Alabama today, too. We give a lot of lip service. In those days, on road trips, we ate in the kitchen of restaurants with our black teammates. The word 'prejudice' never entered our mind. I would look at Walt Moore today and say I didn't know. There was never any racial strife between the white and black players on our team."

The 1940s were a peaceful, orderly time. Kids didn't watch television or drive cars or eat at McDonald's. Nobody talked about the NBA or NFL. John Rackaway, sports editor of the *Mount Vernon Register News,* was the local media source. Hooper and his friends listened to broadcasts of the St. Louis Cardinals baseball games with Harry Carey and Gabby Street.

Hooper wanted to be a baseball player. He slept with his glove by his bed so that it wasn't hard to find when he got up. He and his friends went to a field, chose up sides, and played all day. Mothers had a tough time persuading their sons to come home for dinner.

They bought bubble gum that featured baseball cards. Would you trade a Marty Marion for a Joe DiMaggio? A Ted Williams for a Stan Musial? Harry Brecheen for Hal Newhouser? They could recite the batting averages and pitching statistics of major league players to anyone willing to listen.

Hooper dreamed of pitching in the major leagues. He was 6' 5" and threw very hard. How hard? There weren't any radar guns in those days, but a scout for the New York Giants was impressed enough to offer Hooper a five hundred dollar contract when he was a junior. The major leaguer Ray Blades lived in Mount Vernon and said that he could arrange for a tryout. Hooper opted to attend the University of Illinois because of baseball coach Wally Roettger, a former major leaguer.

"The NBA wasn't something to dream about in the 1940s," Hooper said. "After we won our first state title, I felt I had talent in basketball. But I never sensed I was going to be a college player."

But doors opened for him. After he led Mount Vernon to a second state title, after he set a state tournament record by scoring thirty-six points to beat Danville for the 1950 championship, Kentucky's legendary coach Adolph Rupp sat on Hooper's front porch and begged him to come to Lexington. Bradley, then a national power, recruited Hooper, Riley, and King. Riley and King decided to go to Peoria.

Hooper chose Illinois because the former Illini great Lou Boudreau spent a day with him. They met at Chicago's Comiskey Park on a warm day in June in 1950. Boudreau, then the famed player/coach of the Cleveland Indians, gave him a baseball signed by Boudreau, Bob Feller, and Larry Doby.

Hooper isn't sure where his basketball skills came from: his father was a baseball player, and his brother played football. The first time he got an inkling that he had some basketball talent was when Mount Vernon coach Stan Changnon came to a junior high school practice and worked with him.

"At first, he was pretty awkward," said Scott Gill, a former coach at Mount Vernon. "We played the walk-style of basketball, not run-and-gun. Max couldn't run until his freshman year when he was on the varsity. In our slow style, he could play. Any time you showed up at the gym, he was working hard. He would try to do anything for the good of the team."

Hooper developed into the state's premier player. He was unique, a big man who could play inside or outside. He was taught to shoot a two-handed overhead shot, which he rarely missed. Even though he was the acknowledged star, he worked as hard as anyone on the team.

"That made us a team," Eddie King said. "He had the ability to not take advantage of his position. He had as many assists as anyone. He held us together. We all knew our roles, and no one tried to outshine anyone else."

"Basketball was a finesse game, much more than today: no dunking, no showboating," Hooper said. "No one was concerned about scoring. We gave the ball to the open man, the one who had the best opportunity to score. There were no selfish bones in our bodies."

In 1949, Hooper was the leading scorer in the state finals (eighty-one points in four games) as Mount Vernon beat Johnston City by two in the first round, then swept past Decatur, West Aurora, and Hillsboro to win the school's first state title since 1920.

In 1950, Hooper repeated as the leading scorer in the state finals (104 points in four games) as Mount Vernon completed an unbeaten season with victories over Peoria Spalding (by seventeen), Freeport (by twenty-five), Elgin (by eight), and second-ranked Danville (by twenty-four).

"Against Elgin, we trailed 8–0 at the start," Hooper recalled. Then Changnon called time-out, hitched his pants, and gathered his players around him. He hardly had to say a word.

"He didn't come at you screaming and yelling," Hooper said. "He had a big belly and a smile on his face. He recognized the talent he had on the team. He knew we knew what we had to do because of all the hard work we had done for four years."

Even today, when old-timers and historians talk about the best teams in state history, Mount Vernon's 1950 powerhouse is included with such teams as Thornridge 1972, Collinsville 1961, Quincy 1981, Chicago Marshall 1958, and Taylorville 1944.

"They still remember us," Hooper said. "Even when I go back every year to see a game, the young kids remember those times.

"Yes, it was a special time, just after World War II. Economic times were good, and Mount Vernon, a little town in southern Illinois, came along and won two state championships. We did not realize how well known we were. That is evident when even today those two championship teams are talked about."

2
The 1950s

Segregated Schools:
"Power of the Pointed Finger"

Integration was slow to come to Illinois. The wildfire of racial hatred that burned through the Deep South, especially in Alabama and Mississippi, was less publicized but no less subtle in southern Illinois in the 1920s, 1930s, 1940s, and 1950s.

Towns in Pulaski, Jackson, Franklin, and Williamson Counties were run by southern Baptists and rednecks that had antiforeign or antiblack or anti-Catholic feelings. Route 37, a north-south highway, went through Johnston City. For years, a sign warned: "Nigger, don't let the sun set on your head in this town."

To this day people who have followed the Illinois high school tournament for years are surprised to learn there once was a championship game between members of the Southern Illinois Conference of Colored High Schools that was played between Friday's quarterfinal sessions at Huff Gym from 1942–45.

The conference of all-black schools in southern Illinois covered an area from Carbondale to Cairo, including Lincoln (Brookport), Sumner (Cairo), Attucks (Carbondale), Colp (Herrin), Lincoln (East St. Louis), Lincoln (Edwardsville), Lovejoy, Dunbar (Madison), Dunbar (Metropolis), Douglass (Mounds), and Lovejoy (Mound City).

For several years prior to 1927, the schools had attempted to organize a competitive sports program. In 1927, principal G. V. Quinn of Colp appeared before the IHSA's board of control to discuss the conference's problems. From 1928 to 1941, the conference conducted its own tournament.

In 1942–45, the championship was moved to Huff Gym in Champaign. Few people realized it at the time, but this was the first step toward integration. Carbondale Attucks won in 1942 and 1943 and Mounds Douglass won in 1944 and 1945. In 1946, the tournament was abolished, and the IHSA ruled that all-black schools were eligible to compete with all-white and integrated schools for the state title.

Gene Cross witnessed all of it. He attended Mounds Douglass, an all-black school of 125 students that closed in 1964. In 1944, he scored seventeen points as the Douglass Tornadoes beat Madison Dunbar 49–34 for the "Colored Schools" championship.

After the game, sportswriters wanted to know Douglass's nickname; it didn't have one. But Leonard Tucker, the team's best player—he later became the first black baseball player signed by the St. Louis Cardinals—christened Douglass the Tornadoes. "We want to play like the other Tornadoes," he said.

The following night, the other Tornadoes, from Taylorville, completed their 45–0 season. One newspaper asked: Who are the best Tornadoes?

"We were aware of Taylorville," Cross said. "We saw their title game. They were tough. Johnny Orr and Ron Bontemps were very good. I won't say we could or couldn't beat them. But the state hadn't ever seen a black team play like we did. We did things that weren't supposed to be done."

In Mounds, there were two high schools but one board of education. Mounds was for whites, Douglass for blacks. Geographically, they were located three blocks apart. Ideologically, they were light years apart.

"Growing up, we were too young to understand the deadly principle of segregation," Cross said. "We accepted things as being a matter of fact or part of life. I don't recall any protest or uprising. There were certain things we didn't do and certain places we didn't go."

As coach at Mounds Douglass from 1951 to 1964, however, Cross had a different view of integration. "I saw the unfairness of discrimination as opposed to when I was sixteen and seventeen," he said.

For example, Cross, who was born across the street from the house on Shiloh Road in Villa Ridge, north of Mounds, that he lived in until his death at age seventy-five, never played golf at the nearby Egyptian Country Club. As a youngster, he wasn't even allowed to be a caddie. The club accepted its first black member in 2002.

Cross became a leader in the all-black schools' bid to gain equal standing in the IHSA. He and others called for an integrated tournament. It took a few years to achieve their goal, but the groundwork was laid. It was an idea whose time had come.

The turning point, the event that opened the eyes of school administrators who still clung to the Old South dogma of the 1920s and 1930s, came in 1946, when Mounds Douglass stunned West Frankfort in the regional at Benton.

West Frankfort was 26–2 and ranked number two in the state. They beat top-ranked Champaign, the eventual state champion, in the final of the Centralia tournament. They were coming off of 28–5, 23–9, and 33–5 seasons, but Harlan Hodges's 1945–46 team was best of all. It was led by All-Stater Robert "Cotton" Hughes.

West Frankfort was an all-white coal-mining community. Hughes's only experience with black players was competing against archrival Centralia and its star, Ken "Preacher" McBride. To this day he insists that West Frankfort wasn't a racist community.

Even though the state tournament was supposed to be integrated in 1946, the IHSA didn't designate pairings to schools in southern Illinois. Douglass had to ask white schools for permission. The school had to go as far north as necessary until a white school agreed to play.

B. Floyd Smith, the principal of Benton and the IHSA president, gave permission for Douglass to participate in the Benton regional. And West Frankfort, believing that Douglass would be an easy first-round victim, volunteered to play them.

"There wasn't a great deal of concern when we learned we would play an all-black team," Hughes said. "We figured we were heading to Champaign, and whoever they threw in our way, we could handle them. The fact that they were black, even though there was some prejudice, we weren't concerned about it."

More schools began to question the IHSA's policy. Douglass had no business playing in the regional at Benton. Put them where they belong, critics said. Black schools in southern Illinois continued to ask for complete integration.

It finally happened in the fall of 1953 when Al Willis, then the IHSA's executive secretary, called a meeting in Dongola. All of the schools south of Carbondale were invited to attend. About twenty to twenty-five people showed up, including Douglass coach Gene Cross.

At the outset of the four-hour meeting, Willis said that he was there to get feedback from black schools that had petitioned for an integrated state tournament. If they could obtain a consensus view, he would go back to the IHSA's board of directors to make a recommendation.

"I recall every word that was said," Cross said. "The meeting almost came to blows between white and black schools. All but two white persons spoke against integration. All of the whites talked about possible race riots."

Late in the afternoon, a number of coaches wanted to leave. But Willis said that nobody would leave until a decision was reached. So he gathered all twelve school superintendents around a large table in the center of the room.

"I'm going to ask some questions, and all I want is a yes or no answer," Willis told the administrators. "If the state integrates the district tournament, will your school host the tournament with a colored school assigned to it?"

It was the power of the pointed finger. Willis pointed to one of the administrators who hadn't uttered a word, the superintendent from Anna-Jonesboro. "We will host the tournament," he told Willis. He revealed that, at its last meeting, the Anna-Jonesboro board had voted unanimously to host.

Willis pointed to the other administrator who had sat mute during the earlier discussions, the superintendent from Shawnee–Wolf Lake. He also agreed to host an integrated tournament, adding that his school board also had unanimously voted to support the issue.

Willis knew it all the time. Before he left his Chicago office for the long trip to Dongola, he was aware that the superintendents from Anna-Jonesboro and Wolf Lake had agreed to host tournaments. They were the key to passing the proposal because the two schools had the best facilities.

"Now I am sure that all of you others would like to host the tournament," Willis said. "But since I have the two nicest facilities, I do not need to ask anyone else. The schools that don't like my decision don't have to play in the tournament. Meeting adjourned; the tournament will be integrated."

The first integrated tournament in southern Illinois was a district tournament at Anna-Jonesboro in 1954. There were no problems. Douglass won the district and the regional at Wolf Lake before losing to Mount Carmel and Archie Dees in the sectional at Harrisburg. Mount Carmel later lost to Mount Vernon, which went on to win the state title by beating the all-black Chicago Du Sable.

Integration led to a reduction of all-black schools in southern Illinois. There were mergers between Attucks and Carbondale and Sumner and Cairo. Douglass, Mounds Township, Mounds City, and Lovejoy combined to form Meridian High School.

"The great lesson in all of this," Gene Cross said, "is you shouldn't prejudge people or human nature, that you should give everyone an equal chance. That is all you can expect out of life, that life owes you only one thing—an opportunity."

Hebron: The Giant Killers

Before there was *Hoosiers*, there was Hebron. The popular motion picture was based on Milan's dramatic ride to the Indiana state championship in 1954. Milan High School (enrollment 162) beat perennial power Muncie Central 32–30 on Bobby Plump's last-second basket. Two years earlier, Hebron produced its own David-and-Goliath drama. Led by twin brothers and a 6' 10" center, Hebron became the smallest school (enrollment ninety-eight) to win the Illinois championship and the first to win on live television.

Paul and Phil Judson were born on April 10, 1934. Paul is fifteen minutes older than Phil. Growing up, Paul was an inch taller and two pounds heavier. But fifty years later, when the Hebron team celebrated its golden anniversary at the 2002 state tournament in Peoria, people still couldn't tell them apart.

In the army they switched guard duty. In baseball they switched numbers and fooled the umpire. In college they switched on dates. As high school coaches they once tried to switch teams at halftime, but they forgot to change jackets, and the players caught on quickly.

But they were always serious about basketball. Their older brother Howie, who later pitched for the Chicago White Sox, was a freshman reserve on a Hebron team that reached the first round of the 1940 state tournament. In 1950, Paul was a sophomore starter as the Green Giants posted a 23–5 record. In 1951, they were 26–2 as Phil joined Paul in the starting lineup.

The Judsons' first experience with "basketball" came when they tossed a tennis ball into a coffee can that Howie had nailed up inside the family garage. Later, the twins played with Don Wilbrandt and Ken Spooner on their driveways or at Mau's barn across the street if it was too cold.

"When we played in the driveway, we always played for the state championship," Phil said. "I always wanted to be Champaign and Jesse Clements, my idol. Paul was Centralia and Dike Eddleman. Howie had pictures of Eddleman in his room. The others would represent Mount Vernon, Paris, Taylorville, and Decatur. My father had a trophy for trap shooting and we used it as a state championship trophy. We'd go to Spooner's to play the district tournament, then to our driveway for the regional, then to Wilbrandt's for the sectional, then to Mau's barn for the finals. That was Huff Gym. We played in the hay loft."

They were dreaming, of course. They grew up in a different world. Their graduating class had eighteen students; Hebron played six-man football. The Judson family bought a newfangled television set in 1948. They watched Milton Berle, Navy basketball games, and Kukla, Fran, and Ollie.

The Judsons saw Huff Gym for the first time in 1945. Howie was a sophomore at the University of Illinois, and the family drove to Champaign to celebrate his birthday.

They returned to Huff Gym in 1951, after losing to Elgin in the regional. The school could get only four tickets, so Phil, Paul, Don Wilbrandt, and Don's father drove in his Cadillac, the only Cadillac in town, to see the Saturday finals.

"In 1952, we looked at where we were at, where we sat last year, and realized that was why Coach Ahearn sent us, to get a little atmosphere, to get a feel for things," Phil said. "We never thought of it at the time. Huff Gym was a special place."

They didn't meet Bill Schulz until they got to high school. A year younger, Schulz grew up on a farm four miles west of Hebron. He attended a one-room school for seven years. He was 6' 4" in eighth grade, but he hadn't touched a basketball before Hebron coach Russ Ahearn asked if he wanted to learn to play the game.

"I had milked cows as a farm boy. I had seen only one or two basketball games, but I had never played," Schulz said. "It was hard because I wasn't very well coordinated. But it became enjoyable because I had never experienced anything like it. Once I started, I never thought I'd quit. I wanted to get better."

Howie Judson was pitching for the White Sox at the time. In the winter he became Schulz's private coach. He worked with the youngster on post play. When he was preparing to move to the varsity as a 6' 10" junior, Ahearn gave him a list of things to do to improve—ballhandling, shooting, turnaround jump shot, and getting good position for rebounds.

Ahearn was thirty-five years old when he came to Hebron in 1948. He had been an assistant on John Krafft's staff at Elgin. He wanted to be a head coach, and he knew it wasn't likely that he would succeed Krafft. When he arrived, he had a plan in his pocket.

"I wasn't included in the plan, because he didn't know about me," Schulz said. "But he knew Howie Judson, and he knew about the Judson twins."

Ahearn was called "Duke" or "Napoleon" because of his small stature at 5' 4", and his reputation as a strict disciplinarian. He stressed sportsmanship and character. If a player got out of line, he was dropped. He didn't swear and wouldn't tolerate anyone who did.

He handed out food menus. He cautioned his players to avoid milk and gravy for two days before a game. He recommended drills. During practice, he was the only one who talked. He always carried a brown notebook. Everything he knew or wanted to know about basketball was included. Practices were detailed to the minute: four minutes for this, five minutes for that. He often assigned assistant coach Phil Hadley to write things in the notebook.

Everybody anticipated that 1951–52 would be a special season. Before the first district game at Richmond, Ahearn jotted the number 11 on the chalk board. "Boys, you win eleven games and you will be state champs," he said. Then he walked out.

The team had few set plays. Ahearn figured if a team had a set play, the other team would scout it and be able to defend against it. So Hebron played "alley ball."

Hebron had a tip-off play, an out-of-bounds play under the basket, and a "hey, Paul" play. If the player defending Phil was over guarding, he would holler "hey, Paul," and cut to the basket. Schulz would screen his man, and Paul would throw a baseball pass to Phil for an easy basket. They successfully executed the play twice in the state finals.

Hebron played only seven home games in 1951–52. The gym seated only 550, and the court was seventy-two feet long and forty feet wide. It fit snugly on a stage. There were two ten-second lines. Opponents didn't want to play there. Neither did Hebron.

The Green Giants became the darlings of the media. Phil and Paul filled one scrapbook with newspaper clippings of regular-season games. They filled another with state tournament clippings. They collected newspapers. Every day, they read the four Chicago dailies—*Daily News, Tribune, Herald-Examiner,* and *Sun.* They read John Carmichael, Tommy Kouzmanoff, Jerome Holtzman, Ralph Leo, and Emil Stubits. They read George Sullivan's reports in the local paper, the *Woodstock Sentinal.*

They started 15–0, then lost to Crystal Lake 71–68. It was the only team that scored more than sixty points against Hebron during the season. Fritz Schneider scored thirty-four.

"After we lost, we thought [Ahearn] would say something about it in practice," Schulz said. "He said: 'We ran into a better team. They beat us fair and square. That's the last you are going to hear about it. Let's practice.' He never mentioned the game again. That was great motivation for us."

Later, Hebron avenged its only loss by beating Crystal Lake 61–46 in a regional semifinal at Elgin. In the final, they beat Elgin 49–47, and Schulz scored twenty-four.

After dispatching Barrington and DeKalb by twenty-two-point margins in the sectional, Ahearn was prepared for the trip to Champaign. The team stayed at a hotel north of the downtown area. No television, no radio, no phone calls, no newspapers, no distractions. He didn't even allow the team to go to Huff Gym to watch other games. They ate in the hotel, had meetings, and sat in their rooms.

"We didn't hear about Bruce Brothers [Quincy] or Billy Ridley [Taylorville] or Sharm Scheuerman [Rock Island] or Clarence Burks [Champaign]," Phil Judson said. "Our fans didn't know how we could beat Rock Island after they saw them warm up."

After beating Champaign 55–46 in the first round and Lawrenceville 65–55 in the quarterfinals, Hebron trailed Rock Island by three early in the fourth quarter, then scored fourteen points in a row and went on to win 64–56.

In the championship, Hebron outlasted Quincy 64–59 in overtime. Schulz scored twenty-four, while Brothers led Quincy with twenty before fouling out. Paul Judson scored thirteen, Phil twelve.

Afterward, Al Willis, the executive director of the IHSA, presented the championship trophy in Hebron's makeshift dressing room. There was no formal trophy presentation at the time, and Willis was late, having gone to Quincy's dressing room because he thought they had won. Then the Judsons, Schulz, and the other players went upstairs to be interviewed on television by Chick Hearn, who had done the color commentary of the game with play-by-play announcer Jack Drees.

"For me, I recall two things, the map on the wall at the end of Huff Gym and the jubilation, the people jumping around and screaming," Schulz said. "When they turned the other light out [Quincy] and we were the only light on, we were still on the floor when it happened. That was a big thrill to see Hebron with the only light on, the only team left."

St. Elizabeth: Gone but Never Forgotten

Larry Hawkins, who later coached Pete Cunningham and Cazzie Russell and produced a state championship team at Carver, recalls how he and others in the Chicago public school system viewed St. Elizabeth's program in the 1950s.

"It was the little school that had a great impact," Hawkins said. "They were terrible in football. But they got them all in basketball. In my world, that's where basketball occurred. We watched them and marveled at them. They had some magic."

In the 1950s, Chicago manufactured an assembly line of sleek, talented players who took the city game to another level, earning the respect of doubting Downstaters and raising the competitive bar for future generations.

Art Hicks may have been the best of all. "He was as good as I saw," Hawkins said. "He was a big guy who was in control. When he played 100 percent, he was awesome."

St. Elizabeth coach Art White said that Hicks was "the greatest high school player I ever saw. If he weren't such a good team man, he could average forty points a game."

Hicks, Prentiss Thompson, Tommy Williamson, and Elgin Dorsey led St. Elizabeth to the Chicago Catholic League and all-city championships in 1956 and 1957. They also won the National Negro Tournament in 1957. Hicks scored 1,151 points, or 22.6 per game, while leading the Ironmen to a 48–3 record in 1956–57.

In those years, if you were black and wanted to play football or basketball in the Catholic League, there was only one school you could attend. St. Elizabeth, located at 41st Street and S. Michigan Avenue, was the only all-black high school in the Catholic League. It closed in 1964 for lack of funds.

The Sisters of the Blessed Sacrament were paid a penny a day to teach three hundred boys and girls. The white nuns educated their students about black heritage and warned of the evils of white racists. In the Catholic League, Hicks and his teammates learned that Jim Crow wasn't a man's name but a way of life.

Hicks and Thompson grew up together in the Ida B. Wells housing project at 37th and Vincennes. They started playing basketball at Holy Angels Grammar School, then played in summer tournaments at Sheil House, across the street from St. Elizabeth, and Meyering playground at 71st and South Park.

"You went there to prove yourself," Thompson said. "We looked up to guys like Joe Bertrand, Phil Buckhalter, Sweetwater Clifton, and Leon Hilliard. Some of the pro players, like Woody Saulsberry of the Globetrotters, would play. Wilt Chamberlain was there one day. So were Sam Jones and K. C. Jones. If you thought you were a player, that's where you would be."

"We slam-dunked and played the same triangle offense that the Chicago Bulls used to win six NBA championships," said Lawrence Goolsby, who followed Hicks to St. Elizabeth. "We played fast break, up and down, very physical. Competition was hot. It set the tone for the style that kids play today."

Hicks's mother was a Baptist but wanted her son to have a Catholic education laced with plenty of discipline. A friend recommended De La Salle, which was in the neighborhood, but when Art attended basketball tryouts, a priest told him, "We don't have any Negroes going here, and I don't think we ever will."

Later, Hicks's mother met a woman on a streetcar who said that she had sent her son to St. Elizabeth, also in the neighborhood. Art wanted to enroll at Dunbar or Phillips, where his friends were going, but his mother insisted on a Catholic education.

Thompson was wavering between St. Elizabeth and Corpus Christi (now Hales Franciscan). He chose St. Elizabeth because it played football, his first love, but the Ironmen annually were crushed by Catholic League powers Mount Carmel and Fenwick, so Thompson began to take more kindly to basketball.

Despite his size, 6' 4" and 220 pounds, Hicks didn't play football. He had no other interest except basketball. "As freshmen, we were unbeaten and beat the varsity in practice. I knew when we were juniors we would be great," he said. "We stuck together and built a dynasty."

Art White and assistant coach Charlie Gant were the architects. White, who later became the first black football and basketball official in the Big Ten, lived in the same housing project with Hicks and Thompson. He was the motivator, the shouter, the enforcer. He was a former boxer, and no one wanted to tangle with him. A no-nonsense type on the court, after practices or games he often invited his players to his house for pizza.

Gant, who later coached at Englewood and Dunbar, was the tactician. His players called him "Doctor." He reinforced everything that White preached. He taught Hicks how to play every position and to have footwork like Fred Astaire.

In 1955–56, St. Elizabeth lost its season opener to St. Phillip. Afterward, White gathered his team together and explained their roles. The Ironmen went on to win forty-six of fifty games. They beat De La Salle 57–55 in overtime for the Catholic League championship. Hicks had thirty points and fourteen rebounds, and Williamson converted two free throws in the closing seconds. And they beat Dunbar 64–61 for the city championship at Chicago Stadium, with Hicks scoring twenty-three. A week earlier, Dunbar had finished third in the state tournament.

"That was our time," Hicks said. "We played two types of basketball—black like the Harlem Globetrotters, and white like the Boston Celtics. We used our bodies and minds on a very high mental and physical level."

In 1956–57, St. Elizabeth was even better. Paul Ellison had graduated, and Goolsby replaced him as the playmaker. They beat De La Salle 59–50 for the Catholic League title. Hicks scored thirty in a 63–57 victory over Crane for the city crown. The April 18, 1957, cover of *Jet* magazine featured a picture of White, Hicks, and Thompson posing with the city trophy. "It didn't get any better than that," Thompson said.

But it got a whole lot tougher. Each year, during the holidays, they received an even more important education. White and Gant drove their players to the South to play the best teams in Tennessee, Mississippi, Alabama, Georgia, Louisiana, and Arkansas. What they learned couldn't be found in a textbook.

They saw black men hanging from trees with tar all over their bodies and washrooms that said "Whites Only." They rode on a bus in Nashville and saw signs for "Colored Only," which were for the rear seats. When they stopped to eat, they had to walk around to the back of the restaurant and knock on the kitchen door. Sometimes they would be served, sometimes they wouldn't.

Their reception at all-white Catholic League schools also was inhospitable. At one tournament, an elderly white man who supervised the locker rooms assigned St. Elizabeth to the most dilapidated dressing facility and issued old towels with holes in them. He didn't say a word to the players.

After the Ironmen won their first game, however, the old man was impressed. "I guess you boys will be back tomorrow," he said. When they returned for the championship game, he took them to the best locker room, gave them new towels and big bars of fresh soap. And he shook hands with each of them.

"They didn't call us niggers anymore," Hicks said.

Later, they wondered how it might have felt to participate in the state tournament with the public schools and such Downstate powers as Centralia, Pinckneyville, and Mount Vernon, but the Catholic League wasn't admitted to the IHSA until 1975. School officials tried to arrange for games with two state champions, West Rockford (1956) and Herrin (1957), but they declined.

"We wished we could have played in the state tournament. We saw a lot of our friends from Du Sable and Dunbar going there," Goolsby said. "But it was a great thrill to play in Chicago Stadium. We ruled the city. Our goal was always to play in the city championship at Chicago Stadium."

Hicks had other goals. The boast of Chicago, he was one of the first coast-to-coast recruits. He took his first plane flight to visit the University of Southern California. Northwestern coach Bill Rohr talked to him, but he wanted to go to a Catholic school. Notre Dame was his first choice.

He wanted to go to Notre Dame with his pal, Prentiss Thompson. Parker's Tom Hawkins was there. Hicks was accepted, but Thompson wasn't, so they enrolled at Northwestern. Thompson flunked out after one year, went to North Dakota for two years, got married, and enlisted in the army. Hicks dropped out after two semesters, worked in a steel mill, then decided to return to college. He chose Seton Hall because it was a Catholic school.

If he had stuck to basketball, friends say that he could have played in the NBA or joined the Globetrotters. Instead, he met a professional gambler, Jack Molina, in New York and became embroiled in college basketball's second point-shaving scandal in ten years. He left Seton Hall in 1961 with a contract on his head and federal investigators on his behind. No charges were filed against him, but his basketball career was over.

"My first girlfriend was basketball, my first love affair," he said. "When you do something to break up that relationship, you never forget it. You never forget the first time you made a bad play on purpose. I will always remember it. I feel I would have been a sure NBA player. But I lost my love for the game. I turned it out of my life. I never thought I'd do that."

Chico Vaughn/Joe Aden: Only Fifteen Miles Apart

The mayor of East Cape Girardeau, Illinois, population 448, thumbs through some dusty scrapbooks in the living room of his home near the bridge that spans the Mississippi River, directly across from Cape Girardeau, Missouri, population 35,349.

Joe Aden has served as mayor since 1977. He has an office in City Hall but only puts in about twelve to fifteen hours per week. He has no full-time clerk, no police department, and no fire department.

When East Cape Girardeau was incorporated in 1975, the first item on the city agenda concerned stray dogs; it still is on the agenda today. People from Missouri cross the bridge and dump unwanted dogs on the levee.

But Aden has brokered several civic improvements, including a new sewer system, new natural gas system, and a new cable television system. There are plans for a new park.

Aden continues to thumb through his scrapbooks. He uncovers old newspaper clippings about himself and Chico Vaughn, Dongola, Tamms, and southern Illinois basketball in the 1950s.

Vaughn and Aden were two of the most prolific scorers in state history. They played at the same time (1954–58) at small country schools only fifteen miles apart. They competed against each other in pickup games during the summer and on eight occasions during their high school careers.

"Now it seems so weird, two players so close together at the same time," Aden said. "Television wasn't big then. We had no radio station that covered our games. No newspaper covered us every night. Ray Owen covered some games. So did Merle Jones [of the *Southern Illinoisan* in Carbondale]."

Vaughn/Aden developed into a hotly contested rivalry. In one game in 1958, Tamms beat Dongola as Vaughn scored thirty-six points and Aden scored thirty-four. In a regional game at Anna, Vaughn scored forty-nine and Aden scored forty.

Both of them were chasing the state record of 2,702 career points set by Centralia's legendary Dike Eddleman in 1939–42. Aden had never met Eddleman, but he knew that Eddleman's family roots were in Dongola and that he often spent summers there.

Vaughn emerged as the state's all-time leading scorer. But did he score 3,358 points, as the state record book attests, or 3,331, according to a chart in the hallway outside the gym at Tamms Egyptian High School? Also included in the glass case that commemorates Vaughn's career are a list of other accomplishments, his number 31 jersey, a picture, and a big trophy.

Aden scored 3,033 points according to the state record book. As a senior, he averaged more points (36.6) than Vaughn (36.3). They ranked third and fourth in the nation at the time. But Aden claims that he scored 3,031 points in his career. He averaged 28.3 points for 107 games, Vaughn 32.2 for 104.

"I only wish I was two inches taller [he was 6' 1"] and a step faster," Aden said. "Chico and I both shot from far outside. I thought about how many points we would have scored if we had the three-point line. But I never thought about us playing at a different time so I might have gotten more recognition."

When Dongola retired his number 33 jersey a few years ago, he was honored by school officials, alumni, and townspeople as the "Athlete of the Twentieth Century." His senior class had twenty-five students. The school's enrollment was ninety-nine.

"In the 1950s, every kid from a small town dreamed of going to Champaign [for the state finals]," Aden recalled. "As a freshman in 1954, the coach took us to the state tournament in Huff Gym. Our eyes bugged out. Huff was the biggest gym I had ever seen. Hebron had won the state title in 1952, so kids from small towns began to think that they could go to state, too. We were inspired and motivated by what Hebron had done."

Vaughn was inspired, too. He shot at a net behind Oliver Ray's grocery store in Unity, near Tamms. "I felt I could be someone. I could jump and shoot and handle the ball. I read about Bill Russell, Oscar Robertson, Jerry West, and Wilt Chamberlain. But I never thought I would play against them," he said.

While Dongola was all-white, Tamms (population 750) was mixed. Vaughn and other African Americans couldn't eat in the town's only restaurant. Chico ate sandwiches at the grocery store. "You couldn't go where you wanted to go or do what you wanted to do, but you could go to school," he said.

In the 1950s, Tamms wasn't a basketball town. The school had never qualified for the state finals. Led by Vaughn, the team advanced to the sectional two years in a row but lost to Pinckneyville in 1957 and Herrin in 1958, a year after the Tigers won the state championship.

"Herrin was ranked third in the state," Vaughn recalled. "We were battling back and forth, and the game went into overtime. One of my shots was nullified because it was ruled that I shot from out-of-bounds. When I shot, I often fell out-of-bounds after I released the ball. They took a few shots away from me. We lost in overtime. We got cheated. We had a real good team and finished 26–4. If we had won, we would have gone to the supersectional and maybe played Chicago Marshall [the eventual state champion] in the quarterfinals."

Ray Owen, reporting for the *Cairo Evening Citizen*, wrote a column criticizing the officiating. He thought that Pinckneyville's last-second, game-winning shot shouldn't have counted. The timekeeper disagreed.

"Vaughn took as much abuse as anyone should have to take," Owen said. "They tried to rattle him, but they couldn't."

Vaughn had a very unorthodox shot. He put the ball behind his head with both hands. "I got more distance by putting the ball at the back of my head, like a slingshot," he said. Aden said he had never seen a shot like that. "I wondered how it could go in the basket from that angle—but it did," he said.

"Vaughn was the greatest offensive player I ever coached against, better than Joe Aden or Archie Dees [of Mount Carmel]," said Gene Cross, former coach at Mounds Douglass. He once said that the only player he ever saw who was in Vaughn's class was Jim Stokes, an All-Stater at Mount Vernon in 1952 and 1953. "Vaughn had an unorthodox jump shot that you couldn't teach to defend against. You never would teach anyone to shoot that way. He put the ball behind his head with both hands. He never saw a shot he felt he couldn't make."

It was the best of times for high school basketball in southern Illinois. Mount Vernon won the state title in 1954, Herrin in 1957. Bobby Joe Mason was a legendary player at Centralia. Duster Thomas was producing great teams at Pinckneyville. There were great players: Mason, Vaughn, Aden, Stokes, Dees, Ron Purcell, John Tidwell, Al Avant, Roger Suttner, and Catfish Rollins.

"Basketball was never better in the Deep South than it was in the 1950s," Owen said. "And it was one-class basketball. It was big for a small school, like Tamms, to get to the sectional tournament. That's why Cobden [in 1964] was such a big story."

It also was a time when there were racial issues, with blacks playing against whites, Mount Vernon versus Chicago Du Sable, Vaughn versus Aden, Tamms versus Dongola.

"Vaughn took a lot of abuse in certain games, where the other team would get by with things that he couldn't but didn't let bother him," Owen said. "Tamms was like Cobden. He put the town on the map. Everyone wanted to see Dongola play Tamms.

"Aden was a scrawny kid who played center. He didn't have the finesse or ballhandling ability that Vaughn had, but he knew where the basket was. He scored without much fanfare. Everyone wanted to see him play because he scored so much."

Aden said that he had no understanding of racial issues at the time. As a junior, his all-white team played at Mounds Douglass, an all-black school. "We were one of the first all-white schools to play there. We didn't think anything about it. We were there to play ball, and so were they. It was just another game to us," Aden said.

Vaughn had different experiences. "We had problems with different teams. We were called names, and we were hit by players," he said. "The experience taught me about being a man and having faith in society. You have to show respect to get respect. I can deal with people better than before."

After setting the career scoring record at Southern Illinois University, Vaughn played for eight years in the NBA and ABA. He played with Bob Pettit, Cliff Hagan, and Clyde Lovellette with the old St. Louis Hawks. And he played with Connie Hawkins and Art Heyman on the Pittsburgh Pipers' ABA championship team in 1967. He was out of basketball in 1970.

Since 1988, Vaughn has been employed as a security guard at Meridian High School in Mounds. He never wanted to become a coach. What he is doing now, he said, is more satisfying. He works with handicapped and behaviorally challenged students.

His old school has been converted into a state vocational school: cars are repaired in the gym that Vaughn once played in. The new school opened in 1967. All of his scrapbooks were left with the second of his three wives in Pittsburgh.

"From sixth grade through college, I never missed a day of shooting or handling a basketball, no matter what the weather," Aden said. "Chico and I both came to play. It developed into a pretty good rivalry. It was pretty even over the four years."

Lyons: A Generation Apart

Harold Caffey and Marcus Washington are a generation apart, Caffey a child of the 1940s, Washington of the 1960s. But they share a lot in common, including an addiction to golf.

Caffey was the tenth man on La Grange's 1953 state championship team. Washington was an All-Stater, one of the stars of La Grange's 1970 state championship team.

Willard Johnson, Washington's cousin, also was a member of the 1953 squad. Caffey has been a friend of Washington's family for years. They live a lag putt from each other.

When Washington lost his basketball legs and ceased to participate in recreational league games, Caffey introduced him to golf. They play once a week and reminisce about Ted Caiazza, Chuck Sedgwick, the McRae brothers, Greg Sloan, Ron Nikcevich, Owen Brown, Effingham St. Anthony, Kankakee, and Harv Schmidt.

"I knew about the 1953 team, and Harold watched our 1970 team," Washington said. "He played in a difficult time. It was a difficult era to do what they did, to go to places they went. They all grew from it. In 1970, we had a great experience in a different era."

Lyons Township in La Grange is one of three schools in state history to field two unbeaten championship teams—Lawrenceville (1982, 1983) and Chicago King (1990, 1993) are the others—but the only one to prevail twice in a one-class playoff.

The 1953 team was one of the most dominant in state history. None of its twenty-nine opponents came within nine points. In the state finals, the Lions dispatched Chicago Du Sable by seventeen, Decatur St. Teresa by thirty-two, Pinckneyville by thirteen, and Peoria Central and Hiles Stout by twelve.

After losing to Oak Park in the sectional in 1952, La Grange had high expectations for 1953. Caiazza, Sedgwick, Joel and Leon McRae, and Nate Smith were back. After scoring fourteen points in an opening victory over Argo, however, coach Greg Sloan tore into Caiazza, a 6' 7" junior who had overcome the awkward style that had kept him on the bench as a freshman.

"You have all the potential of being an All-American if you put your mind to it. Why are you passing the ball? You shoot the ball. You can do this," Sloan told him. He scored twenty-three in his next game. As a 6' 7", 235–pound senior, Caiazza averaged thirty.

"Sloan was a tremendous coach," Caiazza said. "He would knock you down, pick you up, praise you, then cut your throat. Everybody who played for him liked him. He had great knowledge of the game and knew how to handle young men."

La Grange's toughest test came against Kankakee and Harv Schmidt before a crowd of fifty-five hundred in the sectional semifinal at Joliet. Kankakee was 26–0 and ranked number one in the state. La Grange was 23–0 and rated number three. Schmidt, a 6' 6" senior who averaged 27.5 points, was the best prospect in Illinois.

"Seldom, if ever, has a Chicago area high school game attracted as much attention," wrote Jerome Holtzman of the *Chicago Sun-Times*.

In one of the most ballyhooed games in tournament history, La Grange prevailed 83–74. Schmidt scored thirty-seven points, but Caiazza had thirty-one, Sedgwick had eighteen (including sixteen free throws, ten of ten in the fourth quarter), and Joel McRae added sixteen.

"Sloan said Schmidt was a great shooter, that he had an uncanny shot, unusual, he threw the ball like a baseball and it went in," Caiazza said. "Kankakee wasn't a running team. The key to beating them was we had to outrun them, outmaneuver them, and be a half-step ahead of them. We had to press and fast break and wear them out. In the third quarter, they had oxygen tanks on the floor. We had them on the run."

Schmidt was obsessed by the game. Like La Grange, Kankakee was a dominant team. The Kays' closest game was an eight-point victory at Quincy. He still believes Kankakee would have won if point guard Paul Weller, who had a slipped disc and didn't play much, had been able to handle La Grange's press. Or if Dick Rapp, who had averaged fourteen points per game but was limited to three shots and four points, had been more of a factor.

"There was great hoopla. Kankakee went berserk. It was fun," Schmidt said. "But there is a downside to getting beat. I've had nightmares about the game a couple of times a month all my adult life. I never got over that loss. It isn't a joking matter."

How good were the Lions? "I won't say we were as good as Thornridge [1972] or Quincy [1981]. But if we had the same training and coaching that improves athletes each year, we could give them a helluva game. Remember, we blew out a Du Sable team (85–68) that finished second in 1954 and revolutionized the game with its fast break," Caiazza said.

After the season, Sloan left for Rich Township in Park Forest. He took his 1955 team, led by Roger Taylor, to the Sweet Sixteen. In his last six years at La Grange, he won 83 percent (120–24) of his games.

After Sloan left, La Grange qualified for the Sweet Sixteen only once until Ron Nikcevich, who had coached Riverside-Brookfield and Tom Kondla to a West Suburban Conference title in 1963, was persuaded to become head coach in 1969. He won a state title in his first season and retired after finishing third in 1994 with 562 career victories.

"He was the most intense, most demanding coach I ever met," said Dave Van Skike, a junior starter in 1969–70. "He was a perfectionist, very organized. I can remember thinking even after we won the state title: 'Oh my God, I have to go back for another year." It was that intense. As good as we were, we never got overconfident. He wouldn't allow it. There was always something we could have done better."

Before the season, Nikcevich met with his team leaders—6' 8" junior Owen Brown, Washington, and point guard Scott Shaw. "He told us we had a leadership role to fill. He introduced us to his concept of defense and talked about the expectations we should have," Shaw said. "He was so big [6' 7"] and tough, someone you didn't mess with. He was so confident and sure of what he was doing. He really meant business. He had every minute accounted for in practice. He was military-like. He hated laziness and selfishness. He had a way of getting your attention and delivering a message."

Nikcevich introduced the 31 defense, a 1-3-1 with man-to-man principles. "Our intention was to display two separate defenses to force an opponent to use two separate offenses to attack us," he said.

Washington, swift and catlike, was at the top of the key in a 1-2-1-1 alignment, then moved to the baseline as a chaser according to ball movement. "He was the greatest defensive player I ever saw in high school," Nikcevich said.

The strategy was to stay in a 1-2-1-1 as long as possible, then recover to a 1-3-1 when the ball penetrated the free-throw line. "The key was to keep the ball between the center line and the free-throw line. We were never compelled to get out of the 31 defense. No one ever solved it," Nikcevich said.

In the 31, Shaw played the point. Steve Heinzelman, a 6' 6" junior, played to Shaw's left, with Van Skike, a 6' 3" junior, to Shaw's right. Brown, an intimidating shot blocker, lurked under the basket. Nikcevich said that Heinzelman was "just as good a defender and rebounder as any kid I ever coached."

Going into the state finals, La Grange was 27–0 and ranked number one in the state. Only five teams had come within ten points of them, but the Lions nearly tripped in the quarterfinals. After building a 52–35 lead at the outset of the third quarter against tiny Effingham St. Anthony, they were lulled to sleep. Brown and Shaw fouled out, and St. Anthony rallied to lead 85–84 before reserve Dave Wehrmeister's tip-in gave La Grange a one-point edge with fifty-seven seconds to play.

St. Anthony's John Miller made one of two free throws to tie at eighty-six. Then La Grange forged ahead for keeps on Heinzelman's short jumper with fourteen seconds left. After a turnover, Washington was fouled, and he made a free throw with two seconds remaining. St. Anthony's Mike Wente scored at the buzzer, but La Grange won 89–88.

Washington had twenty-eight points, thirteen rebounds, and eleven assists, Van Skike scored twenty, and Heinzelman had seventeen points and ten rebounds. Wente led St. Anthony with twenty-six points.

"They were pressing full-court, and I was totally exhausted," Van Skike recalled. "They ran and ran and ran. If it had gone on a few more minutes, they would have beaten us. It would have been like the movie *Hoosiers*. But Heinzelman made that fadeaway corner jumper when we were ahead by one. If he misses, they go down and score and beat us by one, I'm sure. But he made it. That was the kind of year it was."

The following day, La Grange didn't let up. The Lions beat Joliet Central and the tournament scoring leader Roger Powell by eleven in the semifinals, then outscored East Moline 24–10 in the fourth quarter to win 71–52 in the final. Brown had twenty-four points and set a tournament record with twenty-four rebounds.

"How do you put into words a first-year coach winning the state title, a guy who barely knows the way around the school's North campus?" Nikcevich said. "Before you know it, we're riding fire trucks through downtown La Grange."

Du Sable: Where We've Come From

In his 1978 book, *The Du Sable Panthers: The Greatest, Blackest, Saddest Team from the Meanest Street in Chicago,* the *New York Times* sports columnist Ira Berkow describes the story as "a reminder of where in racial terms in America we've come from. But more, it is a reflection of where we are today and why."

Berkow was a child of the 1950s. He was born in K-Town on Chicago's West Side, grew up on the North Side, and attended Sullivan High School. He recalls the glory days of city basketball, players such as Sweet Charlie Brown, Paxton Lumpkin, Tommy Hawkins, Art Day, Howie Carl, Ron Rubenstein, Lou Landt, and Abe Booker, and a time when the Illinois Tech Tournament was more appealing than a trip to Huff Gym.

Basketball was competitive from Altgeld Gardens to Rogers Park. In the first round of the Illinois Institute of Technology (IIT) Tournament in 1956, all-black Phillips beat all-white Senn 49–47 and went on to win the title. All-white Roosevelt was 23–4 and reached the first round of the state finals in 1952.

There was nothing more exciting than the IIT Tournament at the International Amphitheater. All of the city's public schools participated. Games started at 9 A.M., and the last game started at 9 P.M. In the 1953 championship, Du Sable, Brown, and Lumpkin beat Marshall and Day in overtime.

"We would sit all day long and watch," said Berkow, who captained Sullivan's 1956–57 team. "You could smell the stockyards. They had no lockers and one shower for both teams. They gave you a large paper bag to put your clothes in. IIT's floor was panels of wood that would bounce up and hit you in the eye. But it never seemed to bother the good players."

As a fourteen-year-old, Berkow observed the evolution of the game in the city. Until 1954, it was dominated by Jewish kids on the West Side and North Side such as Landt, Carl, Rubenstein, Moose Malitz, Irv Bemoras, Eddie Goldman, Danny Rogovich, and Harvey Babetch. On the South Side, white kids such as Johnny Kerr, Bill Bandemier, Sammy Esposito, and Tommy Jorgensen were standouts. Then Du Sable triggered a new era.

"Du Sable captivated the city, all black players, like the Harlem Globetrotters," Berkow said. "You couldn't wait to see their games. Their names were exciting. Nobody ever saw anything like it before."

Chicago basketball got no respect from Downstaters. Since entering the state tournament in 1928, city schools had rarely been competitive. Schools in southern and central Illinois, from Centralia to Mount Vernon to Pinckneyville to Taylorville to Paris to Decatur to Champaign, were much more advanced in terms of organization, coaching, and community, school, and fan support.

If that wasn't enough, the city offered midyear graduation to students, a rule that scuttled many good teams. In 1953, Du Sable graduated three starters at midyear and lost to La Grange 85–68 in the first round. In 1954, Du Sable lost Curley Johnson, its best defensive player, and Bobby Jackson, its number two scorer.

It took some time to put the team together. Charlie Brown didn't touch a basketball until the summer before he went to high school. He chose Du Sable because his brothers Reggie, Leroy, and Herb were on the swimming team that hadn't lost a meet in ten years. Shellie McMillon transferred from Tilden. Paxton Lumpkin, who hated school, had to be persuaded to attend class.

It wasn't enough to be the first all-black team to qualify for open state finals in Champaign. After losing to La Grange, Lumpkin called his teammates together at center court in Huff Gym. "We will be back here next year," he told them.

"We lost to a dominating team," Charlie Brown said. "We learned that you had to be at your best all the time, that you couldn't slack off. We were outmanned against La Grange. Ted Caiazza was dominant. McMillon couldn't match up to him. In the summer, we went to La Grange to play them. If you play against better players, you get better. We ended up beating them."

Before the 1953–54 season, Jim Brown was named to succeed Art Scher as head coach. Scher, who had guided Du Sable to a 27–3 record the year before, had moved to Sullivan. With Charlie Brown, Lumpkin, and McMillon returning and McKinley Cowsen, Karl and Brian Dennis, Sterling Webb, and Eugene Howard coming up, there were high expectations.

"We felt we were on the verge of something great," Jim Brown said. "The kids took pride in the fact they were black and had a black coach. They knew they could become the first all-black state champion. The newspapers made a lot out of it. The kids were constantly reminded of it."

Jim Brown introduced an exciting, up-tempo, run-and-gun offense and a full-court-pressing defense. The Panthers won their first thirty-one games by averaging ninety-five shots and 82.8 points per game. Critics, mostly from southern Illinois, called it "uncontrolled chaos." Duster Thomas, Pinckneyville's legendary coach, described it as a "five-ring circus."

"But we had a plan, and we knew what we were doing," Charlie Brown said. "It was more instinctive. No one could envision young people having that kind of coordination and cooperation at that time. Today, you don't have it because of so much individual play. We had an opportunity to display our own talents, but it was done in the concept of the team."

Du Sable also had its version of Showtime. That was Lumpkin's time, when the Panthers were ahead by twenty points. He would dribble à la Marques Haynes or his cousin Leon Hilliard of the Globetrotters. Duster Thomas always said that Centralia's

Bobby Joe Mason was the best player he had ever seen. After seeing Lumpkin, however, he made an allowance. Lumpkin was a superior ballhandler, Thomas conceded, but Mason was a better shooter.

The Panthers smashed Lake View 82–65 for the Public League championship. But their 28–0 record wasn't good enough to earn a spot in the Associated Press's final regular-season poll. Downstate, they swept Bowen 87–64, Quincy 80–66, and Edwardsville 89–73, setting up a duel with Mount Vernon for the state title. Mount Vernon, seeking its third crown in six years, had trounced second-ranked Pinckneyville 70–44 in the semifinals. By then, Du Sable was the darling of the crowd.

"We didn't think Don Richards and Al Avant would dominate the game," Jim Brown said. "We felt we would control the boards. We felt our press would be effective against them. We felt we could run."

It didn't happen. In perhaps the most controversial game in state history, Mount Vernon overcame a six-point halftime deficit to win 76–70. Richards, whose eyesight was so poor that he couldn't see the scoreboard, scored a career high twenty-five points, twenty more than his average. Avant, an All-Stater, netted twenty-three.

But the central figure was one of the officials, John Fraser of Alton. He made several critical calls, all against Du Sable. Lumpkin was called for charging on two occasions after making a basket. Charlie Brown was whistled for three traveling violations after converting long jumpers. Lumpkin, Brown, and Karl Dennis fouled out in the closing minutes.

"He turned the game around," Jim Brown said of Fraser. "In the last three minutes, he called key fouls and took the game over. The other official [Joe Przada of Belleville] was fair. Sure, we made mistakes. We didn't protect the key. Richards surprised us. We probably should have called off the press earlier rather than foul. But I still believe the game was taken away from us."

Two years later, Fraser was banned from officiating for life after being convicted of rigging games in the Missouri Valley Conference.

The veteran Chicago sportswriter Jerome Holtzman, who covered Du Sable throughout the season, didn't question the officiating in his postgame story. Avant, the only black player on the Mount Vernon team, claimed that the officiating was evenhanded and that the Rams won fairly. He noted that Du Sable committed nineteen fouls to Mount Vernon's twelve, not a big disparity.

"It's not how many fouls you call but when you call them," Charlie Brown said. "I had been making the same move throughout the season and in the tournament. [Jim Brown] said: 'Don't dribble, don't fake, don't jump, just shoot the ball.' I took a stutter step. I'd plant both feet when I caught the ball, then took a step for a launching pad to shoot the ball. It was called traveling in that circumstance."

Curiously, Charlie Brown, who later starred on Seattle University's 1958 NCAA runner-up with Elgin Baylor and officiated Public League basketball games for thirty years, obtained a film of the Du Sable/Mount Vernon game from Illinois Bell, which sponsored the telecast. To his dismay, the last three minutes had been deleted.

He isn't obsessed by the memory, however. And he isn't bitter. "I let Fraser go a long,

long time ago. I learned more from that one loss than all of the wins," he said. "It taught me how to deal with realities of our society and to learn how to accept them so if it happens again I will know how to deal with it. I tell young kids not to cheat or be bitter. If someone wrongs you, don't get mad, get better."

Rockford: Six Points in One Second

Alice Saudargas, the widow of the former West Rockford coach Alex Saudargas, has ten children, eighteen grandchildren, and six great-grandchildren. She also is mother hen to a legacy that her late husband created.

Her commitment began years ago when the former West Rockford player Rex Parker asked her, "Where are all the trophies?" The high school was closed in 1969 and now is West Middle School. All of West Rockford's history was missing.

In 1997, when she learned that town officials planned to demolish the old building, Alice Saudargas had it declared a local landmark. Then she established a memorabilia room to house West Rockford's 1955 and 1956 state championship trophies and other artifacts, including old letter jackets, yearbooks, trophies, pictures, records, mascot attire, and a portrait of the coach painted by his daughter Patti.

"They made a mistake when they closed West Rockford," said Parker, whose wife was president of the school board in the late 1970s and early 1980s. "It is tough to drive down Rockton Avenue and realize it isn't West Rockford anymore. We're still hoping it can be brought back to being a senior high school."

Rockford has been a basketball hotbed since Mary Pickford was America's Sweetheart. Rockford High won state titles in 1911 and 1919. East Rockford dominated the 1940s under coach Jim Laude, Alex Saudargas produced winning teams in the 1950s and 1960s, Dolph Stanley came to Rockford Auburn and stoked the competitive fires in the 1960s, Steve Goers built a dynasty at Rockford Boylan in the 1980s and 1990s, and Mike Miller produced a state runner-up at Rockford Guilford in 1993.

But West is gone. Built in 1940, West and East were the only high schools in town. The Rock River served as the boundary, dividing the city in more than one way. Rockford is an ethnically diverse community with a large Italian population in the Southwest, Polish and Swedes in the East, and Irish in the West.

Nolden Gentry, a two-time All-Stater on West Rockford's 1955 and 1956 championship teams, grew up on the South Side. He was one of twenty-five African Americans in his class of four hundred. There were five black players on his team. Three black players started on the 1956 team.

"It was a small-town atmosphere even though it was the second largest town in Illinois," Parker said. "The quality of life was good, there wasn't much crime, and parents had little concern about their kids riding their bicycles all over the community. Then things changed in the 1980s."

Economics, integration, and political and racial issues aside, basketball always was king. West and East games were sellouts. The lead story in the daily newspapers, morning and afternoon, almost always was high school basketball.

"I'd go to the barber shop on Saturday and seven or eight guys would talk only basketball, what happened the night before," said Rod Coffman, a standout on West Rockford's 1955 championship team. "The papers even covered the grade school games. They were always looking for future players."

Saudargas arrived at West Rockford in 1947. He coached in Laude's shadow for a few years, won back-to-back state titles, then retired from coaching. He continued to teach, finally retiring in 1979. A diabetic, he died on March 1, 1999. He was eighty-two.

"Alex didn't get the credit he deserved," Gentry said. "He was the kind of person you would fall on a sword for. He was a father figure for all of his players. He could be stern, but I always found him to be extremely fair and very supportive. He brought to coaching a knowledge of different personalities and how to deal with them all."

Known as the "Little Lithuanian," Saudargas was recognized for his signature crewcut, red socks, and bow tie. He was color blind. He once sold pots and pans door to door to supplement his teaching salary of nine hundred dollars. Known for his quiet demeanor on the bench, he never had a technical foul called on him.

"He was Rockford," Parker said. "He was a gentleman. I don't think I ever heard him curse. A lot of people underestimated him. They thought he had the horses, and he did, but he drilled into us that we had to be disciplined to win big."

West Rockford was a dominant team in 1954–55. The Warriors were ranked number one in the state from the outset. They had great size—Nolden Gentry and John Wessels were 6' 7" juniors, and Fred Boshela was a 6' 5" senior. Parker and Coffman were the guards.

They beat Decatur by four in the first round, Lincoln by ten in the quarterfinals, and Pinckneyville by eight in the semifinals. In the final, they were poised to meet their Big Eight rival Elgin, whom they had beaten by six earlier.

West Rockford trailed by thirteen at halftime. The teams were housed in adjoining handball courts in Huff Gym. The Elgin players were whooping it up, and their uproarious behavior could easily be heard next door. Saudargas told his players to listen to Elgin's celebration. "Now go out and show them," he said.

Led by Boshela, Coffman, and Gentry, West Rockford outscored Elgin 20–8 in the third quarter. But Elgin, behind Gary Smith, Paul Hudgens, and Tom Aley, led 57–51 with 2:19 to play. Then, in one of the most bizarre incidents in state tournament history, West Rockford scored six points in one second.

Gentry made a seventeen footer and was fouled after the shot. He converted two free throws. Elgin gained possession but threw the ball to Gary Siegmeier at half-court. Parker was guarding him. Both were wearing number 43.

"The ball was up in the air, and we both went up for it. He was taller than me. The whistle blew, and the official called a foul on number 43," Parker recalled. "The foul had been called on Siegmeier. I walked to the free-throw line and made two free throws. The score was tied at fifty-seven with 2:18 left."

West Rockford went ahead 59–57 on Boshela's basket with 1:35 remaining. Elgin tied on Smith's basket with 1:20 to play. Saudargas diagrammed a final play. Wessels missed a shot, but Gentry tipped it in with fourteen seconds left.

Elgin had time for a last shot, but Smith lost track of it. Coffman, who was guarding him, couldn't believe that Smith wasn't trying to get a shot. He loved to shoot from the corner. Instead, he dribbled back out front as time expired. West Rockford won 61–59.

With Gentry, Wessels, and Bobby Washington returning in 1955–56, West Rockford was a prohibitive favorite to repeat. But it wasn't easy. In the supersectional, they overcame a twenty-nine-point performance by Galesburg's Mike Owens to win 66–64 in double overtime as Gentry tipped in the game-winning basket.

They trounced West Frankfort by twelve in the quarterfinals and Chicago Dunbar by thirteen in the semifinals. But they were taken to the brink by Edwardsville in the final, as Govoner Vaughn scored twenty-eight and Mannie Jackson scored twenty-one. Wessels countered with twenty-nine points, and Gentry and Washington each had seventeen as West Rockford won 67–65.

Mark Lotzer's father was a friend of Alex Saudargas. He enrolled at Rockford Boylan for the quality education it offered. As a sophomore, his 1969–70 team won only five games. His father called Saudargas about transferring. But Dolph Stanley had retired from Rockford Auburn at sixty-five and had been hired at Boylan. Lotzer stayed.

"I was in awe of him," Lotzer said. "We knew he had coached at Taylorville in 1944 and had coached at Beloit College. We went to see his Rockford Auburn teams in the 1960s. He had a certain persona. He was a real legend. He was bigger than life."

As a junior, Stanley took Boylan and Lotzer to the state quarterfinals. As a senior, Lotzer averaged 29.5 points per game and earned a scholarship to Wisconsin. In one game, Boylan outlasted West Rockford 75–73 in double overtime as Lotzer scored twenty-six while West's Ernie Kent had thirty. Boylan trailed by twenty points with 2:30 left in the third quarter and rallied to win.

The program went downhill after 1972 as Stanley began to lose interest—he loved to gamble and play golf and gin rummy. The talent pool dried up, and assistant coach Ken Slimko went to Jacobs in Algonquin. When Stanley retired in 1980 at age seventy-five, school officials looked to Steve Goers, who was coaching at tiny Harvard, Illinois. It was the best decision they ever made.

"When I was hired, Boylan was a football power. In basketball, they had been to the Elite Eight only once, in 1971, Dolph's first team," Goers said. "Dolph told me that I couldn't win at Boylan. It has tough kids and offers a good education, he said, but it is a football school."

His first team was 7–17, but three of his teams finished fourth in the state in the 1990s. From 1996 to 1999, his teams were 117–14, an .893 winning percentage. From 1984 to 1987, Boylan was 113–11, a .911 winning percentage. He coached Sonny Roberts, Danny Jones, Lee Lampley, Durrell Banks, Michael Slaughter, Damir Krupaglia, John Hernandez, and Joe Tulley.

But Goers hasn't won a state title. In fact, Rockford hasn't produced a state champion since 1956. In 1992, Goers's best team lost to Peoria Richwoods by one in the state semifinals.

"The state title is an elusive butterfly. You can't measure a program's success by the state title," Goers said. "The program I have built is most satisfying because we are the Yankee syndrome. Either you love us or you hate us. Success for other schools is measured by how well they play against Boylan."

Elgin: Bill Chesbrough Era

Flynn Robinson grew up in Murphysboro, in southern Illinois, where high school basketball was king in the 1940s and 1950s. For two years, before he moved to Elgin, he played against great players and great teams from Herrin, West Frankfort, and Pinckneyville and heard about the grand traditions at Centralia and Mount Vernon.

Then he met Elgin coach Bill Chesbrough and realized that the game was played differently in Chicago and its suburbs. "Basketball tradition at Murphysboro was nothing like Elgin. It was like going from Division III to Division I," said Robinson, who later played with Wilt Chamberlain on an NBA championship team.

To improve his skills, Robinson often hitchhiked in the summer to a popular playground at 71st and South Park in Chicago, where all of the city's top players tested themselves.

Robinson emerged as one of the best players in Elgin history, alongside Jack Burmaster, Don Sunderlage, Bob Peterson, Bob Survant, Wally Graf, Glen Lose, Gary Smith, Chuck Brandt, Dick Becker, Gary Kane, George Clark, Rick Sund, Tim Jones, Jeff Wilkins, Terry Drake, Rick Hopkins, Terry Mayfield, Sean Harrington, Mark Baugh, Marcus Smallwood, Jesse Henderson, and Marcus Howard.

The tradition was founded in 1924 and 1925, when Mark Wilson, Otto Vogel, and Cliff Adams produced two state championship teams. One of the players was Doug Mills, who later became basketball coach and athletic director at the University of Illinois.

John Krafft carried on the tradition in the 1940s, finishing fourth in the state in 1943, second to Taylorville's 45–0 powerhouse in 1944 with Burmaster, Jim Rager, Howard Kugath, Sam Sauceda, and Karl Plath, and third in 1950. He also reached the quarterfinals in 1945.

"In the 1940s and 1950s, the whole social life of the town was built around high school or church activities," Glen Lose said. "Friday night and Saturday night was the big night, like Quincy or Collinsville. No one could get a season ticket because the gym sat only sixteen hundred."

That was "The Snakepit," Elgin's home floor from 1938 until the new school and what is now known as the forty-two-hundred-seat Chesbrough Field House were built on the East Side of town in 1972. In the old gym, Elgin won 82 percent of its games, including forty-two in a row from 1942–46.

Although Elgin hasn't won as many state championships as Mount Vernon or Centralia, old-timers insist that the program is rooted in a similar sense of tradition.

In 1900, Elgin hosted Chicago Englewood at Sauer's Hall in the first interscholastic basketball game in state history.

It was the tradition that attracted Bill Chesbrough to the Kane County community. Born in Hartford, Connecticut, he attended Syracuse University on a football scholarship. He served in the navy at Great Lakes in the early 1940s and returned to Chicago after World War II. "I didn't know if I wanted to go back to teaching," he recalled. "But I attended an Elgin sectional game at Waukegan. The enthusiasm of the crowd excited me. It was a high-class team. I said I would like to coach at that school one of these days. I got acquainted with the tradition real early."

Chesbrough assisted on Krafft's 1950 team, then became head coach when Krafft retired. No one else was interviewed for the job. From 1950 until he retired in 1985, he won 695 games and took ten teams to the Sweet Sixteen. His 1954–55 team finished second. Four others reached the state quarterfinals.

"I was in the golden years of Elgin basketball," he said. "What I wanted to do was continue the tradition of the school, to be as good or better than Krafft was as a coach. I saw potential because there was a lot of talent in the community."

He was disappointed because he never won a state title and some of his best teams never qualified for the state finals. "But the biggest disappointment was how we lost in 1955 at the end," he said.

In 1999, a statewide panel of sportswriters voted to select the most memorable moment in Illinois boys basketball history: when West Rockford scored six points in one second and went on to beat Elgin 61–59 in the 1955 state championship.

Leading by six with 2:19 to play, Elgin became unglued. West Rockford rallied when Nolden Gentry hit a seventeen footer, was fouled after the shot, and made two free throws. Elgin's Tom Aley threw the ball to Gary Siegmeier, but West's Rex Parker leaped for the ball, and Siegmeier was charged with a foul. Parker made two free throws to tie at fifty-seven.

Gentry tipped in John Wessels's shot for the game-winning basket with fourteen seconds to play. Elgin had a chance to tie, but Gary "Whitey" Smith, an All-State guard, lost track of time. Instead of looking for a shot, he dribbled into a corner as the clock ran out.

"Things happen, maybe for better or worse," Chesbrough said. "You have to forget about those things and move on. Sure, I thought we should have won. Even today, you remember the tough losses more than anything else."

Nobody could claim that Chesbrough wasn't prepared. He always carried a brown spiral notebook and constantly jotted notes during games. He dispatched two or three scouts to a game. One took notes on personal characteristics, another on patterns.

"I have never seen a coach who was as well-prepared for a game as he was. He lived and died with scouting reports," said Lose, a 1953 graduate who later played at Northwestern with Princeton's Joe Ruklick and Hebron's Bill Schulz and assisted Chesbrough from 1962 to 1968.

Rick Sund, an All-Stater in 1969 who played at Northwestern, has served as an executive in the NBA for thirty years, the last two as general manager of the Seattle

SuperSonics. He still marvels at Chesbrough's organizational skills and his keen creative mind.

"I have seen the game evolve . . . new offenses, new defenses," Sund said. "He was ahead of his time. He would devise offenses to create shooting areas where kids could be effective. And he devised defenses that confused opponents all the time."

Elgin's 1957 team was 21–0 and ranked number two in the state. The Maroons, led by 6' 7" Chuck Brandt, 6' 5" Dick Becker, 6' 4" Gary Kane, 6' 5" Ted Tammearu, and 6' 1" Phil Sokody, wanted to accomplish what the 1955 team couldn't. After beating fifth-ranked Bloom, Homer Thurman, and Jerry Colangelo 53–52 in the supersectional at Hinsdale, they felt confident in their mission.

Brandt picked up three fouls in the quarterfinal against third-rated Herrin, and Elgin lost by six. "I thought we should have gotten to the championship game if we kept our heads. Herrin's biggest man was 6' 3". We outsized them and had better shooters," Chesbrough said.

"They controlled the game and didn't let us do what we wanted to do," Brandt said. "We were good but not disciplined. Herrin played a different style of ball, more disciplined, a passing game, high-percentage shots. They didn't rush up and down the floor. We weren't used to that."

The 1973 team was Chesbrough's best. Led by 6' 10" Jeff Wilkins, 6' 7" Terry Drake, 6' 5" Tim Jones, 6' 4" Jay Geldmacher, and guard Tom Koch, Elgin was 22–1 and ranked fourth in the state. The team boasted six Division I players, won the Proviso West Tournament, and beat several good teams, including Proviso East twice, but they couldn't beat their conference rival, West Aurora.

In the state quarterfinals, West Aurora beat Elgin 54–49 in double overtime. "It was devastating. You hear about it to this day. People keep bringing it up, how we blew it," Jones said.

Elgin led by two with a minute left when Koch, trying to stall, was called for failing to advance the ball in five seconds. West's Matt Hicks took a long shot that hit the backboard, bounced on the front of the rim, hit the backboard again, then went in. In the first overtime, Elgin led by two when John Bryant hit a thirty-five footer to tie.

"By that time, I feel Dame Fortune isn't with us," Chesbrough said. "In the second overtime, we didn't respond at all."

Jim Harrington knew about Chesbrough's legend and Elgin's tradition when he was coaching at Chicago Weber in the 1970s and 1980s. At a sectional game at Elgin, he was impressed by what he observed—the town, talent, mix of students, big gym, enthusiasm, administration, and commitment to athletics.

In fifteen years, from 1986 to 2002, he won 290 games and took teams to the Elite Eight in 1987, 1990, and 1998. "I kept the tradition going," said Harrington, whose son Sean became the school's all-time leading scorer with 2,119 points. "I hoped my size eleven shoes could fit into Bill's size sixteen. I didn't want to ruffle any feathers. If I could be half as successful as Bill was, I felt I would be satisfied. But I had to do it my way, the way I felt comfortable."

Centralia's legendary duo: Dike Eddleman (40), perhaps the greatest high school athlete ever produced in Illinois, and coach Arthur Trout, who won 809 games in his career at the school. Photo courtesy of Teddy Eddleman.

Ernie Eveland coached Paris to 590 victories in twenty-one years, including state championships in 1943 and 1947, second-place finishes in 1939 and 1942, and a third-place finish in 1938. His teams won thirty or more games for six consecutive years. Photo courtesy of Linda Eveland Shirar.

PARIS TIGERS - STATE CHAMPS - '43

Paris's 1943 state championship team. Front row, left to right: manager Chester Dahlgren, Delbert Glover, Max Norman, Dave Humerickhouse, Dick Foley, Gordon Taylor, coach Ernie Eveland. Back row, left to right: Don Blair, Paul Pedersen, John Cychol, Nick Swinford, Bobby Cochran. The Tigers, who finished second in 1942, upset second-ranked Moline for the 1943 title. Photo courtesy of Linda Eveland Shirar.

Bob "Chick" Doster led Decatur to the 1945 state championship. He was the tournament's leading scorer with ninety-six points in four games, including eighteen in a 62–54 victory over Champaign for the title. Photo courtesy of the *Decatur Herald and Review*.

Gay Kintner, Decatur's legendary coach, is carried on the shoulders of his players after winning the 1936 state championship. Kintner also produced state champions in 1931 and 1945. Photo courtesy of the *Decatur Herald and Review.*

Coach John Schneiter poses with the starters on his 1962 state championship team. From left: Jim Hallihan, Jerry Hill, Prentis Jones, Jim "Bulldog" Johnson, and Ken Barnes. Photo courtesy of the *Decatur Herald and Review.*

Champaign's 1946 state championship team. Front row, left to right: coach Harry Combes, Earl Harrison, Jim Cottrell, Ted Beach, Fred Major, Rod Fletcher. Back row, left to right: Kirby Know, Bobby Clark, John McDermott, Bill Johnston, Dick Petry, assistant coach Harold Jester. Photo courtesy of Ted Beach.

Coach Harry Combes (left) and Ted Beach were instrumental in Champaign's success in the 1940s. Beach was a two-time All-Stater who later played for Combes at the University of Illinois. Champaign finished fourth in 1944, second in 1945, first in 1946, and second in 1947. Photo courtesy of Ted Beach.

Mount Vernon coach Stan Changnon (left) talks to four of his starters before the start of the 1950 state finals: Bob Brown, Eddie King, Walt Moore, and Max Hooper. Hooper, Moore, and their teammate John Riley were named to the All-State team while leading the Rams to a 33–0 record and their second state championship in a row. Photo courtesy of Max Hooper.

Max Hooper of Mount Vernon (left) drives the baseline and scores on a reverse layup during a 32–27 victory at Centralia's Trout Gym on December 17, 1949. Hooper scored twenty-six of his team's points. Photo courtesy of Max Hooper.

Hebron's 1952 team, the only district team and the smallest school (enrollment ninety-eight students) ever to win a state championship. Front row, left to right: coach Russ Ahearn, Ken Spooner, Paul Judson, Bill Schutz, Phil Judson, Don Wilbrandt. Back row, left to right: Jim Bergin, Jim Wilbrandt, Joe Schmidt, Bill Thayer, Clayton Ihrke. Photo courtesy of the Illinois High School Association/Don Peasley.

Art Hicks emerged as perhaps the most outstanding player in Chicago in the 1950s. He led St. Elizabeth to Catholic League and city championships in 1955 and 1956. Photo courtesy of the *Chicago Sun-Times*/ Phil Velasquez.

West Rockford coach Alex Saudargas (right) and star players Nolden Gentry (left) and Johnny Wessels receive the 1956 state championship trophy from an IHSA official. It was West Rockford's second state title in a row. Photo courtesy of the Illinois High School Association.

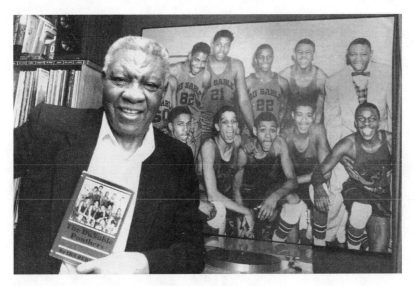

Former Du Sable coach Jim Brown displays a copy of Ira Berkow's book on the 1954 Du Sable team while sitting in front of a picture of the famous squad that lost to Mount Vernon in the 1954 state championship game. Photo courtesy of the *Chicago Sun-Times*/John Booz.

Marshall's George Wilson, a three-time All-Stater, led the Commandos to state championships in 1958 and 1960. Photo courtesy of the *Chicago Sun-Times*.

Collinsville coach Vergil Fletcher won 792 games in his career and state championships in 1961 and 1965. Photo courtesy of the Illinois High School Association.

Chicago Marshall's 1958 state championship team, the first all-black team and the first representative of the Chicago Public League to win the state title. Front row, left to right: Ron Banks, Robert Smith, Lonnie Elliott, Paul Brown, Jimmy Jones, coach Spin Salario. Back row, left to right: Tyrone Johnson, Steve Thomas, George Wilson, Bobby Jones, M. C. Thompson. Photo courtesy of the *Chicago Sun-Times*/Associated Press.

Collinsville's Tom Parker (left), a two-time All-Stater who averaged thirty-two points per game in 1967–68, later played for legendary coach Adolph Rupp (right) at Kentucky. Rupp coached Freeport to third place in the 1929 Illinois high school tournament before becoming the famed Baron of the Bluegrass. Photo courtesy of Tom Parker.

Collinsville's 1961 state championship team, generally regarded among the best in state history. Front row, left to right: Bob Meadows, Ronnie Mottin, Fred Riddle, coach Vergil Fletcher, Bogie Redmon, Bob Basola, Bob Simpson. Back row, left to right: assistant coach Bill Hellyer, Than Brykit, Ronnie Matikitis, Joe Brennan, Harry Hildreth, assistant coach Bert Weber. Front: mascot Marc Fletcher. Photo courtesy of the Illinois High School Association.

Marshall: Remember the Juniors

Marshall's basketball tradition didn't begin in the 1950s with Spin Salario, Art Day, Ralph Wells, and George Wilson. It tipped off in the 1930s with Lou Weintraub, Izzy Acker, Alex Eisenstein, Whitey Siegal, Chicky Zomlefer, and Pee Wee Tadelman.

"The tradition was built by Jews," said Jim Pitts, who played on the 1960 state championship team and the 1961 team that finished third. "Marshall was unique. No city school had it like we did. During the 1950s, Marshall was going through a rapid racial, ethnic, and religious change."

Bosco Levine bridged the gap. As the director of the basketball program at the American Boys Commonwealth and freshman coach, he helped to develop most of the youngsters who enrolled at Marshall. He also was a longtime teacher and athletic director at the West Side school.

Levine was there when Weintraub's juniors (players who stood 5' 7" and under) recorded an historic ninety-eight-game winning streak from 1939 to 1944, the longest in state history. And he was there when Marshall became the first all-black school to win state championships in 1958 and 1960.

At one time, Marshall was 95 percent white with three thousand students. In the 1950s, however, the demographics of the Lawndale neighborhood changed from white to black almost as swiftly as the game changed. Taller, more athletic black players began to dominate in the city.

In 1952, Chicago school officials decided to do away with the junior program. From then on, each Public League school would be represented by only one varsity team. The Catholic League, which had a junior program for players 5' 8" and under, soon followed. For some old-timers, it would never be the same.

"To me, junior basketball was more exciting, like it is more exciting to watch college basketball than the NBA," said the longtime Chicago radio sportscaster Red Mottlow. "They were fast, they could shoot, and they could play defense. It was more of a team game."

Mottlow, who published a book, *Fast Break to Glory: Marshall High School's Ninety-Eight-Game Basketball Winning Streak,* in 2002, recalled when 5' 7" Whitey Rodnick of Manley played on a senior team that upset 6' 6" Sweetwater Clifton and Du Sable in the city playoff in 1941. Manley won three junior titles in five years in the 1930s and was the dominant junior program in the city before Marshall.

In 1943, the Public and Catholic Leagues conducted the first all-city championship at Chicago Stadium. A crowd of 21,742, the largest in state history, saw Marshall beat Mount Carmel 21–12 for the junior title and Mount Carmel beat Kelvyn Park 48–24 for the senior crown.

Marshall's juniors were so popular and exciting that they were the subjects of a *Time* magazine article in 1944, after the streak had reached ninety-four in a row. "They ended the story by saying that obviously they will win a hundred in a row. It put a curse on them," said Mottlow, a 1944 Marshall graduate. "But it's something when your high school is written about in *Time* magazine."

Weintraub was the architect of the dynasty. Quiet, unemotional, and soft-spoken, he never criticized a player in public. If he was displeased, he removed the player, motioned for him to sit at the end of the bench, and gave him a funny look. He was a motivator, not an X's and O's coach.

Acker was the best player. Instead of shooting a two-handed set shot, as most players did in that era, Acker spent hours on the Lawson playground developing a different style. He would jump in the air while holding the ball in both hands and shoot from over his head.

"We were probably the only basketball team that went into the girls' gym and practiced to music," Acker said. "It was a lot of fun. It gave us a sense of rhythm. Mr. Weintraub [which is how he insisted on being addressed] was very inventive. He was the first coach to have a fast break. He also emphasized conditioning. We ran around the school about four times a day."

In those days, the junior program commanded the most attention in the city. There were a lot of good short players. Coaches thought that any player taller than six feet was too clumsy to play. The juniors played a more exciting style than the seniors, with more running and scoring.

"Not until later in life did I realize what we had accomplished and analyze what was happening," said Acker, who never played in a losing game in three years. "My mother took every article and put it away. I have the scrapbooks and show them to my grandchildren. I don't think athletes think about what they are doing at the time, they just do it. It was fun, a great time in my life."

After Weintraub retired, Marshall's juniors won their last city title in 1947 behind 5' 6" guard Seymour "Bimbo" Gantman. The following year, coach Ted Perzanowski moved Gantman to the seniors. He joined 6' 3" Irv Bemoras, an All-Stater who later played at Illinois. With Burt Wilens and Burt Jacobson, they led Marshall to a 28–2 record, the Public League championship, and the state quarterfinals.

In a four-year period from 1957 through 1961, Marshall won thirty-one, twenty-five, thirty-one, and twenty-eight games, lost eleven, claimed two state championships, a third-place finish, and lost a one-pointer in the supersectional. George Wilson became an icon in the city, joining Thornton's Lou Boudreau and Centralia's Dike Eddleman as one of the few three-time All-Staters in Illinois history.

"George could have scored forty points per game if we chose to set him up," Salario said. "But I've always felt when you see a team with a guy who scores thirty to forty points, it is weak somewhere. A team that has balanced scoring will be a winner."

Salario left Marshall after the 1960 season, and his assistant, Harvey Hartenstein, didn't miss a beat. He finished third in 1961, with Jim Pitts, Eddie Jakes, Charlie Jones, Don Jackson, and Ed Franklin, and third in 1965, with Rich Bradshaw, Charles Conway, and Calvin Triplett. After leading Marshall to the Sweet Sixteen in 1966, Bradshaw was generally acknowledged as the state's premier player.

Basketball was sacred at Marshall, Don Jackson said, and basketball players were held in awe. Being a Commando was special. Being a member of the M Club was an honor.

"You were confronted by a lot of temptations—drugs, gangs, women," Jackson said. "It was easy for you to think you were the king and could do whatever you wanted to do. But George [Wilson] and M. C. [Thompson] and Ralph [Wells] carried themselves so well that it made an impression on us."

"There was something special about Marshall, a mystique," said Bradshaw, a two-time All-Stater. "Carver won a state title in 1963 after Cazzie Russell left. But Marshall was always there. They had tradition and great players. Everyone wanted to play at Marshall or beat Marshall."

Luther Bedford knew about tradition, too. Born in Arkansas, he grew up in Rockford. If he hadn't torn up a knee during the last game of the 1955 football season, he probably would have started on West Rockford's 1955–56 state championship team. When Hartenstein left Marshall in 1973, Bedford became head coach. He retired in 1999.

"When I started, we had an advantage every time we played because Marshall had a mystique," Bedford said. "We had a real good program where kids would get other kids to follow them, like Westinghouse is doing now. They don't remember the great teams of 1958 and 1960. They have their own idols."

Joe Stiffend didn't know about George Wilson until he enrolled at Marshall. He was supposed to attend St. Joseph in Westchester, which produced Isiah Thomas, but he chose to stay closer to home. When he saw the state trophies, he realized he had an opportunity to rekindle Marshall's winning tradition.

Stiffend, a 6' 2" jumping-jack center, led the Commandos to fourth place in the Class AA tournament in 1982 and 1983 and the school's first Public League titles since 1966. In the 1983 city final, Marshall beat Collins 67–62 in double overtime, but Stiffend suffered a shoulder injury, which hampered him. Marshall lost to Peoria Central 58–57 in the state semifinals.

"Basketball helped me to mature and taught me to get along with people," said Stiffend, who played at Cincinnati. "In grade school, I played hooky for thirty days. I played with the wrong crowd. My uncle wouldn't let me go outside for two months. It turned me around. I learned you must go to school and do the best you can so you can do well in life."

Bedford believed that his 1981 team was his best. Stiffend, Kelvin Upshaw, and James Horne had beaten Westinghouse by twenty-three and thirty-five points in league matchups but lost by thirteen in the city final.

In 1991, Marshall finished third in Class AA, with Cesare Christian, Arthur Agee, Quadall Kimble, and Rodrico Dale. In 1992, his 22–3 team was ranked tenth in the state but lost to King on a last-second shot in the city semifinals.

"Today, kids only judge success by the number of players who went to the NBA, not by how many went to college or are successes in life," Bedford said. "I still talk to them about the Marshall tradition and the importance of upholding the tradition of the program. Most kids used to buy into it. In the meantime, I still keep the trophies polished."

George Wilson: The Messiah Comes to Play

When he was ten years old, only a few years removed from his roots in Meridian, Mississippi, George Wilson threw in a hook shot to win a basketball game at the Midwest Chicago Boys' Club. A knowledgeable coach named Will Bonner saw him and changed forever how the game is viewed in the city.

Bonner taught Wilson how to play the game. There were only eight players on a team. They wore cotton bottoms and nylon tops. Some had sweat socks, some didn't. It was a new experience for Wilson, who had never seen snow before.

An only child, Wilson had come to Chicago three years earlier to live with his mother in the architect Frank Lloyd Wright's building, the Terrace, at San Francisco and Fulton. It was the best of times, he recalled, and the worst of times.

He took the train to the Chicago Theater to see movies for fifteen cents. Afterward, at Walgreen's at State and Lake, he sat at the counter and ordered a ham salad sandwich on toast, a strawberry milk shake, and a piece of apple pie.

He particularly remembers those stops at Walgreen's because "the white waitresses were so nice to me. Those were bad times for race relationships. There were places we knew not to go, but we were welcome there. That's why Walgreen's is still a great place for me."

Wilson began to explore Chicago during the summer—the museums, Tribune Tower, lakefront, and forest preserves. He attended church every Sunday and didn't miss a day of school or incur a single tardiness from third through eighth grade. The summer before he entered high school, he grew six inches. The following summer, he grew four more.

He might not have been born to be a basketball player, but he learned fast. He enrolled at Marshall, which already had established a great basketball tradition with Lou Weintraub's juniors in the 1930s, Irv Bemoras in the 1940s, and Art Day and Ralph Wells in the 1950s. Day had put Marshall on the statewide map, and Wilson recalled listening to the radio account of the Commandos' loss to Quincy in the first round of the 1955 state tournament.

"In the 1950s, basketball in the city was better than the NCAA, NIT [National Invitation Tournament], and anything else," Wilson said. "Art Day, Clarence Wordlaw, Abe Booker, Frank Burks, Charlie Brown, Paxton Lumpkin . . . they set the stage and we wanted to be like them. They were such an inspiration. It was such a great time in history."

Isadore "Spin" Salario became head coach at Marshall in 1955. He taught Wilson to shoot a right-handed hook. He also taught other things: he made sure his players were in superior condition and taught them to outthink opponents. His philosophy was simple: Score at one end, stop them at the other end, and finish the game ahead by at least two points.

Salario was tough, too. He once threw Wilson off the team for three days for talking back to him. Wilson never dared to tell his parents. He learned to be respectful of someone in authority and "not to let your mouth get you in trouble." He let his basketball talent do his talking for him.

"George was looked upon as a messiah," said Jim Pitts, who starred on Marshall's 1961 team. "No one used that language at that time, but everyone knew he was so good that when he linked up with other talent the West Side's ambition to be the best in basketball was going to come to fruition."

Wilson knew he was that good. He never lacked for confidence. When he was unemployed, he taught Russian but couldn't speak the language. He never let his three-time All-America status go to his head. Salario always said that he could have averaged forty points per game if the offense was geared to him.

"He was braggadocio," said M. C. Thompson, who also starred on the 1958 and 1959 teams. "He came with an 'I will rescue the basketball team' attitude. That was his personality. And he did rescue the team. He had talent and speed. He was faster than any big man. He was a fighter. He always would take a risk."

In 1957, when Wilson was a freshman, Marshall lost to Crane in the city final. But Salario knew he had the makings of a strong team coming back even though Ralph Wells, perhaps his best player, would graduate at midyear.

Wilson was fifteen years old, stood 6' 6", and weighed 185 pounds. The triangle offense was built around him. He was stationed low, with M. C. Thompson on one side and Steve Thomas on the other. Bobby Jones and Tyrone Johnson handled the ball. The object was to get the ball to Wilson for his hook shot. "When I started my move, Steve and M. C. would go to the board because they knew I wasn't going to pass it," Wilson said.

Marshall beat Dunbar 68–59 for the city title, then beat Elgin and Flynn Robinson 63–43 in the supersectional at Evanston. The Commandos continued to romp in the Elite Eight, smashing the defending state champion, Herrin, 72–59 in the quarterfinals, West Aurora and Bill Small 74–62 in the semifinals, and Rock Falls 70–64 in the final.

"I never saw a team that was better than my 1958 team . . . if only because it overcame the psychological barrier of being the first Chicago team to win a state title," Salario said.

"We were the best at that time in history," Wilson said of the 31–0 powerhouse. "Why were we such a great team? We had great talent and a man in control of the players. We had a great support system. Everyone knew their roles. There was no jealousy, no matter who scored. I feel we had the talent and athleticism and quickness to play today."

In 1959, Crane with Tim Robinson was the city favorite. But Marshall beat Crane 61–58 to advance to the supersectional at Evanston. Despite nineteen points and twenty-two rebounds by Wilson and twenty-three points by Thompson, however, the Commandos lost to Waukegan 63–62. Wilson was whistled for three fouls in the first half, and Thompson fouled out.

"That was the most disappointing experience of my life, worse than losing to Loyola for the NCAA championship in 1963," Wilson said. "I'm still bitter today. The game was taken away from us. Even the newspapers criticized the officiating in the game. But you can't go back. I learned from that. We didn't cry. It just motivated us for 1960."

Wilson never forgot. A week later, at the state finals, he had to be restrained when he saw one of the officials from the Waukegan game. Thompson thought that Waukegan's guards, Dick Nixon and Andy Hankins, had more to do with the outcome than the officials. He felt that they controlled the tempo of the game by driving to the basket and putting pressure on Marshall's big men.

As it turned out, Dunbar and Bernie Mills provided even more motivation for 1959–60. Marshall lost to Dunbar by sixteen in the season opener, then lost to the Mighty Men in overtime for the championship of the Illinois Tech Tournament. From then on, the Commandos went on a roll, finishing with a 31–2 record.

In the city playoff, they ousted Carver and sophomore Cazzie Russell in the semifinals, then stomped Crane 79–38 in the final. In the supersectional, they crushed Elgin 71–55. They beat Monmouth by twenty in the quarterfinals, Decatur by twelve in the semifinals, and Bridgeport by twenty-four in the state final. For a coup de grace, they beat De La Salle 88–72 for their third all-city championship in a row.

As a 6' 8" senior, Wilson remained the centerpiece, but junior guard Eddie Jakes was the team's leading scorer in the state tournament with eighty-five points in four games. Ken Moses and juniors Ed Franklin, Charlie Jones, Jim Pitts, and Don Jackson formed an able supporting cast, the backbone of a squad that would finish third in the 1961 state tournament.

Wilson and his teammates realized that they made an enormous impact on history, becoming the first all-black team to win the state title in Illinois. They were aware that Oscar Robertson and his Crispus Attucks team from Indianapolis had accomplished the same feat in Indiana in 1955.

"It is more meaningful now because when I was doing it at the time I was just having fun, going to school, working, playing basketball, planning to go to college," Wilson said. "Years later, I realize it was a great feat in the 1950s with the race climate being what it was.

"It makes me feel good that I didn't let anyone down, my parents, cousins, buddies, coaches, teachers, friends at church, even Mr. Art Sears at the grocery store on the corner of San Francisco and Walnut."

Wilson was recruited by dozens of colleges. When he visited Cincinnati, his hero Oscar Robertson was waiting at the airport to greet him. He signed with Cincinnati and Illinois but opted for Cincinnati. After playing on one NCAA champion and an NCAA runner-up, he started on the 1964 Olympic team and played in the NBA for seven years.

"Everyone knew George was going to be something special," Jim Pitts said. "He was going to be the first one you could see building a dynasty, not Abe Booker or Tommy Hawkins or Art Day. He could build a great team and inspire confidence. He was a young Bill Russell. He could start a fast break with a rebound and end it with a dunk. He showed all we needed was a standard of excellence and we could do anything."

3

The 1960s

Collinsville: Bogie's Hometown

Bogie Redmon is nothing if not loyal. His license plate reads "IL BIG10," a reference to his days playing on Harry Combes's basketball team at the University of Illinois. But Redmon's most cherished memories are of his high school experience in his hometown.

"Collinsville is like an old Greek city-state," he said. "Everything is there. Very seldom do you need to go to another town. Or want to."

When Redmon was growing up in the 1950s, there were no shopping malls or interstate highways or Nikes. Folks shopped at Imber's or Jere's for clothes or Krite Hardware for household needs. Even though the factory had been closed for years, everyone took pride in the Brooks Ketchup Bottle, the world's biggest bottle and now a registered landmark.

But basketball was king. Even before Vergil Fletcher became a legendary coach, taking fourteen teams to the Sweet Sixteen and winning two state championships, Collinsville had established a winning tradition. In 1937, Willard Larson's 27–4 team finished third in state. In 1946, the year before Fletcher arrived, Jack Fabri's 30–10 team reached the state quarterfinals.

"You were really somebody if you were a basketball player," said Sam Miranda, an All-Stater on Fletcher's 1948 team. "You wore your letter sweater every day. You were a special person if you played basketball at Collinsville."

Redmon wore number 54 because Terry Bethel, the star of the 1957 state runner-up, wore the same jersey. When he was four years old, his family moved to 900 St. Louis Road. His father was in the insurance business. Today, Bogie's insurance office is at 405 St. Louis Road. "This always will be home," he said.

Redmon was an outstanding multisport athlete, an All-State end in football and one of the most prolific discus throwers in the state. But he was bit by the basketball bug as a fourth grader when John Finnan, who ran a good program at Webster Junior High School, invited him to play with sixth graders. "I thought it was so cool," he recalled, "to wear my Converse All-Stars around my neck and ride my bicycle to the school to play basketball with the older kids."

Basketball was the hottest ticket in town. It was most prestigious to have two season tickets at midcourt. Lines of one to two hundred people began forming three hours before tip-off. Jack Buck, Joe Garagiola, Harry Gallatin, and other St. Louis sports celebrities spoke at civic clubs or team banquets.

Collinsville expected to win its first state title in 1956–57. Led by a pair of All-Staters, 6' 7" Terry Bethel and 6' 5" Thom Jackson, the Kahoks won their first thirty-four games and were ranked number one. Bethel was named to *Parade* magazine's All-America team with Jerry Lucas and appeared on Steve Allen's television show.

In the state final against Herrin, which lost to Collinsville at Centralia in December, Bethel picked up three fouls in the first five minutes and was forced to sit down, Collinsville shot only seventeen of forty-seven, and Herrin won 45–42. Fletcher said that it was one of the most disappointing losses of his career.

"Nobody will let the 1957 team die," Bethel said. "To them, there never will be a team like 1957, not even 1961."

But Collinsville was 32–0 in 1960–61. The Kahoks had plenty of incentive. Redmon and Fred Riddle, who had transferred from Madison after his sophomore year, were returning starters from a 1959–60 powerhouse that was ranked second in the state before losing to Granite City in the regional at Collinsville.

Fletcher knew it was a special group. Before the first practice, he said, "If anyone doesn't think we can win the state title, go to the dressing room." No one left.

Other starters were Bob Simpson, who had transferred from Madison with Riddle, Bob Basola, and Bobby Meadows. Basola was an unheralded shooter. Meadows, quick and smart, was a superb ballhandler and the disruptive chaser on Fletcher's 1-2-2 ball-press zone defense. The team had more speed and mobility than 1957. Like 1957, it had two All-Staters in Redmon and Riddle.

After Simpson stole the ball in the closing seconds to key a 66–64 victory over second-ranked Centralia in the supersectional, the Kahoks crushed their last three opponents by margins of twenty-three, thirty-seven, and thirty-four points to be acclaimed as one of the top five teams in state history. Redmon scored ninety-two points in four games and Riddle scored seventy-six to finish first and second among tourney scorers.

It almost didn't happen. On the night before the second game, Redmon grabbed a rebound and came down on the foot of Harry Hildreth, suffering a hairline fracture of his tibia. It was speculated that he would miss the rest of the season. "It was devastating. We knew we had a chance to win the state title. Our dream was crushed," assistant coach Bert Weber said.

Fletcher contacted the St. Louis Cardinals trainer, who worked on Redmon's ankle like it was Bob Gibson's right arm. Miraculously, Redmon was back after twenty-three days. He missed only nine games. The Kahoks never missed a beat.

"It was a little crack," Redmon said. "But I was worried how good I would be when I came back. Could I still do it? But it was the best thing that ever happened to our team. When I went out, it gave others [particularly Ronnie Mottin] a chance to do things. It gave us more balance."

"Today, everyone talks about chemistry," Riddle said. "Everyone on that team liked each other, worked hard, and had a goal to be state champion. It was like magic that, in the course of a game, someone would step up if something happened. Fletcher was unique. He molded a lot of people who came in as young boys and turned them into men."

After two-time All-Stater Rodger Bohnenstiehl failed to punch a ticket to the state finals in Champaign in 1963 and 1964—his 26–3 and 28–1 teams lost to Centralia in the supersectional at Salem—Fletcher turned in his best coaching job in 1964–65, guiding 6' 3" center Dennis Pace and a bunch of guys named Harry, Steve, Jack, and Don to the state championship.

Pace didn't try out for the freshman team because he didn't think he was good enough. Fletcher discovered him in gym class. "He blue-collared everybody to death," Fletcher said. "He couldn't out-finesse anyone, but he outworked everyone."

The team had no one taller than 6' 3". Even Fletcher didn't expect them to win the state title. In December, after they lost to Decatur MacArthur, the coach said that it was the worst game a Collinsville team ever played. But they bounced back and were ranked number eight in the state after the regular season.

"They were fundamentally sound," Fletcher said. "Nobody executed the ball-press better. They set a school record for steals."

"After we showed we could beat anyone in the area at the lower levels, we were very confident that we could be successful," Pace said. "We had five of the quickest sets of hands around. You couldn't pass the ball around us. Someone would get a hand on it and deflect the ball. We kept teams off balance all the time."

Pace made fourteen of his first fifteen shots, including eleven of twelve in the first half, as Collinsville crushed Lawrenceville 82–58 in the supersectional. The Kahoks smashed Lockport 70–45 in the quarterfinals, then beat Chicago Marshall and Rich Bradshaw 76–64 in the semifinals. In the final, they held off Quincy's late rally to win 55–52; Pace had fifteen points and ten rebounds, Jack Darlington scored seventeen points, and Don Birger scored eleven. Steve Gauen was the point guard, and Harry Parker, who later pitched for the St. Louis Cardinals and was Tom Parker's older brother, was another scoring threat. Pace was the tournament scoring leader with 112 points in four games.

"You wanted to play for the purple and white," Pace said. "You didn't want to do anything to jeopardize it. They'd write your name on the street because you were a basketball player. It was a very rewarding experience. You were a nobody, but you became a somebody because you played for a successful team."

Today, it isn't the same. The family-owned businesses on Main Street are gone. The TeePee, the old hangout for high school students, now caters to junior high students. Basketball isn't the only game in town, as it once was. Kids have developed loyalties for soccer and hockey.

The current coach, Bob Bone, who played on Fletcher's teams in 1970–73, recalls the old days. He idolized Redmon and Bohnenstiehl. In 1973 he thought his team could win the state title, but the Kahoks lost to New Trier in the quarterfinals.

He still coaches the ball-press, implements Fletcher's old rules, and talks about the tradition that oozes from every brick in Vergil Fletcher Gymnasium, but he concedes that "outside stuff" has a negative impact on the program. He claims that coaching his oldest son has been the highlight of his career.

"In the old days, you wanted to wear that uniform, you wanted to go to all the games, you wanted to be part of the basketball program. There was a lot of pride in the town," he said. "Now there is a different feeling. Kids have so many options now. There are so many other activities that take attention away from basketball."

Vergil Fletcher: A Winner and a Visionary

After coaching Collinsville to the 1965 state championship, his second in five years, Vergil Fletcher was invited to speak at a clinic at Lewis University in Romeoville.

"Do you want to know how we won the state title?" Fletcher asked the large gathering of high school coaches.

"Yes," they responded. And they proceeded to get out their clipboards and notebooks.

Fletcher told Lewis's 6' 8" center to stand under the basket. Fletcher threw him a high pass. He caught it. "Now turn around and shoot it," Fletcher said. He did.

"That's how we won the state title," Fletcher said. "We don't fast break, and we don't allow a hook shot."

"He always tried to do things simple," said Frank Pitol, who played for Fletcher and was a longtime assistant. "His idea was not to do everything but do what you can and do it well. Other coaches said they didn't need to scout Fletcher's teams because they knew what they were going to do. They just didn't know how to stop it."

Fletcher had a lot of ideas and a lot of rules. For years, before the first preseason practice session, he distributed a four-page, typewritten list of dos and don'ts to every varsity candidate. Called the "Kahok Code," it defined the values, principles, and requirements of Fletcher's program.

"As an athlete," Fletcher said in the code, "you cannot do some of the things other students do. If you think more of smoking, drinking, dating, long haircuts, staying out late at night, or riding around in automobiles (hot-rodding), then you are not willing to pay the price and it is best for you not to take out a uniform. To be on a championship team, you have to be a champion yourself."

Fletcher was strict and uncompromising. He didn't tolerate profanity, loafing, alibis, tardiness, or dating on the night before a game. Players had ten o'clock curfews before a school day or game and practiced on Thanksgiving Day, Christmas Day, and New Year's Day.

The father of one of Fletcher's players, a minister, admonished Fletcher that he shouldn't practice on Thanksgiving. Fletcher told him that he would run the basketball program, and the minister should run his church.

"You've got to be the boss," Fletcher said. "You can't let the players or their parents decide what is best for them or the program."

An older brother of one of Fletcher's star players, Kevin Stallings, now head coach at Vanderbilt University, tried to persuade the coach to change his offense to take advantage of Kevin's shooting skills. "There's the door," Fletcher told him. Later, Stallings's brother came to his senses and apologized.

"Egotism is defined as an anesthetic which deadens the pain of stupidity," Fletcher said.

There was no room for egos in Fletcher's system. Even though he produced many great players—Sam Miranda, Chuck Kraak, Ray Sonnenberg, Bob and Norm Schaulat, Terry Bethel, Thom Jackson, Bogie Redmon, Fred Riddle, Rodger Bohnenstiehl, Dennis Pace, Tom Parker, Mike and Marc Fletcher, Richard Knarr, Kevin Stallings, Richard Keene, and Bob Bone—all of them understood that the key to success was teamwork.

"I was a good player, but I made All-State because I played at Collinsville," said Bone, who played on Fletcher's worst team (3–19) in 1971 and has served as head coach at Collinsville since 1985.

"I got recognition because I played for Fletcher, because of the respect he had and the program had. There were a lot of perks for playing at Collinsville. You didn't realize how big he was until after high school, when you see what else is out there. Then you realize how special it is to play here."

Pace, the star of the 1965 state championship team, called Fletcher the Vince Lombardi of basketball. "He had three or four plays and one basic defense, and he made you play the way he wanted you to play. You couldn't play the way you wanted to. He prepared his players to do the things he wanted you to do on the floor under any condition. He knew if we did what he wanted, we would be successful," he said.

Few coaches in state history have enjoyed as much success. In thirty-two years at Collinsville, from 1946 to 1979, his teams won 81 percent (747–170) of their games. He made fourteen state tournament appearances, including state titles in 1961 and 1965, second place in 1957, third place in 1978, and fourth place in 1950.

In the 1960s Fletcher was virtually unbeatable. During an eleven-year span, from 1959–60 to 1969–70, his teams won 89 percent (283–34) of their games. He won 87 percent of his home games, once winning sixty-two in a row. In 1965–68, Tom Parker became the school's all-time leading scorer with 2,041 points. As a senior he averaged 32.9 per game.

"He gave his heart and soul to you and only asked that you do what is right," said Parker, who later was a three-time All-SEC player at Kentucky. "To play for him, you had to have your act together, mentally and physically. He set a stage for success. He was highly organized and disciplined and professional. He created an environment to succeed. You didn't want to let him down."

You didn't want to make him mad, either. Thom Jackson, an All-Stater on the 1957 state runner-up, said he was told that Fletcher "was the meanest son-of-a-bitch alive." When he coached football from 1946 to 1963, he was known to put on a leather helmet, get in a three-point stance, and demonstrate how to block and tackle.

"If he wasn't happy, he didn't have to say anything, he only had to look at you. We called it 'the look.' You knew you had done something wrong," Jackson said. "He taught me that a man has one basic thing, your word. That's all you have. If you ever break that, you've lost everything."

Fletcher changed with the times. He even let his hair grow. When he realized that Parker was a superb shooter with range from twenty to twenty-five feet, he scrapped his inside game to allow Parker to roam freely. Parker's single-game record of fifty points in the final of the 1967 Carbondale tournament still stands. Later, he installed a more up-tempo offense with perimeter shooting.

When he graduated in 1961, after starring on one of the best teams in state history, Bogie Redmon asked Fletcher, "Coach, did you know what we were doing? Did you know we were sneaking out on dates on weeknights? Did you know we were doing things that you didn't want us to do?"

"I knew," Fletcher said. "I knew you didn't go straight home. But what could I do? You were winning."

Winning is one thing that never changed. "As a team, you always believed you were going to win, and most likely the other team didn't believe it could beat you," said Marc Fletcher, the coach's son and an All-Stater in 1974.

Vergil Fletcher also was a visionary. In 1956 he pulled a copy of a unique defensive concept out of a file cabinet in his office. It said "ball-press" on it. "Let's try this. Let's put this in tonight," he told his assistant, Bert Weber. It was a 1-2-2 zone press that revolutionized the game.

"The emphasis was on pressuring the ball," said Weber, who played for Fletcher for two years and assisted him for eight. "The trick was to anticipate where the ball was going, then intercept it. Bobby Meadows [who played the point on the 1961 state championship team] said his job on the press was to figure out what the guy with the ball wanted to do, then not let him do it."

St. John's coach Lou Carnesecca observed Fletcher demonstrating his ball-press defense at a clinic and declared that it wouldn't work at the college level. A year later, he began using it. John Wooden made it famous at UCLA.

"I didn't learn anything in college that I didn't learn in high school," Redmon said.

"He had plays that were so innovative that no other coach would think about them," said Terry Bethel, an All-Stater on the 1957 state runner-up. "There never was a man who believed in fundamentals as much as he did."

Fletcher had one regret. After winning 794 games in thirty-six years at Mount Pulaski, Pana, and Collinsville, he didn't have an opportunity to surpass the state record of 809 career victories set by Centralia coach Arthur Trout. In 1978, he wanted to give up teaching and the athletic director's job. He only wanted to coach one more year.

Instead, the school board voted 5–2 against him. The only favorable votes came from his wife, Violet, and the school superintendent, Fred Riddle Sr., whose son was an All-Stater on the 1961 state championship team. So Fletcher quit. He wanted 100 percent support and didn't get it.

"He was well-established as a legend in the state and the community," Marc Fletcher said. "I saw how he was admired by so many college coaches who came into the house. He created a tradition that withstood the test of time. Even when times changed, it is remarkable that through those years, he was able to keep it going."

Carver 53, Centralia 52:
Smedley's Game-Winning Shot

Old memories die hard. In Centralia, where the basketball team has won more games than any other high school in the United States, they still recall one unforgettable loss more than forty years ago.

"Next to the deaths of my twenty-one-year-old son in a car accident and my forty-six-year-old wife due to cancer, the 1963 loss to Carver was the worst experience of my life," Centralia coach Bob Jones said. "We won thirty-two games in a row, but we lost two one-point games. That's what you remember, the losses."

Life hasn't been the same since the game for Anthony Smedley, either. The 5' 7", 135-pound sophomore was added to the ten-man tournament squad almost as an afterthought by coach Larry Hawkins. Yanked off the bench to provide defensive pressure, he stole the ball and swished a seventeen-foot, left-handed shot to win one of the most dramatic state championship games in history.

Smedley's defining moment lasted only nine seconds.

When Centralia's Cliff Berger lofted an eighteen footer from the baseline that was partially blocked by Carver's Robert Cifax at the buzzer, Smedley was sitting on the bench.

It was an ironic twist. A year earlier, Carver and the great Cazzie Russell lost to Decatur 49–48 in the last state championship game played at old Huff Gym.

Ken Maxey, Joe Allen, Cifax, Gerry Jones, Charles Glenn, and Curtis Kirk never forgot. They formed the nucleus of the 1962–63 team. Following the loss to Decatur, on the bus trip back to Chicago, they vowed to return to the state finals.

Hawkins said that he was as optimistic about 1963 as he had been in 1962, but he had a new game plan. He took his squad to small farming communities to let them understand other cultures and learn other coaching philosophies and playing styles.

Centralia was on a mission, too. Legendary coach Arthur Trout had guided the Orphans to three state championships, but they hadn't won a state title since 1942. "We were totally dedicated to winning the state championship in 1963," Herb Williams said. "Every day for four years, we got up at five A.M. to practice at six. We knew about the great tradition at Centralia, and we wanted to continue it."

The Orphans were ranked number one in the state. Williams and Ron Johnson were All-Staters. Don Duncan, Johnson's backcourt mate, was almost as good. And 6' 8" junior Cliff Berger was an All-Stater in 1964 who later played at Kentucky.

In the supersectional, Centralia crushed Collinsville 69–48. Collinsville coach Vergil Fletcher said that his Kahoks didn't have to worry about Centralia's guards, only Williams and Berger. So Jones installed a new offense. Johnson scored thirty points, and Duncan had twenty-five. It was one of Fletcher's most humiliating defeats.

In Champaign, Centralia trounced Metropolis 74–45 in the quarterfinals and nudged Springfield Lanphier, Calvin Pettit, and Mike Rodgerson 50–46 in the semifinals.

In the other bracket, Carver's road to Champaign was littered with potholes. Going into the Chicago Public League playoff, the Challengers were unranked. They had lost five games, including a twenty-five pointer to Gary (Indiana) Roosevelt and a thirty-one pointer to Rockford Auburn.

"It took some time for Hawkins to get us together," said Maxey, a sophomore who was asked to choreograph the offense. "We had a speed game and a slow-down game. Hawkins wanted someone who would implement his philosophy on the court, not be too creative outside the offense, but be mindful of protecting the ball and quick enough to get the ball up and down the floor."

They dispatched Harlan 57–51 in the city final, Waukegan 54–41 in the supersectional at Evanston, Geneva 57–50 in the quarterfinals, and Peoria Central and the tournament scoring leader Craig Alexander 40–37 in overtime in the semifinals.

Ironically, in the closing seconds of the fourth quarter against Peoria Central, Hawkins also called Smedley off the bench to provide pressure on defense. He took a pass from Maxey and converted a twenty-five footer at the buzzer to force overtime.

In the championship game, Hawkins had three concerns: how to contain Williams, whom Jones described as "the best 6' 3" rebounder ever to play in the Assembly Hall," how to contain Johnson, who was averaging twenty-eight points per game, and how to prevent Centralia's attacking defense from neutralizing Carver's size advantage.

Williams quickly discovered that he was in for a tough evening. "Early in the game, Cifax was taking a jumper from the corner, and I went out to get him. Normally that shot would be back in the stands. But the higher I leaped, the higher he went, and the shot went in. I knew the game was on from that point."

Hawkins confounded Centralia's defense by assigning Allen to bring the ball up the court. "He was the first 6' 7" guard," he said.

To stifle Johnson, Hawkins devised a four-man zone with a chaser on Johnson. He finished with eighteen points but converted only eight of twenty shots.

It all came down to the last fifteen seconds.

Williams made a turnaround jumper with thirty-five seconds to play to give Centralia a 52–51 lead. It was only his second shot and his only basket of the game.

With fifteen seconds remaining, Allen threw the ball away, Williams grabbed it, and Centralia called time-out. Hawkins called for Smedley.

"We weren't supposed to call time-out when we got the ball in the closing seconds," Jones said. "It gave them time to put Smedley into the game. The referee put his hand on the ball after our kids broke and delayed the inbounds play and disrupted our strategy. That set up the steal."

At that point, Hawkins said he was in disarray. He was happy that Centralia had called time-out. He needed a moment to catch his breath, devise a strategy, and put Smedley into the game.

"I wish I could say I had a brilliant thought," Hawkins said. "Cifax had lost the ball, and I had to get him out of the game. I had to get somebody in. Smedley had the quickest hands. We had to steal the ball and put the ball in the basket. I got him in because he was a good shooter and the kind who could play in a hot minute. The average kid wilts. But I knew he wouldn't, even though he was a sophomore."

Smedley was the most surprised person in the crowd of 16,183 when he was summoned off the bench. "Hawkins had just called a make-it-or-break-it play, and it didn't make it," Smedley said. "He had to come up with something else. He put me in for defensive pressure. Oh, great, I have a chance to go into the game. I'm supposed to pressure whoever gets the ball."

Duncan inbounded the ball to Williams, who was defended by Allen. He was instructed to hold it until Duncan or Johnson took it out of his hands. But he never saw Smedley, who slapped at the ball, stole it, dribbled into the corner, and launched the game-winning shot.

"The ball goes to Williams. Allen is behind him, and I'm at the side of him," Smedley said. "He is aware that Joe is behind him. He looks and turns and gets ready to pass. I hit up on the ball. I recall his eyes buckle, and I snatched the ball. I was on the baseline about seventeen feet from the basket, in the corner, in front of the Centralia bench. I knew I had enough time. To me, it was automatic. I took one rhythm bounce and shot. I knew it was in, all net."

"Smedley was a gunner, an automatic shooter," Maxey said. "We called him 'The Golden Arm.' That spot on the baseline, that was his spot. He did it instinctively. He never thought about it. For him, it was a natural reaction to take the shot."

The game wasn't over, however. Centralia called time-out with six seconds to play. Smedley was replaced. Berger missed a last shot. Bedlam. Hysteria. Joy. Tears.

Williams was distraught. He sat on the bench and buried his face in a towel. He had to be prodded to accept the second-place trophy, then hurried off the floor. Centralia was heartbroken.

"Smedley saw an opportunity, and he seized it," said Williams, who has had years to reflect on the moment. "At the time, I thought we were robbed. The town still believes we were cheated. But I wasn't fouled. Lots of people said I was, but it wasn't called. I was totally crushed. We had worked so hard. It is one of those things that you never get over. But you have to accept it. You realize you did the best you could, but it wasn't meant to be."

Smedley never capitalized on his magic moment. He and Maxey were named co-captains of the 1964 team, but Smedley saw little playing time due to disciplinary reasons. He attended junior college, joined the army, received a bad conduct discharge, and worked as a counselor in a juvenile court for fifteen years. Now he is unemployed and living in Wisconsin.

"Fame works in different ways," Maxey said. "For Smedley, it took him too high up. He didn't improve his skills like he should have. He didn't elevate his game to the point where his game and his reputation were compatible. He never regained that moment of glory."

Cazzie Russell: In a Class by Himself

Before there was Cazzie Russell, there were Tommy Hawkins, Gerald Junior, and Darius "Pete" Cunningham. They grew up in Altgeld Gardens, a self-contained housing project on Chicago's far South Side, and put Carver High School on the map.

Altgeld was built in 1949. There were two roads in and two roads out. It was a close-knit community with its own grocery store and its own high school. Residents kept their lawns green, windows open, and doors unlocked. They had contests to judge the most beautiful lawns and gardens.

At Carver, there was no emphasis on sports. The school didn't field a football team. Tommy Hawkins and William Saxton, two outstanding basketball players, enrolled at Parker (now Robeson), sixty-three blocks to the north. Football players opted for Tilden, eighty-four blocks away. If you wanted a more academic-oriented curriculum, you went to Parker or Harlan, thirty-six blocks away. Teachers didn't want to work at Carver.

Tommy Hawkins influenced many youngsters. He had a hoop in his backyard. When he realized he could dunk, he raised the basket. To get in shape, he ran on a track surface in combat boots and jumped rope. He was an All-Stater at Parker in 1955, an All-American at Notre Dame, and he played for the Los Angeles Lakers in the NBA.

Larry Hawkins arrived at Carver in 1956, fresh out of George Williams College. He was hired as a physical education teacher but was appointed head basketball coach "because nobody else was there to do it." He consulted Eddie O'Farrell, Parker's legendary coach, and persuaded Bill McQuitter and Roy Credelle to organize a feeder system to keep Altgeld kids in Altgeld.

Junior, who played on an Amateur Athletic Union (AAU) team with Tommy Hawkins, and Cunningham, who graduated in 1961, were the first great players produced in the program. As a sophomore, Pete scored ninety points against Morgan Park and averaged thirty-five points per game. The media suddenly began to pay attention to Carver.

"No one knew about Carver until then," Cunningham said. "I never asked how many points I scored in a game. I think I scored more than two thousand in my career, but no one kept statistics in those days. No one got recognition like the kids get today."

Cunningham saw a promising youngster named Cazzie Russell coming up. He played a half semester with Russell when he was a senior and Cazzie was a sophomore and Joe Allen was a freshman. "I sensed there was something special with Cazzie," Pete said, "the way he could handle the ball, how he took things that coach Hawkins taught him and put them to work. I didn't know he would be that big and still be able to do those things."

When Russell arrived at Carver, however, his favorite sport was baseball: he wanted to be a catcher or outfielder, not a power forward. "Growing up, I didn't know anything about basketball," he said. He wanted to be a major leaguer. He once had a tryout with the Chicago White Sox.

But Larry Hawkins discovered him in a gym class. He was 6' 2" as a freshman, but Hawkins projected him as a 6' 5" senior. He wasn't very athletic; he couldn't run fast or jump high. But he had size, smarts, and an insatiable work ethic. He was dripping with potential, and he was eager to learn.

"What caught my attention was his work ethic," Hawkins said. "He was the kind of guy who paid attention to whatever you talked about. He would be in the gym all the time, trying to learn moves. He wanted to play basketball while he was getting ready to play baseball.

"He wanted to learn to play guard at a time when kids his size were playing center. He was determined that he could play that position. He was the first guy on the floor and the last to leave. As great as he was, he would do whatever the team needed him to do to win."

Russell credits Hawkins for putting his life in order, for teaching him how to play basketball from the floor up, and for recommending that he attend Michigan to establish his own identity by leading a struggling program from the outhouse to the penthouse. Crisler Arena, home of the Wolverines, forever will be known as "the house that Cazzie built."

"After a gym class, Hawkins said he wanted to see me," Russell said. "He wanted me to drive and make layups. Two other kids missed. My approach was I didn't want to miss. He taught me how to play the game, the basic fundamentals. It was a blessing. When I came back for my sophomore year, I had developed so much that I took everyone by surprise."

He started to make his mark as a sophomore, leading Carver to an unbeaten record and the city frosh-soph championship. As a junior he led Carver's varsity to the city semifinals. As a senior he emerged as the state's premier player while leading Carver to second place in the state tournament. A *Chicago Sun-Times* poll in 2002 singled him out as the number one player in the history of city basketball.

"Playing basketball in the city taught me how to be aggressive, how to be tough, how to keep my composure," said Russell, who played in the NBA for thirteen years. "You couldn't be a cream puff and play in Chicago. Physically, I wasn't going to get beat because I wasn't in shape."

At Carver, Larry Hawkins taught him more than how to dribble, pass, and shoot. Cazzie knew that if he didn't go to class, he wouldn't play. He learned work ethic, priorities, and discipline. Hawkins wanted his athletes to be well-rounded, not one-dimensional.

"He would tell guys what to do and go out of the gym and come back and he could tell if you had practiced what he told you. He found out who he could depend on," Russell said. "He taught me about responsibility, that you can't play ball and run in the street. I learned there are no shortcuts to success."

Russell became a role model in the community. He began eating in a different line in the cafeteria. As a freshman, he ate hamburgers and fries; as a sophomore, he switched to vegetables and salads. He took a course in public speaking, sang in the glee club, and was president of the student council.

Despite the presence of Russell, Allen, who later played at Bradley, and Gerry Jones, who later played at Iowa, Carver wasn't expected to challenge for the state championship in 1962. Du Sable was ranked second in the state, and Carver, which lost five games in the regular season, wasn't rated at all.

"The state tournament wasn't our goal, just the next game," Larry Hawkins said. "But we knew we had a very good team. We didn't play many places where we could be seen, so no one knew much about us. They would have to learn about us on the floor for the first time. They couldn't prepare for us."

In fact, few people knew about Cazzie Russell until he arrived in Champaign. Carver beat Marshall 47–39 for the Public League championship, then ousted St. Patrick 48–42 in the supersectional at Northwestern's McGaw Hall in Evanston.

Carver and Russell leaped into everyone's consciousness by stunning top-ranked Centralia 56–50 in the quarterfinals, snapping the Orphans' twenty-eight-game winning streak. Leading 31–25 at halftime, Carver broke away as Russell scored all of his team's eleven points in the third quarter. He finished with twenty-two points; Allen had sixteen.

In the final, Carver rushed to an early 13–2 lead against Decatur. But three twists of fate helped to turn the tide. An apparent Carver basket was disallowed because a faint whistle had sounded, signaling for a time-out. And Joe Allen, Carver's muscular 6' 6" center, suffered a knee injury and was sidelined for the remainder of the game.

"That's when the game changed, and they began to come back," Hawkins said. "He was dominating. We would have won easily if he had stayed in the game."

In the closing seconds, Carver guard Bruce Raickett inexplicably tossed the ball to Decatur guard Jerry Hill. With the game tied, Decatur held for a last shot. Ken Barnes was fouled with six seconds left and made one free throw for a 49–48 victory. Russell was magnificent in defeat, finishing with twenty-four points and fifteen rebounds.

"The [Raickett] incident at the end was unfortunate," Hawkins said. "We got thousands of letters from people who commiserated with him. We still talk about it from time to time. It was a growing experience. How can you forget it?"

Russell remembers Allen's knee popping out, Raickett throwing the ball away, and his mother constantly asking, "When are you guys going Downstate?" But what disturbed him most of all was the off-the-ball foul call on Curtis Kirk that allowed Ken Barnes to make the winning free throw.

1962 laid the foundation for what was to come. The following year, Cazzie was gone, but Allen, Jones, Kirk, Robert Cifax, and Ken Maxey returned to lead Carver to the state championship.

"Mayor [Richard J.] Daley came in 1962 when we lost and said he would be back in 1963 when we win. He did," Hawkins said. "After 1962, people knew where Altgeld was and what it was. After 1963, people from Altgeld had great respect.

"I don't know anyone in Altgeld who wasn't keyed into it. It was a great source of pride for the whole community. No one sold drugs or robbed anyone or shot anyone. It was just about some kids who made a name for themselves and their community."

Pekin: Four Years of Glory

Rich Hawkins didn't want to move from Peoria to Pekin, but the eleven-year-old sixth grader didn't have a vote in the decision. His father was a basketball coach, not a diplomat. He never ran a democracy. Now the high school gym is named in his honor.

Dawson "Dawdy" Hawkins had success written all over him. In his native Nebraska, he had coached a state championship team and a state runner-up at Lincoln Northeast. He moved to Peoria Central in 1949, finished second in the 1953 state tournament, and qualified for the state finals in 1954, 1956, and 1959.

One of Hawkins's bitterest rivals was Pekin. Founded by Italian and German immigrants in the 1880s, Pekin is located on the Illinois River a few miles south of Peoria. A strong union town, most people carried a lunch pail to work. Now many residents work at Caterpillar in Peoria.

In the 1950s and 1960s, the mostly all-white community had a racist reputation. There was a neighborhood called Dago Hill. Most of the population had southern roots. For years, a sign at the city limits warned: "Niggers, don't let the sun set on you."

In those days, the school's nickname was the Chinks. The name was derived from Pekin's sister city, Peking, China. It was changed to the Dragons in 1978. The students voted overwhelmingly to retain the old name, but a Chinese American organization applied pressure, claiming that it was demeaning. The school administration ordered the students to come up with a new name.

Politics and prejudices aside, Pekin (population thirty-five thousand) was a sports-minded community. The basketball team had placed third and fourth in the state finals in the 1930s under Frenchie Haussler and in the 1940s under Red Lewis and had qualified for the Sweet Sixteen in 1957 and 1960 under Bob Cain.

After the 1960 season, the coaching position opened up when the school board elevated Cain to the principal's chair. To everyone's surprise, Hawkins expressed interest. Once he applied, his hiring was a no-brainer.

"To me, he was the finest basketball coach in the state," said Fritz Joesting, chairman of the school's athletic committee. "The people in Pekin, the basketball fans, knew how good he was. They hated him when he was at Peoria Central, but they turned that hate into love."

Why did he choose to move to Pekin? After all, Peoria Central has enjoyed one of the richest traditions in state history, since it won the first state title in 1908.

"I think he wanted another challenge," Joesting said. "It was a good challenge because we didn't have much for several years. We told him we wanted to go to Champaign within five years. He said it would take him four years."

It did. Hawkins produced state titles in 1964 and 1967. His 1965 and 1966 teams lost in the supersectional. In four years, his teams won 91 percent (115–11) of their games.

He couldn't wait to get started, to put his stamp on the program. He ordered his players into the gym in the summer, a violation of IHSA rules. He chained the doors so no one could get in or out. They worked out for two and a half hours for three to four days a week in a hot gym. He taught them the fundamentals of defense.

Meanwhile, assistant coach Duncan Reid worked with the eighth graders at Edison Junior High. Reid, who later won more than six hundred games while coaching at Lincoln and Rock Island, was brash and abrasive but a superb teacher.

"Hawkins and Reid were a good match," said Amel Massa, a senior starter on the 1964 championship team. "Both were very solid tacticians, real fundamentalists, and passionate about conditioning."

Summers in Pekin meant open gym at the high school, open morning, noon, and night. Kids would ride their bicycles to the gym and shoot hoops, find a pickup baseball game in the afternoon, then return to the gym at night for more hoops.

Hawkins orchestrated the whole symphony. He took his players to the summer league in Peoria. It was the only time they experienced playing against quick black athletes. The 1964 state champions were the first ones to play there.

"In central Illinois, Dawdy Hawkins is still the king whenever there is talk about the greatest coach ever," said former Thornridge coach Ron Ferguson, who later served as athletic director at Bradley University. "He has to rank among the top ten coaches of all time."

Hawkins was an innovator, a visionary. He spent 80 percent of each practice on defense, especially full-court press. He believed that the key to winning is defense and conditioning. On offense, he played to his strength. In 1964, he took advantage of Dave Golden's perimeter shooting. In 1967, with Fred Miller and Barry Moran, he focused on an inside game. "Don't be set in one way, know your bread-and-butter," he said.

Hawkins said that his 1963–64 team was the best he had produced in terms of shooting and ballhandling. Golden, a 5' 11" junior guard who earned All-State recognition in 1964 and 1965 and later played at Duke, averaged fourteen points per game. Jim Sommer, a 6' 3" senior center who later attended a Division III school in Ohio, averaged fifteen. He was the tallest starter.

Golden, Sommer, Massa, Jim Couch, and guard Ron Rhoades lifted their expectations at the Pontiac tournament, where they upset highly rated Waukegan before losing to the defending state champion, Carver, by one point in the final. "We sensed we would play with the best teams in the state," Golden said.

Pekin, which lost its last regular-season game at Moline, was 21–3 and ranked eighth in the state. In the regional final, they overcame a fourteen-point deficit to avenge an earlier loss to Peoria Limestone 85–80. In the sectional, they beat Peoria Woodruff as a last-second, game-tying shot went in and out. In the supersectional, they scored only three points in the first quarter and trailed by ten before rallying to oust Streator 61–46.

They got better. They crushed Glenbard East 84–43 in the quarterfinals and Rock Island Alleman 69–36 in the semifinals. But awaiting them in the final was Cobden, the sentimental favorite with four starters standing 6' 5" or taller.

"We talked about how they would be the crowd favorite because they were the smallest school [to qualify for the state finals] since Hebron," Sommer said. "To beat them, we had to be strong fundamentally, box out, keep them off the boards, take good shots, and not try to ram the ball down the middle."

It was Hawkins's finest hour. He purposely had his team wait in the tunnel of the Assembly Hall until the Cobden team went onto the floor. Then he sent his players out with them as the mostly pro-Cobden crowd cheered loudly.

Hawkins's game tactics were on the mark, too. He spread his offense to tire his taller and slower opponents and to force fouls. Pekin converted sixteen of nineteen free throws, built a seven-point halftime lead, and won 50–45. Golden scored eighteen points, Couch twelve.

In 1964–65, Pekin was expected to return to the Elite Eight. Led by Golden, Couch, Rhoades, and sophomore Fred Miller, the team was ranked second in the state. Hawkins later said that the team had more talent than the 1964 and 1967 state champions. But they lost to Lockport 67–61 in the supersectional. Earlier, they had beaten Lockport by twenty-seven points in the Pontiac Tournament.

"The 1964 championship was my greatest happiness, and 1965 was my biggest disappointment," Golden said.

In retrospect, the 1965–66 team probably went as far as it could have gone. With only one senior starter, Pekin won twenty-six games before losing to Joliet Central in the supersectional.

Miller, a 6' 4" senior, and Moran, a 6' 5" junior, were the headliners in 1966–67. Miller later played at Illinois, Moran at Northwestern. They were supported by Mark Freidinger, Rich Hawkins, Doug Jones, Tom Vucich, and Dave Martin.

"Miller was our star, but his work ethic set the example and was a driving force," Rich Hawkins said. "Everyone had a goal. We were more businesslike. From the start, we thought of the state tournament."

Pekin split four games with Peoria Central. They lost twice in conference play to finish second to the Lions. But they beat Hawkins's old school in the final of the Pekin tournament and, most importantly, in the sectional final at Peoria.

"That was the state championship," Miller said. "Rhea Taylor and Steve Kirley were Central's leaders. Both teams were 22–2 after the regular season and ranked eighth and ninth in the state. Physically, they were the toughest team we faced."

After that, Pekin romped to its second state title in four years, winning by margins of thirteen, twenty-four, sixteen, and sixteen points. They ousted Springfield and Dave Robisch 77–61 in the semifinals. In the final, they beat Carbondale 75–59.

"We made adjustments. We overcame our lack of size," Rich Hawkins said. "We used a switching man-to-man press and sagged in the middle. Then we switched to a zone press in the second quarter against Carbondale in the state final and turned the game around [outscoring Carbondale 18–6 in the second period] because they weren't prepared for it."

Miller scored thirty-six points to tie a final game record (set by Mount Vernon's Max Hooper in 1950) that stood until Thornridge's Boyd Batts scored thirty-seven in 1972. And he converted sixteen field goals (of twenty shots) to tie another record that still stands.

Hawkins retired in 1974. After suffering with Alzheimer's disease for six years, he died on Father's Day in 1997. He was eighty-two.

"Some people aren't aware that he was a Little All-America football player at Nebraska Wesleyan in 1933," his son said. "He was always surprised that he made his mark in basketball."

Cobden: In Memory of Tom Crowell

Forty years later, Chuck Neal still can't talk about the tragic accident that took the life of Tom Crowell without tears welling up in his eyes. He rarely mentions it, even to his family. Some teammates never heard the story.

"What always has stuck with me is had I not lied to my father and gone where we were supposed to go, it may not have happened," he said.

Neal, his younger brother Jim, Ken Flick, Ken Smith, and his cousin Jim Smith grew up in Cobden, a small agricultural community located fifteen miles south of Carbondale. In 1964 they rekindled memories of Hebron's 1952 Cinderella team and had basketball fans throughout the state wondering what an Appleknocker is.

In those days, Cobden had a population of nine hundred. The tracks of the Illinois Central Railroad split the town, creating "the widest Main Street in the world." Folks celebrated victories at Fuzzy's Tavern, Flamm's Restaurant, or the pool hall. The senior class included six basketball players and seventeen other students.

They learned the value of a dollar before they learned how to dribble. They picked strawberries, blueberries, apples, peaches, and tomatoes for sixty cents an hour. For entertainment, they drove five miles to the A&W Drive-In in Anna.

"We didn't realize what we didn't have because we didn't have anything to compare it to," Jim Neal said.

The Neals, Flick, and the Smiths came together in fifth grade. Flick, who was born in Golconda, moved to Cobden when he was six. In 1957 the Neal family arrived from DeKalb. For two years the Neals, Flick, and the Smiths dominated grade school tournaments in southern Illinois.

One piece of the puzzle was missing, however. And the Neals' father, a local dentist and school board member, found it. He persuaded Dick Ruggles, a young and promising coach at conference rival Hurst-Bush, to move to Cobden in 1962.

Ruggles seemed out of place in Cobden, like a surfer. He grew up in Quincy, Massachusetts, walked on Southern Illinois's basketball team, and played with Chico Vaughn. After obtaining a master's degree in recreation and administration, he accepted a job at Hurst-Bush. Then Cobden came beckoning.

"He had a [New England] accent in his speech. Mix that with our hillbilly accent and we couldn't understand what each other said," Ken Smith said. "He was very disciplined with a capital V. He emphasized conditioning, a lot of running and stair-climbing. He wouldn't tolerate not being a team player."

Ruggles evaluated his players and determined that they had great size—Chuck Neal and Flick were 6' 6", Jim Neal and Ken Smith were 6' 5"—and skills. So Ruggles introduced a rotating offense that created movement among the big kids.

They won twenty-nine of thirty-one games in 1962–63, losing to McLeansboro and the Burns brothers, Jim and John, in the sectional. Flick got married during Christmas break and was forced to drop out of school when the team was 11–0. He returned for his senior season and earned All-State recognition.

Then they lost Tom Crowell. Chuck Neal, Ken Smith, and Crowell planned to go swimming on a warm day in May. Chuck knew that his father didn't want him to go to Little Grassy Lake because it was known to have a big dropoff. So Chuck said they would go to Lamer's Pond. But they went to Little Grassy.

"Chuck and I decided we would swim across the cove," Ken Smith said. "We both told Tom to stay where he was, in a shallow place. He said he would. We got halfway across and I turned around and looked and saw that Tom was struggling."

Neal went ahead and tried to get help. Smith swam back and desperately tried to save Crowell's life. "It was the most horrible experience I ever had, even worse than Vietnam," Smith said. "He kept fighting me and he kept going under and he was gone. Hardly a day goes by that I don't think about it. I think about what Tom could have been."

Crowell was a 6' 2" point guard and the team leader. The players devoted the 1963–64 season to him. To this day, no one at Cobden wears Crowell's jersey, number 35. The trophy room is named in his memory.

Flick chose to rejoin the squad, but Cobden had a rule that married students couldn't participate in athletics. So they changed the rule and petitioned the IHSA for permission to play a married student.

Ruggles rotated Jim Smith and Bob Smith in the fifth spot. Ken Smith had superior ballhandling skills, so he assumed Crowell's role of floor general. Pressing defenses were ineffective because they used their height advantage to pass over shorter opponents.

On October 1, the first day of practice, Ruggles told them, "Men, if we work hard and get a little luck, we can be playing on the last day of the year."

"He never said another word," Jim Neal said. "I still get chills remembering him saying that. Gosh, he really thinks we can do this, play on television, play at Illinois."

Despite their celebrity, the Appleknockers took a lot of grief from Merle Jones, a longtime sportswriter with the *Southern Illinoisan* in Carbondale. He said that Cobden couldn't contend for the state title because it was too small and couldn't beat bigger schools that played better competition.

Cobden started 11–0, lost a two-pointer to McLeansboro in the final of the McLeansboro Holiday Tournament, then went on another eleven-game winning streak before losing by two points in overtime to Albion in the final game of the regular season. Earlier, they had beaten Albion by thirty points. They were unranked in the Associated Press's final regular-season poll.

Cobden's season almost came crashing down in the regional final at Anna. Tamms, which had lost earlier to Cobden by twenty and fifteen points, was trailing by one but stalled for the last shot. Ted Cleghorn missed a fifteen footer. "He got his shot from his spot but missed it," Chuck Neal said. "If he had made it, nobody would be talking about Cobden."

It didn't get any easier. The Appleknockers beat Harrisburg and All-Stater Guy Turner by four points in the sectional final. In the supersectional at West Frankfort, they outlasted Pinckneyville and All-Stater Ben Louis 68–66 in triple overtime.

"We weren't afraid of any team," Chuck Neal said. "It was five against five, not small school against big school. We weren't in awe of bigger guys or bigger schools. We felt our five were as good as anyone in the state."

In the quarterfinals, playing in the sixteen-thousand–seat Assembly Hall in Champaign, Cobden beat Galesburg and All-Stater Rick Callahan 60–57. In the semifinals, they dispatched Decatur and All-Staters Charlie Currie and Jack Sunderlik 44–38.

"Decatur was favored to win the state title after Centralia and Collinsville lost," Chuck Neal said. "Their players chanted: 'We're going to make apple sauce' as they went past our locker room. After they beat Evanston in the quarterfinals, Currie shook hands with the Evanston players, but he wouldn't shake our hands after we beat them."

Cobden had emerged as the darling of the tournament. The team mascot, Roger Burnett, the Appleknocker, wore a maroon hat and bib overalls with a red handkerchief hanging out of the back pocket. Before the championship game against Pekin, he placed five apples at center court and received a five-minute ovation.

Pekin coach Dawson Hawkins was up to the occasion. He didn't want to lose a psychological battle before the war began. He refused to send his players onto the floor until Cobden took the first step. So both teams came out of the tunnel together, to the cheers of the pro-Cobden crowd.

The adrenaline finally wore off. Cobden's starters had been stretched to the brink in previous games while Pekin won by margins of fifteen, forty-one, and thirty-three points. Its starters, including All-Stater Dave Golden, were well-rested. Pekin got off to a 15–8 lead in the first quarter and held on to win 50–45.

"They spread us out, and we had to foul," Ruggles said. "We couldn't chase them. I thought we were better than Pekin, but they held the ball and spread us out and we got anxious.

"In the middle of the third quarter, we tried to go after them, and that's what Hawkins wanted. We moved our feet too slow. We couldn't chase Golden and Ronnie Rhoades."

Ken Smith kept waiting for something to happen, for Cobden to strike back in the third quarter as it had done all season. But the Appleknockers never responded. "I remember it was like we were playing with a flat basketball," Smith said. "We couldn't get going."

Smith scored seventeen points, but he was the only Cobden player in double figures. Golden scored eighteen, Jim Couch scored twelve. Pekin converted sixteen of nineteen free throws, Cobden only three of ten. Flick, who averaged fifteen shots a game, was limited to only six shots and four points.

The next day, the team returned home on the Illinois Central. It was only the second time the train stopped in Cobden. It had stopped to pick up the team to go to Champaign and to drop them off with the second-place trophy. Over five thousand people greeted them. One of the cheerleaders was Mildred Crowell, Tom's sister.

"Since then, I've always been a dreamer. It was like a storybook," Jim Neal said. "It was a real-life experience of believing you can do it and knowing someone else believes you can do it, too. I wouldn't trade that era for anything. It doesn't make a difference where you grow up, it's what you do with the experience. But it still hurts because we lost."

Rich Herrin: "A Gem of a Man"

When Rich Herrin moved from Okawville to Benton in 1960, he arrived in a mobile home, a house on wheels "so you can go down the road when they fire you," according to Dr. William Swinney, president of the school board.

Benton, Herrin was told, was a basketball graveyard. In the first twenty years after the South Seven was founded in 1940, Benton hadn't won a conference championship. In fact, Benton hadn't won a single conference game in twelve of those twenty years. The school's best records were 7–5 in 1953 and 6–6 in 1954.

Benton was a football town. The Rangers won a conference title in 1957 with John Bauer and Harry Stewart. Terry Thomas was an All-Stater. Jim Lovin and Red Lowery were stars. Benton and West Frankfort engaged in a Thanksgiving Day rivalry.

Basketball coaches were football coaches who didn't start working with the basketball team until the football season was over. No one attended the games in the old fourteen-hundred–seat gym that had been built as a WPA project in 1942. You could show up before tip-off and get a seat.

All of that changed in 1961, when Herrin took Benton to the state finals for the first time since 1933. Led by Terry Thomas, Tom Whittington, and Wiley Hall, the Rangers were 17–13.

They committed only three turnovers while beating Belleville 65–59 in the supersectional. "It was the most flawless game I ever coached," Herrin said. "And it inspired young kids to play basketball." They lost to Peoria Manual 54–51 in overtime in the state quarterfinals. But it was a beginning.

"I never saw anyone so consumed with basketball, twenty-four hours a day. He had tunnel vision," Terry Thomas said.

In twenty-five years at Benton, Herrin won 521 games. When he left to become head coach at Southern Illinois University, where he won 225 games in thirteen years, the new forty-four-hundred–seat gym had been named in his honor, two numbers had been retired—Doug Collins's number 20 and Rich Yunkus's number 40—and thirteen banners recalled state tournament appearances from 1928 to 1992. Everything but a state title.

"It was very disappointing not to get to the Final Four," Herrin said. "We had our chances. In 1961, we led by fourteen points late in the third quarter against Peoria Manual but scored only three points in the last eleven minutes. In 1984, Everette Stephens stole the ball with 1:34 left and made a layup to tie, and we lost to Evanston in overtime."

Herrin employed an unsophisticated system. "There are no secrets in basketball," he said. "The only secret is how to motivate kids to play with intensity. You must be fundamentally sound. I try to outwork everyone and convince my players that there is more work off the court than on it."

He insisted that the game be fun and exciting, or the kids won't want to play and the fans won't want to watch. That's why he coached a run-and-gun offense. "If you are having fun, you can work them harder. You are an entertainer. That's how to draw fans," he said.

People stood in line in the snow to buy tickets. Before games, all the store windows in the square were painted. There were pep rallies. Benton never had an away game because more Ranger fans attended away games than fans of the home team. The players portrayed a unified image with their maroon bags, maroon blazers, white shirts, black pants, and black ties.

"As long as Rich Herrin was here, basketball was a big thing," Rich Yunkus said.

The gym was open from 7 A.M. to 11 P.M. five days a week. The team scrimmaged at night. On school days, the team worked out from 7:30 until 8:20 in the morning, during study hall, in the last hour, and during physical education class and then practiced from 2:15 to 6:00 P.M. Two nights a week, Herrin drove Yunkus and Jim Adkins to the gym to play one-on-one.

The players had to be home at 9:30 the night before a game. Herrin would call and ask parents to put their sons on the phone. He would drive around the neighborhood to see if everyone was at home. On Saturday nights, he imposed an 11:00 curfew, but he still showed up to see if each player was at home.

"My girlfriend was at my house one time," Yunkus said. "He said she couldn't be there, and my mother had to drive her home. We have been married for thirty years. He set an example for us. No one worked harder."

Jim Adkins got the message when he arrived in Benton. Born in Fleming in the mountains of southeastern Kentucky, he moved from a town of 150 to Benton (population seventy-five hundred) when he was in eighth grade. His father was a coal miner, and Benton offered a better opportunity for him and his family.

"I didn't realize what I was getting into at first," he said. "After my freshman year, that's when it hit me. I'd go into the gym lobby and see the pictures of players going back to the 1920s. 'Wouldn't it be great to get my picture on the wall?' I'd say to myself. Then I realized I was living in a hotbed for basketball."

Adkins's picture hangs in the gym today. Adkins and Yunkus were All-Staters on the 1965–66 team that was unbeaten and ranked number one in the state. But they lost to Galesburg 73–71 in the state quarterfinals when Dale Kelley made a thirty-footer. Thornton, which lost to Benton 70–63 in the Centralia Holiday Tournament in December, beat Galesburg for the state title.

"It was the most devastating loss I ever was involved with," said Adkins, who later played at Alabama. "I still think about it. I took the last shot that rimmed out, a step across half-court at the buzzer. We thought we let the whole town down."

In 1966–67, Yunkus was back. At 6' 7", he formed a formidable double low-post combination with 6' 8" Greg Fustin. Jerry Hoover was the point guard, and Danny Johnson was a promising sixth man. For the second year in a row, the Rangers were unbeaten and ranked number one in the state at the end of the regular season. But they lost to Carbondale 59–53 in the supersectional.

"It was my most disappointing experience," said Yunkus, who later was an All-American at Georgia Tech and played for the Atlanta Hawks in the NBA. "I let me and the town down. We felt we were better and bigger than the 1966 team. Four of us went on to play at Division I colleges. We understood the game."

Benton had beaten Carbondale twice in South Seven play, but Carbondale went on to finish second in the state. "When we saw Carbondale lose to Pekin in the state final, we knew we were better, that we should have won the state title," Yunkus said.

"It was my best team," Herrin said. "We felt we were as good as other great teams in state history. We had dominant people."

Benton made another run at the state title in 1970–71. The Rangers were 24–1 and ranked fourth at the end of the regular season. They were unselfish, deep, and well balanced. They won the Centralia Tournament, and no one was named to the all-tournament team. Hugh Frailey, Dennis Smith, and Dave Lockin were the leaders.

In the state quarterfinals, Benton lost to Oak Lawn and C. J. Kupec 71–58. Oak Lawn led 52–50 with 2:15 to play when Dennis Smith fouled out. Herrin had implemented a triangle-and-two defense to contain Oak Lawn's leading scorers, Kupec and Jim Bocinsky, but Brett Arnold broke loose for twenty points. "They were scared, but we couldn't get ahead," Smith said.

In 1974–75, Benton was 27–0 and ranked fifth in the state. But 6' 8" Rob Dunbar missed the last seven games with a knee injury, and the Rangers fell to Olney, which was coached by Ron Herrin, Rich's brother, in the sectional.

In 1983–84, Benton was 24–7 with three Division I players—Randy House, Bruce Baker, and Kai Nurnburger. House played on three teams that qualified for the state finals, then played four more years for Herrin at Southern Illinois University. But the memory of the loss to Evanston in the 1984 quarterfinals still haunts him.

Benton led by six with 1:35 to play and had the ball. But Evanston, sparked by Everette Stephens, rallied to win in overtime. Earlier, Benton had upset Carbondale in the sectional final. Carbondale, which had beaten Benton twice in conference play, was 28–0 and ranked fourth in the state at the time.

It wasn't the same after Herrin left. JoJo Johnson, Danny's son, was the *Chicago Sun-*

Times Class A Player of the Year and led coach Rod Shurtz's team to third place in the 1992 state tournament. He was the tournament's leading scorer with 121 points in four games.

"He was all about hard work and preparation," Yunkus said. "I never played on a team that was better prepared and better conditioned. He was all about being competitive. He said you can beat people with better talent in business or sports if you are more competitive."

Herrin always told his players, "Remember, when you are in public, your actions, what you say and what you do, because there is a little kid who idolizes you who will do exactly what you do or say."

"He is a gem of a man," said former Thornridge coach and Bradley University athletic director Ron Ferguson, a close friend. "He is one of the most humble men I have ever known in coaching. Of the ones who are successful, there are not very many who are humble. He built a program that ranks right up there with Quincy and Collinsville. Not many coaches get the gym named after them."

Galesburg: The John Thiel Era

Galesburg is one of the oldest towns in Illinois, dating to 1837. It was established as a railroad hub, but the Santa Fe and Burlington pulled out years ago. Other industries left, too.

When the Outboard Marine factory closed in 1978, three thousand jobs were lost. In 2002, Maytag, the city's biggest employer, closed its big plant after fifty-two years, costing sixteen hundred more jobs.

But Galesburg is a survivor. It is Knox College, the Orpheum Theater, and Seminary Street. Most of all, it is Carl Sandburg. In the 1950s and 1960s, however, it belonged to John Thiel.

That's right, John Thiel, a basketball coach, not a poet. "Basketball was a way of life when Thiel was there," said Bob Morgan, a 1954 Galesburg graduate who coached in the grade schools for thirty-two years. "Women wore dresses and men wore suits to games on Friday and Saturday night. It was the big social event of the week. Basketball was the talk of the community in the off-season. How good will the team be next year? Can we go to state?"

In the 1960s, Churchill and Lombard junior high schools drew thirty-five hundred to eighth and ninth grade games at the high school gym. In one divorce settlement, a man said that his ex-wife could have the car and house but not his season tickets.

Galesburg won a state championship in 1913, and Gerald Phillips produced several good teams in the 1930s and 1940s, but the program had slipped badly. The team played in a small gym at the old high school on 7th and Tompkins. When Thiel was hired as an assistant coach in 1955, he figured it was a stepping stone to a more promising job in a basketball-minded town.

"In the 1950s, the town wasn't gung-ho about basketball," said Jimmy Carr, who started on Thiel's 1959 team that finished third in the state tournament, and later did color commentary on Galesburg radio broadcasts for twenty-four years. "Interest was lacking. Then Thiel became head coach in 1956, and his first team was 26–3. The town went basketball-crazy after that. Everybody wanted to play. Basketball players were treated like celebrities. It was the only game in town."

Born in Beloit, Wisconsin, Thiel was an outstanding athlete. He played baseball in the Chicago White Sox farm system, but basketball was his first love. He played professional basketball with the Milwaukee Hawks. He and Hall of Famer Bob Pettit were roommates before the NBA team moved to St. Louis.

At that point, Thiel had a career decision to make. He was married with two children. He needed to settle down. He wanted to coach. He read about an opening for an assistant at Galesburg. After one year, head coach Frank Adams unexpectedly moved to Knox College, and Thiel was promoted.

In eighteen years he won 82 percent (396–90) of his games, finished second in the state in 1966 and 1968, third in 1959, and took four other teams to the state quarterfinals.

"He was revolutionary," said Barry Swanson, who played on the 1966 state runner-up and later coached at Galesburg. "He gave blacks a chance to play. He was idolized by many people and resented by others, but his philosophy was to play the best, black or white. He met with some resistance early. But to him, winning was everything, no matter what it took."

Fred Mims, a black man who moved from Garland County, Alabama, to Galesburg when he was three, said that Thiel gave him opportunities and self-esteem. He started on Thiel's 1968 state runner-up and now is associate athletic director at the University of Iowa.

"Most people didn't know him," Mims said. "He wanted you to conduct yourself as though you represented the team and the school. After I left Galesburg, people who had heard about the town talked about the respect they had for the program."

"We played the most exciting basketball of any high school team around in the 1960s and 1970s," said Bob Morgan, who helped to develop many of Thiel's players. "He coached a pro-type offense, no set plays, a backyard style. The kids loved it."

What they didn't like was to go one-on-one with the coach. When he was young, until 1966, he went one-on-one with the guards for thirty to forty minutes. He once broke his son Zack's jaw in a Sunday night workout. He could shoot free throws blindfolded. He once made three hundred in a row.

"He believed in winning. Losing wasn't part of his life," said Dale Kelley, the star of the 1966 state runner-up. "And he was able to get his players to believe in that same mindset. He told me that someone was working to get better than me when I was sleeping. So I shot the ball against the ceiling. I believed what he said. He was a great teacher. He left no doubt what he wanted you to do."

Mike Owens, an All-Stater on Thiel's 1956 team who later assisted Thiel before becoming head coach at Galesburg, said that Thiel was "the fiercest competitor I ever saw." He was fun to play for, very positive, and his players worshipped him. "He did more in a practice situation to prepare for a game and scrimmaged more than anyone I ever came in contact with," Owens said. "He would set up a three-hour scrimmage on Saturday and go one-on-one with you, maybe for an hour without stopping."

Owens scored twenty-nine points, but Galesburg lost to the eventual state champion West Rockford 66–64 in double overtime in the 1956 supersectional at Moline's Wharton Fieldhouse. The Silver Streaks rushed to a fifteen-point lead, but West Rockford's 6' 7" John Wessels and 6' 7" Nolden Gentry gradually wore them down. Gentry tipped in a missed shot for the game winner.

"It was devastating. We didn't get over it for awhile," Owens said. "Everyone who watched the game said it was one of the best games they ever saw."

In 1957, with Doug Mills and Elbert and Albert Kimbrough, Thiel shelved his up-tempo style and slowed down to stun Rock Island and Don Nelson 21–19 in the sectional. The team finished 23–7, losing to Collinsville by two in the quarterfinals.

By most accounts, his best team was in 1958–59 with All-Stater Bumpy Nixon, who had transferred from Quincy, Dave Cox, Ralph Cannon, Jimmy Carr, and Otis Cowan. They were ranked number one in the state, beat second-rated Herrin 73–69 in the quarterfinals, then lost to West Aurora and Bill Small 74–61 in the semifinals.

Some argued that Thiel's 1963–64 team was his best creation. Rick Callahan and Mike Davis led the Streaks to a 24–4 record, but they lost to Cobden 60–57 in the state quarterfinals. "That was the best team I saw at Galesburg, better than 1966," said Dale Kelley.

In 1964–65, Galesburg was ranked seventh in the state, but Thiel was hung in effigy. His team lost to Pekin and Quincy in the regular season and to Quincy in the sectional. Some folks felt that the team should have gone farther. Quincy went on to finish second in the state.

The 1965–66 squad, led by Kelley, Barry Swanson, Terry Childers, Bob Jasperson, and Roland McDougald, won eighteen in a row, beat Springfield and Dave Robisch by four in the supersectional, and upset top-ranked, unbeaten Benton 73–71 in the quarterfinals and Belleville and Joe Wiley 65–64 in the semifinals. But they were buzzsawed by Thornton, LaMarr Thomas, Jim Ard, and Rich Rateree 74–60 in the final.

"I felt so bad for Thiel. He never won a state title," said Kelley, who hit a last-second, half-court shot to beat Benton. "I shot only three of thirteen for twelve points against Thornton. They were tall and quick. They played box-and-one, and I couldn't get the ball. Rateree had the game of his life [twenty-four points]. And we were exhausted."

Thiel also had to settle for second in 1967–68 when Mims, Leon Luckett, Ruben Triplett, Dave Wood, and Jim Reinebach lost to Evanston and Bob Lackey, Farrel Jones, and Ron Cooper 70–51 in the state final. The Streaks were 27–3, and Mims insisted that it was Thiel's best production.

"It was the all-time best combination of players that Galesburg ever had, better than 1966," Mims said. "There were a lot of hard workers, no egos. We were assured of our abilities."

After the 1972–73 season, Thiel retired. "He was tired," his wife said. He applied to coach at Southern Illinois University but didn't get the job. He was asked to be an assistant at Iowa, but the pay was inadequate. He died in 1988 at age sixty.

In 1976, Owens coached Galesburg to a 27–4 record. The team lost to the eventual state champion Morgan Park 53–48 in the quarterfinals. Earlier, the Streaks upset top-ranked and unbeaten Peoria Richwoods in overtime in the regional.

Galesburg didn't return to the state finals until 1998, when 6' 5" Joey Range and 6' 6" Rod Thompson led coach Mike Miller's Streaks to a 30–3 record. They lost to Chicago's Whitney Young 61–56 in the state final. Range finished as the school's all-time leading scorer with more than twenty-three hundred points.

By then, the Thiel days were almost forgotten. Almost.

"He had a temper, and he had a reputation for making life miserable for officials," said Marilyn Thiel, his widow. "He would get very upset if he thought it was a bad call. One time, he left the floor and sat in the bleachers because he was so upset with the officiating. He said he wanted to see if it looked as bad from up there as it did on the floor."

Thornton: Lipe, Lou, LaMarr, Lloyd

Thornton was so big in the 1930s and 1940s, with coach Jack Lipe and Lou Boudreau, as big as Centralia with Arthur Trout and Dike Eddleman, that the Harvey school could take on the IHSA and not back down.

Lipe's Flying Clouds, led by Boudreau, Dar Hutchins, and Tommy Nisbet, finished 1–2–2 in the state tournament in 1933–35. Afterward, Lipe had a falling out with the IHSA over its policy of not funding schools that qualified for the state tournament. The IHSA made money, the schools didn't.

Lipe led a revolt, urging other top schools such as Centralia, Paris, and Decatur to boycott the tournament. They chose not to rock the boat, but Lipe's courageous stand led to changes in IHSA policy. Still, from 1941 to 1947, Thornton opted not to participate in the state tournament.

Since 1948, Thornton has written a distinguished chapter in the state series, winning one title and claiming three seconds, two thirds, and a fourth. Coach Bob Anderson's 1966 state champion is recognized as one of the best teams in history. Coach Rocky Hill's 1995–97 teams won ninety-three of ninety-seven games.

All-Staters? The Boudreau Room in Thornton's gym, which houses decades of trophies and memorabilia, recalls the greats of the past: Boudreau, Hutchins, Bill Berberian, Roy Johnson, Russ McKibben, Bob Caress, Leon Clark, Harry Hall, LaMarr Thomas, Jim Ard, Herschel Lewis, Lloyd Batts, Curtis Watkins, Phil Gary, Darren Guest, Lamont Robinson, Tracy Webster, Michael Allen, Tai Streets, Melvin Ely, Erik Herring, and Antwaan Randle El.

"What amazed me was how Thornton kept its winning tradition going in football and basketball," said Sam Cameli, a 1952 Bloom graduate who was Thornton's basketball coach from 1983 to 1993. "Thornton has produced great athletes for so long despite the problems that have arisen in the community and the school. There is not another school in the state where you have an opportunity to coach such great athletes year after year."

Nobody understood the tradition better than Bob Caress. He grew up a few blocks from Thornton. Boudreau's mystique was ever present. His father played with Boudreau on the 1933 state championship team, but he was killed at the battle of Leyte Gulf in the Philippines in World War II. Bob never knew his father.

Growing up, Boudreau took an interest in Bob Caress. So did his cousin, Bob Anderson, who coached the 1966 state championship team. He listened to away games on the radio and showed up at six o'clock for home games to see the sophomores warm up.

"There was so much interest in Thornton's program, you wanted to be a part of it," Caress said. "You always felt that wherever you went, it was a big deal for other people, that they were in awe of Thornton. I remember other teams watching us during warm-ups. We were like the New York Yankees."

Bill Purden grew up in the tradition. A 1946 Thornton graduate, he played for Lipe. He watched Boudreau and the Flying Clouds and dreamed of having the same degree of success. After coaching for six years in Iowa, he became Thornton's head coach when Tommy Nisbet left for New Trier in 1957.

The first thing Purden did was call Iowa coach Bucky O'Connor. He spent a weekend with O'Connor and his assistant, Sharm Scheuerman, looking at films. At Thornton, he installed the same system that O'Connor had used to win the Big Ten title. He also inherited two outstanding assistants: Bob Anderson, who succeeded him in 1966, and Ron Ferguson, who later coached Thornridge to state championships in 1971 and 1972.

"Purden was a great coach," said Ferguson, who played for Lipe in 1945. "He was big on scouting the officials. He was very much ahead of a lot of coaches with new ideas in basketball. Had he not left for college coaching in 1965, he would be one of the legends in high school basketball."

In eight years, Purden won six conference championships and took four teams to the Sweet Sixteen. His 1959 team, led by Paul Jackson and Andy Wilson, was 27–3 but lost to West Aurora and Bill Small in the supersectional. His 1961 team was 27–3 and second in the state. His 1962 team, led by Clark, lost in the supersectional. His 1965 team, led by Harry Hall and Rich Hallbert, was 28–3 and finished fourth.

In 1961, Thornton was coming off of a 14–13 season. Caress had missed six weeks with two dislocated legs. Clark was a 6' 7" junior who hadn't played as a freshman after moving into the district. They lost twice to Bloom but trounced the Trojans 73–58 in the sectional final as Caress scored twenty-six points.

The Wildcats beat Morton by twelve in the supersectional, edged Springfield by two in the quarterfinals, and overcame a fourteen-point deficit to upset Marshall's defending state champions on Al Dehnert's game-winning shot in the semifinals. But they were crushed 84–50 in the final by Collinsville's unbeaten team led by Bogie Redmon and Fred Riddle.

In 1965, Thornton was ranked number one, but the Wildcats were upset by Quincy

64–59 in the semifinals, as Hall was limited to eleven points, and LaMarr Thomas and Jim Ard were hobbled by injuries.

Thomas and Ard returned in 1966. Anderson replaced Purden, who had left for Wyoming. While Purden reminded his players of Bob Knight, a stern taskmaster, Anderson reminded them of Ray Meyer, a player's coach who exuded the knowledge and discipline of a Purden without the temper or hard edge.

"Purden was a very good coach, great with strategies and tactics," Thomas said. "But there was a more relaxed style with Anderson, a freedom to develop a greater sense of team and confidence. He helped to make us all better."

Thornton didn't miss a beat when Hallbert broke an ankle early in the season. Bob Landowski stepped in. At 6' 7", Ard was a formidable inside presence. The Wildcats' 1-3-1 press wore out opponents, and Thomas was the best athlete in the state. "LaMarr was quiet, but he was the boss," Anderson said. "If he wanted the ball, the kids gave it to him."

Thornton was ranked third in the state behind unbeaten Benton and York at the end of the regular season. They had lost to Benton at the Centralia Tournament, but they beat Wheaton Central by four in the supersectional, then trounced New Trier by fifteen in the quarterfinals and Decatur by twenty-two in the semifinals.

In the final, they confronted the high-scoring Dale Kelley and a Galesburg team that had ousted Benton in the quarterfinals. They implemented a box-and-one to frustrate Kelley. Anderson assigned Rich Rateree to guard Kelley, who went to his right all the time. When Rateree was picked, Thomas got in Kelley's path. Rateree played the game of his life, scoring a career high twenty-four points. Kelley shot three of thirteen and was limited to twelve points. Thornton stormed to a twenty-two-point halftime lead and won 74–60.

"The most important lesson I learned at Thornton was a sense of equality," said Thomas, who chose to play football at Michigan State. "We had conflicts, but there was a sense that you were going to be treated fairly in class and on the sports field. We learned discipline, a sense of responsibility, and the importance of education. It was a great foundation."

In 1969, Lloyd Batts was a junior but already well on his way to becoming the leading scorer in school history. Thornton was 30–2 but lost to Waukegan 63–61 in the supersectional on Vernon Martin's tip at the buzzer. Earlier, Thornton had lost to the state champion Proviso East on Jim Brewer's buzzer-beater.

"It was a big disappointment that we didn't go farther with Lloyd," Anderson said. "I still dream about that loss to Waukegan, the mistakes I made, how we went scoreless for the last four minutes, if I had done this, if I had done that."

Thornton didn't return to the state finals until 1983, when Sam Cameli, who had been out of coaching for ten years, took Darren Guest, Lamont Robinson, and Tyrone Thigpen to third place. They lost to Springfield Lanphier 54–52 in the semifinals.

In 1984, Guest and Robinson returned, but Thornton lost to St. Joseph 52–50 in the quarterfinals, as Guest missed eleven of thirteen free throws. In 1993, Cameli's last team, led by Michael Allen, lost to Proviso East in the supersectional.

Rocky Hill rekindled the tradition. He had idolized LaMarr Thomas and the 1966 team. His father had season tickets. Because of a change in boundaries, he graduated from Thornridge in 1974. He was on the sophomore team when Thornridge won the 1972 state title. He guided Thornton's sophomore team to fifty-nine victories in a row before becoming head coach in 1994.

His 1995 team went 30–2, upset Kevin Garnett, Ronnie Fields, and top-ranked Farragut in the quarterfinals, but lost to Peoria Manual for the championship.

In 1996, Thornton was unbeaten and ranked number one at the end of the regular season, but the Wildcats lost to Sergio McClain, Marcus Griffin, and Peoria Manual in the final.

Peoria Manual won its fourth state title in a row in 1997, beating Thornton in the semifinals. It was a matchup of the two top-rated teams in the nation according to *USA Today*. The Wildcats led early 18–4, but Peoria Manual rallied to win 65–62.

"I still hurt because we could have won three state titles in a row," Hill said. "Instead, we are the best team that never won it. Any other year we would have won, but we had the misfortune to play Peoria Manual, another great team, in the same years. Not a day goes by that I don't think about it."

Billy Harris: The Fastest Gunslinger of All

Billy Harris was born too soon. On city playgrounds, he was tagged "The Kid" because he was a shooter nonpareil. If the three-point line had been in effect at the time, his coach claimed that he would have averaged fifty to sixty points per game. It wasn't an exaggeration.

"His jump shot was classic, flawless. His rise and release were so quick that you couldn't stop him even if you were on top of him," former Dunbar coach Jim Foreman said. "I keep remembering the game where he made twenty-one of twenty-two shots, and nobody believed it. He was as good or better than players who went to the NBA, but he was a victim of circumstances."

Circumstances weren't kind to Harris. He never fully grasped the concept that basketball is a team game, that defense wins championships. He shot twenty-five footers like others shot layups.

"I never saw a shooter like him, before or since," said Chicago attorney Herb Rudoy, who once represented Harris. "The only shooter I can compare him to is Chuck Person of Auburn, who played in the NBA for twelve years. Billy never saw a shot he didn't think he could make. He had no conscience. He could miss ten shots in a row and never think twice about taking an eleventh shot."

No one argues that Harris wasn't a great offense-minded player, a pure shooter, but that was his only interest. To be a professional, Rudoy said, a player must have other skills. Harris could shoot, but he didn't have a total game. In the end, that made him a car salesman.

"City basketball has always been the real game, which is putting the ball through the hole. The guy who shoots the best wins," Harris said.

Harris couldn't adjust. After helping to put Northern Illinois' program in *Sports Illustrated*, he bounced around the NBA and the ABA. He even played in the Philippines, and then he quit.

He hit rock bottom. He made a living as a pimp for a while, before his mother put a stop to it. Later, he was a drug dealer. He admits that he made some bad decisions in his life, but he never spent a night in jail.

After thirty years, he is still bitter. "I never did anything to hurt anyone but myself," he said. "I gave away more dope than I ever sold on the street. I always had a conscience. But talent can be a curse. I was born to play basketball, to do it well, but I had those dreams shattered."

Harris was born on Chicago's South Side, in an area known as "the Gap." Later, his family moved to the Robert Taylor Homes, a notorious housing project in the shadow of Comiskey Park.

He got serious about basketball when he was nine years old. It was cheaper to play than other sports. All you needed was a pocketful of S&H green stamps to purchase a Voit basketball. His older brother Willie, who was an all-city player at Dunbar and an All-American at Wilson Junior College, was a great influence.

"Willie said I had to see his brother, who he said was very good and wanted to come to Dunbar," Foreman said. "He brought Billy by the school before the season, and they played the damndest one-on-one in the full court that I ever saw."

"What made me different from others is I had a desire to be the best," Harris said. "I didn't want to be some other guy. Every time I went out, I went out with the intention of being the best. There is a time when that isn't true, but you have to have that mentality."

Even today, more than thirty years after he established himself as a playground legend and perhaps the most prolific shooter ever developed in the Chicago Public League, people still marvel at his skills and recount their favorite Billy Harris stories.

"Billy had an aura, a personality," said Lloyd Walton, who played at Mount Carmel, Marquette, and in the NBA. "When he walked in a gym, he grabbed all the attention. And he would back it up. He invented trash talking, but in a fun kind of way."

Walton recalls a hot summer day in 1975 when Harris's team met Walton, Bo Ellis, LeeArthur Scott, Louis Gray, and Bill Robinzine in a game at the Martin Luther King Boys' Club.

"Everyone was waiting for Harris to do something spectacular," Walton said. "Robinzine was playing defense at the top of the key. Harris dribbled right at him, then stopped at the free throw line. He jumped in the air, put the ball behind his back twice, then finished with a jump shot.

"Everything Billy did was spectacular, from his conversation to the way he played the game. If he was playing today, he'd be a first-round draft pick. But it wasn't his time. What happened to him is the way it was in those days, for all of us. You have to move past it."

Harris didn't enroll at Dunbar as a freshman. He had good test scores, so his mother wanted him to attend Lindblom, a superior academic school. Billy passed the entrance exam, but he wasn't permitted to play on the varsity basketball team as a freshman. So he transferred to Dunbar.

A 6' 3" guard, he averaged twenty-six points per game as a junior and thirty-three as a senior. He scored fifty-seven against Du Sable in 1969, including forty-one in the second half, and made twenty-seven of thirty-nine shots. Old-timers compared him to the former Carver star Pete Cunningham, who once scored ninety points in a game in 1959. He was named to the All-State team with Thornton's Lloyd Batts, Proviso East's Jim Brewer, and Champaign's Clyde Turner.

Harris was recruited by dozens of major colleges, but Foreman had a social conscience. He persuaded Harris to attend Northern Illinois. Why? Because NIU had a program for minorities. By choosing NIU, Harris opened the door for ten other black students to go to college.

"There were no guarantees associated with it," Harris said. "If you were a blue-chip athlete, you would open the doors for others. The bottom line is my generation was the first to get a sniff of formal education. My parents were from Mississippi and worked on farms. They didn't know anything about recruiting. Luckily, I ended up at a place where they took care of me."

Today, however, he has regrets. If he had to do it all over again, he says he would have enrolled at Kansas. He was recruited by Kansas assistant Sam Miranda, who was a familiar face in the inner city in those days. Kansas coach Ted Owens showed up at his home after he had announced for NIU and told him that he had made the worst decision of his life.

Harris went to NIU with James Bradley of Gary (Indiana) Roosevelt, another celebrated player, and Cleveland Ivy of Carver. They beat Indiana when the Hoosiers were ranked fifth in the nation. They were 21–4 and earned the first national ranking in school history, but it wasn't good enough to earn a bid to the NCAA tournament or NIT.

As a college senior, he averaged twenty-four points per game, but there were flaws in his game. "He couldn't guard his hat," NIU assistant coach Emory Luck said. "He was the wildest kind of alley player you'd ever want to see," NIU coach Tom Jorgensen said. But NBA scouts loved his offensive skills.

Harris still recalls how he scored thirty-eight points against Ed Ratleff and Long Beach State in New York's Madison Square Garden, then was devastated when Ratleff was selected in the first round of the NBA draft while he was invited to a tryout.

He was drafted in the sixth round of the 1973 NBA draft by the Chicago Bulls, but general manager Pat Williams and coach Dick Motta got tangled up in a power struggle. When Williams resigned and fled to Philadelphia, Motta dumped all of Williams's draft choices. Harris was one of his last cuts at training camp.

"One reason he never got into his own with the Bulls was their style of play," Foreman said. "We tried to be as wide open as we could, but the Bulls were more structured."

"I have a renegade nature," Harris said. "When I went through that experience with the Bulls, I was ready to stop playing. When you set a goal, then find out that all that glitters isn't gold . . . well, I got angry. I couldn't accept it."

Harris believed that the system was racist. In his view, many white players whom he judged weren't good enough to play in the NBA were taking up spots on rosters that they didn't earn.

"I never got a chance," he said. "There was no support mechanism for black athletes in Chicago. If I was in New York, I could have made it. People knew I was something special. The only one who stood up for me [*Chicago Sun-Times* sportswriter Lacy J. Banks] lost his job and had to go to court to get it back. No one else went to bat for me."

"He wasn't receptive to team play or playing defense," Foreman said. "His idea of the game was to get to the other end of the court first and put the ball in the hole. He had no peer as a shooter, but there were questions about his defense."

Harris didn't think he had to sell himself. Hadn't he proven himself? In the summers, he beat up the pros. He led his team to a pro-am championship. He led the league in scoring. He made NBA players admit that he was the best. Wasn't that enough?

"I was born too soon," he said. "Guys are signing million-dollar contracts today with a game I had thirty years ago.

"There is a lot of racism out there, people putting their agendas ahead of what is right. That isn't real. What is real is when you pick up a ball and go against someone one-on-one on the bricks, and they say I am the best to ever play the game. That's what is important, the only thing that isn't jaded."

4

The 1970s

Two-Class System: David vs. Goliath

Chuck Rolinski had a vision. Ron Felling admitted that he couldn't see beyond the city limits of Lawrenceville.

In the 1940s, 1950s, and 1960s, basketball was king in small towns from Pinck-neyville to Pittsfield to Paris. People filled high school gyms on Friday night to cheer their local teams. For many, it was the social event of the week. But something was missing.

It was becoming clear that large schools were beginning to dominate the state tournament series and that small schools couldn't advance beyond the regional or sectional levels.

Hebron gave purists something to cheer about in 1952 when it became the small-est school (enrollment ninety-eight students) to win the state championship. It was Illinois's version of the motion picture *Hoosiers* that will be replayed as long as the game is played.

But it only happened once again. In 1964, Cobden (enrollment 160) emerged as the darling of the state tournament. The team with the endearing nickname, the Appleknockers, lost to Pekin in the state final.

More and more, the Elite Eight was filled with teams from Chicago and its suburbs, Peoria, Galesburg, Quincy, Rockford, Collinsville, and the Quad Cities. Small-town folks, the tournament's chief supporters for years, weren't buying tickets.

No one recognized the problem more clearly than Chuck Rolinski, who joined with Quincy coach Sherrill Hanks to form the Illinois Basketball Coaches Association in 1971. The son of a coal miner, Rolinski graduated from Illinois State University in two years because he wanted to coach at Toluca High School.

From 1956 to 1990, Rolinski's teams won 649 games. He took three teams to the supersectional. His 1966–67 team was 17–10 but lost to Pekin's state championship team 77–64. His 1972–73 team was 22–6 but lost to St. Anne and Jack Sikma. His 1983–84 team was 29–1, losing to Hoopeston 51–48 in overtime.

"For a small school, it was the ultimate to win a regional," Rolinski said. "But things tighten up in the sectional. I wanted to fight for a chance to win a regional, not the state title. My argument was the system discriminated against small schools. In many areas, it was impossible for small schools to win a regional against bigger schools."

His plan called for two classes. Class A would include all schools with enrollments under five hundred students. Class AA would include all larger schools.

"I wanted to give small schools a chance, some equality, an identity of their own," he said. "The power was shifting from small schools to larger schools in industrial areas of the state. You could see the talent gap widening."

Rolinski's proposal was met with much negative criticism. Some purists still insist it was the worst idea since long pants. Although he initially panned the idea, Lawrenceville coach Ron Felling concedes that the two-class system did more for him and his community than Mickey Mouse did for Walt Disney. "I wasn't for the two-class system at first," Felling said. "When Rolinski had his vision, I would have voted against it. I didn't want watered-down basketball. But I didn't have any vision. It came out well. Who has benefited more than me and Lawrenceville and other small towns? The state might never have heard about Jay Shidler without the two-class system."

Felling won state titles in 1972, the first year of the two-class format, 1974, 1982, and 1983. He finished third with Shidler in 1976. His 1982 and 1983 powerhouses, led by Marty Simmons, won a state-record sixty-eight games in a row. Simmons earned the Mr. Basketball Award as the state's top player.

"Lawrenceville had a rich basketball tradition before I got there," Felling said. "But it had never won a state title. In 1972, we broke through. It put our town on the map. But it never would have happened without the two-class system. We couldn't have competed with Thornridge [the Class AA champion] in the state finals. We needed to find our own niche."

Rolinski launched his campaign in the spring of 1968 when the Illinois Athletic Directors Association, an organization that Rolinski helped to form, met to discuss class basketball.

Harry Fitzhugh, executive director of the IHSA, attended the convention. He favored the one-class, one-champion format, and he didn't appreciate Rolinski's attempts to change the system. He took it as a personal attack against his administration.

"I didn't think [Rolinski's plan] would work," Fitzhugh said. "With two classes, you would never have a true state champion. Every once in a great while a Hebron or a Cobden will come along. But very rarely, not often enough to make a difference. I didn't see a need for change. But I was wrong."

Members of the IHSA's board of directors were impressed by Rolinski's proposal, however. They suggested that Rolinski select nine coaches and administrators to polish his plan, then meet with the IHSA's Legislative Commission.

When Rolinski returned, he was asked to debate the issue with Duster Thomas, Pinckneyville's legendary coach, who favored the one-class system. Afterward, the commission voted 17–2 to toss Rolinski's plan off the ballot.

Enter Louis Schreiter, who served as superintendent at Carrollton from 1960 to 1972. He got involved in the dispute at the urging of Carrollton basketball coach Dick Hamann. "They needed an administrator to push things," Schreiter said. "Each year we would see Quincy, Jerseyville, and larger schools get a free pass to the Sweet Sixteen. I thought, 'If it is good for kids at big schools to play in postseason basketball, it must be good for small schools.' I was happy to play a part in it."

Schreiter attended an IHSA meeting in Jacksonville, which drew seventeen school administrators from the Carrollton area. "The report came back that it was decided

17–0 that we weren't interested in class basketball," Schreiter recalled. "I said it can't be right. I didn't remember a vote."

Schreiter was furious. He called the IHSA and suggested that a survey be taken of all high school administrators in the state to determine if there was any interest in a two-class format. The IHSA argued that a survey wasn't in order.

So Schreiter mailed a survey to nine hundred high schools. He received more than seven hundred replies. Of those, the vote was three-to-one in favor of class basketball.

Schreiter and other supporters met with the IHSA. "Any way you cut it, I have twenty-four ounces of yes votes and only eight ounces of no. It is three-to-one for class basketball. We think you ought to take a vote of the schools," Schreiter told Fitzhugh.

Schreiter threatened to go directly to the state legislature if Fitzhugh didn't agree to a vote. Fitzhugh continued to bide for time, postponing the vote. In desperation, he arranged for a meeting between Rolinski and Du Quoin principal Howard Tweedy. He hoped that Tweedy could change Rolinski's mind and kill the plan, but Rolinski refused to cave in.

The IHSA's board of directors ordered Fitzhugh to appoint a blue-ribbon committee to come up with a plan that would be voted upon by the full membership. The nine-man committee included Rolinski, Schreiter, Tweedy, principal Paul Blakeman of Pontiac, and basketball coaches Ron Ferguson of Thornridge, Will Slager of Chicago Christian, and Jim Brown of Du Sable.

Rolinski argued for two classes, Blakeman wanted three. Slager didn't approve of either proposal. When it was revealed that there were seventy-two schools with enrollments between five hundred and 750, Rolinski raised the dividing point to 750 for his two-class proposal. Two plans were submitted, Rolinski's and Blakeman's. But Tweedy, president of the IHSA board, said that only one plan would be recommended.

The vote was 4–4. Brown hadn't voted. He wasn't sure which plan was best for Chicago, and he was holding out for the Public League champion's direct entry to the state finals.

As a member of the IHSA's basketball advisory committee, Brown was well known throughout the state. In 1966, Public League champion Marshall had lost to New Trier in the supersectional at Northwestern's McGaw Hall in Evanston. Afterward, Marshall's angry students tore up the neighborhood and Evanston, and Northwestern officials voided the agreement to bring the city champion to McGaw. In 1969, after Hirsch lost to Proviso East in a controversial finish in the supersectional at Hinsdale Central, Public League officials called for a change. "Everybody agreed it was the right thing to do," Brown said.

Rolinski reminded Brown that his plan called for the Chicago champion to go directly to the state finals, not a suburban supersectional. Brown voted for the two-class plan, breaking the tie. Later, it was accepted by a 321–290 margin.

When Fitzhugh saw small schools outdrawing large schools at the state tournament, he declared that the IHSA's decision to adopt the two-class plan was "one of the crowning achievements" of his ten-year administration. "The basketball group did a great job of making the transition and did a good job of selling the idea to the schools," he said. "I wasn't in favor at first. They changed my mind completely."

Thornridge: The Best There Ever Was

Before the 1971–72 season, Thornridge coach Ron Ferguson gathered his players together to outline their goals for the coming campaign, but team leader Quinn Buckner interrupted: "If we win all of our games, we'll accomplish all of our goals."

Perhaps no team was ever saddled with higher expectations than Thornridge in 1971–72. That the Falcons from south suburban Dolton emerged as the best team in state history was a tribute to the leadership of Ferguson and Buckner, extraordinary quickness and ballhandling skills, and a pressing defense that intimidated all opponents.

"I never saw a better team," said Peoria Manual coach Dick Van Scyoc, who coached for forty-four years and won more games (826) than any coach in state history. "I was proud that we lost to them three times [and finished fourth in the 1972 state tournament]. We didn't lose to an ordinary team."

Statistics set Thornridge apart from all other great teams—from Taylorville 1944 to Marshall 1958 to Collinsville 1961 to Quincy 1981 to Peoria Manual 1997. The Falcons went on to win fifty-eight games in a row, a state record that stood for ten years. In a 33–0 season, Thornridge never allowed an opponent to come within fourteen points. The Falcons averaged 87.5 points while permitting fifty-three. In the state finals, they won by margins of twenty-eight, twenty-nine, nineteen, and thirty-five points. Their coup de grace, a 104–69 thrashing of Quincy, is the standard by which all other championship games are measured. It was a Rembrandt compared to so many Warhols.

"I don't know of any team better," said St. Patrick coach Max Kurland, who won 658 games in thirty-five years. "What impressed me most was Buckner, his competitive spirit, the way he hustled up and down the court no matter what the score was. That attitude spread to other members of the team. I've never seen a better leader in high school basketball than Buckner."

Ferguson knew he had the makings of another championship contender. His 1970–71 team had survived in the state final, beating Oak Lawn by one point when Jim Bocinsky's last-second shot from the baseline bounced off the rim. But his 1971–72 squad was better, quicker, more talented, and more experienced. From the outset, Ferguson recognized that it could be something special.

A quiet, personable man, Ferguson had coached in the shadow of district rival Thornton of Harvey, a perennial power that had finished second in the state in 1961, fourth in 1965, and won the state title in 1966. As sophomores, Buckner and Boyd Batts were awed by Thornton's Lloyd Batts, a two-time All-Stater who was Boyd's older brother and Quinn's boyhood idol. Lloyd had graduated in 1970. This, they felt, was their time.

Buckner came from good roots. His parents were educators. His sister is superintendent of District 214, which includes Thornton, Thornridge, and Thornwood. His full name is William Quinn Buckner. He was called Bill, his father's name, for his first two years in high school. As a junior, however, he told Ferguson to inform the media that he wanted to be called Quinn. He wanted to establish his own identity.

Buckner considered UCLA but chose Indiana because he wanted to stay closer to home and play for coach Bob Knight. And he was influenced by his father, who was a lineman on Indiana's 1945 Big Ten championship football team that included George Taliaferro, Pete Pihos, and Ted Kluszewski.

"My father [who died in 1986] understood I had an ability to lead guys before I did," Quinn said. "He talked to me about being prepared and helping my teammates to understand what they needed to do. He drove me to what I have become. He taught me how I had to grow up as a young African American in society."

Ferguson's job was to make sure everybody was on the bus, no easy task. Batts and Greg Rose were gifted players, but they sometimes listened to a different drummer. In the state final, Batts set records with thirty-seven points and fifteen rebounds, while Rose scored twenty-six points, and Buckner contributed twenty-eight points, eleven rebounds, and seven assists.

Batts was a free spirit. He couldn't understand why he had to go to school to play basketball. He had the attention span of a toddler in a sandbox. On one occasion, during a time-out, Buckner noticed Batts admiring some girls in the bleachers rather than listening to Ferguson's instructions. With his huge hands, he grabbed Batts by his neck, shook him several times, and warned him never to do it again. Batts got the message.

"People still talk about what we did," said Batts, who played professionally in Belgium, France, and South America for fifteen years. "It gives me a special feeling inside, to know that thirty years ago we accomplished something that people still remember."

Rose loved music more than basketball. He had to work to support his family. He taught himself to sing and play drums when he was ten. His father died when he was eleven, and his mother was ill. He had two children, born when he was a sophomore and junior in high school. He got home from gigs at local nightclubs at 4:30 A.M., slept until seven, then went to school.

He knew Thornridge would have a good basketball team because Ernie Dunn and sixth-man Nee Gatlin were junior high school teammates. Later, he met Buckner, Batts, and Mike Bonczyk.

But Rose couldn't enjoy basketball. As a senior in 1972–73, he was an All-Stater. He attended Thornton Community College but didn't get along with the coach and dropped out. He continued to play his music. In 1981, he went to California to pursue his dream of becoming a professional musician.

Buckner said that the trick to keeping Batts's and Rose's minds on the game was to pass them the ball and let them shoot. "Then they'd be happy. All I ever cared about was winning," he said.

Bonczyk, who was named to one All-State team with Buckner and Batts, later played at Illinois State and coached at high schools in Kansas and Illinois. Like Buckner, he was a team player who never meddled in the lives of his teammates unless it affected the outcome of a game. "For us, it was all about winning, not individual goals," he said. "That separates the great teams from the good ones. We played roles. We were so unselfish. It wasn't about me, it was about all of us."

Today, as an executive for one of the world's largest telecommunications companies, Ernie Dunn has more of an appreciation for what he experienced in 1971–72 than ever before. He had grown up in the shadow of his more publicized brother, Otis, who was a star player at Thornton. At Thornridge, however, he had an opportunity to do his own thing.

"When you are in the midst of it, you don't realize how good it is," Dunn said. "It was a great team, five guys who could play five positions. It taught me that, if you work hard, you reap a lot of benefits. We learned how to deal with people and different situations, just like in the business world."

It wasn't a big team, even by standards of the day. Batts was the tallest at 6' 7", Buckner and Rose were 6' 3", Gatlin was 6' 2", Dunn was 6' 1", and Bonczyk was listed at 5' 9" but looked closer to 5' 7". Buckner was the most physical athlete on the floor, but Batts was more athletic and agile than anyone his height or taller.

"They were unique," said Ferguson, who resigned after the season to become an assistant coach at Illinois State and later served as athletic director at Bradley University. "Everyone recalls Buckner's leadership, our quickness, our press, our athleticism, our discipline. What I remember most of all was all five starters could handle the ball. No one had to be hidden. Every starter could take the ball down the floor. I've never seen a team that could handle and pass the ball so well."

To take advantage of their speed and teamwork, Ferguson devised a 1-2-1-1 zone press to disrupt opponents—Rose flapping his long arms in front of the inbounds passer, Bonczyk and Dunn pressuring on the wings, Buckner roaming in midcourt, looking to intercept a pass, and Batts lurking under the basket, braced to scare the daylights out of anyone who dared to break the press.

In its defining moment, the press drove Thornridge to a 32–11 margin in the second quarter en route to the Falcons' record thirty-five-point victory over Quincy in the state championship.

"At halftime, I asked somebody if there was a back exit we could take to get to our bus," said Quincy coach Sherrill Hanks, whose team had fallen behind 57–26. "We had scouted them, and we knew what to expect. But you couldn't defend against it. They were so quick and so smart. They anticipated everything we tried to do. They were the best team I ever saw."

Buckner, now a basketball analyst for ESPN, said that he had more fun playing basketball in 1972 than he ever experienced in college or the NBA. A consummate leader, he was selected as the seventh player in the 1976 NBA draft even though he averaged fewer than ten points per game as a senior at Indiana.

"We were ahead of our time," he said. "Basketball hasn't changed in the last thirty years. You still put as much pressure on people as you can. We were unique, great athletes who understood how to play the game.

"It was the best time of my life. It framed my life. I was doing something I loved to do with friends I knew all my life. When it was over, we had a better perspective. It was the end of a great era. We were ready to take the next step in our lives."

Bob Dallas: Down on the Farm

When Bob Dallas drove into Ridgway for the first time, he pulled into a gas station. The owner was a member of the school board. He told Dallas that he wouldn't be in town for very long, that the Catholics would drive him out. Dallas said that religion and politics had nothing to do with his game. He became head coach and stayed for forty-five years.

"I didn't want to coach, but I wanted to be close to home," Dallas said. "I figured I would have the job for a year or two, then go back to farming or manage a paint store."

After his first team finished 3–21, Dallas figured it wouldn't be long before he returned to his father's 550–acre farm located midway between Marion and Harrisburg. But he won nineteen games in his second season and twenty-four in his third.

"I knew I was a bad coach after my first year," he said. "But I hated to go out with a bad record. So I read books and watched games. I learned basketball is a game where you learn every day. The more you coach, the better you get."

Dallas got better. He won 781 games before retiring in 2001. Only three coaches in state history won more—Dick Van Scyoc, Arthur Trout, and Vergil Fletcher. His 1973 team won the Class A title, and his 1974 team reached the quarterfinals.

He developed some outstanding players. Roger Suttner, a seven footer, played at Kansas State. Ron "Moose" Stallings, the school's scoring leader with 2,643 points, played on Louisville's Final Four team in 1972. Brent Browning led Ridgway to the 1973 state title, scoring 105 points in four games.

Dallas has only one regret: he wasn't given an opportunity to win eight hundred games. Instead, he was forced to retire. The school board wanted a new regime. When he resigned as a teacher, school officials assumed that he had resigned as coach, too. They hired Robert Patton, Dallas's assistant for ten years, as the new coach.

"I just wanted a chance to win eight hundred games, more than Trout [809], more than any coach ever won at one school," he said.

Dallas's career filled several scrapbooks. He put Ridgway on the map. Located off Route 1, up the road from Cave-In Rock, Horseshoe, and Equality and about nine miles west of the Ohio River, it was the only school in Gallatin County. The town had a population of a thousand, and the high school had an enrollment of 250. It drew students from Ridgway, New Haven, and Cottonwood.

Now all that is left of the "Popcorn Capital of the World" is one gas station, two grain elevators, and Cox and Son Funeral Home. The old school on Karber Street, where the 1973 state champions played, where Suttner, Stallings, and Browning played, closed in 1994. Students now attend Junction High School on Route 13.

In the 1950s, Shawneetown was the power in the region. Led by Garrison New-som, Shawneetown was 32–1 and reached the state quarterfinals in 1955. Ridgway had never won a regional. When Dallas wasn't hired at Shawneetown, he opted for Ridgway.

When he arrived, Roger Suttner was a freshman. So were Don Sanders and John Schmitt, who later assisted Dallas for twenty-nine years and earned a reputation as the winningest junior varsity coach in the state. Sanders, who earned a scholarship to Kansas State with Suttner, later covered Ridgway basketball for the *Ridgway Weekly* and the *Vienna Times*.

Suttner was a skinny 6' 4", 150-pounder who never touched a basketball until eighth grade. As a junior, he was a seven-footer. In 1959, he was named to the All-State team, but he wanted to be a farmer, not a college basketball player.

"In physical education class, I learned to lay the ball up from the right and left sides," Suttner said. "Dallas touted me to the colleges and called the newspapers."

The University of Illinois coach Harry Combes showed up. So did Kentucky's Joe B. Hall and Kansas State's Tex Winter. Suttner impressed them with his left-handed hook shot. He chose Kansas State over Purdue. As a senior, he was the top center in the Big Eight.

He was drafted by the Philadelphia Warriors in the seventh round, but he was tired of basketball. Besides, Wilt Chamberlain was playing with the Warriors at the time, so Sutter knew he wouldn't play much, if at all. So he taught school in Kansas for six years, worked in the coal mines for ten years, and now drives a truck for a company in Harrisburg.

There wasn't anything that Moose Stallings didn't think he could do. He played on teams that won 104 games in four years. As a senior in 1967–68, he averaged 37.7 points per game. In back-to-back games, he scored career highs of fifty-eight points against Galatia and fifty-nine against Grayville.

Dallas saw Stallings for the first time in a grade school tournament game. Dallas was one of the referees. Stallings scored fifty points, but his team lost 53–52. Dallas knew that he was something special. When he graduated, he chose Louisville over Illinois, Florida, Kansas, Georgia, and Michigan.

Everything Stallings did bordered on the spectacular. His forte was a reverse layup with a finger roll. Two or three opponents were assigned to defend against him in every game, but his team still averaged a hundred points. However, losses to Benton and Rich Yunkus in 1967 and to Carrier Mills in 1968 ended Stallings's dream of play-ing in the state finals.

Stallings bragged that he invented the art of partying, and no one who knew him offered a dissenting view. Dallas told college recruiters that if they opened up Stallings's head, all they'd find would be girls and beer.

"I was a wild boy," Stallings said. "If it wasn't for the coach, I'd be in a prison in-stead of working at one [now retired, he formerly worked for the Illinois Department of Corrections]. He gave me a guiding light."

Browning came under Dallas's spell when his father took him to high school games as a fourth and fifth grader. Brent had heard about Suttner and Stallings. He knew Ridgway had a winning tradition in basketball, but Dallas scared him to death.

Later, Browning learned that appearances aren't always what they seem to be, at least in Bob Dallas's case. Dallas was refereeing one of Browning's eighth-grade games. Afterward, he told Browning's coach that he was impressed with the youngster's head fakes and thought that Brent had a future in high school.

"That was enough for me," Browning said. "I started to work harder. I wanted to play in high school. Sure, coach was very demanding. We practiced very hard. He believed his team might lose because the other team was better. He would never have a team lose because the other team was in better shape."

After finishing 16–9 in 1971–72, with Browning and three other starters returning, Dallas felt that he had the makings of an outstanding team for 1972–73. Up to then, Ridgway had never won a regional.

Ridgway lost its opener to Enfield and was unranked in the Associated Press's final regular-season poll. But they went on to win thirty-two games in row, capping the greatest season in school history by beating Kaneland of Maple Park 54–51 for the Class A championship. Mike Dixon scored twenty points, Browning eighteen.

Browning, a 6' 2" senior, was an All-Stater. Danny Stevens was the best point guard that Dallas ever coached. Dixon was the team's best all-around performer. Dennis Pearce, a 6' 3" center, was an outstanding defender. Mike Fromm was a good defender and rebounder. Jeff Drone, a junior, was a good shooter.

In the regional, Ridgway beat Eldorado by three points. In the sectional, they rallied from an eleven-point halftime deficit to beat Carrier Mills. In the final, they trailed by ten points but rallied to beat Waltonville. In the supersectional, Ridgway edged Pinckneyville 57–56 on Stevens's free throw with eight seconds to play.

Browning scored forty-five points as Ridgway ousted Petersburg Porta 85–79 in the quarterfinals. Earlier, Browning and Stevens watched St. Anne and 6' 8" Jack Sikma, a future NBA star, dismantle Cerro Gordo 88–70. "We can beat them," Browning said. "We belong here."

Ridgway won 73–51. Dallas's game plan was to take advantage of his team's quickness and keep Sikma and his taller but slower teammates running between the free-throw lines. The strategy paid off. By the third period, St. Anne was exhausted.

In the final, Ridgway led Kaneland by ten at halftime. Kaneland, with Steve Lynch scoring twenty-seven points, closed to one and shot for the lead. But Stevens was fouled and converted two free throws. He scored his team's last six points, and Ridgway won by three.

"They played together," Suttner said about the 1973 team. "They were better as a unit than any team I ever saw."

Today, there is nothing at Junction High School to remind visitors that Bob Dallas once coached in the county and built one of the most successful programs in the state. The gym wasn't named after him. After the consolidation, Ridgway's trophies were stored away, never to be displayed again. The picture of the 1973 state championship team has disappeared.

"It is sad that he didn't have a chance to have a day in the sun on his way out the door," said Browning, now an investment banker in Batavia. "He began coaching in 1955 and should have had an opportunity to bow out gracefully, with his head up."

Jay Shidler: Ride with Shide

On the first day of practice before the 1975–76 season, Lawrenceville coach Ron Felling asked all of his players to introduce themselves to senior Jay Shidler, shake his hand, and throw him the ball.

"If you will play with him, get him the ball, look for him, he will get you shots and take you to Champaign, to the Big House," Felling told them. "We're going to ride with Shide."

And so they did. Shidler emerged as one of the most exciting players in state history. He personally put the fledgling Class A tournament in prime time. It was desperately searching for an identity, and Shidler, Felling, and Lawrenceville established one.

"I wasn't for the two-class system at first. But I didn't have any vision," Felling said. "Who has benefited more than me and Lawrenceville and other small towns? The state might never have heard about Jay Shidler without the two-class system."

What they saw was unforgettable. In 1975–76, Shidler scored 1,013 points, averaging 32.7 points per game, as Lawrenceville won twenty-nine of thirty-one games and finished third in the Class A tournament. He set a state finals record with 157 points in four games, including forty-eight in a semifinal loss to Oneida ROVA and forty-five in a consolation victory over Buda Western. Nobody else on his team scored more than twenty-eight.

"He was the best athlete I coached," said Felling, who produced four state championship teams, including two 34–0 powerhouses in 1982 and 1983. "He was my kind of guy, a picture shooter. He had everything going for him when he was going up for a shot. His mechanics were so good. He could jump so well. He had great explosiveness with his legs. He always had control of himself when he was shooting. He was born to shoot."

Shidler wanted to be a baseball player. When he was young, he played with his older brother Dennis. His father threw batting practice, and his mother shagged flies. A catcher, he thought he was more skilled in baseball than basketball. "My brother played basketball against bigger and stronger kids," Jay said. "I recall being better than the others and getting more attention from coaches. But I didn't focus on basketball. I always liked baseball more."

As he got older, however, he got bit by the basketball bug. Dennis became a star on Lawrenceville's varsity, scoring more than two thousand points from 1967 to 1970. He recognized his younger brother's talent. In seventh grade, Jay was jump shooting while others were trying to perfect a set shot. His star was rising.

In 1972, when Shidler was in eighth grade, Lawrenceville won the first Class A championship behind Mike Lockhard and Joe and Rick Leighty.

In 1974, he was a sophomore starter on Felling's second state championship team. He made two key baskets in the second overtime as Lawrenceville upset second-ranked Cerro Gordo 77–72 in the quarterfinals. In the final, he scored fourteen, while Rick Leighty had twenty-four points in a 54–53 victory over Ottawa Marquette.

In 1975, Lawrenceville was elevated to Class AA because its enrollment was thirteen above the limit. The team was 21–5, losing to Olney in the first round of the regional.

Lawrenceville returned to Class A in 1975–76, and Felling suspected that he had a player who could take him to Champaign for the third time in five years. His suspicion was confirmed when Shidler scored forty-seven points to beat Thornridge in the championship game of the Carbondale Holiday Tournament.

"We were a bunch of small country kids [no one taller than 6' 2"] who played their butts off and played great defense," Shidler said. "The other players made so many sacrifices to get the ball to me. That was the game plan. They knew if we were going to win, they had to get the ball to me."

Shidler became a celebrity. To remove oil from his hair, his mother began bleaching his hair blond beginning in 1972. Nicknames followed: Bionic Boy, Blond Bomber, White Lightning. He was embarrassed by the publicity, but a legend was born.

More than 14,300 showed up for the third-place game in 1976 to see Shidler challenge the tournament scoring record of 152 set by Springfield's Dave Robisch in 1967. He needed forty-one to eclipse Robisch's standard, and Felling predicted he would do it.

Shidler scored thirty-one in the first half against a Buda Western team that had lost only once in thirty-two games. He finished with forty-five for the game and 157 for the four-game run, an average of 39.3. His record stood for twenty-five years, until Westmont's Pierre Pierce scored 159 in 2001.

"I don't know what all the fuss was about," Shidler said. "We were raised by modest standards. We always were told that no matter who you are, there is always someone who is better. I was never impressed by my own accomplishments. To me, it was just another day at the office, and life goes on."

Like it or not, however, Shidler was a cult figure.

"He was Elvis to us . . . beads, necklace, blond hair, white shoes," said Doug Novsek, an All-Stater on Lawrenceville's 1982 state championship team. "What people saw in Champaign was what we saw all the time. He was the reason a lot of us started to shoot. It was all Jay. Everyone came to see him.

"Marty [Simmons] had more success at Lawrenceville than Jay, but Jay attracted more attention. Marty is the best player in school history, the all-time leading scorer and rebounder, but Jay will forever have that reputation because he had that flair."

Simmons, who led Lawrenceville to a state-record sixty-eight victories in a row in 1982 and 1983 and was Illinois's Mr. Basketball in 1983, said that Shidler was his boyhood idol. "He was the best high school player ever to play the game. He was the man," Simmons said. "He could score points so easily. He was a legitimate jump shooter. If they had the three-point line in those days, God knows how many points he would have scored. He shot thirty-footers like no one else."

The three-point line was adopted in 1987. A Lawrenceville assistant said that he charted the last two games of the 1976 tournament, visualized where the three-point line would have been, and computed that Shidler would have scored sixty to sixty-five points in each game, rather than forty-eight and forty-five.

Shidler wasn't impressed. "It would have been fun. But I really think [the three-point line] is a bad thing for high schools because kids get in their minds that they need to shoot behind this line and try to learn to shoot that far out when they have no business shooting from there. It's too early to be involved. It creates bad habits," he said.

For Shidler, it was a matter of necessity. When he was young, playing against older and bigger kids, he couldn't get close to the hoop and was forced to shoot from twenty to twenty-five feet.

Unfortunately, his star faded after high school. Many thought he would attend Indiana. The Hoosiers had just won the NCAA championship, and Felling and Indiana coach Bob Knight had developed a relationship. He also considered Illinois State.

Late one night, he got a call from Indiana assistant Bob Weltlich, who asked, "Are you coming to Indiana or not?"

"It didn't sit well with me; it turned me off," Shidler said.

Kentucky made a late sales pitch. After observing Shidler at all-star games in Pittsburgh and Dayton, coach Joe B. Hall persuaded him to visit the Kentucky campus. He wanted to play for an NCAA champion, and he believed that Kentucky was in a good position to win. He also was impressed with twenty-three-thousand-seat Rupp Arena, Kentucky's tradition, Hall's up-tempo style, and a proposed million-dollar home for players.

"It sounded great to a kid from Lawrenceville," Shidler said. "I knew I was going to Kentucky on the day after my visit. It was everything I was looking for."

Shidler started every game as a freshman. He scored twenty points against Indiana. It turned out to be one of the highlights of his college career. As a sophomore, he started with Kyle Macey on Kentucky's 1978 NCAA championship team. As a senior, he was the sixth man. Hall changed his philosophy, switching from a guard-oriented to an inside-oriented offense. Shidler's confidence was shattered.

"I never beat my own drum," he said. "Even today, I am embarrassed if someone wants me to autograph something. I couldn't understand why they wanted my autograph when I'm no better than anyone else. Maybe I have a talent to do something that someone else can't do, but what does that matter?"

The Chicago Bulls drafted him in the ninth round. He played well at training camp, well enough to make the team, he thought. But the Bulls signed Ronnie Lester and Sam Worthen, their top two picks. It was the first time that Shidler had failed to make a team. He was crushed.

Later, he played for one year with a professional team in Scotland. But at twenty-seven, he lost his competitive fire. He returned to Kentucky to obtain his degree. He did baseball broadcasts on a Lexington radio station. Now he is the bar manager at Applebee's Park, home of Lexington's Class A baseball team. It isn't far from Rupp Arena.

"I like the sounds and smells of a ball park," he said. "I still think baseball was my best sport."

Bloom: Tales from Hungry Hill

Jerry Colangelo and Wes Mason were friends. Because of their basketball backgrounds, they met on several occasions at sporting events. Basketball was their game, but fun was their fame. They never passed up a good time.

Most importantly, they played significant roles in the long-playing basketball drama at Bloom Township in Chicago Heights, Colangelo in the 1950s and Mason in the 1970s. They would have filled a table at Savoia's Restaurant with Pete Coppa, Augie Bamonti, Verl Sell, and other members of the Bloom Mafia.

Colangelo grew up on Hungry Hill, a lunch-pail, blue-collar neighborhood of Polish and Italian immigrants. "I learned about my roots before *Roots* became popular," he said. His only regret is that he never played on a state championship team.

"I thought my life was over," he said, recalling Bloom's last-second 53–52 loss to Elgin in the 1957 supersectional at Hinsdale. "I drove around all night in my father's station wagon. But the sun rose the next day, and life went on.

"That was the most devastating loss of my career. It was the most important thing of my life. We thought we were going to win the state title. Losing in the NBA finals was something that happened, but it wasn't life or death. That was what it was for me in 1957."

By the time Mason arrived at Bloom in 1963, Colangelo had left for Phoenix, where he became general manager, then chairman of the board and chief executive officer of the Phoenix Suns and later managing general partner, chief executive officer, and chairman of the board of the Arizona Diamondbacks.

Mason, who was born in Beloit, Wisconsin, became one of the most popular coaches in the state. He produced five Sweet Sixteen qualifiers from 1972 through 1979, including a pair of Class AA runners-up in 1974 and 1975. He also developed ten All-Staters in ten years and sent more than twenty players to Division I colleges, including the 1974 Player of the Year, Audie Matthews.

"Wes was the only coach I know who could beat you by thirty points and you wanted to have a drink with him after the game," said former Thornridge coach Ron Ferguson.

"He was a good ambassador for the game," said Verl Sell, who co-owned a bar with Mason called I'd Rather Be in Philadelphia from 1979 to 1984. "I never heard him say a negative word about another human being, a redeeming quality. And I can't think of a player who didn't like him. He was a player's coach and a people's person."

Larry McCoy, a 1971 All-Stater who later played at the University of Wisconsin, said that Mason had a reputation for not missing too many meals and not passing up a cold beer. "He loved to party, but there was no smarter coach," McCoy said.

When Mason died of colon cancer in 1991, Ferguson, Sell, and, appropriately, Mason's bookie were among the pallbearers. He once said: "It's not so much that I like to win, it's just that I can't stand to lose." It would have been a fitting epitaph.

Basketball was a winning tradition at Bloom before Mason arrived and took it to another level. The 1950s were the golden years. The south suburban school produced championship teams in football, basketball, baseball, and track and field.

Colangelo, Leroy Jackson, Chuckie Green, Homer Thurman, Jim Bouton, Bobby Bell, Grady McCollum, Fred Macklin, Morris Cortez, and Roger Elliott were some of the school's outstanding athletes of that era. Bouton later pitched for the New York Yankees.

Coach Bert Moore said that McCollum was "the finest young man I ever coached, the best basketball player I ever saw," and that Thurman, an All-Stater in football and basketball and a state high jump champion, was "the best athlete I ever saw."

"We had great classes, great athletes, great coaching," said basketball star Bobby Bell. "We dominated everyone. The atmosphere was good because the players did everything together. We had all nationalities, and it all worked out great. We had strong feelings for one another, a lot of love, a lot of memories."

In those days, Chicago Heights was a polarized, divided community. The middle class had moved out. Sports was the one unifying factor. There was great pride in being a Bloom athlete. They were treated as celebrities, and they inspired and motivated other athletes to achieve.

"We were able to forget our differences on Friday and Saturday nights, when Bloom was playing," said Robert McCoy, a star on Bloom's 1974 and 1975 state runners-up. "But there was nothing to bring us together with the other sides of town other than sports."

The 1955–56 team was led by McCollum, who had transferred to Bloom from a small school in Mississippi and showed up for practice as a junior. His transcript was written on a page from a spiral notebook. Before the supersectional game against Oak Park, he was ruled ineligible because he had turned nineteen. Without McCollum, Bloom lost 62–57 and finished with a 22–6 record.

With Thurman, Colangelo, Bell, Green, and Paul Goebel returning in 1956–57, Bloom had high expectations. The Trojans were 22–1 and ranked fifth in the state. They beat Rock Island and Don Nelson 74–58, but they lost to unbeaten and second-ranked Elgin 53–52 in the supersectional.

"When Gary Kane hit a shot at the end of the game, it was something like John Paxson's shot to beat us in the NBA finals," Colangelo said. "Then Bobby Bell's last shot went around and around and came out. And we finish 27–2. I couldn't believe it."

"If I had made that last shot, it wouldn't have counted," Bell said. "There were eight seconds left on the clock when I came down. I shot from the top of the key but missed it. Our scorekeeper said it wouldn't have counted. I thought it would have. I still think about it. I still think we were good enough to win the state title."

Mason produced great teams and players in the 1970s: Matthews, Larry and Robert McCoy, Raymond McCoy, Kelvin Small, Mark Barwig, Larry Lowe, Emir Hardy, Gary

Clark, Richard Thomas, and Claude White. He won 317 games in fifteen years and retired in 1984.

"He wasn't a coach who believed in X's and O's," said Glen Giannetti, who played for Mason in 1972 and 1973 and later coached at Bloom from 1990 to 1995. "But he was a powerful personality who knew how to deal with kids from different social backgrounds. He knew how to put them together. You don't understand if you didn't play for him. You'd learn to respect what he did.

"From a young kid's eyes, Bloom was like the New York Yankees. Everybody talked about Homer Thurman. The Bloom-Thornton rivalry was the most intense in the south suburbs. It was a hot seat, and Wes loved sitting on it."

Mason's lifestyle proved his undoing, however. He failed to land a spot on Illinois coach Lou Henson's staff, and he sought to succeed Joe Stowell at Bradley but lost out to Dick Versace.

"I always felt alcohol kept Wes from becoming a basketball name known coast to coast," said Bloom graduate Mike Downey, now a sports columnist for the *Chicago Tribune*. "He drank so hard, and so long into the night, that I believe it became common knowledge in the Illinois coaching community and scared off out-of-state universities that might have hired him.

"Less successful high school coaches from the south suburbs began advancing to the collegiate level. I never heard him bitch about it or begrudge his coaching pals a thing. He was happy for them. Yet his own progress froze. He was a big man in Chicago Heights, but he never hit the coaching heights he should have."

His teams didn't quite make it, either. His 1973–74 team, led by Matthews's spectacular 28.8 scoring average, won thirty of thirty-three games but lost to Proviso East 61–56 in the state final. His 1974–75 squad, led by Robert McCoy and Small, was trounced by Chicago Phillips 76–48 in the state final. It marked the only time in history that a school had lost in the state championship two years in a row.

"Wes was disappointed in 1974 and 1975 when he finished second, but he never felt he got the short end," Verl Sell said. "He recognized that he didn't have the best team."

Mason's most disheartening experience happened in 1979, when his 27–3 team lost to Lockport 43–20 in the supersectional at Joliet. It was the worst loss of Mason's career. He wasn't prepared for Lockport's stall. He was crushed. He never took another team to the Sweet Sixteen.

Bloom returned to the Elite Eight in 1989 and 1990 with coach Frank Nardi and two-time All-Stater Brandon Cole. After the 1989–90 season, Nardi, a 1954 Bloom graduate, served as Bloom's principal from 1990 to 1994. Cole became the leading scorer in school history. He later played at DePaul.

In 1989, Cole scored sixty points in two games, but Bloom lost to Peoria Central 62–61 in the state quarterfinals. In 1990, Cole scored fifty-three points in two games, but Bloom lost to Quincy 54–51 in the quarterfinals. He finished with 2,517 points in his career, among the top fifteen in state history.

"When I took over from Wes Mason, the great athletes were gone," Nardi said. "Wes once said to me: 'I really apologize because I'm not leaving you very much at all.'

When I was a senior, we were the first Bloom team to win twenty games [under coach Dale Love]. We set the tone. We saw it coming."

East Leyden: 104–4 in Four Years

Glen Grunwald didn't look like a basketball player. Even North Carolina coach Dean Smith said so. He was tall and skinny and weak and shy. He was self-conscious about his dark horn-rimmed glasses. In eighth grade, he played the tuba in the school band. He used to correct his coach's grammar.

He was a prankster. He once scared his basketball coach to death by lining up at split end during a football scrimmage. He lived across the street from the school, but he didn't like walking around the block so he cut a big hole in the fence so he could get to class more quickly. He ranked number one in his class.

Grunwald met East Leyden coach Norm Goodman when he was nine. East Leyden's fieldhouse had opened, and Goodman was supervising when he spotted the gangly youngster. "You take this basketball and practice every day," Goodman told him.

In grade school, Grunwald played on a basketball team that didn't have a hoop in its gym. He shot at a light on the wall, pretending it was a basket. In sixth grade, he began to work with Ken Belza, who taught him footwork and basic moves and made the game fun to play.

The youngster began to improve and grow at the same time. He was 5' 10" in sixth grade and 6' 6" in eighth grade. He realized that he had some talent, that he was taller than everyone else, and that he was scoring a lot of points.

"I had a nontalented group of seniors when Glen was a freshman," Goodman said. "I told them in the spring that there is a kid who is coming in, and he is skinny and weak, and you will be his supporting cast. They protected him. He averaged twenty-seven points as a freshman. He was one of the first players who showed an up-and-under move before anyone else had the move."

Grunwald turned East Leyden into a powerhouse. In his four years, the Eagles were 20–3, 21–4, 28–1, and 25–1. Two of his teammates were Tom Dore and John Hendler. After they left, Eric Karg led the team to a 24–1 record. Then Ron Lindfors was the driving force in a 27–1 season. After four years, the Eagles were 104–4, the best four-year record in state history.

But Jack Gregg, who has kept statistics for East Leyden's football and basketball teams for more than fifty years, insists that the 1984–85 team was best of all. Led by Mike Griffin, who later played on Michigan's NCAA championship team, Bernie Tompa, and Dino Devinere, the Eagles were 27–2. They upset top-ranked Proviso West and Michael Ingram 64–62 in overtime in the sectional final but lost to the eventual state champion, Mount Carmel, 37–34 in the supersectional.

There were more pleasant memories during Goodman's twenty-nine-year career. His teams won 549 games, including a state-record 108 in a row during the regular season. He produced fourteen conference champions and three Sweet Sixteen qualifiers. But he never got to the state finals.

"We couldn't win the big one," Goodman said. "Something always happened to beat us in a big game, in a regional final or sectional final or supersectional. I thought we were always well prepared. But we just couldn't get over the hump."

Goodman's teams were nothing if not well prepared. When Grunwald enrolled at Indiana, coach Bob Knight said that he was one of the best coached players he had ever seen. Michigan coach Steve Fisher called Griffin the ultimate role player, totally unselfish, willing to do whatever was necessary to help the team win.

Goodman seemed out of place at East Leyden, a Jewish coach in an Italian neighborhood. Franklin Park was a segregated, blue-collar community. Surrounded by industry, it had a good tax base and a thriving school system.

Old-timers recalled basketball coaches Rip Watson in the 1930s and Dale St. John in the 1940s. They remembered outstanding players such as Harry Kossack, Frank Pruter, the Doss twins, John and Richard, and Jimmy Rodgers, who later coached the Boston Celtics.

There were no blacks in the community. Hendler said that he didn't meet a black person until he was a sophomore and "never got to know them" until he went to college. But Hendler and his teammates experienced black culture and a different style of basketball when they played in Maywood or at Margate Park in the summer.

When Goodman was hired in 1957, he knew East Leyden was in over its head as a member of the South Suburban League, which featured Thornton, Bloom, Lockport, and Kankakee. The school moved to the Interim Association (later the Des Plaines Valley, then the West Suburban Gold), and Goodman formed his philosophy.

"We knew we weren't going to press anyone like Proviso East," he said. "We decided to build the greatest defensive team that the area had ever seen. We wanted to be known for something, defense rather than speed and athleticism."

Goodman, who became head coach in 1961, didn't win any popularity contests. "You didn't like him, you feared him, but you respected him," Hendler said. But he cared for his players. He counseled them and helped them to go to college.

Most of all, he and assistant Jerry Wainwright taught in-your-face defense. A former Marine, he was tough and demanding. Some parents thought he was too harsh, but his players understood that if they worked hard, they would get better, especially if they played good defense.

"I never understood that you had to continue to work on your sport," said Dore, who transferred from West Leyden in Northlake to East Leyden as a junior. "I couldn't believe all the work they put in. I got in better shape and realized why they won."

Under Goodman's choreography, it all came together. In the 1960s he produced two outstanding players in Jim Bradof and Ken Norgaard. They starred on teams that were 21–6, 23–2, and 21–5. The 1965 team lost to Thornton 65–57 in the supersectional.

Then Grunwald enrolled. He was an All–Chicago Area selection for four years, an unprecedented achievement. His first team lost to St. Patrick 69–67 in the regional, and his second team lost to St. Patrick 67–65 in the regional final.

In 1974–75, Grunwald, Dore, and Hendler were 24–0 and ranked number one in the state after the regular season, but they lost to Proviso East 72–60 in the supersectional at East Aurora. Afterward, a frustrated Grunwald slammed his fist through a door on his way to the locker room. "I felt this was a team that could win the state title," Grunwald said. "We had a lot going for us . . . huge size, good guards. We were mostly dominant until Proviso East. But they weren't afraid of us. We had trouble with their press, and I didn't play very well [seventeen points, ten rebounds]."

"It was devastating," Dore said. "For a couple of days, I didn't want to talk to anyone or see anybody. At school, everybody said: 'Did you hear they lost last night?' It stayed with me all these years.

"Maybe [the eventual state champion] Phillips was a better team. But we felt we should have gone Downstate, that we could have been one of those teams that people talk about for a long time."

In 1975–76 Dore was gone, but Grunwald and Hendler returned, and East Leyden was 24–0 and ranked second in the state. In the regional final, however, Hendler suffered a severe ankle sprain, and the Eagles lost to Weber 73–68.

Grunwald was one of the most widely recruited players in the nation. He chose Indiana over Illinois, Kentucky, North Carolina, and DePaul. He wanted to play for Bob Knight. Before he left for Bloomington, however, he blew out his left knee in a pickup game. He captained Indiana's 1981 NCAA championship team with Ray Tolbert and Isiah Thomas, but he never was the same after the injury.

"Personally, I had a disappointing college career," said Grunwald, who later was general manager of the Toronto Raptors in the NBA. "I never was able to be the player that I thought I could be. We won the NCAA, Big Ten, and NIT. But I wasn't the biggest part of it."

"I always will wonder how good he could have been, what he would have done in college," Goodman said. "He was the best defensive player I ever coached. There was no one he couldn't guard."

Skeptics claimed that Goodman couldn't win without Grunwald, Dore, and Hendler, but he proved them wrong. Karg, Lindfors, Lou Fashoda, and Mark Danhoff were 51–2 in two years. The 1977 team lost in the regional, and the 1978 squad lost to St. Joseph and Isiah Thomas 73–67 in the sectional.

Finally, the 108–game regular-season winning streak was snapped by Maine South 64–61 on December 28, 1978, in the East Aurora Tournament. It spanned four years and ten months.

"We learned that basketball is a game, that at some point in your life you have to stop playing," said Hendler, now a director of local sales for Worldcom Telecommunications in Vienna, Virginia.

"It was disappointing not to go to state. As I reflect and page through my scrapbooks, I realize it was a painful experience. It struck me more when I got to college [Wake Forest] and heard what my teammates had accomplished. I knew my team was as good as others, but we didn't get to state."

Chicago Carver's Cazzie Russell, singled out in a *Chicago Sun-Times* survey as the most outstanding basketball player in the history of the Chicago Public League, grabs a rebound during the 1962 state championship game against Decatur. Carver lost 49–48. Photo courtesy of the *Chicago Sun-Times/* Associated Press.

Pekin's 1964 state championship team, which beat Cobden 50–45 for the title. The team was directed by coach Dawson Hawkins (standing, left) and assistant Duncan Reid (standing, right), who later built one of the state's winningest programs at Rock Island. Top players were guard Dave Golden (20) and Jim Sommer (44). Photo courtesy of Rich Hawkins.

An estimated crowd of five thousand waited at the train station in Cobden to welcome the Cobden basketball team upon its return after finishing second in the 1964 state tournament. It was only the second time that the Illinois Central stopped in Cobden. The other time was when it took the team to Champaign a few days earlier. Photo courtesy of the Illinois High School Association.

Coach Rich Herrin won 521 games in twenty-five years at Benton. Later, he won 225 games in thirteen years as head coach at Southern Illinois University. Photo courtesy of the Illinois High School Association/ *Champaign News-Gazette/* Brian K. Johnson.

Thornton's Lamarr Thomas drives past Galesburg's Roland McDougald to score a layup during the Wildcats' victory in the 1966 state championship. Photo courtesy of the *Chicago Sun-Times*/*Chicago Daily News*/John F. Jaqua.

Billy "the Kid" Harris of Chicago Dunbar was one of the most prolific scorers in Chicago Public League history. An All-Stater in 1969, he was a playground legend before the three-point line was adopted. He averaged twenty-six points per game as a junior and thirty-three as a senior. In one game he scored fifty-seven points, forty-one in the second half. Photo courtesy of the *Chicago Sun-Times*/*Chicago Daily News*/Gary Settle.

Quinn Buckner holds the state championship trophy and stands with teammates Greg Rose (44) and Nee Gatlin after Thornridge overwhelmed Quincy 104–69 for the 1972 Class AA championship. The Thornridge team has been recognized as the best in state history. Photo courtesy of the Illinois High School Association.

Bloom coach Wes Mason, who guided the Trojans to second-place finishes in the 1974 and 1975 Class AA tournaments. Photo courtesy of the Illinois High School Association/ *Champaign-Urbana Courier*/Phil Greer.

Ridgway's 1973 Class A championship team. Front row, left to right: Mike Fromm, Brent Browning, Dennis Pearce, Mike Dixon, Danny Stevens. Back row, left to right: coach Bob Dallas, John Cross, Tony Cox, Jeff Drone, Jim Doyle, Don Wathen, Martin Duffy, assistant coach John Schmitt. Photo courtesy of Bob Dallas/Hood's Studio.

Lawrenceville's sensational Jay Shidler, who averaged 32.7 points for thirty-one games in 1975–76 and led his team to third place in the Class A tournament. In the last four games he scored 157 points. Photo courtesy of the Illinois High School Association/*Champaign-Urbana Courier*/Phil Greer.

East Leyden's Glen Grunwald was a three-time All-Stater and one of the best players in state history who never reached the state finals. Photo courtesy of the *Chicago Sun-Times*/*Chicago Daily News*/Don Bierman.

Glenn Rivers (25) was a three-time All-State selection at Proviso East in 1978–80. But while the Maywood school won four state championships from 1969 to 1992, Rivers never played in Champaign. Photo courtesy of the *Chicago Sun-Times*/Perry C. Riddle.

Isiah Thomas (11) led St. Joseph of Westchester to second place in the 1978 Class AA tournament. Photo courtesy of the *Chicago Sun-Times*/Don Bierman.

Jeff Baker (22) led Maine South to the 1979 Class AA championship to cap one of the most improbable stories in the history of the state tournament. Photo courtesy of the *Chicago Sun-Times*/ Charles Kirman.

Michael Payne (42) and Bruce Douglas led Quincy to a 33–0 record and the 1981 Class AA championship. Photo courtesy of the Illinois High School Association/ United Press International/Kurt Baumman.

Lawrenceville's Marty Simmons (50) shoots over the outstretched arm of Herscher's Scott Meents during the semifinals of the 1982 Class A tournament. Lawrenceville won 47–45 in overtime and went on to win the state title. Photo courtesy of the Illinois High School Association/Associated Press.

Quincy coach Sherrill Hanks won 354 games in fifteen years and produced state runners-up in 1965 and 1972. "He built a great program, and he wanted you to know it," Rock Island coach Duncan Reid said. Photo courtesy of the Illinois High School Association.

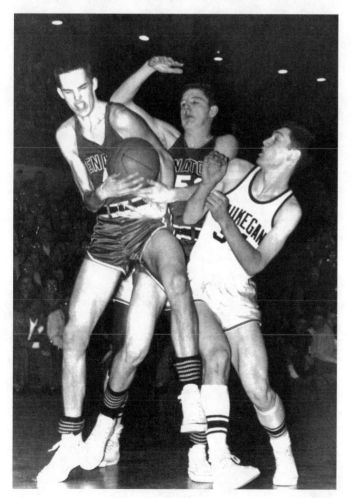

Springfield's Tom Cole (left) maintains control of the ball as he battles teammate Tom Frick and Waukegan's Kit Gordon (right) during a semifinal game in the 1959 state tournament. Springfield won 64–40 and went on to win the state title. Photo courtesy of the Illinois High School Association/United Press International.

Lawrenceville coach Ron Felling waves to Lawrenceville fans after his team defeated Flanagan for the 1983 Class A championship. It was Lawrenceville's second state title in a row, extending its unbeaten streak to a state-record sixty-eight games. Photo courtesy of the Illinois High School Association/ Associated Press/Kate Stallmeyer.

Mount Carmel's Derek Boyd, an unheralded sophomore who scored the winning basket in the Caravan's 46–44 victory over Springfield Lanphier in triple overtime for the 1985 Class AA championship, is hoisted on the shoulders of his jubilant teammates. Photo courtesy of the *Chicago Sun-Times*/ United Press International/Michael Meinhardt.

Jim Hlafka: Home, Sweet Home

Here is a trivia question that nobody outside of Macoupin County can answer: What is the name of the high school that went unbeaten in a season but didn't win a state basketball championship?

Bunker Hill.

In 1983 Bunker Hill went 29–0 but didn't qualify for the state finals. The team lost to Madison 53–52 in overtime in the sectional. Three months later, the IHSA awarded Bunker Hill a forfeit victory after ruling that Madison had used an ineligible player.

So Bunker Hill finished 29–0 but has nothing to show for it. Madison, which lost to Marty Simmons and Lawrenceville's unbeaten powerhouse in the supersectional, still has a 1983 sectional banner hanging in its gym.

Jim Hlafka prefers it that way. As the coach at Bunker Hill for forty-three years, he never sought the spotlight. In fact, he didn't even seek the job. But once he got it, he opted to stay put. He loved what he was doing and didn't want to do it anywhere else.

Hlafka won 755 games. Only Centralia's Arthur Trout (809) and Ridgway's Bob Dallas (781) won more at one school. And only five coaches in state history won more games.

During a four-year span from 1980 through 1984, his teams won 101 of 108 games, a .935 winning percentage. He won ten regional titles but never a sectional. If it bothered him, it never showed. He had offers to go elsewhere, including five colleges, but he chose to stay at Bunker Hill.

"I didn't do it for the money," he said. "My goal always was to win twenty games and get the most out of my kids that I could. I had the best of both worlds, coaching good kids and having a school and fans that backed me. I could do as I pleased."

He thought seriously about trying to surpass Dick Van Scyoc's record of 826 career victories, but he didn't let his ego get in the way of his devotion to his players, his school, and his community. After finishing 11–15 in 2001–2, he retired. "I wasn't happy with myself," he said. "I didn't do a very good job. I had expected a good season, but it was my worst record in many years. I don't feel I got the maximum effort out of my kids. So I resigned."

Hlafka grew up in Gillespie, thirteen miles north of Bunker Hill. He earned a scholarship to St. Louis University and played one year for coach Ed Hickey. He dropped out because his father couldn't work. Later, he attended Eastern Illinois University, then got a job as a teacher and coach at Piasa Southwestern. He wanted to be a basketball coach.

One day, while playing cards at the VFW lodge in Gillespie, Hlafka's father heard that there was an opening at Bunker Hill. Hlafka interviewed for the job and got the support of board members Melvin Buhs (the father of future Bunker Hill star Terry

Buhs), George Ash, and Clinton Dey. His first salary in 1959–60 was twenty-three hundred dollars to teach and five hundred dollars to coach four sports, supervise intramurals, and serve as athletic director.

"There was not a lot of pressure on me from the alumni to win," Hlafka said. "I was told not to practice on Sunday, not until after 1 P.M. I practiced on Sundays for forty-two years. They told me: 'We don't care if you win or lose, but we want you to be competitive.' It was a good environment to work in."

Bunker Hill (population seventeen hundred), located west of Staunton, was founded in 1873 as a stagecoach stop on the route from Springfield to St. Louis. In 1948 a tornado destroyed the town and killed twenty-seven people. The high school's enrollment is 179.

There are several homes in the community that Abraham Lincoln once slept in while the young lawyer was riding the central Illinois circuit. One of five standing statues of Lincoln in the United States stands in Bunker Hill. There is a flagpole in the main intersection (no stoplight) where an old bandstand once stood.

"It is a whole different world from the inner city," said David James, who was born near old Sportsman's Park in St. Louis but played for Hlafka and later coached with him for fifteen years. "It is heaven on earth, the first time I saw green grass and a drinking fountain by the barber shop."

Hlafka's initial recollections of Bunker Hill weren't so pastoral. "When I was growing up in Gillespie, Bunker Hill was a pushover. It was a nice town, but why would anyone want to coach there? It was a graveyard. That was its reputation," he said.

Even after Hlafka arrived, it took a few years before his program began to command respect. In 1962, when Denny Bruckert and Kevin Downing led the team to twenty victories, it was seeded last among nine teams in the county tournament.

"I was enthused when I came here," he said. "I recalled Hebron had won the state title [in 1952] and proved small schools could win. We were 6–18 in my first year. But everyone was so nice to me. They supported the team. The kids wanted to work. Why would I want to leave a situation like that?"

Hlafka never lost his passion for the game. He was a stickler for being on time. When school ended at 3:20 P.M., his players had to be on the practice floor at 3:25. He once drilled his players for six and a half hours on Thanksgiving Day.

"He made practices hell," James said.

"But he never screamed," said Terry Buhs. "The reason we played so hard was because we wanted to please him."

Hlafka copied Hickey's run-and-gun, let's-go offense, but he prided himself on his skills as a defensive coach. He attended a camp conducted by Vergil Fletcher and befriended the legendary Collinsville coach. They talked frequently, and Hlafka picked up Fletcher's triangle offense and ball-press defense.

Hlafka also copied some of Fletcher's rules. He stressed teamwork. He didn't like publicity in the newspaper. He wouldn't permit his players to wear the floppy haircuts that were popular in the 1960s, only flattops. No smoking, no drinking. Players wore red blazers and ties to away games.

"He told us: 'Girls are here to stay, but basketball is for right now. I put my wife second. So why can't you put your girlfriend second?'" said James.

He was big on slogans: "Press, force, and fatigue"; "The dog is back, but the caravan keeps moving on"; "Defense never rests"; "Ain't no stopping us now"; and "Play defense, defense wins."

Terry Buhs was the best player Hlafka ever produced. In 1966–67, Buhs and James led Bunker Hill to a 24–3 record. Buhs, a 6' 4" senior, was one of the leading scorers in the St. Louis area, averaging 26.7 points per game. He was named to an All-State team that included such celebrated players as Dave Robisch, Tom Parker, Greg Starrick, and Rich Yunkus.

To improve Buhs's skills, Hlafka took him to Collinsville to work one-on-one against Parker, Ron Burton, and Dennis Arnold, who led the 28–3 Kahoks to the state quarterfinals.

The object of Hlafka's offense was to give the ball to Buhs in the post. He wanted Buhs to shoot more, but Buhs didn't shoot enough. He wanted the ball to go inside and encouraged his players to have patience until they got a high-percentage shot. He had six or seven offenses for every type of situation.

Buhs drew major college coaches to Bunker Hill for the first time. He chose Southern Illinois over Michigan, Kansas, Illinois, Kansas State, Michigan State, and St. Louis. He made his first plane flight to visit Michigan coach Johnny Orr, but he chose SIU because coach Jack Hartman reminded him of Hlafka.

James, who was called "Jesse" by his high school teammates because of his shooting style, moved to Bunker Hill in fourth grade following a murder near his home in St. Louis. He didn't know a basketball from a grapefruit before then. He played on Saturday mornings, and Hlafka, suspecting a shooter was in the making, came by every day to watch.

As a junior, James played with Buhs. As a senior, he played on a 22–5 team that lost in the regional final. He attended Southern Illinois University at Edwardsville as a walk-on. He was hired as a teacher and coach at nearby Staunton. In 1973, Hlafka persuaded him to join his staff with a promise that he would be the head coach in three years. But Hlafka didn't quit.

The old gym was filled in the 1970s and 1980s. There is a sign in the gym, one of Hlafka's favorite slogans: "Victory favors the team that makes the fewest mistakes." It is adjacent to James Hlafka Hall, the school's trophy room.

But the atmosphere changed in recent years. Some felt that Hlafka was over the hill, that he had lost his edge. Others, like Buhs, said that they had more respect for him because he continued to win without talent.

One of Bunker Hill's oldest fans, seventy-six-year-old Sterling "Dunnie" Allen, who moved from Kentucky to Bunker Hill in the 1940s, noticed that something was missing. "All the kids loved him and wanted to play for him," Allen said. "But in the last few years, he said kids didn't want to listen anymore. Parents spoiled them, let them have cars. They didn't want to practice hard. They weren't as dedicated as they were fifteen to twenty years ago." Ultimately, it led to Hlafka's retirement.

Chicago Public League: Rise to Power

In the 1930s and 1940s, softball was the most popular recreational activity in Chicago. Sweetwater Clifton's legend began in softball, not basketball. It was said that he could hit a softball farther than Chicago Cubs slugger Bill Nicholson could hit a baseball.

City basketball was a double dribble. Blacks weren't permitted to play with whites. The best players—Agis Bray, Iron Man McKinnis, Hillary Brown, Nugie Watkins, Runt Pullins, Bernie Price, Goose Tatum, Toots Wright, Fat Long, Kid Oliver, Draggy Underwood, Inman Jackson—snubbed high school competition and joined the Brown Bombers, Savoy Big Five, Harlem Globetrotters, Olde Tymers, and other semi-pro teams.

"There was nothing intriguing about high school ball," said Watkins, a Du Sable graduate who once captained the Brown Bombers. "Today, playing in high school means something to a kid. He could get a college scholarship and could get to the NBA. He has something to look forward to.

"But when we were in high school, there was nothing beyond that. If we got a scholarship, it was to a black college in the South. From there, we came back home. Black kids didn't have any NBA to look forward to."

The city game got no respect. Catholic League schools hired coaching specialists, but the Public League hired gym teachers who coached in their spare time. Kids participated in three or four sports and never played basketball in the spring or summer. In Centralia, Mount Vernon, Paris, and Pinckneyville they were only concerned with winning basketball games.

"Downstate, there was a basketball hoop nailed to every garage," said Abe Booker, an All-Stater at Wells in 1954. "In the city, it took a long time before the park district built outdoor basketball courts."

"Basketball was a positive influence. It was one of the few things we could do," said Nelson Brown, a 1942 Du Sable graduate. "It was how the athletes met each other. It got fellas going to school. In my neighborhood, guys were either musicians, scholars, or basketball players. You had to excel in something."

In an era when few players were taller than 6' 3" and the term "athleticism" hadn't been invented, most teams adhered to a walk-the-ball-up-the-court, pattern style, copying the coaching strategies of Centralia's Arthur Trout, Pinckneyville's Duster Thomas, Taylorville's Dolph Stanley, and Paris's Ernie Eveland.

There were no jump shots, no dunks, and no run-and-gun. Players executed set shots from certain spots on the floor. Teams ran figure eights or weaves, the forerunner to the motion offense or passing game. Pivot men blocked or set picks but rarely shot.

Du Sable changed the tone and the tempo in 1954. At the same time, there was an influx of great black players: Booker, Charlie Brown, Paxton Lumpkin, Shellie

McMillon, Art Day, Clarence Wordlaw, Tommy Hawkins, George Wilson, Mel Davis, and Ralph Wells. Marshall made significant statements in 1958 and 1960. Carver added exclamation points in 1962 and 1963.

"Kids saw more and got exposed to more. They began to say: 'We can do that.' Basketball began to open doors outside Chicago," said Larry Hawkins, who coached Carver's 1962 state runner-up and 1963 state championship team.

"Du Sable changed the game," Booker said. "Jim Brown's philosophy was new, run and score seventy-two to seventy-five points. If they did, he expected to win. City kids began to travel and mingle with other players. We began to learn different styles and concepts."

George Wilson, who led Marshall to state championships in 1958 and 1960, said that basketball in the city in the 1950s "was better than the NCAA and the NIT and anything else."

Wilson said that older players such as Booker, Day, Wordlaw, Lumpkin, and Charlie Brown set the stage. "We wanted to be like them. They were such an inspiration. It was such a great time in history," he said.

In the beginning, kids played at Carter playground, 71st and South Park, the South Side Boys' Club, Wabash YMCA, or St. Elizabeth because the high school programs were weak and disorganized. They idolized McKinnis, Pullins, and Hillary Brown, who attracted big crowds on Sunday mornings on Carter playground or Saturday nights at Savoy Ballroom. They copied their styles and dreamed of following in their sneakers.

"If Runt Pullins or Hillary Brown were going to be on Carter playground, everybody would be there," said former Du Sable coach Jim Brown, who once played for the Brown Bombers. "They were the role models, the sports heroes of that time, the guys the kids worshipped. There were no black heroes in major league baseball or other professional sports."

Tommy Hawkins and Cazzie Russell grew up across the street from each other in Altgeld Gardens, a large housing project on Chicago's far South Side. Cazzie helped Tommy construct the only basketball hoop in the neighborhood. That's where they developed their skills before going to the big playgrounds.

"On the playgrounds, I learned how to play physically," said Hawkins, who later played at Parker, was a two-time All-American at Notre Dame, and played in the NBA for ten years. "I learned what it was to protect a reputation. The other guys would say: 'Okay, big fella, show me.' Just because you averaged twenty-five points in high school, it didn't mean anything on 71st Street."

Charlie Brown and his friends staked out a court at Washington Park. Novices competed at one end, the more skilled players at the other. Everyone's ambition was to be good enough to be chosen to play at the big guys' end. On the playgrounds, the only rule was no blood, no foul.

"If you wanted to be a player, you had to play there," Brown said. "People surrounded the court. If you won, you kept playing. If you didn't, you sat down. We'd show up at ten in the morning and come home at ten at night. Sometimes we had to shovel snow off the court."

Interest swelled, coaches got more serious about X's and O's, individual skills improved, the tempo speeded up on offense, and the defense pressed all over the court. Influenced by Du Sable, the game became more specialized and more aggressive.

The milestones came gradually. South Shore, coached by Tony Maffia, became the first Public League team since 1931 to place in the state finals, finishing third in 1944. Du Sable became the first all-black team to qualify for open state finals in 1953, then finished second in 1954.

Marshall became the city's first state champion in 1958. Marshall, Crane, Du Sable, and Carver were the dominant programs in the 1950s and 1960s. From 1973 to 2002 eight other schools—Hirsch, Phillips, Morgan Park, Manley, Simeon, King, Whitney Young, and Westinghouse—claimed ten state titles.

"Chicago became a hotbed for college recruiters in the 1970s," said Mark Aguirre, an All-Stater at Westinghouse in 1978 and 1979 who was a two-time All-American at DePaul and played in the NBA for fourteen years. "A lot of schools had good team concepts, which was good for the state tournament. But Chicago had a lot of kids who possessed individual talent, who could play one-on-one.

"They were able to do everything: fast break, handle the ball, shoot, pass, rebound. There were so many good players in the city. You went everywhere to play against them, to test yourself, to show them that you wouldn't back down."

A new breed of player emerged—Aguirre, Eddie Johnson, Rickey Green, Bo Ellis, Billy Lewis, Sonny Parker, Donnie Von Moore, Darius Clemons, Levi Cobb, Terry Cummings, Russell Cross, Mo Cheeks, Ken Norman, Deon Thomas, Joe Stiffend, Hersey Hawkins, Ben Wilson, Nick Anderson, Tim Hardaway, Marcus Liberty, Jamie Brandon, Juwan Howard, Rashard Griffith, Kiwane Garris, Kevin Garnett, Ronnie Fields, and Quentin Richardson.

"It was the best thing that anyone could do, playing on the city playgrounds," said Hardaway, a 1985 All-Stater at Carver who later played in the NBA for thirteen years. "I had to show people I could play the game every night. They said I was too short and couldn't shoot over people or couldn't play defense or couldn't go to the hole and make plays or run a team."

Hardaway, who idolized Isiah Thomas while growing up, said that playing on the playgrounds was as tough as banging in the NBA, "because it was a bunch of guys who played street ball and had enough talent to be in the NBA but didn't get any breaks."

Rich Bradshaw, an All-Stater at Marshall in 1965 and 1966, met one of them on a playground at Adams and Springfield. He was a 6' 1" freshman; Johnny Burton was 5' 10". They played one-on-one.

"I thought I was pretty good, and I was going to kick his butt," Bradshaw said. "He beat me so bad and sent me home. I could almost cry. He was a basketball player. He went to Dunbar for one year, then went to Marshall but didn't play."

"Isiah was the one we looked up to," Hardaway said. "We loved how he played the game, his charisma, how much fun he had while playing, the confidence he showed on the floor. I could see myself being him.

"But the playgrounds will make you or break you. It makes your body tougher and your mind stronger. They will knock you down, elbow you, and fight you. Either you will learn to play the game and not take any stuff or you won't play at all."

Isiah Thomas: Hoop Dreams and Disneyland

Isiah Thomas has been a celebrity since he was a teenager. He led Indiana to an NCAA championship and starred on the Detroit Pistons' two NBA championship teams. He escaped from the streets of Chicago's West Side by learning how to play a game better than anyone else and emerged as an American icon.

But some hoop dreams turn into nightmares. He still can't get over the memory of one defeat that affected him more emotionally than losing to Michael Jordan and the Chicago Bulls.

After finishing second to unbeaten Lockport in the 1978 Class AA tournament, Thomas and his St. Joseph teammates felt that they were destined to win the state title in 1979. "We were the best team in the state going into the season," Thomas said. "Our determination and commitment to winning was better than everybody else's."

St. Joseph was on target to accomplish its mission. After the regular season, the Chargers were ranked third in the state behind unbeaten Quincy and Proviso East. But their dream imploded in the sectional championship.

Against De La Salle, St. Joseph was nursing a one-point lead in the closing seconds. Thomas did a 360 to the basket, but referee Dan Chrisman ruled that he charged into John McHale. It was his fifth foul. Coach Gene Pingatore inserted sophomore guard Kenny Williams in the lineup to run out the clock.

However, Williams didn't follow Pingatore's instructions. He broke free on the baseline, but he missed a layup. De La Salle rebounded and called time-out. St. Joseph argued that there was only one second left. De La Salle coach Jerry Tokars insisted that there were four or five. The officials settled for four.

Albert "Moochie" Williams, a 5' 7" junior and the tenth man on the roster, swished a twenty-footer to beat St. Joseph 59–58. Some accounts reported it as closer to thirty feet. Ironically, the previous summer, Thomas taught the youngster how to shoot.

"It was the most disappointing loss I ever had in basketball," Isiah said. "I'm not over it to this day."

After Thomas's Pistons lost to the Boston Celtics in game five of the NBA's Eastern Conference playoff in 1987, after Larry Bird had intercepted Isiah's pass and tossed the ball to Dennis Johnson for the game-winning basket with one second left, a reporter said to Thomas, "This had to be your toughest loss."

"No," Isiah said. "My toughest loss was to De La Salle as a senior in high school."

Pingatore agrees. "That was the most devastating loss that I have felt in thirty years of coaching. That was the team that I felt could win [the state championship]," he said.

"It was the end of a fairy tale," Isiah said. "We had brought the community together from a racial and social standpoint. We went to school every day and interacted and laughed and played basketball. We were in Disneyland.

"When [Moochie] made that shot, it was over. When we went back to the school, we hung out in the parking lot until three o'clock in the morning. Everybody realized that was the end, not of the team, but the end of Disneyland."

Thomas's world began on Chicago's West Side, in Garfield Park, near Congress and Homan. He was the youngest of seven boys and two girls. Later, the family moved to the Austin area, to Division and Latrobe. Much of Isiah's time was spent at Our Lady of Sorrows Parish and Youth Center, where his mother worked.

He began to play basketball at age three. It was a good way for his mother to keep an eye on her youngest child and to keep him away from the violent street gangs that infested the West Side. There were tournaments on Saturday and Sunday after mass. Isiah became a halftime show, dribbling and shooting free throws.

Thomas's mother wanted him to attend a Catholic high school. He wanted to enroll at Weber because most of his teammates from Resurrection grade school went there. His second choice was Gordon Tech. He admired Gordon Tech's LeeArthur Scott and Hales Franciscan's Sam Puckett. In fact, he chose to wear number 11 because of Puckett, an Isiah-type guard who scored more than twenty-six hundred points in 1967–70.

"But none of those schools wanted me," Thomas said. "They said I was too small to play."

Isiah went to a tournament at St. Joseph in Westchester. Pingatore introduced himself. He had become head coach in 1969 and brought in the school's first black players in 1974. When St. Joseph clinched its first conference title in 1975, Isiah, then an eighth grader, was in the stands. He was impressed with the spirit and the fact that two former teammates at Resurrection, Ray Clark and Andrew Cooper, had chosen St. Joseph.

"Pingatore was the big thing," Isiah said. "When he showed some interest, my brothers and sisters said to give the place a look. They liked it. Pingatore took me under his wing. He made me feel comfortable and made me feel that he would have a personal hand in my development."

Pingatore said that he knew from the first time he scouted Thomas that the youngster was special, but he and other coaches weren't evaluating Isiah. They went to Resurrection to see Tyrone Brewer, a talented 6' 4" prospect.

"Then Resurrection came to our tournament at Thanksgiving," Pingatore recalled. "All of a sudden this kid catches your eye. He dominated the game. Where did he come from? He dominated every game I ever saw him play. His personality and charisma showed right away. He was thirteen and took over the game. He stood out from everybody else. He never ceased to amaze me."

Thomas and Brewer followed Resurrection teammates Ray Clark, Carl Hill, and Elgin Jones to St. Joseph. Anthony Young, who grew up in the Austin neighborhood, and Hector Gonzalez, who played at St. Barbara's in Brookfield, came along. They forged a friendship and built a foundation for a program that won a state title in 1999, finished third in 1987, fourth in 1984, reached the Sweet Sixteen on four other occasions, and established Pingatore as one of the state's most successful coaches.

Dennis Doyle saw it unfold before his disbelieving eyes. Now the coach at Willowbrook, Doyle was Pingatore's assistant for eleven years in the 1970s and 1980s. His first season at St. Joseph was Isiah's sophomore year. The team was 16–10.

"You could see things starting to grow with Isiah and Ray Clark. It took off from there," Doyle said. "The environment was electric when Isiah was there. People didn't believe that St. Joseph could continue what they started in 1978. But they did."

How good was Thomas?

"Quinn Buckner was bigger but couldn't do other things," Doyle said. "Rickey Green was faster but didn't do other things. Isiah was a better all-around player. He made other players better. Glenn Rivers didn't have a point guard mentality; Isiah did. He worked harder than anyone I ever saw."

Thomas and Clark—"as good a pair of guards as I ever saw," Pingatore said—led the 1977–78 team to a 31–2 record and second place in the state tournament. They beat Fenwick to win the Proviso West Holiday Tournament for the first time. In the state quarterfinals, they beat Westinghouse and Mark Aguirre 63–60. In the final, they bowed to Lockport 64–47.

"It was a magical season," Pingatore said. "We had never been through anything like this, a young school that hadn't done anything statewide. I don't know if we could have beaten Lockport on another day. It didn't matter. Hey, we finished second in the state."

The 1978–79 team figured to be even better. When they beat Proviso East and Glenn Rivers at the Proviso West Holiday Tournament, they knew that destiny was in their hands.

"We never thought about losing," Brewer said. "In our minds, it wasn't possible. We just thought about playing and winning. How devastating was it to lose to De La Salle? To this day, I still wonder how [Moochie] could get off a shot in four seconds. I haven't recovered yet."

After the season, Pingatore informed the family that Isiah was being recruited by dozens of colleges. His sister, Ruby Thomas Carlson, evaluated the academic standing of each school, and his brothers evaluated the coaches. His mother and brothers wanted him to attend DePaul. Ruby wanted him to go to Indiana.

Notre Dame was Isiah's first choice. He had promised Bro. Alexis Kalinowski, who had coached Isiah at Our Lady of Sorrows, that he would attend Notre Dame. However, Irish coach Digger Phelps called and said that he had given his last scholarship to John Paxson. Isiah's second choice was Iowa, but coach Lute Olson left for Arizona. Indiana was his third choice.

"We fought so much over his decision," Ruby said. "Nobody wanted him to go to Indiana but me. We finally agreed that Bobby Knight was the best coach for Isiah. He would help him develop into a better basketball player. Isiah thought so, too."

Knight visited the Thomas home to confront his mother, brothers, and sisters. He was very persuasive. "I am missing one player from winning the national title, and that is your son," he told Mary Thomas. "I guarantee if he comes to Indiana, he will develop into a strong man and be able to deal with any situation that he comes in contact with."

"It didn't surprise me when he announced for Indiana," Pingatore said. "He wanted to play for the best. He knew it would take the best to take him to the next level."

Maine South: The Biggest Upset of All

When Maine South's basketball team showed up for its semifinal date with East Moline in the 1979 Class AA tournament, officials at the entrance gate wouldn't let them in because, they argued, "they don't look like a basketball team."

"They had to get a copy of the tournament program [which included a picture of the team] to see if it was really us," recalled Dan Fiddler, the team's 6' 4" center. "It was a snapshot of the whole season. It didn't matter who we beat, people didn't think we were any good."

Maine South won thirty-one of thirty-two games, fifteen by margins of three points or less, and capped its fairy-tale season by being booed in the Assembly Hall while executing a game-winning strategy, then beating previously unbeaten Quincy's unbeatable full-court press to win the state title.

"I've covered the Super Bowl and the World Series, and I've covered Don Shula, Michael Jordan, Magic Johnson, and Pat Riley," said guard Jay Huyler, who was a television sports anchor in Miami for nine years. "But my biggest sports impression always will be winning that state title."

It was no accident that Fiddler, Huyler, Jeff Baker, Chris Theodore, John Crowl, Brian Sir, and Tim Loeffler accomplished what few others thought they could. With coaches Quitman Sullins and George Verber, they began plotting their trip to the 1979 state finals when they were in fifth grade.

Baker, Huyler, Theodore, and Sir lived within a few blocks of one another. From fifth grade on, they played on a basketball court in Huyler's backyard. In eighth grade, Baker, Huyler, and Fiddler played on a park district all-star team. They played together again at Lincoln Junior High School.

Togetherness wasn't their only virtue. They were smart, too. Fiddler, now an anesthesiologist who does open heart and brain surgery procedures in Medford, Oregon, ranked number one in his class. Huyler was number four. Sir went to law school and now is chief operating officer for a Chicago-based financial services company. All nine seniors earned college degrees.

Baker was the only one recruited by Division I colleges. The 6' 4", 165-pounder was athletic but not an efficient perimeter shooter. Big Ten schools showed no interest. They said that he could run and jump but wasn't a good enough shooter to play guard in college. But he scored 2,512 points in high school and was an All-Southwest Conference selection at Texas Christian.

"When we were freshmen, we won twenty games and started to talk about winning the state title," Baker said. "We felt we had the ability to win state if we stayed together."

Nobody outside of Maine South had that feeling. They acknowledged that Bernie Brady, who won 323 games, was an outstanding coach. His 1969–70 team lost in the supersectional, and his 1973–74 squad was ranked number one in the state. The basketball program had a solid tradition. People thought that they were good but never good enough to get Downstate. They would fold against city teams or tough competition.

Sullins and Verber were determined to change that image. When Brady resigned to become athletic director in 1974, he promoted Sullins. His first team, led by Player of the Year Pete Boesen, was 23–4 but lost in the supersectional.

Sullins had his eye on the Class of 1979 all along. He knew that it had the potential to be special. He assigned Verber to teach man-to-man defense, and he insisted that his players participate in the toughest summer leagues in the Chicago area.

Conditioning was Sullins's top priority. His preseason program for nonfootball players called for weightlifting, two days of long-distance running, and three days of sprints.

Sullins, born in Booneville, Mississippi, played basketball at Murray State, then played with the Goodyear Wingfoots of the National Industrial Basketball League and the Pittsburgh Pipers of the ABA. He coached at Vienna, Illinois, and Blytheville, Arkansas, before coming to Maine South as Brady's assistant. He was very knowledgeable about the game, well organized, and a strong disciplinarian.

"You always believed that at the end of the game he would have an offensive strategy to find a way to get around the defense," Sir said. "He expected you to give a hundred percent, and he had zero tolerance for anyone who didn't."

Sullins clearly defined the role of each player. Baker and Fiddler were the shooters, Theodore played inside, Huyler was the passer, and Crowl was the point guard and outside shooter. "We didn't have the best talent," Huyler said, "but we were the best-coached team."

Sir may have been the team's most valuable player. He was expected to be a starter, but he broke his elbow a week before the season opener, so he settled for being the sixth man. But Sullins ordered him to terrorize Baker in practice.

"Brian was our unsung hero, our defensive specialist," Baker said. "Sullins told Brian to guard me. He didn't want me to get the ball. He told him to stay with me like glue. We pushed and shoved and punched each other. Brian did everything he could to stop me. Coach wanted me to be more intense."

Baker emerged as an All-Stater, one of the state's most prolific scorers. He scored eighty-nine points in the state finals, including twenty-six on ten-of-fifteen shooting against Quincy in the championship. He also led his team with thirty-five rebounds.

"Baker probably had as good a year as anyone has had in one season," Verber said. "We went to Baker in close situations. He had a knack for coming through in big games, and we had confidence that he could do it."

Maine South wasn't a total surprise in 1978–79. After rallying from a twelve-point deficit to beat highly rated De La Salle in the championship of the East Aurora Tournament, Sullins knew that his team was capable of going to the state finals.

After the holidays, Maine South was the only unbeaten team in the Chicago area. Television sportscaster Tim Weigel designated the Hawks as the number one team, but Proviso East and St. Joseph were ranked first and second by the *Chicago Sun-Times*. And the Associated Press's statewide poll tapped Quincy as number one.

Then Glenbrook South punctured Maine South's balloon in overtime, snapping the Hawks' sixteen-game winning streak. But they quickly recovered.

In the regional, they dispatched Maine East and Gordon Tech. In the sectional semifinal, trailing Arlington by four points with fifty seconds left, Fiddler blocked a shot at the buzzer, and the Hawks won in overtime. In the final, they overcame a five-point deficit in the fourth quarter to oust Elk Grove.

In the supersectional at Northwestern, they edged New Trier West 65–64, as Fiddler tipped in his own missed shot with two seconds to play. It was Maine South's only lead in the game.

"We ran a play that I was supposed to pass to Theodore or Baker," Fiddler said. "Chris was tightly guarded, and Baker ran out-of-bounds with a man on him. You can't pass to a man who is out-of-bounds and comes back, so I didn't have any other choice but to shoot an eighteen footer with four seconds left. I missed, but nobody blocked me out. I charged in, grabbed it, and tipped it in."

That set up a quarterfinal rematch with De La Salle, which was favored because of its massive 6' 8", 6' 6", and 6' 6" front line that featured Darryl Allen and Mike Williams. Tony Brown, who later played at Indiana, stood out in the backcourt. They had upset Isiah Thomas and St. Joseph in the sectional final.

Maine South won 37–27 in a game that drew boos from the crowd, even from its own fans, but Sullins earned great respect from rival coaches and basketball purists. His brilliant strategy enabled the Hawks to overcome De La Salle's size.

Maine South held the ball, forcing De La Salle out of its 2-3 zone defense. Coach Jerry Tokars's team hadn't played man-to-man all year. When Tokars removed Williams and ordered his players to go man-to-man, the Hawks ran their motion offense and scored on shuffle cuts and backdoor plays.

"People didn't want to see a delay game, but we didn't come down to put on a show, we came to win the tournament," Sullins said. "Some people enjoy run-and-gun basketball, but people who know the game enjoy the strategy part of it. We did what we had to do to beat a team with superior talent."

In the semifinals, Maine South overcame a ten-point deficit in the last five minutes to beat East Moline 77–76 in overtime. Baker, who had been limited to a season low of twelve points against De La Salle, tallied thirty to spark the comeback.

In the final, Maine South wasn't intimidated by Quincy's three-quarter, 1-3-1 zone press that had dismantled opponents throughout the season. Crowl was the key. A consummate setup man, he drew a double team to one side of the big floor, then passed to Huyler, who created three-on-two situations, which led to layups, and thirty-three-of-fifty shooting. Huyler still holds the Class AA championship game record with twelve assists.

When Quincy coach Jerry Leggett finally realized that his team couldn't disrupt Maine South's offense and force Crowl and Huyler to commit turnovers, he called off the press. But it was too late, as Maine South won 83–67.

"I convinced the kids they were better conditioned and smarter than any other team," Sullins said, "that we could run these offenses and defenses, and if we played together, we could beat anyone."

5
The 1980s

Glenn Rivers: Doc Makes House Calls

The first thing you should know about Glenn Rivers is that he didn't become associated with his popular nickname, "Doc," until he went to college.

The second thing you should know about Rivers is that the most devastating loss of his basketball career—at any level—happened in a sectional semifinal in his last high school game.

The third thing you should know about Rivers is that he insists that his favorite coach was Glenn Whittenberg at Proviso East in Maywood, not Al McGuire at Marquette or Pat Riley in the NBA.

The last thing you should know about Rivers is that "the biggest regret of [his] life" is that he was a three-time All-Stater but never led his team to the state finals in Champaign.

"High school was the best of times," he said. "I loved college and the pros, but that was competitive more than fun. High school was all I knew, all I wanted at that point in my life. The pros became a goal and a dream. But I had other things—the media, my wife, my family. In high school, it was only about basketball."

Rivers was dubbed "the basketball nerd" at his twentieth high school reunion. He didn't talk to girls. He never had a girlfriend. He attended only one homecoming dance and one prom. His mother made him go to his senior prom. He arrived late and left early.

"Basketball was my life," he said. "I didn't miss a Proviso East game, except for punishment from my parents for talking back to a teacher in class, from first grade to when I played. I cried when they lost."

Grady Rivers recalls that his youngest son played basketball ever since he could dribble. In the basement, he would dribble around two support poles and perfect his spin moves. He was the first freshman to play on Proviso East's varsity. His older brother, Grady Jr., was a senior.

"When he was playing in sixth grade, I began to see something special in him," his father said. "No one could stop him. He was playing against older kids. Grady was a better shooter, but he didn't have the great desire that Glenn had to succeed. Glenn wanted to be a professional basketball player. And he did everything he had to do to achieve that goal."

As a freshman, he attended a summer camp in Milwaukee. Marquette coach Al McGuire and his assistant Rick Majerus were there. The Milwaukee Bucks and Philadelphia Warriors conducted a scrimmage, but they had only nine players. They needed a tenth.

"Hey, Doc, get down here," McGuire shouted to Rivers.

Glenn didn't know who he was talking to.

Then Majerus said it, too.

Rivers joined the scrimmage.

"All the kids called me 'Doc,' and it stuck," Rivers said. "But locally I was still Glenn. When I decided to go to Marquette, the Chicago newspapers said Glenn, but Milwaukee said Doc."

Julius "Dr. J" Erving was an icon at the time. To this day, however, Glenn isn't sure how McGuire and Majerus arrived at the name.

Glenn was greatly influenced by his uncle, Jim Brewer, the star of Proviso East's 1969 state championship team, and his cousin, Walt Williams, another starter on the 1969 team. Brewer and Glenn's father, a Maywood policeman, made sure that the youngster "didn't do anything stupid."

He still recalls that his "biggest memory and scariest moment" was in 1969 when Hirsch was beating Proviso East, Brewer, and Williams by fifteen points with six minutes to play in the supersectional game at Hinsdale Central. But the Pirates rallied to win 47–46.

"Glenn was the hardest working young boy I remember," Williams said. "He tried the same move for an hour until he got it right. In his backyard, when the older kids came, if he didn't get picked, he'd pick up his ball and wouldn't let them use it.

"He and Isiah Thomas emerged at the same time. Isiah was unstoppable. He could break Proviso East's press when he wanted to. I never saw anyone else do that. Doc was high-flying, a spectacular player. He changed a lot of things at Proviso East. He was a cult hero in the community."

Maywood was a great place for a young kid to grow up if he wanted to play basketball. Everyone gathered at 10th Avenue Park on Washington Boulevard. Isiah Thomas, Mark Aguirre, and a lot of players from Chicago's West Side showed up.

In the late 1970s, Aguirre, Thomas, and Rivers triggered an explosion of fan interest in high school basketball that attracted record crowds to the Proviso West Holiday Tournament and commanded multimedia attention. Aguirre was the most valuable player at Proviso West in 1977, Thomas in 1978, and Rivers in 1979. So many people wanted to see the games that fire marshals had to padlock the doors for safety reasons.

Michael Finley knew about Rivers and the Proviso East tradition, about the 1969 and 1974 state championship teams. In 1980, his sisters were cheerleaders at Proviso East, and he tagged along with them and sat on the floor to watch Rivers, Ricky Wilson, and the nation's top-ranked high school team.

"Basketball has always been the most popular sport in Maywood, on the playground or in school or in the backyard. Everyone wanted to be a part of it," said Finley, who was an All-Stater on Proviso East's 1991 state championship team, an All-Big Ten player at Wisconsin, and now is a standout with the Dallas Mavericks in the NBA. "Proviso East's gym was the place to be on Friday and Saturday. There was a big picture of the 1974 state championship team celebrating in the fieldhouse. I always asked: 'What is that all about?' I always felt it would be a great feeling to win a state title."

So did Rivers. He never dreamed about being an NBA player, only about playing on a state championship team. As a senior, he attended the Bill Cronauer's camp in Georgia. It was the first time he had ever played against someone outside Chicago. He won the camp's MVP, slam dunk, and playmaker awards. He played against Sam Perkins, Derek Harper, Vern Fleming, and James Banks.

He credits his development to Whittenberg, an ex-Marine who was a drill sergeant of a coach. "He scared hell out of me. He reminded me of Bear Bryant. He was a high school version of Bob Knight. But he was a great coach. He made me an NBA player," he said. "He defined your role. He told you what he wanted you to do. If you went outside that role, you had to deal with him. That's why his teams were so good. You could score, but you had to play defense if you wanted to play. At the end of the day, I played thirteen years in the NBA because I was hard-nosed and a defender."

Whittenberg didn't play any favorites. He played only man-to-man defense. He said that zone was a sign of weakness. "He was the most strict disciplinarian that Proviso East ever had," Grady Rivers said.

At an Elks Club meeting, someone asked Whittenberg why he wasn't starting any white players. "Because they aren't any good," he said. "I don't care what color they are, white or green, if they aren't any good, I won't use them."

Whittenberg and Rivers never qualified for the state finals. In 1978, they lost to St. Joseph and Isiah Thomas in the sectional. In 1979, they were ranked second in the state but lost to De La Salle in the sectional. In 1980, they were ranked number one in the nation but lost to De La Salle 62–52 in the sectional.

"The last one was the most frustrating thing I ever went through," Rivers said. "I was convinced we were the best team and would win the state title. Then I could see my dream slipping away. There was no bigger dream in life than to play in Champaign and win the state title."

Rivers had twisted his ankle in the regional, and he was hobbling. He was limited to thirteen points. Proviso East's other star, Ricky Wilson, a free spirit whom Whittenberg considered only slightly less talented than Rivers, missed the team bus, showed up at the end of the first quarter, and didn't play until the second half. He finished with seventeen points.

De La Salle, led by Dan Burich's twenty-six points, led by fifteen at halftime and nineteen with four minutes to play. Rivers was scoreless in the second half and fouled out with two and a half minutes remaining. He was inconsolable in the locker room. Even Whittenberg started to cry.

Marquette coach Al McGuire and assistants Rick Majerus and Hank Raymonds tried to cheer Rivers up. "You have bigger and better days coming," McGuire said.

"No, this isn't just high school," Rivers told him. "I'm leaving not being a state champion. You never recover from something like that."

But Rivers recovered. His high school experience left an indelible footprint on his life and paved the way for future success. "Whittenberg and the Proviso East environment gave me a love for something," he said. "If you work hard enough, no matter where you are from, you can do what you want to do. Some have to work harder than others, some aren't as talented as others, but you can succeed if you work hard."

Quincy: The Hanks/Leggett Feud

Duncan Reid, an old coaching rival who admired his craft and enjoyed watching other craftsmen, defined the career of former Quincy coach Sherrill Hanks as Grant might have appraised Lee. "He built a great program," Reid said, "and he wanted you to know it."

How great? When Hanks left Alton to become head coach at Quincy in 1961, the school didn't offer season tickets and didn't have designated seats in the gym. Today, Quincy has thirty-two hundred season-ticket holders. No other school in the state comes close.

"I wasn't the smartest coach who ever lived," Hanks said. "I prided myself that I could see all ten players on the floor. I never carried a chalkboard. My philosophy? Let your players dictate the game. If a kid can shoot, let him shoot. Let the players play. I didn't hold them back from what they could do."

Hanks had fun coaching, and his players, including Larry Moore and Jim Wisman, had fun playing. As a senior, Moore took 706 shots, and Quincy finished second in the state. Wisman, who married the coach's daughter, played on teams that went 28–5, 26–2, and 22–8.

Hanks didn't invent Quincy basketball. Sam Storby coached the Blue Devils to the 1934 state championship, upsetting defending champion Thornton and Lou Boudreau. George Latham, who later coached at Waukegan, won 250 games from 1945 to 1956; he finished third in the state in 1951 and second in 1952. Because of Latham's success, Hanks applied for the job at Quincy.

"I never had been to Quincy," Hanks said. "After a few months, my wife Sondra said, 'Coach, I don't like it here.' I said, 'Stick it out a few more months and finish out the year. If you still feel that way, we'll leave.' She fell in love with the town."

Located on the Mississippi River, Quincy is a long trip from the Quad Cities, Galesburg, Springfield, or Collinsville. "It isn't a river town, it is an overgrown country town," Hanks said. "It grows on you."

From 1961 to 1975, Hanks won 80 percent (354–89) of his games. He never won a state championship, but he claimed two seconds and a third and put an indelible stamp on his program, an unmistakable swagger, and you knew it.

Jerry Leggett enjoyed even more success. From 1976 to 1990, he won 81 percent (330–77) of his games, a state and national championship, a second, a third, and two fourths. His 1979–82 teams won sixty-four games in a row. His 1981 team is ranked among the best in state history.

Quincy's five-thousand-seat gym, which opened in 1957, is in a class by itself. The pregame ceremony, with the Blue Devil mascot running through a tunnel of smoke onto the floor, often persuades opposing coaches to keep their teams in the locker room so they won't get caught up in the hoopla. Quincy has won 86 percent of its home games. Hanks's teams never lost more than three in a season. Leggett's teams won seventy-two in a row.

It shouldn't come as a surprise that Hanks and Leggett weren't the best of friends. In a clash of giant egos and conflicting personalities, Hanks prevailed because he was John Wooden to Leggett's Gene Bartow. Hanks was more popular. Despite his success, Leggett remained an outsider to many people.

They never had a relationship. There was a great distance between them. They never talked. Jane Leggett, Jerry's widow, claims that Hanks never congratulated her husband after winning the 1981 state title. But Hanks spoke at the team's celebration.

"A week after Jerry took the job, before we moved to Quincy, Hanks asked Jerry to come to town," Jane Leggett recalled. "He told Jerry, 'Don't mess with my people and my money-backers. I'm at Quincy College, and don't mess with my supporters.' Jerry never had anything to do with Sherrill from then on."

Hanks was dynamic, resourceful, dapper, a classy dresser. He always had a flair to him. He contracted a charter bus service from Burlington, Iowa, to transport his team to away games. He chartered a train to Galesburg. He had a radio show on Saturday and a television show on Sunday. An innovator, he set the Illinois Basketball Coaches Association into motion.

"He was a class act," Wisman said. "He did more for his players from a personal standpoint, building character, ethics, principles. He was a good bench coach. He was great at making decisions in the last ten to fifteen minutes of a game. I rarely saw him make a mistake that put his team in jeopardy. But I recall several times how he put his team in a position to win."

Leggett upstaged Hanks by expanding the dressing room, painting it blue and white, laying down a blue carpet, and installing wooden lockers, a television set, a computer/film room, and a weight-training facility. He irritated Hanks's friends by intimating that his teams were better. But no one questioned Leggett's work ethic or coaching credentials.

At his funeral in 1998, Bruce Douglas, the star of Leggett's 1981 state championship team, gave the eulogy. He said: "He believed in his players, believed you play like you practice, held us to high standards, hated mediocrity."

Douglas, Quincy's all-time leading scorer with 2,040 points, said that Leggett was "one of the two or three greatest high school coaches of all time. He had plans and plays for every situation, which made him unique among other coaches. He made the game fun to play. His approach to the game was entertaining."

Keith Douglas, Bruce's older brother, was an All-Stater on Leggett's 1979 state runner-up. He said that Leggett "was the greatest coach I ever played for," even though he quit in 1978 after Leggett suspended him for two weeks for staying out too late.

"Leggett was like Bob Knight, the strictest disciplinarian I ever played for," Keith said. "It was hard for him to deal with young people. You did it his way or hit the highway. I came to respect that. I never had any intention of sitting out my senior year. We patched things up."

Keith tipped off what was the golden age of Quincy basketball. In the next four years, the Blue Devils were 32–1, 26–3, 33–0, and 32–1. The 1981 powerhouse, led by

Bruce and Dennis Douglas and 6' 10" Michael Payne, generally is regarded as the second best team in state history, behind Thornridge 1972. They beat second-rated Lincoln in the sectional final, then swept their last four games by twenty-eight, twenty-five, thirty-one, and twenty-nine points.

"It's hard to imagine there ever was a better team than us," said Bruce Douglas, who later played at the University of Illinois. "We had speed, size, and versatility. I remember Thornridge. My brother Jerry played against them in 1972. They had all the things that make you great, too. We would have loved to play them."

After winning sixty-four games in a row, Quincy was expected to win its second state title in a row in 1982. But in the semifinals, the Blue Devils were upset by Chicago's Mendel Catholic 53–52 on Mike Hampton's game-winning shot.

"When you win that many games, you have a lot of things go right," Bruce Douglas said. "For the first time in sixty-five games, we had some things go wrong against Mendel. I recall missing a one-and-one, I remember Dennis grabbing the ball and losing it between his legs out-of-bounds, setting up their last shot."

After Hampton's shot, Quincy set up a play that it had practiced many times, one of Leggett's favorites. Bruce tipped an alley-oop pass, but it rolled off the rim. They executed the same play to beat Chicago Marshall 62–61 for third place.

"One of the good things about winning is you understand losing," Bruce Douglas said. "Winning is an attitude and a character. You don't know a winner until you see him lose."

Devastated by their loss in the afternoon semifinal, the Blue Devils were going through the motions in the consolation game. They trailed Marshall by ten points with three minutes to play when Leggett called a time-out.

Bruce Douglas, now a minister, delivered the sermon. "We're not going out like this," he told his teammates. "We put our hands together and looked at each other," he said. "We played the last three minutes on heart. Everything had to go right and we had to have a miracle to win the game."

Leggett was succeeded by Loren Wallace, who had produced winning teams at Lincoln and Bloomington before coming to Quincy in 1990. In thirty-two years he won 671 games. He was the youngest coach to win six hundred games and the only coach to have thirty-one consecutive winning seasons. His 1998 team finished third in the state.

"You couldn't coach in Illinois and not know about the Quincy tradition," he said. "I knew there was a lot of pressure to win here. I was replacing Jerry Leggett, and I knew it would be a problem after what he had done. But I was at Lincoln after Duncan Reid left with a 30–1 record and a number one ranking."

Coaching at Quincy is unlike anywhere else. Basketball is a social event, the only game in town in the winter. Two television stations and two radio stations cover the team. It is a college atmosphere at the high school level.

"Eight years ago, at a meeting of all faculty members of the Quincy public schools, the superintendent said that no one had to worry about losing his job—except that man," said Wallace. "And he pointed to me. If he loses, he said, he'll be gone tomorrow."

Lawrenceville: 68–0

Because of his well-documented off-the-court shenanigans, Ron Felling was often characterized as a free spirit. It wasn't an exaggeration. His boyhood idol was Hot Rod Hundley. A sign in his office described his lifestyle: "To hell with conformity."

Felling was known as a partygoer, womanizer, drinker, and carouser. He reveled in his reputation as a lady's man. When the community sponsored a roast in his honor, he mooned the mayor and the crowd.

A role model he wasn't, but he was a great coach, and that's all he really cared to be. In sixteen years at Lawrenceville, he won 83 percent (388–77) of his games and four state championships, set a state record of sixty-eight victories in a row, and produced such outstanding players as Marty Simmons, Jay and Dennis Shidler, Doug Novsek, Rick Leighty, and David Brooks.

"I was a renegade, a crazy guy. A lot of people didn't understand me. I couldn't play for me," Felling said. "But after all the crazy things I had done, all I wanted to do was make a name for myself.

"I felt people didn't have a lot of respect for me. I wanted to do something that no one else had ever done. I wanted it written on my tombstone: 'If you messed with him on the basketball court, he would beat your ass.' Today, when people think of Lawrenceville, they think of the basketball program."

And they think of Felling.

"He is one of the great names and coaches in Illinois high school basketball history," said former Thornridge coach Ron Ferguson. "He could coach and motivate players as well as anyone I ever knew. Players loved him and wanted to play for him. He made basketball fun to play."

His reputation as a free spirit preceded him. At one time, he could have picked any high school coaching position he wanted. School officials from all over the state wondered how they could lure Felling away from Lawrenceville. But they backed off when they learned of his extracurricular activities.

"The shame is he never was a head coach at the college level," Dennis Shidler said. "He would have been a great college coach. What was special about him was he could relate to all types of kids and get the most out of each one.

"He could scream and make you feel the size of an ant, then turn around and put his arm around you and make you feel like a giant. Kids understood it. But some administrators, faculty, and parents didn't want to understand it. But he got results."

"He is the best teacher of the game that I have ever been around," said Novsek, who has coached at four Division I colleges. "Twenty years later, I say things and do things with kids that he did with me, and it works. There were days when you hated him, but you knew he knew what the game was about."

"He was the best high school coach in state history. His record speaks for itself," said Simmons, who later played at Indiana and Evansville and now is head coach at Southern Illinois University at Edwardsville. "He was a great motivator, a great bench coach, a great teacher, a great shooting coach, so fundamentally sound."

Simmons, who led Lawrenceville to 34–0 records in 1982 and 1983, was Illinois's Mr. Basketball in 1983, and was the number five scorer (2,986 points) in state history, said that there were days when he came home from practice and told his father that he didn't want to play anymore, that Felling was unfair, too tough.

"My father said to get my ass up to the IGA, file an application, and help at home. That was the last thing I wanted to do," Simmons said. "Felling challenged me over and over again. You don't like it when it is going on, but that is what made me a good player. That's what competition is all about, how you react when you are challenged."

Born in Terre Haute, Indiana, Felling attended a small country school with a graduating class of twenty-seven students. He was kicked off the basketball team at Indiana State after attempting a hook shot at the free-throw line during a game. He arrived in Lawrenceville in 1963 and became head coach in 1967.

Lawrenceville, on the Illinois/Indiana border about ten miles west of Vincennes, Indiana, was a town of fifty-seven hundred before the Texaco Oil Refinery closed. "There was nothing to do but play basketball and watch the stoplights change," Felling said.

A basketball tradition already had been established. Joe Fearheiley had taken three teams to the Sweet Sixteen in the 1950s, and Felling's predecessor, Ken Pritchett, had produced Sweet Sixteen qualifiers in 1965 and 1966. Old-timers remembered Jim Wright, Larry Breyfogle, Al Gosnell, Bob Montgomery, Al Rudesil, and Mike and Greg Ritchie.

Felling wanted to be even better. He built a system and put his indelible stamp on it. Fifth graders ran the same offense as the varsity. They shot the ball like Leighty, Shidler, Simmons, Novsek, and Brooks. "I need your minds, not your bodies," he told his players.

"I just set out to be the best basketball coach I could be, and I knew shooting was the most important aspect of the game," Felling said. "It doesn't take a genius to watch Jerry West shoot a jump shot. Proper technique is important. It starts with balance and footwork. You can't build a house if the foundation is out of whack."

Felling put a swagger in the program. "He was the most charismatic, hard-working, attention-to-detail, intense individual I have ever encountered," Dennis Shidler said.

Looking back, Felling thinks that he could have won six or seven state championships. He settled for four titles (1972, 1974, 1982, and 1983) and a third-place finish (1976). Only one other coach, East St. Louis Lincoln's Bennie Lewis, has won four state titles.

Ironically, Felling was opposed to the two-class system that was introduced in 1972. But nobody benefited more than him. He doubts that his 1972 and 1974 teams could have contended with larger schools such as Thornridge or Proviso East. He wonders if Jay Shidler would have become a rock star with only one class.

But he thinks that his 1982 and 1983 powerhouses could have won under any circumstances. "You have a chance to do something that you can tell your grandkids about," he told his players.

"You wanted your team picture to be on the wall like the 1972 and 1974 teams," Novsek said. "As a player, you'd see the jerseys of Dennis and Jay Shidler on the wall and want your jersey to be there, too."

Felling had Simmons and Novsek, but he needed a point guard, a floor leader. Jeff Gher had broken a hand and didn't play much as a sophomore. He had decided not to play as a junior, but when Felling handed him the ball, he was hooked.

"That's when I knew we were going to be good," Simmons said. "He was the missing link, the guy who turns good teams into great teams. He and Felling weren't on best of terms, but Felling had no ego in that circumstance. He knew he needed Gher if he was going to win the state title."

The 1981–82 team averaged 78.8 points, while its opponents were limited to 56.6. Simmons averaged twenty-five points per game, Novsek 24.5. Novsek finished with 2,193 points in his career.

In the quarterfinals, Novsek scored twenty-five and Simmons had twenty-three as Lawrenceville ousted Benton 75–62. In the semifinals, they barely got past Herscher and 6' 9" Scott Meents, as Simmons made a last-second basket to force overtime and Novsek converted a free throw to produce a 47–45 victory. In the final, in a duel of the state's two top-rated teams, Lawrenceville beat Monmouth 67–53, as Simmons scored twenty-one and Novsek scored twenty.

The 1982–83 team was led by Simmons, a 6' 5", 230-pounder who was nicknamed "the Mule" and "Moby Dick" and "Great White Whale" by Felling for his stubbornness and overwhelming presence around the boards. He scored 1,087 points, an average of 31.9 per game. The team averaged seventy-nine points, its opponents fifty-two.

"He didn't have great height or great speed or great athleticism, but he had a sense of how to play," Felling said. "He had something pushing him that a lot of guys don't have. He was wanting to learn and wanting to be good."

Lawrenceville had its toughest test in the state quarterfinals against a Chicago Providence–St. Mel team that would win the Class A title in 1985. The Indians broke to a 16–4 lead, but St. Mel rallied behind Lowell Hamilton and Michael Parker. Lawrenceville won 56–54, as Simmons scored all of his team's twenty-three points in the second half.

In the final, in a matchup of the state's two top-rated teams for the second year in a row, Simmons had twenty points and ten rebounds as Lawrenceville beat Flanagan and seven-foot Bill Braksick 44–39 to complete an unprecedented 68–0 sweep.

"In the hotel room before the last game, Felling was sick as a dog, taking penicillin. There was a lot of emotion, tears in his eyes," Simmons recalled. "I will remember the scene until I die. It is what makes Lawrenceville special. He reminded us of where we were at, our last game, what the game meant, what we meant to him. He told us that teams with the best talent and the best coach don't always win. But he said we had a burning desire to win and compete. That is what separated us from other teams. We knew what we were going after. We wouldn't have been satisfied with anything less than 68–0."

Mount Carmel: One of a Kind

Chicago's Mount Carmel High School has a rich football tradition that dates to the 1920s. Donovan McNabb, Simeon Rice, Tony Furjanic, Chris Calloway, Nate Turner, Terry Brennan, Mel Brosseau, Ziggy Czarobski, Frank Pinn, Dan Shannon, and Elmer Angsman played there. Coach Frank Lenti has produced nine state championship teams since 1988 and has won 88 percent (222–30) of his games in nineteen years.

That's not all. Chris Chelios, one of the best defensemen in the history of the National Hockey League, got plenty of ice time at Mount Carmel. And coach Bill Weick built one of the strongest wrestling programs in the state.

Basketball? Mount Carmel won three Chicago Catholic League titles in the 1940s and beat Marshall for the city championship in 1965. The sport didn't command a lot of space in the school yearbook, even less in the minds of the students.

"Kids came to Mount Carmel to play football, not to play basketball," said Ed McQuillan, who coached basketball from 1978 to 1988. "Hockey was bigger than basketball. What was the attitude toward basketball? It clearly was a football school."

"When I went there, I saw all the football trophies," said James Farr. "The coach talked to me about basketball players who had played there—Bob Frasor, Lloyd Walton, Greg Carney, Craig Robinson. I thought there is some basketball interest there. But my friends wondered why I was going there."

Melvin McCants wondered, too. As an eighth grader, he and Lowell Hamilton were touted as the best basketball players on the West Side, but he loved baseball. He wanted to be the next Richie Zisk. He chose Mount Carmel over basketball powers Simeon and Crane because he wanted to get away from his neighborhood.

"Mount Carmel was a football school. Basketball wasn't a big sport there. At that point, I wasn't thinking about basketball very seriously," he said. "It was an academic thing. The first day I got there, I was shocked because it was an all-boys school. I told my mother I wanted to transfer. She said I was going there for an education, not for girls."

Chris Calloway knew it was an all-boys school, but he didn't know about the football tradition. He learned soon enough. The swift wide receiver played on one Prep Bowl champion, then played on three Big Ten championship teams and two Rose Bowl winners at Michigan and played in the NFL for eleven years.

"Due to my height [5' 10"] and size, I was better at football skill-wise. But I enjoyed basketball more than football," he said. "I took football to the basketball floor. I wasn't a great offensive player, so I made up for it with hustle and defense."

In 1984–85, McQuillan blended Farr, McCants, and Calloway with a pair of promising sophomores, Derek Boyd and Sam Smallwood, and produced the first private school champion (large schools) in the history of the state tournament. A week earlier, Chicago's Providence–St. Mel won the small-school crown.

"I felt it was a great challenge, coming from 55th Street," said McQuillan, a South Sider who graduated from St. Ignatius in 1961. "I admired the school's athletic tradition. It got Notre Dame–type notoriety. The Public League had more talent from year to year, but the Catholic League was highly disciplined with an emphasis on strong coaching and fundamentals."

McQuillan tried to promote Mount Carmel as "the place to play basketball." He ran grade school tournaments and invited all Catholic grammar schools to participate. Public grammar schools came, too. He outrecruited De La Salle for McCants. He thought that Farr could develop into a good player when others dismissed the 5' 9" youngster.

In 1983–84, the Caravan was 24–5 but lost to Thornton in the sectional. McCants was the only junior starter. McQuillan saw potential for the future, but he reminded McCants and Farr that they had to demonstrate more maturity and leadership.

In preparing for 1984–85, McQuillan knew that he had to persuade Farr to accept the role of floor leader if the team was going to be successful. But he conceded that there were at least four other Catholic League schools that might be better. "I didn't expect us to win the state title," McCants said. "I knew we were good, but I didn't think we were that good."

It took a while to get untracked. Mount Carmel started 1–2 in the Catholic League and finished third with a 10–3 record. In late January, however, the Caravan crushed Providence–St. Mel 61–39, as the 6' 8", 220-pound McCants had twenty points and ten rebounds and outplayed Lowell Hamilton.

"At that point, we felt we could beat anyone," McQuillan said.

Mount Carmel won its last eighteen games in a row, including victories over St. Rita (by ten) and Leo (by twenty-five) in the regional to avenge earlier setbacks.

"We were on a mission," Farr said. "When we beat Leo in the regional final, that was when I knew we had a chance to win state. Leo had won the Catholic League title with Randy Doss, Tyrone Dowd, and Chris Henderson. They were ranked number seven in the state, but we destroyed them."

In the supersectional, the Caravan snapped Leyden's sixteen-game winning streak 37–34. Earlier, Leyden had upset top-ranked Proviso West in the sectional final. McCants had sixteen points and nine rebounds, Farr scored eleven, and Smallwood had no points but ten rebounds. Leyden star Mike Griffin (seventeen points, twelve rebounds) fouled out with 1:33 to play and his team trailing 33–30. "It was the biggest victory in school history," McQuillan said of the Leyden game.

Hardly anyone recalls the 56–43 quarterfinal victory over Hersey and the 60–51 semifinal win over Cahokia, but everyone has vivid memories of the 46–44 double-overtime victory over Springfield Lanphier for the state title.

Lanphier had beaten second-ranked Chicago Simeon, the defending state champion, by four in the quarterfinals to emerge as the tournament favorite. Ed Horton, the Lions' 6' 8" center, was Illinois's Mr. Basketball. As a sophomore, he had played a key role in Lanphier's drive to the 1983 state championship.

"We had to stop Horton, but we felt McCants could handle him. We weren't in awe of him," McQuillan said. His strategy was to go to McCants early and try to get Horton in foul trouble. Instead, McCants got into early foul trouble. He was sidelined for thir-teen-and-a-half minutes, took only four shots, and was limited to four points.

"I felt I had to put the team on my back and keep us in the game until Melvin came back," said Farr, who scored a season high thirty points on eight-of-fourteen shooting and fourteen-of-fifteen free throws. "I was driving, trying to get to the bas-ket, trying to take every opportunity I could to score."

"James played the best game I ever say him play," McCants said. "He won the game for us."

Mount Carmel led 38–30, but Lanphier tied at forty-four as Horton scored eleven in the fourth quarter. Then Lanphier slowed the tempo, and Mount Carmel didn't get a shot in the last three minutes. Lanphier played for a last shot, but Horton missed, and McCants blocked Wali Abdul-Rahim's shot.

In the first overtime, Lanphier played for a last shot, but William Horton, Ed's brother, missed. McCants and Smallwood combined to hold Ed Horton without a basket for twenty-and-a-half minutes.

In the second overtime, Lanphier again played for a last shot with 1:31 remaining. Willie Grier missed, and McCants rebounded with six seconds left. With two seconds left, a floor-length pass to McCants was deflected out-of-bounds by Ed Horton, set-ting up the final play.

Calloway inbounded the ball. The other players set up in a straight line: Farr, McCants, Boyd, Smallwood. Farr was the first option. He popped out to the corner but was covered. The second option was McCants going to the hoop for a lob, but he was covered, too. Then Boyd stepped up. He was all alone.

"He wasn't supposed to take the last shot," McQuillan said. "He was one for ten at that point. We told Boyd to go for the ball, and when [Horton] got off McCants and went to him, then Calloway would lob to McCants for a ten-footer. But Boyd was so wide open that Calloway gave him the ball. Later, he apologized to me for not do-ing what I said to do."

Boyd made a left-handed ten-foot jumper from the baseline to win one of the most exciting games in state history.

"I had to make up for not shooting well through the whole game," Boyd said. "The play was designed to go to me. I wasn't surprised. In the huddle, when the coach called the play, I knew it was designed for me."

McQuillan shook his head. He said McCants was the first option, then Farr or Boyd. "We've never run that play all year," he said.

"It was very nerve-wracking," Calloway said. "I didn't want to make a turnover that would turn the game around. The play was to McCants, but he was covered. Then the play was to Farr, who was covered. I was hoping someone would get open. I saw Boyd flash to my left, off a pick on the baseline."

"I don't think we got much respect," Farr said. "People thought we were a fluke. Even to this day, some of my friends kid me about going Downstate. They always will think that Mount Carmel is a football school."

Springfield: Bragging Rights

Bob Nika grew up in what was popularly and derisively known as the North End of Springfield, three blocks south of Lanphier High School. It was a rural atmosphere, hardly the Beverly Hills of Sangamon County, which was how Springfield High was perceived.

"I was proud to be a North Ender," said Nika, a 1955 Lanphier graduate who coached his alma mater to a state championship in 1983 and seconds in 1977 and 1985.

"I always thought Springfield was a good team, and one day we'd kick their butts. There was a fierce rivalry in the 1940s and 1950s because of economics. The perception was they were rich and had inflated grades and Lanphier was poor, a blue-collar school. We thought they looked down on us. We were envious of them. They had it, we didn't, we wanted it."

"Springfield thought they were better. We didn't like them," former Lanphier star Kevin Gamble recalled. "They were homeowners, we were renters."

"We didn't know the history of Springfield basketball," former Lanphier star Ed Horton said. "We were kids and hungry to play. We knew about Nika and [Arlyn] Lober. We looked forward to the city tournament at the Armory in January. That was for bragging rights. It was North versus South. It was very competitive."

Springfield had a tradition with coaches Mark Peterman and Ray Page and great players such as Tom Cole, Bob Trumpy, and Dave Robisch. Peterman, who won 532 games in his career, coached the Senators to the 1935 state championship, while Page produced a state champion in 1959.

Lanphier's first graduating class was in 1937. The school won its first city tournament in 1953. "It was bigger than winning the state—until you got to state," Nika said.

"Other than summer basketball, we didn't know Springfield kids. If you went south of Jefferson Street, you were in a different country. It was like the Mason-Dixon Line. Kids didn't hang out together. In those days, we didn't have anything in common. It was all economics. They were doctors and lawyers, and we were truck drivers and janitors."

Lanphier began to gain a measure of respect—on the basketball court, at least—when Lober, who won 423 games in his career, took three teams to the Elite Eight in the 1960s. The breakthrough came in 1963 when Calvin Pettit and Mike Rodgerson led the Lions to a 29–5 record and third place in state.

Springfield started to take notice. Lanphier became the city's dominant program under Nika, who had played and coached under Lober. In 2002, Craig Patton coached Lanphier to second place in the Class AA tournament. Meanwhile, Springfield has qualified for the Sweet Sixteen only once since 1967.

But Springfield had an image: it had Ray Page. In six years, he took six teams to the Sweet Sixteen, a milestone he shared with Pinckneyville's Duster Thomas. With no more worlds to conquer in basketball, he ran for public office. For eight years, he served as Illinois's superintendent of public instruction.

"He was a wonderful guy, a master psychologist," said Tom Cole, an All-Stater on Page's 1959 state championship team. "He was like a father to everyone on the team. He didn't treat everyone equally, but he would give you a kick if you needed it. He had an aura about him. He was the boss. I had more fun playing for him than in college."

Old-timers still recall the "measles incident" that probably had more to do with developing the 1959 champions than any scrimmage or game plan. There was a measles epidemic in Springfield, so Page sent his players home. Then he decided to conduct practice the next day.

"I called Cole's house. He was the captain. But he was at his girlfriend's house," Page recalled. "I didn't want them to go anywhere but home or church, not to the theater or anywhere else because they might sit next to someone who had the flu or measles and put them out of the tournament."

Page called Lynn Neff. He wasn't home. Neither were Jim Wienties or George Mathis. He called Cole's father. "Tell Tom to tell the other players that if the game doesn't mean more to them than this, I won't spend Sunday at practice," he said.

On Sunday morning, the entire squad showed up at Page's house. "He said he was so disappointed. He said he might stop coaching. Tears were running down his cheeks," Cole said.

The players apologized and said they wanted to practice. Page ran them ragged for an hour and a half. "It was a psychological approach to make them work out of a situation that they had gotten themselves into," he said.

Trumpy played for Page for two years. He was an All-Stater in 1962 and 1963. One of the outstanding multisport athletes in state history, he also was an All-State end in football and a state long jump champion in track and field. He chose the University of Illinois for football, then played ten years for Paul Brown and the Cincinnati Bengals in the NFL.

But he never forgot his roots. "If you won the city tournament, it was for bragging rights," Trumpy said. "You might win the state title, but it was more important to win the city tournament, more important than winning the conference title."

Robisch came to Springfield as a sophomore in 1965, when his father enrolled at Concordia Seminary. Why Springfield High instead of Lanphier? Robisch said that his father "looked around town and determined that Springfield was best for his son."

As a 6' 7" junior, Robisch averaged 23.5 points. As a 6' 9" senior, he averaged thirty-one and led his team to a 30–4 record and third in the 1967 state tournament. He set tournament records with 152 points and seventy-seven rebounds. He scored forty-seven versus Quincy, forty-one versus Pekin, and thirty-nine versus West Rockford.

"It was a good decision to go to Springfield High," said Robisch, who later played on a Kansas team that lost to UCLA in the Final Four and played for thirteen years in the NBA and ABA. "The city tournament was *the* moment in basketball during the season. There was pride in where you went to school."

By the time Robisch left town, the balance of power had begun to swing toward

Lanphier. Lober's 1971 team, led by Jim Kopatz, finished fourth in state. After he retired in 1974, Nika was promoted. His 1977 team, behind Tim Hulett and Mike Watson, was 28–5 and lost to Peoria Central 72–62 in the state final.

"We were super overachievers," Nika said. "We were unranked in the state poll and not favored to win the regional. We were behind 19–2 in the quarterfinal [against New Trier] and 17–4 in the semifinal [against Chicago De La Salle]. We were down by three with 1:13 left in the state final, then ran out of gas. We had great chemistry but no All-Staters. The most amazing thing of all was getting to the state final."

The 1982–83 team was special, and everybody knew it. Kevin Gamble, a 6' 7" senior, was an All-Stater. He later played at Iowa and in the NBA. Ed Horton, a 6' 7" sophomore, was Illinois's Mr. Basketball in 1985. He also played at Iowa, in the NBA, and overseas.

The keys to success, however, were guard Moose Nika, the coach's son, who averaged eighteen points during the state tournament while opponents sagged on Gamble and Horton, and the coach's decision (when the team was 13–0) to bench point guard Mark Alsteadt and insert Clarence Briggity into the starting lineup.

"Briggity was a good ballhandler, a bulldog who wouldn't let anyone take the ball away from him," Gamble said. "And we knew we'd have to play half-court in the state tournament."

Lanphier wasn't ranked at the end of the regular season, having lost to Decatur MacArthur in a conference matchup and to Urbana and Morton in the Pekin Tournament. But they beat Lockport 46–45 in the supersectional on Leslie Lee's seventeen footer with one second left. The Lions edged Thornton 54–52 in the semifinals and dispatched Peoria Central 57–53 in the state final, after blowing an eight-point halftime lead. Gamble scored nineteen points, Horton eighteen.

"It taught me how to be a winner," said Gamble, who now is head basketball coach at the University of Illinois at Springfield (formerly Sangamon State). "When you do something that no one has ever done, it can't be taken away from you. We were so close as a group, 1983 at Lanphier and 1987 at Iowa, even more than the NBA."

"We put Springfield back on the map," said Horton, who is Gamble's assistant at Illinois-Springfield. "Winning in 1983 was more satisfying than winning the Mr. Basketball trophy. We had bragging rights for the next ten years."

Horton was back in 1984–85, but his supporting cast was lacking. Wali Abdul-Rahim was a scoring threat, but Nika felt better when Pat McGuire and Paul Piphus were handling the ball. However, Piphus sprained an ankle with eight seconds left in the semifinal and couldn't play in the final.

Mount Carmel won 46–44 in double overtime on Derek Boyd's basket at the buzzer. James Farr paced the Caravan with thirty points. He converted fourteen of fifteen free throws.

"If we had Piphus, we would have won by ten to twelve points," Nika said. "No one could guard Farr. We played four different kids on him. Piphus was our best defender. He could have stabilized Farr and run our offense. But he said he couldn't play.

"I went numb when Boyd made that shot. It was a terrible feeling. He was the only guy to throw to, the screen man, and he was open."

Ben Wilson: Too Young to Die

It was one of the largest funerals in Chicago's history. A former mayor stood in line for hours to view the casket. The Reverend Jesse Jackson delivered the eulogy. Members of the board of education attended, and so did businessmen and community leaders, all to pay respects to a seventeen-year-old basketball player.

Ben Wilson was more than a promising athlete. In two years, he had gone from the last man on a sixteen-member frosh-soph squad to the top-rated prospect in the United States. And he had touched the hearts and minds of thousands of teenagers.

Then he was dead, the victim of an assassin's bullet, a mindless act. On the eve of the opening game of the 1984–85 season, eight months after he had led Simeon to the state championship, he was shot by a gangbanger who picked him out of a crowd because he was taller than everyone else.

"When you look back on what happened to him so fast, you must have known it was his destiny for things to end so quickly," Simeon coach Bob Hambric said.

Nearly twenty years after the tragic event, Hambric still is haunted by those circumstances. On the dates of his birthday (March 20) or the anniversary of his death (November 21), people bring it up. His mother wrote a book, *Benji with Love*. It was only four chapters long; three were devoted to her son's death.

Basketball fans still argue over which college Wilson would have chosen: Illinois or DePaul? Coaches Lou Henson of Illinois and Joey Meyer of DePaul attended the funeral, but Hambric cautions not to rule out Indiana, pointing out that coach Bob Knight made a rare visit to personally recruit Wilson.

"People still ask those questions," Hambric said. "I know which school he was going to attend, but I won't divulge it. I say let him rest in peace."

Tim Bankston was the reason that Wilson enrolled at Simeon. They played basketball at Chatham YMCA. They hung out together when Bankston was a seventh grader and Wilson was a sixth grader.

At the time, Bob Hambric was supervising a biddy basketball program at Chatham YMCA. He said that he never had any intention of coaching at the high school level. But in a quirk of fate, he agreed to do a favor for Simeon athletic director John Everett, whose son was involved in Hambric's biddy basketball program.

"Everett asked me to try to help build the program at Simeon," Hambric recalled. "I came for two weeks [in 1974] and have been here for twenty-seven years. But I didn't have any aspirations to be a varsity coach."

In January 1980, after a series of disciplinary problems and charges that the program was out of control, school officials offered the job to Hambric. In twenty-three years he has 528 victories and has won 80 percent of his games, one state championship, and three Chicago Public League titles.

"You have to want to go to school, conduct yourself in a certain fashion, and look a certain way," he said. "Folks who know basketball know there was a new wind that blew in in 1984 that changed basketball in the Public League forever.

"Simeon had a real impact on the style of basketball that is being played today. We were one of the first that could play either style, up-tempo or slow or pattern. We showed that Chicago teams were not just ripping and running down the floor, that we had direction to what we were doing and had discipline."

Bankston, Rodney Hull, Bobby Tribble, and Kenny Allen arrived at Simeon at the same time. That same year, Hambric became varsity coach. His first team, led by Andre Battle, Tony McCoy, and Marcus Alderson, went 28–1 and lost to Westinghouse in the semifinals of the Public League playoff.

"That was the starting point, when people started to talk about Simeon," said Hull, who later played on a Final Four team at Kansas. "It was the beginning of something big."

It took awhile for Hambric and his assistants, George Stanton and Bill Alderson, to put the program together. Bankston didn't play as a freshman. A self-confessed "knucklehead," he often skipped class. Tribble came to Simeon to play baseball, his favorite sport. He didn't join the basketball team until his sophomore year. Hull planned to enroll at Dunbar or Lindblom. After visiting Simeon, however, he changed his mind.

Hambric wasn't a player's coach. He was all business, no nonsense. If the players wanted to have fun, they joked around with assistant Bill Alderson, not Hambric. He checked egos at the door. His players had to be unselfish, disciplined, and in shape. He wouldn't tolerate anything less.

"Some of his best players are walking the hallways," Bankston said. "Everyone can't play for him. He didn't treat anyone like a star, not even Ben Wilson. His favorite saying was: 'I am the star maker.' You had to be committed."

They practiced six days a week, no exemptions. They practiced in the summer, no excuses. College coaches were told not to bother his players during the season, no exceptions. When Iowa tried to recruit Deon Thomas, the state's Mr. Basketball in 1989, Hambric banned them from the school.

Hambric's players thought he was running a Marine boot camp. Later, they realized he was teaching them how to play the game and how to be a student of the game. He is proud that six of his former players are coaching high school basketball.

Ben Wilson arrived at Simeon with little fanfare. He was skinny and only six feet tall. As a freshman, he was the last man on a sixteen-man roster. He played sparingly. His teammates remember that he was very cheerful, eager to play, and that he ate a lot. "We didn't sense he had great talent or potential," Hull said.

But he never stopped working to improve his skills. He lived near the Chatham YMCA and worked out every day, constantly bugging Hambric to help him get better. He and Bankston played one-on-one until midnight at Perry Park on 85th and Cottage Grove. Later, they played against Mark Aguirre, Rickey Green, J. J. Anderson, and other professionals at St. Ashlem's gym.

When Wilson showed up as a sophomore, he had grown three inches, and Hambric promoted him to the varsity. "He wanted to improve," Hambric said. "Whatever you showed him, he would work on it until he mastered it. Then he would come back for more, to learn something else."

It all came together in 1984. After losing to Collins in the quarterfinals of the Public League playoff in 1983, the entire squad returned and laid the groundwork for a successful season by winning the John McLendon summer league tournament.

Kenny Allen was the glue. He scored only five points in the state finals but did all the little things—rebounding, setting picks, defending, taking offensive fouls, and providing leadership. At 6' 9", Laurent Crawford was a good player, but he was disruptive. When he transferred to King, Hull moved into the pivot, Allen was installed at power forward, and everything fell into place.

From the outset, it figured as a Simeon versus Robeson duel for the city championship. Robeson had beaten Simeon in 1983, but Simeon had prevailed in the summer, on Thanksgiving, and in the final of the Mayor's Christmas Tournament. At the end of the regular season, Simeon was 23–1 and ranked number five in the state. Robeson was 23–3 and rated number seven.

In the city playoff, Simeon beat Carver and Tim Hardaway for the fourth time. In the championship, the Wolverines edged Robeson 44–42. With two seconds left, Bankston stole the ball and passed to Tribble, who completed a three-point play.

Downstate, Simeon didn't overwhelm any opponent, but the Wolverines played with intelligence, patience, and poise. They dispatched Rock Island 48–44 and third-rated West Aurora 67–48 and spoiled top-ranked Evanston's bid for an unbeaten season 53–47 in the championship. Bankston had twenty-five points and twelve rebounds, while Tribble scored fifteen points, and Hull blocked seven shots.

After the season, Wilson was invited to the Nike All-America Camp, where he was designated as the number-one junior in the nation. He wasn't just a tall kid who played around the basket but a mobile 6' 8" version of Magic Johnson who could shoot, rebound, pass, handle the ball, and play any position. "Folks were amazed at his ability," Hambric said. "In those days, 6' 8" kids who could do what he could do were still a rarity."

On an unseasonably warm day in November, as the team was preparing to depart for the Thanksgiving tournament in Rockford, Wilson and his girlfriend took a stroll to the corner store, a block away from the school, during the noon break.

Ironically, Hambric and Wilson had a habit of eating lunch together every day—except for that day.

Two gangbangers were on the school grounds to do some personal business with other Simeon students. They went into the store to look for them. Outside, they approached Wilson and tried to pick a fight. They ordered Wilson to walk around them. When Wilson ignored them, one pulled out a pistol and shot him.

"Someone ran to tell me that Ben had been shot. I thought they were kidding," Hambric said. "He was laying against a fence next to a house when I got there."

"I'll always wonder how good he could have been," Bankston said. "Some people talk about Kevin Garnett. I think Ben would have been better."

King: The Landon Cox Era

No one stirred up more controversy and won more games in such a short period of time than King coach Landon "Sonny" Cox. Love him or hate him, you had to admit that he never was boring.

In twenty years, Cox won 85 percent (503–89) of his games. He won state championships in 1986, 1990, and 1993, was second in 1987, and third in 1989 and 1999. He played for the Chicago Public League title eight times in nine years, winning five. He boasts the highest winning percentage in state history.

Cox produced some of the most celebrated players of the 1980s and 1990s—Efrem Winters, Marcus Liberty, Levertis Robinson, Jamie Brandon, Johnny Selvie, Rashard Griffith, Thomas Hamilton, Michael Hermon, Imari Sawyer, and Leon Smith.

Controversy? Cox was routinely accused of recruiting violations. He had to forfeit some games during one season for using an ineligible player. Public League coaches once threatened to boycott him. The IHSA investigated him. King's principal was demoted after a *Chicago Sun-Times* investigation revealed that Efrem Winters's grades had been changed to allow him to qualify for a college scholarship. In the book *Raw Recruits* by Alexander Wolff and Armen Keteyian, Cox was accused of accepting payoffs to deliver players to colleges. In all cases, Cox was never implicated in any wrongdoing.

"Once we started to win, kids wanted to play at King," Cox said. "At that time, King was a television school. As counselor, my job was to recruit kids who wanted to come to King to learn about television.

"It was okay, but when people began to talk about recruiting for basketball, it was a dirty word. When I did recruit them for television, I made sure they were 6' 4" and 6' 5". I got criticized, but it was within the rules."

Almost to a man, his players stand behind him. They credit him for teaching them fundamentals and teamwork, making them go to class, keeping them off the streets and out of gangs, and sending them to college.

"He taught me that whatever your goal is, you can achieve it if you work hard enough and put in the time," said Levertis Robinson, one of the stars of the 1986 state championship team who later played at Cincinnati.

"He was the best thing to happen to a lot of kids from the inner city," said Tracy Dildy, a 1985 graduate who was an assistant coach at Auburn. "He gave us something positive to focus on. I saw a man who cared about his players, what a father's role is. I couldn't understand why people criticized him."

Selvie was Cox's proudest achievement. He was twice accused of drug possession and had to wear a monitor on his wrist for thirteen months before being acquitted of all charges. Cox hired a lawyer to represent him and served as his guardian. "He got through things that few kids would overcome," Cox said.

"I was caught in the wrong place at the wrong time. They [the police] made an example out of me because of who I was at that time," said Selvie, an All-Stater on the 1990 state championship team. "It was the worst experience of my life. But I wanted to prove to everyone that I wasn't that kind of person. It pushed me harder and harder to get an education."

It took time, but his persistence paid off. He attended Trinity Valley Community College in Texas for three weeks, then came home. He sat out for a year, then enrolled at Eastern Utah University in Price for two years. Then he went to New Mexico State for two years. He played professionally in Spain for six months, earned his degree at New Mexico State in 1997, then returned to Chicago. He assisted Cox for four years, then was head coach at Lindblom for two years before becoming head coach at Bogan.

"King didn't have a good reputation," Selvie said. "People on the outside looking in didn't know what was going on. They were jealous about the basketball program and didn't want us to be successful. If it wasn't for what [Cox] did for me, I would be in the streets and be behind bars like everyone thought I would be. But he pushed me and motivated me to succeed."

Cox, born in Cincinnati, was into music before basketball. He dreamed of being the next Charlie Parker. He and the jazz great Joe Henderson came to Chicago in 1962. Henderson continued on to California to pursue his musical career while Cox opted to stay. He played music on the South Side, working seven nights a week and two matinees, but also got into teaching and coaching in the public school system to supplement his income.

When he was first approached about becoming head coach at King, he turned it down. "They had good teams but never won. I found out that except for three players, they were all thugs and gang members," Cox said.

Efrem Winters and Reggie Woodward begged him to take the job. Cox gave them a list of demands. When they agreed to follow his program to the letter, he accepted the job in 1982.

"At that time, Chicago basketball was helter-skelter," Cox said. "Except for [Harlan coach] Lee Umbles, I didn't see any direction that the city programs were going. [Simeon's] Bob Hambric had a plan, too. At Phillips, Herb Brown did a good job. They always looked two or three steps ahead of everyone else."

Cox had a plan. He attended clinics, installed a summer program, and put the 6' 8" Winters on a conditioning program. And he picked the brains of other city coaches whom he respected, coaches he wanted to beat.

"He had a swagger about him," Selvie said. "He liked to win. He wasn't a follower but a leader. He liked a lot of attention and dressed very professionally. He was the first coach I ever saw who wore suits every day. His players wanted to be like him . . . dress in expensive suits, drive a nice car, and wear a Rolex watch. He was a role model who did it legally."

Cox's 1982 team with Winters and Woodward lost to Vocational in the city quarterfinals. Dildy's teams lost to Marshall in the 1983 semifinals, to Simeon in the

1984 semifinals, and to Tilden in the first round in 1985. "It was part of the building process. But they got over the hump in 1986," he said.

"I remember the loss [to Tilden] as if it was yesterday," Robinson said. "We were 23–2 and ranked number three in the state. Simeon was ranked number two. Tilden had only one guy over six feet tall. We were overconfident. We were looking ahead to Simeon. We were determined to come back in 1986."

Robinson was the only returning starter. But Marcus Liberty, a junior, had transferred from Crane. Reggie "Cato" King was the point guard; Cox said that he was the best floor leader he had ever coached. David Weatherall was a rugged defender. Emmett Lynch and King formed a reliable pair in the backcourt. The Jaguars were 21–1 and ranked third in the state. Simeon was unbeaten and ranked number one in the nation.

In the city final, King beat Simeon 49–46 as Robinson and Weatherall took turns defending Nick Anderson, Illinois's Mr. Basketball. They beat Evanston by two in the quarterfinals, second-ranked Peoria Manual by seventeen in the semifinals, and Rich Central and Kendall Gill 47–40 in the final. Robinson held Gill to five points on two-of-fourteen shooting.

Liberty was Illinois's Mr. Basketball in 1987. Jamie Brandon and Johnny Selvie were promising but inexperienced freshmen. Liberty took an overachieving team as far as he could, putting on one of the most sensational performances in the history of the state tournament. He had forty-one points and fifteen rebounds in the state final, but King lost to powerful East St. Louis Lincoln and LaPhonso Ellis 79–62. In four games, he scored 143 points.

King dominated in 1990. The all-senior team was led by Brandon, who was Illinois's Mr. Basketball, Selvie, Fred Sculfield, Ahmad Shareef, and Damian Porter. Freshman Rashard Griffith came off the bench. Brandon finished as the number three scorer in state history with 3,157 points.

"He was doing things in high school that they are doing now in the NBA," Selvie said. "I believe he could have gone into the pros if they were drafting high school kids in 1990."

Brandon, Selvie, and company beat Westinghouse by thirty-five in the city final. They beat West Aurora by eight in the quarterfinals and ended East St. Louis Lincoln's bid for a fourth consecutive state title in the semifinals by eleven, then broke away in the second half to beat Gordon Tech and Tom Kleinschmidt 65–55 in the final to complete a 32–0 season. Brandon scored twenty-five, Selvie had seventeen points and eleven rebounds, and Kleinschmidt tallied twenty-seven.

Led by the twin towers, seven-foot Rashard Griffith and 7' 1" Thomas Hamilton, and guards Ronald Minter and DeWarren Stewart, King was even more dominant in 1993. They finished 32–0, crushing Westinghouse by twenty-five in the city final, Proviso East by twenty-eight in the quarterfinals, Danville and Keon Clark by thirty-one in the semifinals, and Rockford Guilford by thirty-six in the final.

Despite all of his success, however, Cox never enjoyed the respect of his peers. His swagger, bluster, arrogance, and razor-sharp tongue turned them off. That irritated him more than a probing sportswriter, an IHSA investigation, a nagging parent, or a college recruiter who refused to play by his rules.

"I got to the top of the mountain," he said. "I don't know if anyone will do all the things I have done in so short a time."

East St. Louis Lincoln: Four Titles in Eight Years

Bennie Lewis is retired now. He lives in a comfortable home on the East Side of East St. Louis. He loves to play pool and go fishing. And he loves to replay memories of more than thirty years in coaching, including four state championships.

Born in Jackson, Mississippi, Lewis came to East St. Louis as a first grader. He starred on Tree Harris's 27–1 team in 1957, then went to Langston University in Oklahoma and emerged as the school's all-time leading scorer. For four summers he was a waiter on a Chicago-to–Los Angeles train.

But pool and fishing came first. His mother used to take him fishing when he was young; he got hooked. Now he fishes for bass, crappies, blue gills, and catfish at Pinckneyville Lake.

He started to play pool at fifteen. He shined shoes at the Brown Bomber, a barber shop with a pool hall next door. "I could make more money if I worked in the pool hall on weekends," he said.

During the week, between games, Lewis used to play bank eight with friends at Garrett's in Madison or Poor Bob's in Eagle Park. Now he has a custom pool table in his family room, a gift for winning his last state championship in 1989.

Life is good, but despite winning four state titles, as many as Lawrenceville's Ron Felling and more than any other coach in state history, Lewis doesn't command much respect.

He had several obstacles to overcome. East St. Louis was a football power with coaches Wirt Downing, Fred Cameron, and Bob Shannon, who produced six state championship teams. Lincoln was treated like a stepchild. It used basketball to establish its own identity.

When close friends Todd Porter and Tyrone Jackson opted to enroll at Lincoln instead of East St. Louis, the school was known for its outstanding girls basketball and track teams, for Jackie Joyner (Kersee) and Tina Hutchinson. There was only one gym, and the boys had to practice after the girls.

After Porter and Jackson graduated, after LaPhonso Ellis, James Harris, Cuonzo Martin, Vincent Jackson, and Chris McKinney left, Lewis could reflect on a record of achievement. His teams qualified for the Sweet Sixteen eight times in eleven years.

"I get respect outside the area, but not here," Lewis said. "Outside the area, they say

I achieved a great thing. But here, they say the kids did it, not me. They say I had a good program, but you can't win anything without good players.

"But I've seen good players who didn't win, so someone has to coach them. I know what it takes to win. A high school coach doesn't have his choice of players, not like college or pro, but he must teach them how to think and how to win."

East St. Louis was a bustling town when Lewis was growing up. If you wanted a job, you could work at a packing house or Granite City Steel. Nobody was hungry. Then "the black troubles," as Lewis describes them, erupted in 1967. Businesses started to move out. People moved out, too. Leadership collapsed. Aldermen seized power from the mayor. Educators warned that the school system would prosper as long as there were two high schools, but Lincoln was closed in 1998.

"The bitterness never will go away," Lewis said. "Lincoln now is a middle school. The four state championship trophies are there. East St. Louis doesn't want anything to do with Lincoln. The rivalry was too intense."

Lewis won 497 games at Lincoln, then took Darius Miles and East St. Louis to the state quarterfinals in 1999 and third place in 2000 before retiring. He produced state champions in 1982, 1987, 1988, and 1989 and a third-place finisher in 1990.

Looking back, he said that his 1981–82 squad, led by Porter and Jackson, was his best. "The word was out among my critics that I couldn't win the big one. That hushed them up," Lewis said.

"Some said he was soft, but he wasn't," Porter said. "He wanted to win a state title, and I felt we could take him there. He knew the game, but he needed some talent."

Lewis was big on conditioning. His players ran up a hill to the freeway fifteen to twenty times a day. He practiced three hours daily. He didn't tolerate showboating or back talking. "You had to listen to me, not outsiders," Lewis said. "Anyone can draw up a play or set up a defense. But where do you find players to run it? You must teach your system and make the kids believe in it."

Porter and Jackson believed. So did Clarence Cannon, Edward Wilson, and Jimmy Ike. They were the nucleus of Lincoln's first Sweet Sixteen qualifier, the 1980 squad that finished 20–4 and lost to Effingham in the supersectional at Carbondale. "We made great progress," Lewis said. "Now we had to work harder to get to the Elite Eight."

In 1981, Lincoln was 19–3 and ranked ninth in the state after the regular season, but they were upset by East St. Louis in the regional final. More disappointment.

"We had to start all over again," Lewis said. "We worked out in the summer. I picked up guys to go to the gym. We had to learn how to win, not just to compete."

Before the 1981–82 season, Porter and Jackson sat down with the other seniors and said, "This is our year. We won't let it go past us like we did last year. It is our last year, our last chance to go to state."

Porter and Jackson were 6' 5", and Mark Dale was 6' 7". The guards, Darryl Morgan and Calvin Phiffer, were 6' 2". They had speed and athleticism. They only had to guard against overconfidence.

Lincoln was 24–1 and ranked behind unbeaten Quincy, the defending state champion, and Westchester St. Joseph at the end of the regular season. Their goal was to play Quincy, which had beaten them the previous year in a controversial game in which Quincy shot fifty-seven free throws to Lincoln's seven.

But it didn't happen. After beating Murphysboro and Arlington by fourteen-point margins, Lincoln slipped past Chicago Marshall and Joe Stiffend 57–54 in the semifinals. They watched on television in their hotel as Chicago's Mendel Catholic snapped Quincy's sixty-four-game winning streak 53–52 on Mike Hampton's shot in the other semifinal.

"That was the end of the world," Jackson said. "We wanted Quincy. In our minds, we had something to prove. But Coach put everything in perspective. He said it would have been great to play Quincy, but now we were going to play the better team."

In the final, Lincoln outlasted Mendel 56–50. Leading by two in the fourth quarter, Jackson, despite having four fouls, blocked Hampton's jumper, grabbed the ball, and preserved the victory. Porter had twenty-two points and ten rebounds, while Dale had twelve points and twelve rebounds.

In 1986–87, Lincoln was braced for another big season. LaPhonso Ellis, Chris Rodgers, and James Harris were returning from a 20–7 supersectional qualifier. The front line was overpowering, with 6' 9" Ellis, 6' 7" Rodgers, and 6' 8" Harris. The guards were Lawrence Bradford and Mark Chambers.

How good were they? Lewis thought they would go undefeated, but they lost to Lincoln (Illinois) in the final of the Collinsville tournament. In the sectional final, they beat Collinsville as Ellis grabbed a loose ball and scored the game-winning basket.

In the state quarterfinals, Lincoln trailed Oak Forest 24–6 in the first quarter and by twelve at halftime. "We never had heard of them. We were so overconfident. I called two time-outs in the first quarter," Lewis said. He went to a man-to-man defense in the third period, and Lincoln rallied to win by six.

In the semifinals, Lincoln beat Quincy 55–49, as Rodgers picked up the team when Ellis was triple-teamed. In the final, Lewis tried several defenses to contain King's Marcus Liberty. None worked. Liberty scored forty-one points, but Lincoln prevailed 79–62 as Ellis scored twenty-seven and Harris scored twenty-three.

With Ellis returning, Lewis expected a repeat in 1987–88. Cuonzo Martin was a promising sophomore, and Vincent Jackson was a talented junior. Lewis told 6' 7" Bryant Stevenson to rebound and pass, then go to his spot and take pressure off of Ellis.

Lincoln lost four games in the regular season but was dominating in the state finals, winning by margins of twenty-eight, twenty-four, seventeen, and eight points. They hoped to meet Chicago Simeon and Deon Thomas in the final, but Chicago St. Francis de Sales and Eric Anderson upset the Wolverines in overtime in the quarterfinals. In the final, Lincoln beat de Sales 60–52, as Ellis outscored Anderson 26–23 and Martin contributed twenty.

In 1988–89, Martin, Vincent Jackson, Chris McKinney, and Sharif Ford returned. Rico Sylvester added more punch in the backcourt. Lewis persuaded 6' 8" Ron Willis to play center.

Lincoln was a four-time loser in the regular season and wasn't expected to contend with Chicago King or Peoria Manual in the state finals. But they won two of the most exciting games in tournament history to claim their third title in a row.

In the quarterfinals, Lincoln beat East Aurora 72–70 as Martin stole the ball and threw to Ford, who tossed in a thirty-footer at the buzzer. In the final, Vincent Jackson scored the game-winning basket at the buzzer as Lincoln outlasted Peoria Central 59–57 in triple overtime.

"It was the most exciting game I ever coached, the best game I have ever seen or played in or coached in or been involved with," Lewis said. There wasn't anything else to be said.

Andy Kaufmann: Making a Point of His Own

Jacksonville was playing Chatham Glenwood, and Andy Kaufmann, who was on his way to becoming the second-leading scorer in state history with 3,160 points, wasn't into the game.

"He wasn't playing hard, just lackadaisical," Jacksonville coach Mel Roustio recalled. Roustio removed him from the game.

"You stink tonight," Roustio told him.

Kaufmann mumbled something.

"What did you say?" Roustio asked.

"I'm bored," Kaufmann said.

"Bored? How in the world can you be bored in this competitive situation?" Roustio said.

"Because I can get out there and score any time I want to," Kaufmann responded.

Fifteen years later, Roustio was recounting the incident. Here was a kid who led the state in scoring for three seasons in a row by averaging thirty-two points per game from 1984 through 1988, scored fifty points on three occasions, converted 90 percent of his free throws, and prided himself on his one-on-one skills.

"Think about it," Roustio said. "He wasn't being smart-alecky. He was sincere and honest. He was so confident in his ability. He was the type of kid that you said, 'If he doesn't get hit by a bus coming to the gym, he will score thirty-two points in the game.' You could count on it."

Kaufmann said that he was greedy. He wanted to score points. If he missed a free throw, he was upset because he knew it would take away from his point total. He described missing a free throw as a lack of professionalism. He converted more free throws (912) than any player in state history.

"My game was to score," he said. "I had dribbling skills, shooting skills, a quick first step, hand-to-eye coordination, maneuverability, timing, and strength. I wasn't scared of kids who were more athletic and taller than me."

He still holds several state records, including the most consecutive games scoring twenty points or more (seventy-three) and the most consecutive games scoring ten points or more (ninety-seven). Yet his name is rarely mentioned among the state's all-time greats.

Kaufmann was consumed with scoring points but not setting records. He wanted to play in college, but he never had a desire to play in the NBA. He knew who Chico Vaughn (the state's all-time scoring leader) was, but he wasn't driven to surpass Vaughn's career record.

As a sophomore in 1986, his Jacksonville team lost to Quincy by one point in the regional. As a senior in 1988, his team finished 25–4 but lost to Peoria Manual and David Booth 88–86 in the supersectional at Peoria.

"It was the worst game of my career," Kaufmann recalled. "I scored fourteen points. It was like playing in slow motion. I couldn't move. I felt like I was being pulled down by fifty-pound weights. I was used as a decoy for the first time. We were out of synch."

He lives in his parents' old house in Winchester. In the backyard is the 10' by 10' concrete slab that his father built, where he and his lifelong buddy Jimmy Evans, his brothers Kevin and Chad, and his cousin Tony Cox had played for years. After he completed his eligibility at the University of Illinois, he declined an offer to play overseas and said that he wasn't interested in playing for a CBA team in Texas because it was too far from home.

He chose Illinois over Iowa, Purdue, and Arizona because he wanted to play close to home. His grandfather had been captain of the Iowa basketball team of 1920, but Andy liked the Illinois campus and was particularly impressed with Dick Nagy, coach Lou Henson's chief assistant.

For the last several years, he has worked as a residential care worker for blind children at the Illinois School for the Visually Impaired in Jacksonville. He is into golf. He is an eight-handicapper. He named his daughter Annika, after Annika Sorenstam, the star of the LPGA tour.

Kaufmann's childhood had no room for golf, however. He loved to participate in football, basketball, and baseball, but his father persuaded him that to be an outstanding athlete, he had to specialize in one sport. If he played all year round, he could develop into a complete player. Why basketball? Because he only needed a ball and a hoop to polish his skills.

Kaufmann and Evans played on the Winchester Wolverines from fifth through eighth grade. They would pick up bottles of Mountain Dew, play on the concrete slab in the backyard or at the church near the square or on an asphalt surface on the playground. Then they'd dribble to the community park and play until dark on a concrete court. As eighth graders, they led their team to the state championship.

Andy had a passion for the game. In fourth and fifth grade, he read books by Pete Maravich. He wore out a pair of sneakers in three weeks, then had to tape the soles to hold them together. There were holes in the soles and rips in his socks. He ended up playing on his toes.

"He was as hard-nosed as they come," said Evans, who often traveled to Jacksonville to play with his old friend. "He was a great scorer. No one had a desire on offense like he did. He was unique. He minded his own business. Some people got the wrong impression that he was cocky or stuck-up. There was a lot of jealousy because he was so good. But he never changed."

Kaufmann was lured to Jacksonville, especially by the wooden court at the YMCA. He couldn't obtain a key to the gym in Winchester, but he could play against better competition, including Illinois College players, in Jacksonville.

Andy's father was born in Jacksonville. He had graduated from Jacksonville Routt in 1952. So the family moved to Jacksonville, and Andy attended Routt as a freshman. But he didn't enjoy it. He dominated practice but wasn't allowed to start on the varsity. In a junior varsity game, he had thirty-two points and sixteen rebounds in the first half. In the first half of a game at the Waverly Tournament, he had thirty-nine points and twenty-nine rebounds, then played only four minutes in the next game.

Routt was a football school; it had just won a state championship. So Andy decided to transfer to Jacksonville, which had a reputation as a basketball school. The team played in the twenty-five-hundred-seat Jacksonville Bowl, one of the best basketball arenas in the state. Built in 1954, it resembles Pinckneyville's Thomas Gym, which was opened two years earlier. Today, Kaufmann's number 34 jersey is on display. A large white banner with his name and number in bold red letters once hung from the ceiling, and his number is the only one ever retired by the school.

Kaufmann also opted to switch to Jacksonville High because of coach Mel Roustio, who had coached Andy in the Prairie State Games. "He was all basketball. He was charismatic. I wanted to be a part of his program," Andy said.

Roustio, who won 541 games at seven high schools in thirty-seven years before retiring in 2001, first saw Kaufmann in a junior high school game in Winchester. "He was head-and-shoulders above the players he was playing against," Roustio said. "He was a big boy among little boys. He had great ballhandling skills for a big kid. He had great confidence shooting the ball. Because of his physical prowess, he could do what he wanted to do."

Kaufmann broke all the stereotypes. He was a thick-legged, barrel-chested, 6' 5", 220-pound white kid who wasn't a very good leaper. He compensated in the trenches with his physical stature and his soft hands. He was a scorer, not a shooter. "I'm convinced that over three years there were excellent athletes who were assigned to guard him who thought they would stop him, but his massiveness and ball skills frustrated them," Roustio said. "He spent so many hours on ballhandling drills and perfecting the spin moves of a 5' 7" player."

Illini assistant Dick Nagy took a liking to Kaufmann. Many critics who thought that he was too slow, lacked athleticism, and couldn't jump were surprised at how successful he was at Illinois. As a junior, he averaged twenty-one points per game and was a second-team All–Big Ten selection.

To Andy, the biggest insult was losing a one-on-one match in a game of ten. He and Jimmy Evans played one-on-one with older kids and young adults all over town. It was a form of instant gratification. Friends said that he took it too seriously. If he lost, his pride took a big hit, but he mastered the art.

"I had one-on-one skills. No one on the Illinois team wanted to play me one-on-one," he said. "One-on-one is purely competitive. To be a great one-on-one player, you had to have a quick first step, body control, and good hand-and-eye coordination. If you don't have a quick first step, you're out of the game unless you have a fadeaway shot falling backward into the second row of the bleachers."

He hasn't picked up a basketball in a while. He prefers a Big Bertha driver. He enjoys his job, family, and friends.

"He had the talent to go to the pros," Jimmy Evans said. "But he didn't want to leave home. He had other priorities. He never thought about making big money in the pros. He had to satisfy himself. He is happy with his life."

East St. Louis Lincoln vs. Peoria Central: Triple Overtime

Peoria Central's Chuck Buescher realized the dream of every high school coach when his 2002–3 team won the Class AA championship. But he never will forget the disappointment of losing the 1989 title to East St. Louis Lincoln.

"I show the game once in a while to our team," Buescher said. "Maybe I'd watch it three hundred times if we had won. But I think I've only watched it five times in the last thirteen years.

"It was a great game. I had a great group of kids for four years. We were 32–0. To see them lose, it was hard. But it was one of the great games in the history of the state tournament. To be honest, I couldn't recall how many overtimes we played."

It took three overtimes, the most ever in a state final, for East St. Louis Lincoln to beat Peoria Central 59–57. Vincent Jackson scored the game-winning basket at the buzzer. It was Lincoln's third state title in a row. It was only Peoria Central's third loss in its last sixty-two games.

"It was the most exciting game I ever coached, the best game I've ever seen," Lincoln coach Bennie Lewis said.

"We could have played for two more days, and it still would be a two-point difference," Buescher said.

Lincoln star Cuonzo Martin, who later was an All-Big Ten player at Purdue and now is an assistant on coach Gene Keady's staff at Purdue, said that it was his best experience in basketball.

"There is nothing better than high schools fighting for a state title," Martin said. "We won the Big Ten title, but 1989 was more exciting. Even when you watch it on film today, it still is exhausting and fun."

At the end of the regular season, Peoria Central was 25–0 and ranked behind Chicago Simeon in the Associated Press's final poll. The Lions, who were 27–2 the previous season, were led by guard Chris Reynolds, 6' 7" Mike Hughes, and 6' 5" Charles White.

Lincoln was 21–4 and ranked seventh with three starters returning from its 1988 state championship team—Martin, Vincent Jackson, and Chris McKinney. Lewis added 6' 8" Ron Willis and guards Rico Sylvester, Marco Harris, and Sharif Ford to bolster the lineup.

Martin said that the 1988–89 team was better than the 1987–88 team that featured LaPhonso Ellis: "We had more overall talent. The 1988 team was bigger, but the 1989 team had better athletes. In the summer, we were in the gym every day playing against Ellis and the guys from the 1982 state championship team. We were ready to roll when the tournament came around."

Both teams survived quarterfinal scares. Peoria Central edged Bloom and Brandon Cole 62–61. Lincoln got past East Aurora 72–70 when Martin stole the ball with three seconds left and threw it to half-court to run out the clock (to force overtime), but Ford grabbed it and tossed in a thirty-footer at the buzzer.

In the final, Lincoln broke out to a 9–0 lead, but Peoria Central rallied for a 26–23 halftime advantage. Hughes had eleven points, but Peoria shot ten of twenty-four. Martin and Jackson each scored ten, but Lincoln shot nine of twenty-seven.

"When we got the early lead, we thought they weren't very good," Lewis said. "But they came back, and we knew it would be a dogfight."

"They zone, and we don't shoot well from the perimeter in this game," Buescher said. "We had a good shooting team, about 52 percent for the season. But we were twenty-three of sixty-two and made only two of twelve threes. And Hughes was zero of six on threes."

Peoria was limited to six points on three-of-fifteen shooting in the third quarter, and Lincoln forged ahead 37–32. Then Peoria turned up the defensive pressure and forced a tie at forty-six.

In the first overtime, Peoria led by two with 1:30 left when Buescher called for four corners. Reynolds attacked the basket and missed a layup as Ford blocked his shot. Reynolds fouled in frustration, then said something to referee Bill Vangel as he walked away and was charged with a technical foul.

"[The frustration foul] was the proper call, but he [Vangel] can't call a technical on Reynolds," Buescher said. "The referee can't decide the game, the players must do it. What did Reynolds say? I don't know. I never asked him. But he didn't cuss."

"I don't remember what I said," said Reynolds, now a minister and an assistant athletic director at Notre Dame. "I wasn't a person to cuss, not a person to use bad words. But in the heat of battle, I'm not sure what I said.

"But I did say something to him as we were walking down the court. I'm not in his face, just a seventeen-year-old who said something to him and offended him. I couldn't believe he called a technical in that situation. It decided the game."

With 1:18 left, Jackson made two free throws, and Sylvester made two more to give Lincoln a 50–48 lead and the ball.

With thirty-seven seconds left, Lincoln was called for holding the ball for five seconds, and Peoria regained possession. Reynolds missed a three-point shot, but the ball went out-of-bounds, and Peoria regained possession and called time-out with six seconds to play.

Lincoln switched to a man-to-man defense for the first time. Peoria called another time-out to adjust. Reynolds missed a shot from the top of the key, but Hughes re-bounded and scored on a baseline shot over Jackson to tie at fifty at the buzzer.

"I think Hughes pushed off," Buescher admitted.

In the second overtime, the score was tied at fifty-two, and Peoria had possession, but Tyrone Howard missed a twelve-footer from the right wing with two seconds to play.

At the outset of the third overtime, Hughes took a three-point shot that went down and came out. "That was the first time I thought we're not supposed to win," Buescher said. "The ball was down and in and came out."

Later, White made a three. Then Sylvester looked to pass, hesitated, then converted a three-point shot. "Sylvester was one player I thought they would leave open during the game," Lewis said. "He made two threes. I thought they'd slack off him. He was a good outside shooter."

"That was the biggest shot of the game, as big as Jackson's that won the game," Buescher said. "We defended well, and he still made it."

Reynolds converted two free throws to tie at fifty-seven with twenty-nine seconds left. Then Jackson made the game-winner at the buzzer.

"We were trying to hold the ball for the last shot," Martin said. "I was doubled up in the paint, so it would have been tough for me to get a shot. Jackson or McKinney were the best bets. But if you have to pick one guy to take it, it would be Jackson, a really great athlete. It was an unorthodox shot, but it was the same follow-through he always had."

Lewis said that McKinney was his team's best outside shooter, "but he couldn't handle the pressure." He said that the last play was designed for Sylvester to shoot from the top of the circle or for McKinney to shoot on the side, but Jackson came from the other side, hollered "gimme the ball," split two defenders, and took the shot. He shot off the wrong foot, but that was his style.

"He was the tough guy on our team," Lewis said. "You couldn't scare him. He wasn't afraid to take the last shot."

"You can't defend any better," Buescher said. "Jackson goes to his left, his weak hand. He pulls up and knocks it down with two guys [Reynolds and Hughes] hanging on him. He was off-balance. He shoots off the wrong foot. But he makes it."

"We were devastated," Buescher said. "My first reaction was: 'How will my kids take it?' They beat us the only way they could beat us—with no time left."

Jackson finished with sixteen points, and Martin had twenty-one. Hughes paced Peoria with twenty-one, while White had twenty. But Hughes shot ten of twenty-five, and Reynolds made only two of twelve shots and was limited to ten points.

"I'm still devastated about that game. To this day, I can never think about it without thinking we were robbed," Hughes said. "In my head, we still are 33–0. I never will accept that loss. I knew we were a better team. History might say we lost, but I can never accept it."

"I still don't believe it happened, like someone had killed me," White said. "We lost on a shot that he [Jackson] couldn't even see. He never could make it again.

"But even though we lost, I'm glad I played in it. It was an historic event and set the stage for others to say there are good players outside Chicago. It was the greatest game ever played in Illinois."

To this day, Reynolds believes that he cost Peoria the game. "I cried for a week," he said. "I thought about the effect that game had on the coaches, fans, and players, when you cause your team to lose in the manner I did.

"What I said to the referee was all about me. I was selfish. When I talk to kids today about the story, I explain at the time because of our success it seemed that life revolved around us. When you see your name in the newspaper, you begin to think you are pretty important.

"But you must learn that, regardless of success, life isn't about you but about you using your talents to better society and improve circumstances around you. It is never all about you."

6
The 1990s

Move to Peoria: March Madness
Finds a New Home

Nobody thought it would happen. Even Steve Kouri, the Peoria lawyer who conceived of the plot to steal the prize, had doubts that the heist could be pulled off. After seventy-seven years, why would the boys state basketball tournament leave Champaign-Urbana?

"I was at a Super Bowl party, and a friend whispers to me that he heard someone in a bar in Bloomington say that Illinois State was going after the state tournament," he said. "I thought it was ludicrous that it would move. But I also thought the prize is so big that I at least had to make an inquiry. Maybe there is something to it."

That's how it all began, as a rumor, like on a soap opera. When the final episode of the drama had finally played out, on May 2, 1995, the IHSA announced that its showcase events, the boys Class A and Class AA tournaments, would move to Peoria in 1996.

There was anticipated outrage from traditionalists who reminded us that the tournament had been conducted on the University of Illinois campus since 1919, first at the Men's Old Gym Annex, then at Huff Gym, and finally at Assembly Hall.

"The announcement came as a kick in the stomach to thousands of basketball traditionalists," wrote Loren Tate of the *Champaign News-Gazette*. "The Assembly Hall was the dream, the goal, the obsession of every Illinois youngster who bounced a dribble off his foot in the family driveway, of every teenager pretending he was Kenny Battle or Kendall Gill competing in the Elite Eight."

Could anyone ever feel the same about Peoria? The Assembly Hall, it was argued, is an architectural masterpiece. Opened in 1963, it remains a one-of-a-kind facility, a Rembrandt among so many watercolors. By comparison, Carver Arena, the new site of the state tournament, is just another gym.

As it turned out, tradition wasn't a factor; it was all about the money. But IHSA officials, who began looking for ways to rekindle interest in the tournaments and address complaints about price-gouging by Champaign-Urbana merchants and hotel owners in the early 1990s, never anticipated a change.

"I didn't dream of what we could do differently," said David Fry, then the IHSA's executive director. "Yes, there were proposals out there. But it will be hard to beat what is available [in Champaign-Urbana]. I didn't think the proposals that would come in would be significantly advantageous to the IHSA. But Peoria really wanted it."

Kouri arranged for a meeting in Peoria with Jim Flynn, an assistant executive director of the IHSA. He wanted to see if the rumor had any truth to it, if there was even a scant possibility that the state tournament might be moved. He expected the meeting to last fifteen minutes. Instead, they talked for three hours.

"Let me get this straight: You don't feel appreciated in Champaign?" Kouri asked Flynn.

"No," Flynn said.

"What would you say if I said our community would give you a financial incentive to come here?" Kouri asked.

Flynn smiled.

"Are you saying what I think you are saying?" Kouri asked.

"Yes," Flynn said. "But is your facility available for those two weekends?"

"Yes, we have the dates," Kouri said.

In truth, Kouri didn't have them at the time. In preparing for what he expected to be a brief meeting, he never thought the issue of dates would come up. "But I knew we could make it work if we got the tournament," he said.

"I felt dramatically different when I walked out of the room than when I walked in," Kouri said. "This thing might move, I thought. No one will believe it. I felt, hey, we can get this thing if we do it right."

Flynn thought so, too. Unlike other IHSA officials, he thought that the tournament would move. Champaign-Urbana and the University of Illinois, which owns the Assembly Hall, were taking the IHSA for granted. "They never believed the tournament would leave the town," Flynn said.

So nobody blinked when the Assembly Hall raised its rental fee, demanded a higher percentage of merchandise sales and gross receipts, and began charging for parking. For years, tournament visitors had been complaining about rising prices for lodging. For those and other reasons, tournament attendance had declined dramatically in the 1980s and 1990s.

"We had to find a way to get people back and generate more interest in the tournament," Flynn said. "It got to the point where Champaign-Urbana didn't budge, and the other communities said, 'Give us a chance to show you what we can do.' I knew Peoria's bid would be a good one."

Kouri and other members of the organizing committee—Greg Edwards, Bill Roeder, John Butler, and Tony Pisano—met with civic leaders and businessmen and were assured that they would receive complete cooperation. Caterpillar, the city's biggest industry, made a financial commitment. The hotels, always the biggest hang-up in Champaign-Urbana, jumped on board.

It got even better when Kouri met with Bradley University athletic director Ron Ferguson, a former basketball coach at Thornridge who was well respected within the IHSA. "I think they want to spruce up the tournament, more than games, but I don't know what it is," Kouri told Ferguson.

"They want a Fan Jam, and we can do it in the exhibition hall [sixty-six thousand square feet] next to Carver Arena," Ferguson said. He pulled a flyer from the NCAA's Final Four tournament out of a drawer. It was a promotion for the NCAA's Fan Jam, a fan-friendly carnival that offered basketball-related games for adults and children, a sideshow to the main event.

"A light bulb went on," Kouri said. "We could do it. We could enhance the tournament and give the IHSA something that Champaign-Urbana couldn't."

March Madness Experience was born: shooting contests, interactive games, reality games, youth clinics, and fan entertainment with an Oktoberfest or Taste of Chicago atmosphere. When the IHSA told Peoria that fifteen thousand dollars in corporate sponsorship wasn't enough, Kouri raised $120,000 for the first year.

But first Peoria had to get the tournament. For the first time, the IHSA put its prize event up for bid, and Peoria wasn't the only bidder. After receiving a list of specifications from the IHSA, Champaign-Urbana and Illinois State University also submitted bids. They had six weeks to put together a proposal. After the 1995 Class AA tournament, Fry and his staff examined the bids and made a decision.

"It was a no-brainer," Flynn said. "Peoria was a unanimous choice."

"The Peoria proposal was superior," Fry said. "But the question within the IHSA was: How can we sell the departure from tradition? The only minus was Carver Arena [compared to the Assembly Hall]. But there were so many pluses."

Peoria proposed no rental fee for Carver Arena, a cash contribution to the IHSA, use of the exhibition hall for March Madness Experience, guaranteed lower rates for hotel rooms for three years, free lodging for the teams a block from the arena, no charge for sale of tournament programs and other merchandise, and guaranteed sellouts for both tournaments.

"They said they wanted to make Peoria the capital of high school basketball in the United States—and they have," Flynn said.

March Madness Experience was Flynn's brainchild. The tournament desperately needed something to lure its old fan base and the younger generation. "We had lost our families, and coaches weren't bringing their players to the tournament," Flynn said. "There was nothing for them to do. Champaign-Urbana once staged a carnival in the Illinois Armory, a dance and cheerleading contest, but it lasted for only a decade. We had to come up with something—and we did."

The IHSA surveyed its membership. What did school principals think about the move? How important was tradition? University setting? Costs?

"People said the tournament isn't about the arena, it's about players, games, and fun," Fry said. "Peoria had everything except the Assembly Hall. But not too many people seemed to mind. When I went into the March Madness Experience for the first time, it blew my mind."

The event, masterminded by Roeder, who supervises special events and activities for the Peoria Park District, annually draws about eighty thousand people, more than the state tournament.

Not everybody signed on to the new adventure. Tim Johnson, a state legislator, proposed a bill in the Illinois General Assembly to keep the tournament in Champaign-Urbana. Peoria fought the bill, and it was killed in the rules committee.

"We knew we had one run at the mountain," Kouri said. "We had to make it work now. We had to make it almost impossible for the IHSA to say no. We had to give them an offer they couldn't refuse."

Proviso East: Three Coaches, Four State Titles

Tom Millikin came to Proviso East in Maywood in the late 1950s, before the demographics turned from white to black, before the sport of choice turned from football to basketball, and before the west suburban community turned into a combat zone.

He was a country boy from Pinckneyville, an all-white mining town in southern Illinois. In 1948 he had played on a state championship team under the legendary coach Duster Thomas.

Bill Hitt remembers when it all changed. He was a senior at Proviso East when the school and the community experienced its difficult transformation from white middle-class to African American, when it exploded with a series of race riots.

The first outbreak occurred in October 1967. The school was closed for a week. The Illinois National Guard was present. In April 1968, after Dr. Martin Luther King Jr. was assassinated, the school again was closed for a week. There was tear gas in the halls. Students were forced to sit in their homerooms.

"There was a complete disruption of the educational process," Hitt said. "In a year or two, Maywood went from a white to a black community."

"Race always has been an issue," said Walt Williams, a starter on the 1969 state championship team. "We had our share of problems, but we got along pretty well. When you grow up in an all-white or all-black neighborhood, that is what you know. When you have to face the other race, you must learn to deal with them. Our coaches helped us to deal with the issue."

During the civil rights struggle of the 1960s, Proviso East was the focal point for a wide diversity of views: traditional, racist, nonviolent, and militant. Fred Hampton, a Proviso East graduate and a leader of the Black Panther party, used the school as a podium to voice his views.

"We were oblivious to it until fights started to break out in the hallways and in the cafeteria," said Jim Brewer, the star of the 1969 state championship team. "White guys had the attitude that it was them against the black students."

Brewer was approached to boycott the 1968–69 season based on the school's resistance to some demands that Hampton and others had proposed. Brewer's mother and Walt Williams's mother, Brewer's sister, opposed the idea. They argued that one thing didn't have anything to do with the other.

"If I boycotted the season, I felt it would ruin everything I had worked for," Brewer said. "It was a time of growth. We are where we are today because we went through those times. It was so much more than just being a basketball player."

Millikin and his players—Brewer, Williams, Billy Allen, Harvey Roberts, Pete Bouzeos, Keith Rash, Ira Carswell, John Munchoff, and Ralph Sykes, who grew up on the streets and playgrounds of Maywood—were in the middle of it. They were expected to contend for the 1969 state championship after beating Evanston at the close of the 1967–68 season, before Evanston went on to win the state title. But the school was targeted by political opportunists and card-carrying racists who wanted to use the team for their own interests.

"There was utter chaos in the community," Millikin said. "There were so many negative things going on that every time there was a disturbance, we would be on the six and ten o'clock news. But the basketball team was so positive. They were so great for the school and the community."

The players hung out together. They played basketball on the 10th Street playground and ate ribs and burgers at Stimey's Ribs on 10th and Madison. The black players took Bouzeos, the only white starter, under their wing.

Defense was the hallmark of the team. Millikin hosted dinners every time the Pirates held an opponent to fewer than forty points. He and his wife JoAnn prepared seventeen dinners. The players preferred burgers to salad, pizza, or spaghetti. On one occasion, Millikin ordered twenty-seven Double Whoppers to go.

Proviso East went 30–1. The lone setback was a four-pointer at Galesburg in early December. The Pirates went on to win twenty-five games in a row, capping the season with a 58–51 victory over Peoria Spalding for the state title.

Along the way, they had to hurdle several roadblocks. They barely got past Chicago Public League champion Hirsch 47–46 in the supersectional at Hinsdale Central, rallying from a sixteen-point deficit in the fourth quarter.

In their 52–44 quarterfinal victory over Waukegan, Brewer suffered a severely sprained ankle. But he came back to play in the semifinal against Champaign Central, thanks to an ice massage by Illinois trainer Bob Nicolette. Proviso East won 37–36, as Brewer made two free throws with two seconds left.

"It was the most satisfying experience of my life, more than winning a ring [in the NBA]," Brewer said. "I was one of the leaders and one of the guys who kept the goal alive throughout a lot of adversity. Everyone won in that situation, not just the team, but the whole community."

Williams said that winning the 1969 state title was "like a godsend. We were fighting one year, whites against blacks, then hugging a year later. The 1969 team started the Proviso East tradition. Everybody remembers 1969, even more than 1974 and the 1990s. It was a triumph of race relations."

The seeds for the 1974 state title were planted in 1969, when seventh grader Joe Ponsetto purchased season tickets. He attended every home game. The players were his heroes. "They showed me what we could do. They allowed us to have chips on our shoulders," Ponsetto said. "When I got there, we didn't expect to lose."

As a junior, Ponsetto was the sixth man on a 22–5 team that lost a one-pointer to Elgin in the supersectional. Most observers believed that the 1973 team, led by All-Stater Larry Yates, was superior to 1974. With only two senior starters, Ponsetto and Buck Dobbins, the Pirates weren't touted as one of the top teams in the Chicago area in the preseason.

The team didn't have a dominant player à la Brewer, but Ponsetto, Dobbins, Michael Stockdale, and Jerry Montgomery were groomed in the Maywood school system. The fifth starter was Roderick Floyd, a junior transfer from Alabama who became an All-Stater in 1975.

The coach was Glenn Whittenberg, Millikin's handpicked successor. A former Marine drill sergeant, he was a no-nonsense type who preached fundamentals and didn't take any lip. "He could get along without you if you shot your mouth off," Ponsetto said. "As long as you went along with the program, he was funny and very humble. He told us what to do and left it up to us to do it."

Proviso East lost to Willowbrook 48–37 in its opener. At the Proviso West Tournament, they lost to Elgin and Proviso West. Then senior Eugene Davis, who went into a funk after losing his starting job to Montgomery, began to provide a spark.

They went on a roll after dusting New Trier 82–66 to end the regular season. They beat Elgin 67–57 in the supersectional, Chicago Public League champion Morgan Park 75–55 in the quarterfinals, and Breese Mater Dei 64–42 in the semifinals, then rallied in the fourth quarter to beat Bloom 61–56 for the state title, as Ponsetto had twenty points and fourteen rebounds.

Hitt struggled. He was 20–8 in his first season but 15–11 in his third. The school district was losing good athletes to St. Joseph, Fenwick, and other schools. He added Walt Williams to his staff along with Lawrence McCall and Gene Mobley, two elementary school coaches who were committed to the school.

The 1989 team went 22–6 and nearly upset Gordon Tech and Tom Kleinschmidt in the first round of the sectional. The 1990 squad went 25–3 and lost to St. Joseph in the sectional. With Sherrell Ford, Donnie Boyce, and Michael Finley returning for the 1990–91 season, Hitt had very high expectations.

The Pirates finished 32–1 and were regarded as one of the best teams in state history, more talented than the 1992 squad that went 33–0. But they stumbled in the tournament. They were nearly upset by Nazareth in the sectional final, trailed Thornwood in the supersectional, nudged Libertyville by three in the semifinals, and beat Peoria Manual by seven for the state title.

"People wrote that we were one of the best teams of all time, but we struggled in the tournament," Hitt said. "From the sectional to the state final, we never played our best. Usually the team that wins the state is playing its best ball at the end of the year. This team didn't. It is a tribute to them that they were able to win without playing at their best."

With Jamal Robinson, Kenny Davis, and Ray Gay returning in 1991–92, Proviso East was a prohibitive choice to repeat. The Pirates were unbeaten and ranked number one at the end of the regular season, but Robinson was the tallest player at 6' 4".

At Proviso West, they trailed Westinghouse and St. Joseph by double digits and won. They trailed Oak Park by fifteen but prevailed. In the state finals, they beat Thornridge by eight, Collinsville by two, Westinghouse by seventeen, and Peoria Richwoods by eleven.

"You don't normally look at a team with that lack of size and think they will go 33–0," Hitt said. "But they showed me a lot of character. They bonded as a unit and didn't want to lose. They weren't as spectacular as 1991, but they played so well together."

Mary Wilson, mother of slain high school basketball star Ben Wilson, touches her son's head during the wake, which was attended by thousands of mourners in Simeon's gym. Photo courtesy of the *Chicago Sun-Times/* John H. White.

King coach Landon Cox stands between his "Twin Towers," 7' 1" Rashard Griffith (left) and 7' 3" Thomas Hamilton. Griffith and Hamilton led King to a 32–0 record and the 1993 Class AA championship. Cox also coached King to state titles in 1986 and 1990. Photo courtesy of the *Chicago Sun-Times/* Bob Ringham.

Jamie Brandon of Chicago King, a three-time All-Stater who led his team to the 1990 Class AA championship and the number one ranking in the nation, closed his remarkable career as the third leading scorer in state history with 3,157 points. Photo courtesy of the *Chicago Sun-Times/* Bob Black.

Members of East St. Louis Lincoln's 1988–89 team lift the state championship trophy after beating Peoria Central 59–57 in triple overtime. Photo courtesy of the Illinois High School Association/United Press International/Stephen Wamowski.

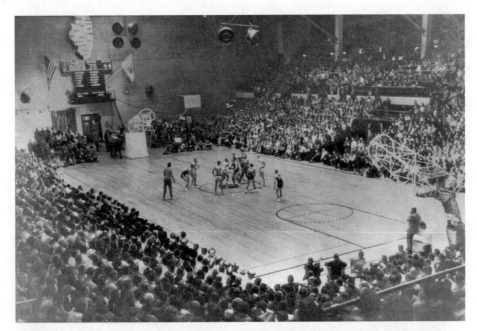

Huff Gym on the campus of the University of Illinois in Champaign was the site of the Illinois high school basketball tournament from 1926 through 1962. One of the distinguishing features was the map on the south wall of the sixty-nine-hundred-seat facility. Lights designated the sites of the Sweet Sixteen finalists. As each team lost, a light would go out, until there was only one remaining, the state champion. Photo courtesy of the Illinois High School Association/Associated Press.

The Assembly Hall on the campus of the University of Illinois in Champaign was the site of the boys Class A and Class AA high school basketball tournaments from 1963 through 1995. Considered an architectural wonder when it was built, the sixteen-thousand-seat arena was the showcase for some of the most exciting finishes in tournament history. Photo courtesy of the Illinois High School Association/Jeff Soucek.

Carver Arena in Peoria has been the site of the boys Class A and Class AA high school basketball tournaments since 1996. The twelve-thousand-seat facility is part of the Peoria Civic Center, which also includes a massive exhibition hall that houses the March Madness Experience. Photo courtesy of the Illinois High School Association/Jeff Soucek.

Tom Millikin, coach of Proviso East's 1969 state championship team, proudly displays the big trophy. Millikin also started on Pinckneyville's 1948 state championship team. He also served as principal when Proviso East won the state title in 1974. Photo courtesy of the Illinois High School Association.

Proviso East coach Glenn Whittenberg talks to his players during a time-out. Whittenberg guided his 1973–74 team to the Class AA championship. Photo courtesy of the *Chicago Sun-Times*.

Proviso East coach Bill Hitt congratulates his team during a pep rally after winning the 1991 Class AA championship. Hitt's 1992 squad also won the state title. Photo courtesy of the *Chicago Sun-Times*/Ellen Domke.

Ed Horton (24) of Springfield Lanphier, who was Mr. Basketball in Illinois in 1984–85, attempts to grab a loose ball under the basket in the state championship game against Mount Carmel. Horton scored twenty-one points, but Lanphier lost in double overtime 46–44. Photo courtesy of the *Chicago Sun-Times*/United Press International/Bruno Torres.

Michael Finley (24) teamed with two other All-Staters, Sherrell Ford and Donnie Boyce, to lead Proviso East to the 1991 Class AA champi-onship. Photo courtesy of the *Chicago Sun-Times*/Bob Black.

Brian Feezel (20) played a key role in Pittsfield's drive to the 1991 Class A championship. Photo courtesy of the Illinois High School Association/ Jim Reiter.

Andy Kuba (50) led Staunton to the 1993 Class A championship. Photo courtesy of the Illinois High School Association/ Associated Press.

Peoria Manual's Brandun Hughes (42) attempts to shoot over Westinghouse's Tyjuan Finley during the first half of the Rams' 81–76 victory in the 1994 Class AA quarterfinals. Peoria Manual went on to win the title, its first of an unprecedented four in a row. Photo courtesy of the Illinois High School Association.

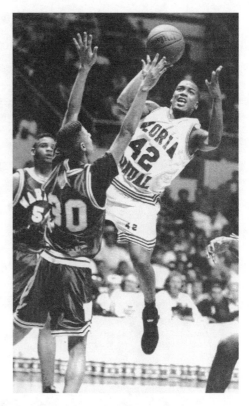

Peoria Manual's Dick Van Scyoc (center) gives a pep talk to his 1993–94 team during the state championship game against Carbondale. Van Scyoc closed out his forty-five-year career with his 826th victory, the most in state history. Peoria Manual won 61–60. Photo courtesy of the Illinois High School Association/Jeff Soucek.

Bennie Lewis, chewing on his traditional cigar, coached East St. Louis Lincoln to 497 victories and four state championships, including three in a row from 1987–89. Photo courtesy of the *Chicago Sun-Times*/Associated Press.

The father/son combination of Sergio McClain (left) and coach Wayne McClain led Peoria Manual to an unprecedented four state championships in a row from 1994 to 1997. Sergio played on all four teams, while his father assisted Dick Van Scyoc on the 1994 winner and was head coach of the other three. Photo courtesy of the Illinois High School Association.

Mark Aguirre of Westinghouse, a two-time All-Stater in 1978 and 1979, later became the college player of the year at DePaul and an NBA all-star. Photo courtesy of the *Chicago Sun-Times*/*Chicago Daily News*/Martha Hartnett.

Frank Lollino, a former University of Illinois football player, was the flamboyant coach who built Chicago Westinghouse into a state basketball power in the 1970s and 1980s. He coached Mark Aguirre, Eddie Johnson, and Hersey Hawkins, three future NBA stars. Photo courtesy of the *Chicago Sun-Times*/Bob Langer.

Westinghouse's Kiwane Garris lofts a shot against Bloom during the Proviso West Holiday Tournament in 1992. Garris, a three-time All-Stater, led Westinghouse to the Chicago Public League championship game in 1991 and 1993 and to third place in the Class AA tournament in 1992. Photo courtesy of the *Chicago Sun-Times*/Joel Lerner.

Pittsfield: They Play Basketball, Too

In twenty-three seasons as Pittsfield's basketball coach, Dave Bennett won 527 games and produced one state championship team, four Elite Eight qualifiers, a state-record ten Sweet Sixteen teams in a row, eleven sectional champions, and eighteen regional winners. He never had a losing record.

Not bad for a football town. It is not an exaggeration to assert that Don "Deek" Pollard put Pittsfield on the map, and Bennett made certain that it stayed there.

In Pittsfield's gym, there is one picture that reminds visitors of the legacy of Pollard, the former football coach. His teams won a state-record sixty-four games in a row in the late 1960s and early 1970s. The picture is of the 1970 team, which was unbeaten and unscored upon. On the back of the main grandstand of the football stadium, there is a huge sign that states: "Pittsfield Saukees, 64 consecutive victories / IHSA state record / Illinois' winningest football team."

When Bennett arrived in 1975, he didn't know anything about Pittsfield. Oh, he had heard about the football team when he was an assistant football coach at Alton. In fact, he served as Pittsfield's football coach from 1979 to 1981.

"At the time, I wanted to be a football coach," he said. "I felt I had a better grasp of the game after I worked under Ed Yonkus [at Alton]. He was one of the best. But now I'm glad that I stuck with basketball."

Bennett came to Pittsfield because it presented a great opportunity and a greater challenge. Recently divorced, he had custody of his three children and felt that a small town would be a comfortable environment for them to grow up in.

From a coaching standpoint, there was nowhere to go but up. Pittsfield hadn't produced a state qualifier since 1970, its first since 1949. The school had never been to the state finals.

Pittsfield, the seat of Pike County, is located in a little valley between the Illinois and Mississippi Rivers. "The land between the rivers," it is called. After games, fans meet at the Red Dome Inn on the square.

"There was no pressure at all," Bennett said. "When I was hired, I was told that the football team was struggling, not doing as well as they hoped, and they wanted me to help. I felt I was a football coach just hanging out in the gym."

But Bennett soon got serious about basketball.

Before Bennett, there had been no practices on Wednesday (church night), the players didn't know how to practice, they weren't in shape, and everyone had a different shooting technique.

After Bennett, there was a 9 P.M. curfew before games, practices were treated like games, body piercing, facial hair, or tattoos were unacceptable, and players were required to wear dress shirts and slacks to games.

He emphasized fundamentals, conditioning, and defense. He organized grades seven through twelve so that all teams ran the same practices, drills, offenses, and defenses. He started a summer league in 1979 and began sending his teams to summer camps in 1984.

Playing in the Assembly Hall in Champaign became a dream for all kids growing up in Pittsfield. Tracy Shelton, the leading scorer on the 1979–80 team that lost to the eventual state champion Luther South in the quarterfinals, said to Bennett as he walked into the huge building for the first time: "Coach, you sure could put a lot of hay in here."

In 1990–91, Pittsfield expected to see the Assembly Hall again. The previous year, the Saukees were 30–2, the most victories of any Bennett-coached team. They were ranked second in Class A at the end of the regular season, but they lost to Norris City in the state quarterfinals.

The team had lost its leader, David Bess—"the most intense player I ever coached," according to Bennett—but three starters returned: 6' 5" Tony Baker, point guard Brian Feezel, and David Fox. David Marable was the third guard, and sophomore Jamie Sweeting had transferred from Perry, fifteen miles from Pittsfield.

With six losses, however, Pittsfield was unranked at the end of the regular season. The team had to overcome a lot of adversity. Sweeting, who came off the bench during the regular season, became a starter in the regional. Troy Taylor suffered a stress fracture. Josh Townley was ill. At one point they played five games in eight days.

Feezel described a loss to Augusta Southeastern as the "low point" of the season. "At that point, I wasn't even thinking about getting back to the state finals. We had some new people, and we weren't meshing. Baker wasn't playing like an All-Stater, and we weren't playing well on defense," he said.

Ironically, Feezel, who ranked second in a class of one hundred, couldn't get motivated. He thought that the 1990 team was better—Bennett said that it was the most talented team he had ever coached—and he was kicked out of a few practices.

"Coach was looking for me to be more of a leader than I wanted to be," said Feezel, who now practices corporate law in St. Louis. "It was a new role for me. Bess was the leader in 1990. Coach thought everyone else was looking up to me, and I wasn't used to that role. For a long time, we couldn't coexist."

Sweeting wasn't sure he was in the right place. He favored baseball, but there weren't enough players at Perry, so the sport was dropped. He feared consolidation was coming. Where would he go to school? Griggsville? Pittsfield?

As a freshman at Perry, which had an enrollment of sixty, Sweeting scored forty points against Meredosia. But the team won only two games. His father decided to move to Pittsfield. In three years, his son played on a state champion and became the school's all-time leading scorer.

Sweeting credits Bennett for bringing out the best in him. He didn't change his shooting style, but he taught him defense, something Sweeting had never thought about before. "He was an intimidating presence. I knew he was a good coach, but I was scared of him," Sweeting said. "He brings the best out of you, but you wonder if it is because you want to please him or if you are afraid of what will happen to you if you mess up."

Baker, who was the first All-Stater in school history, seriously considered quitting the team. "The coach was riding me hard. I was inconsistent. He kicked me out of one practice because he felt I was too cocky," he said.

He went home and told his father that he was quitting, that he couldn't take it anymore. "You're not quitting," his father told him. Nothing more was said. In the last four games, Baker led the Saukees with seventy-five points and forty-one rebounds.

Baker was born in Terre Haute, Indiana, and attended high school in Washington, Indiana. He moved to Pittsfield midway through his sophomore year. Baker tried to talk his father, a pastor, into staying in Indiana. He had played against Hoosier legend Damon Bailey and knew all about the tradition of Indiana basketball.

When Baker transferred to Pittsfield in December, Bennett called the coach at Washington, Indiana. "You got the best Christmas present you'll ever get. If he had stayed here, he'd be my next All-American," the coach told him.

"I didn't know what a Saukee was," Baker said. "Washington had twelve hundred students and the second largest gym [seventy-three hundred] in Indiana. Pittsfield had 450 students and a gym that seated eleven hundred. I saw the sign on the football stadium and heard Deek Pollard's name. I realized they had a football tradition, but I didn't know how good the basketball team was."

It didn't take long to find out. For the next eight years, Pittsfield posted a record of 203–35, an .853 winning percentage and an average of twenty-five victories per season.

In 1990–91, the turnaround came when the regional tournament began. "We didn't care about the regular season, only the state tournament once it started," Feezel said. "We remembered what happened in 1990. Our whole attitude was focused on the state tournament. We wanted to get back there and not let what happened last year happen again."

"Nobody thought we should be there but us," Baker said. "The secret of our success was we came together as a team. We ate and drank and slept basketball once the state tournament began. During the regular season, I think we felt too much pressure of living up to expectations based on the previous year."

As the tournament went along, Pittsfield kept getting better and better. The Saukees never hit a wall, not even a bump. In the supersectional, they avenged their earlier loss to state-ranked Augusta Southeastern 61–44.

In the last four games, Pittsfield capped a 28–6 season, winning by margins of seventeen, thirteen, seventeen, and ten. Their defense was so suffocating that opponents simply couldn't score. The Saukees smashed Williamsville 42–25 in the semifinals and Seneca 45–35 for the championship, thanks to a late 18–9 run.

"If you can get a group of kids that believe in themselves and the system, they don't have to be the greatest athletes to be a championship team," Bennett said. "Our motto that year was: Hard as you can, smart as you can. Too many kids worry about not failing. You must be courageous enough to accept challenges."

Staunton: They All Came Together

None of the principal characters in Staunton's drive to the 1993 Class A championship were born in Staunton. But somehow, some way, they all came together to lead a football-minded community to basketball heaven in one glorious season.

Coach Randy LeGendre was born in Clinton, Iowa. A week before school began in 1970, Staunton football coach Fred Brenzel announced that he was moving to Edwardsville. LeGendre was hired to fill the staff vacancy. He was head basketball coach from 1973 through 1975 and 1991 through 1995.

Assistant coach Dave Lamore was born in Grant Park, Illinois, south of Chicago. In 1969, he began a twenty-one-year career as a coach and teacher at Livingston. In 1990, he was hired at Staunton.

Andy Kuba, the team's leading scorer and rebounder, was born in Belleville, but his parents grew up in Staunton. After his father graduated from college, the family returned to Staunton.

Kevin Meyer, the team's second-leading scorer and rebounder, also was born in Belleville but grew up on a farm in Staunton.

Brad Skertich was born in Washington, Illinois, but moved to Staunton when he was four after his father was hired as an elementary school principal. Football was Brad's favorite sport.

Ron Hampton was born in Livingston, four miles south of Staunton. His father was the varsity basketball coach, but the school had an enrollment of only sixty students.

As a sophomore, Hampton averaged twenty-one points per game. He knew some of the players at Staunton and had attended LeGendre's summer camps. He felt that Staunton would have a good team in 1992–93 and wanted to be a part of it. So he asked his father if the family would move before his junior year. "We couldn't have won the state championship without Ron Hampton," Kuba said.

Staunton wasn't supposed to win the state title for several reasons. It enjoyed a well-earned reputation as a football town. Fred Brenzel was inducted into the Illinois High School Football Coaches Association's Hall of Fame in 1981. In the trophy case in the elementary school, two football jerseys have been retired, none in basketball. Robert Spagnola, an All-State halfback in 1944, wore number 27. And Larry Kuba, Andy's father, an All-State halfback in 1959 who set a school rushing record of 1,414 yards, wore number 26.

After LeGendre was hired, Brenzel told him, "This is a football town." People stood ten deep at football games. Brenzel purposely scheduled games on Saturday night, not on the traditional date of Friday night for other schools, because he wanted people to come to see his teams.

Imagine Brenzel's reaction when LeGendre guided his first varsity team to a conference championship in 1974, the school's first conference title since the 1950s. The town was waiting for a winner, something to cheer about.

LeGendre knew he had the makings of something special. In 1991–92, the team was 17–9 and won the Macoupin County Tournament but lost to Bunker Hill in the regional final.

Kuba had higher expectations for the 1992–93 squad. In other years, the team goals didn't go beyond winning the conference, the county tournament, and the regional. "If we achieved those three goals, we felt it was a successful season," he said.

LeGendre was optimistic, too. "This is our year," he told his players on the first day of practice.

"We were naïve. What is he talking about?" Skertich said. "Kevin Meyer and I had been to the state finals in Champaign for three years and sat in Section A and watched the championship games. 'How neat it would be to experience this,' we said to ourselves. What would it be like? We had never won a regional."

LeGendre had a better view: "I saw ability and attitude. They were tough, intelligent kids. All were honor students [Kuba ranked number one in a class of eighty and studied chemical engineering at University of Illinois]. I felt we had the talent to play at state based on teams I had seen in Champaign."

There was no panic after Staunton lost its opener to Breese Central 66–53 and started 2–2. Both losses were to Class AA teams, Meyer and Skertich were coming off the football team, and the players didn't begin to mesh with Hampton until Christmas.

"We knew we needed Hampton," LeGendre said. "He had more pressure on him to perform. We wouldn't have won the state title without him. He was our point guard, our floor leader, a great ballhandler, and good outside shooter. He came into his own in the last half of the season, when we really needed him."

LeGendre and Lamore, who did a lot of scouting, assigned roles. Hampton was the floor leader, the 6' 5", 195–pound Kuba and the 6' 5", 210–pound Meyer were the go-to guys, the primary scorers, the 6' 2" Skertich was the defensive stopper, and Jeremy May filled in the blanks. They ran a triangle offense.

With four losses in the regular season, Staunton didn't impress the media. They were unranked in the Associated Press's final poll, which was headed by Pinckneyville and McLeansboro.

"No one thought about Staunton until we got to Champaign," Kuba said. "We don't play powerhouse schools in the state." The team started to jell in the postseason. Hampton scored fifteen of his nineteen points in the second half, as Staunton ousted St. Elmo 70–66 in overtime in the sectional semifinal. Then Meyer netted twenty-three as Staunton defeated Litchfield for the third time 71–55 to claim the school's first sectional title. They began to sense that they might be a team of destiny.

"It gave the team confidence that someone will step up on any given night," Hampton said. "Coach LeGendre was a calming force. In the huddle, we never got rattled. Being in close games, you can't be rattled. We won six overtime games during the season. We were tested every night."

In the supersectional, Staunton overcame a six-point deficit with twenty-six seconds to play to nip Bridgeport Red Hill 65–64 in double overtime. Kuba had twenty-six points and eleven rebounds.

Red Hill missed a free throw, Kuba hit a three-pointer, Red Hill missed another free throw, and Kuba hit another three-pointer at the buzzer to force overtime. In the first overtime, Meyer fouled out and Staunton trailed by three, but May made a three-pointer with no time left after first ensuring that his feet were behind the three-point line. In the second overtime, Staunton trailed by one when Kuba missed a shot, then tipped in the rebound at the buzzer. "It was a miracle that we won the game," Kuba said. "Part of our success was we didn't know what we were getting into."

It was hard to ignore the size and majesty of the Assembly Hall, however. The school sold more than two thousand tickets for the Elite Eight games. The players had never played in a gym where people were seated behind the backboards.

It took them awhile to get unwound. In the quarterfinal, Riverton broke out to an 11–0 lead before Staunton restored order and prevailed 52–43. In the semifinals, they beat state-ranked Hamilton and 6' 8" Kurt Meister 52–42.

In the final, Staunton was in for a surprise. They anticipated a matchup with state-ranked Cairo and 6' 7" Tyrone Nesby. But Hales Franciscan, an all-black school from Chicago, upset Cairo 69–67. Even so, Lamore had scouted Hales thoroughly.

Hales was bigger, faster, quicker, and deeper than Staunton. They played a fast-paced style and posed matchup problems. In his scouting report, Lamore said, "We can't run with them. We have to control the tempo. We must box out."

Staunton followed its game plan to the smallest detail. The ball touched a lot of hands, consuming a lot of time. "Screen out! Put your butt on them! Keep them off the boards!" LeGendre shouted constantly. On defense, Skertich shut down Greg Wood, Hales's All-Stater, limiting him to nine shots and eight points.

Staunton led 33–30 at halftime, but Hales led by two with less than two minutes to play. Kuba made a basket and was fouled by Wood, his fifth. After a time-out, Kuba made a free throw. After Hales scored, Hampton made two free throws, and then made two more to seal the 66–62 victory. Kuba had twenty-six points and fourteen rebounds, Meyer scored twenty, and Hampton scored thirteen.

"It was sad," said Meyer, who now works for an architectural firm in Belleville, "because we realized our careers were over. It was difficult to take my jersey off. We sat in the locker room for a long time. It was a life-changing experience."

"It took a long time to sink in," said Skertich, who now is principal of an elementary school in Bunker Hill. "It means more now, and every year as it goes by I appreciate it more. When you are seventeen, you are naïve, having a good time. Now I realize what it meant to accomplish something, where we started from and how we ended up. We put Staunton on the map in some ways."

Kuba, who now works for Bridgestone/Firestone in Akron, Ohio, never realized his dream to play basketball at a major college. Illinois coach Lou Henson invited him to walk on. He led his team to the intramural finals for two years.

"Sometimes I wish I had gone a different route," he said. "But I could relate my basketball experience to everyday life. You can do things that people say you can't do if you believe in yourself and other people you are working with.

"We didn't have a tradition like other schools, but we were all competitive. For months, even years later, I didn't know what we had done. Man, I should have stopped to enjoy the moment when I had it. Then it was all over."

Peoria: "Cradle of the Crossover Dribble"

The hip-hop generation doesn't have much of a sense of history—music, sports, or politics. It recalls Peoria Manual's unprecedented four state championships in a row in the 1990s, but it often confuses who coached all of them.

Meanwhile, old-timers from the Big Band and Elvis eras remember that the River City was producing good high school teams, coaches, and players long before "playing in Peoria" became a tagline to a comedian's monologue on late-night television.

Well, nobody is laughing about Peoria basketball.

In his book, *Big Game, Small World: A Basketball Adventure,* the *Sports Illustrated* reporter Alexander Wolff describes Peoria as "the cradle of the crossover dribble." The fancy handle, he learned, had dissed the dunk as a primary subject among the trash-talking elite.

Since 1987, Peoria has emerged as one of the most fertile grounds in the country for developing young talent, from Jamere Jackson to Lynn Collins to David Booth to Chris Reynolds to Mike Hughes to Howard Nathan to Brandun Hughes to Sergio McClain to Frank Williams to Shaun Livingston. Central is no longer the dominant program; Manual and Richwoods have become very competitive. Fierce coaching rivalries fueled the fire.

"I felt a lot of people looked down on us because they didn't hear about us. They always heard about big names from Chicago," Mike Hughes said. "But we put Peoria on the map, tough kids from the streets. They always play as though they have something to prove, to show they are as good as or better than great players from other areas."

In 1988, Central's Chris Reynolds and Mike Hughes attended the Nike All-America camp, the first two Peoria products to attend a big-time summer camp. Reynolds was rated third among all point guards, behind Kenny Anderson and Bobby Hurley. After he returned, he received calls from Notre Dame's Digger Phelps, Duke's Mike Krzyzewski, and Kansas's Roy Williams. Duke offered a scholarship to Reynolds before Hurley, but he chose Indiana.

"Before that, he wasn't being recruited like that. He wasn't that highly thought of. But now we had national exposure," Peoria Central coach Chuck Buescher said. "Peoria kids found out they were as good as Chicago, maybe better. College recruiters found out, too."

It took a while to change the landscape and the perception. In the 1940s, Peoria's schools were segregated, and few blacks participated in athletics. Central, once the only high school in the city, remained dominant. Manual was good in football and baseball. Central qualified for the state finals once in eighteen years, Manual once in twenty-five years.

"Chicago and New York basketball was all about hoopla, flash, and dunking. But Peoria was all fundamentals," said David Booth, a two-time All-Stater at Peoria Manual in the 1980s. "A lot of guys from Chicago were very athletic, but their fundamentals weren't there. They didn't have an understanding of the game.

"Basketball is 70 percent mental. Larry Bird wasn't a great athlete, but he knew the game. I wasn't a great athlete, but I played ten years professionally because I knew the game. Off the court, you were taught how to carry yourself and understand what basketball can do for you after you quit playing."

Interest in basketball began to soar in the 1950s with the emergence of Bradley University as a national collegiate power and the Peoria Cats of the National Industrial Basketball League. Dawson Hawkins arrived from Nebraska to lead Peoria Central and Hiles Stout to second place in the 1953 state tournament. At Manual, Fred Marberry, who later played for the Harlem Globetrotters, generated a lot of excitement.

"Coaching had a lot to do with it," former Bradley coach Joe Stowell said. "The influence of Hawkins and Dick Van Scyoc, Duncan Reid and Chuck Buescher, Wayne Hammerton and Bruce Boyle. Their success stimulated other coaches to be competitive and inspired more kids to participate."

Bruce Boyle continued Central's tradition. He became head coach in 1972, following the legacy of Salen Herke and Dawson Hawkins and preceding Chuck Buescher. His 1974 team finished third, and his 1976 squad was ranked sixth in the state before losing to Manual in the regional final. But his 1977 team, led by Dwayne and Ernie Banks and Percy Neal, won the school's first state title since 1908.

After beating Manual 41–40 in the regional final and Galesburg in overtime in the sectional final, the Lions went on a roll. Although no one averaged more than fourteen points per game, they used a matchup zone devised by former coach Harry Whitaker to confuse opponents who hadn't seen it before. In the last four games, they won by margins of fourteen, twenty-seven, twenty-one, and ten points to complete a 29–2 season.

"Hawkins changed Central's image in the 1950s," Boyle said. "It was known as 'Bow-Tie High' because upper-class kids went there. They had their own cliques. Hawkins told them if they wanted to play basketball, they couldn't belong to fraternities. It played on the kids."

Richwoods opened in 1957. Hammerton, who had coached at tiny Atwood-Hammond for six years, joined the Richwoods staff in 1964 and became head coach in 1970. When he retired in 1996, he had won 578 games and two state trophies—second in 1992 and fourth in 1975.

In his first season, however, Hammerton had to rent a private gym for ten dollars a session to give his team practice time. Basketball wasn't a priority. Richwoods had a reputation as the New Trier of central Illinois, a lot of rich kids who didn't work hard and had a lot of other things to do besides play basketball. But Hammerton knew he was working in a gold mine.

"My first Richwoods team had six kids who were 6' 4" and taller," he said. "I never saw so much height. I realized there was more talent in larger schools than anything I had at a smaller school where you built your program around one player."

While Van Scyoc and Wayne McClain were building a powerhouse at Manual, and Boyle and Buescher were producing winning teams at Central, Hammerton and his successor Bob Darling took Richwoods into the twenty-first century. For twenty years, before it closed, Peoria Spalding was a factor, claiming three state trophies, including second in 1969.

"We knew we couldn't compete unless we got our kids into the gym. At first, I and two assistants had to play so we would have ten on the floor," Hammerton said. "Later, we had seventy to eighty kids in the gym during the summer. We created a monster, but that's what we had to do to compete."

Richwoods emerged as a state power in 1974. The Knights, led by junior Chris Williams and sophomore Derek Holcomb, were 24–1 and ranked second in the state before losing to Peoria Central in the sectional final in double overtime.

In 1975, Williams and Holcomb were back, and Mark Smith was a sophomore. Richwoods was 24–1 and ranked third in the state, but the Knights lost to state champion Phillips in the semifinals when Holcomb was sidelined with a knee injury.

In 1976, Richwoods was 25–0 and ranked number one in the state. But the Knights lost to Galesburg 85–79 in overtime in the regional final at Galesburg when Holcomb fouled out in the fourth quarter. Holcomb and Smith were neutralized by Galesburg's Mike Campbell and Scott Kelley. They had beaten Galesburg by ten earlier in the season.

"This was our best team," Hammerton said. "It was one of those games you never, ever forget. It was total bedlam. I've been in a lot of big games at Galesburg but never experienced such a loud crowd. I literally had to yell in each kid's ear during timeout. I still replay that game over and over."

Richwoods also qualified for the state quarterfinals in 1980 with Terry Cole and Doug Altenberger, reached the Sweet Sixteen in 1985 with Randy Blair and Keith Singleton, and finished second in 1992 with All-Stater Troy Taylor.

"It is a small enough town where all the kids know each other and play against each other in the summer," Hammerton said. "Schools want to keep the tradition going. Everyone wants to play. Every school is getting good players." In the summer, at State Park or Carver Center or Proctor Center, kids from Peoria, Morton, East Peoria, Bartonville, and even kids from Chicago and the Quad Cities tested each other.

"It was put up or shut up," said Charles White, a Peoria Central star in the late 1980s. "If you talk the talk, you better be able to walk the walk and come to play. There were classic battles, maybe better than the games in February and March. People started to see that we could play big-time. Recruiters came to see us play, too."

"That competition gives you an attitude and a maturity," Sergio McClain said. "If you don't come with your game, you won't play. Playing on the streets gives you a mentality that you can't back down from anybody.

"Manual kids [in the 1990s] came from the street, not the suburbs. We stayed in the hood. We had a me-against-the-world attitude. Peoria basketball is team-oriented. We feel we know the game better than Chicago or anyone else. We have better coaches, too. They taught us how to think on the court and use our common sense."

Dick Van Scyoc: 826 Career Victories

Looking back on his forty-five-year career, Dick Van Scyoc said that his most memorable achievements were that he never was fired and never missed a game. The fact that he won 826 games, more than any coach in Illinois history, had more to do with longevity than talent.

"I never dreamed I'd be where I am," Van Scyoc said. "I never had a goal to surpass Arthur Trout as the winningest coach in state history. I always watched the great coaches and admired them—Trout, Thomas, Evers, Changnon, Hawkins, Eveland, Cabutti—but I never dreamed of doing what they did."

Born in Eureka, Van Scyoc played on a regional basketball champion, but baseball was his favorite sport. A left-handed pitcher, he was scouted by the Boston Red Sox, who paid his bus and train fares to Danville to perform in a game.

After volunteering for a four-year European tour of duty in the army and graduating from college with a degree in philosophy, he worked out for the St. Louis Cardinals but was only offered a Class A contract. So he decided to teach and coach at the high school level.

He coached baseball at Armington, outside of Bloomington, went to Hittle Township, now Olympia, and then landed as basketball coach at Washington in 1951. In 1962 he took his team to the state quarterfinals. He was happy and didn't plan to leave.

Peoria Manual offered him a job in 1955, but he turned it down. Peoria Central was the dominant program in town, and Manual, which practiced and played its games at junior high schools, "didn't look like it was going anywhere at that time."

In 1966 Van Scyoc changed his mind. He asked friends if Peoria Manual could ever be as good as Peoria Central. They said that it could: Manual had talented athletes and potential, but they had to be motivated and developed. Van Scyoc accepted the challenge, even though he had never coached a black athlete, and Manual was mostly black.

"When I came to Peoria Manual, I was caught between Ken Heinrichs [football] and Ed Stonebock [baseball]," he said. "Both had had great success. Basketball was something they did between fall and spring. The kids didn't care about basketball."

After two subpar years, Van Scyoc wondered if he had made a mistake. He tried to promote the program but wondered if he could ever turn the corner. His father reminded him that nothing comes easy, so he kept working hard.

"It was a sleeping giant, and you hoped it would not wake up," said former Peoria Richwoods coach Wayne Hammerton, who won 578 games in thirty years before retiring in 1996. "There was talent but a lack of discipline. In the 1970s, it was Peoria Central and Peoria Richwoods. All of a sudden, Manual came into it."

Mike Davis, Wayne McClain, Bobby Humbles, Jamere Jackson, Howard Nathan, David Booth, and Brandun Hughes came along. So did Sergio McClain and Marcus Griffin. It was the beginning of a dynasty that produced an unprecedented four consecutive state championships in the 1990s.

Van Scyoc started workouts at 6:30 in the morning, no nonsense, no earrings, no profanity; keep your mouth shut, pull up your pants, and do what you are told. He introduced a weight-training program that Iowa coach Bucky O'Connor used to increase strength and jumping ability. The turning point came in 1972, when Manual finished fourth in the first Class AA tournament.

"I didn't have hours when I coached," he said. "My goal was to play the best competition we could. You don't get better by beating someone by fifteen to twenty points. We wanted to pass everybody, and now everybody wants to get where Peoria Manual is."

"He had a unique rapport with kids," said longtime assistant coach Chuck Westendorf, who has been married to Van Scyoc's daughter Gwen for thirty-one years. "Although he came from an all-white background, he was always fair. He was tough but treated everyone fairly. Word traveled quickly through the community. He treated his kids well."

"The kids knew I believed in them," Van Scyoc said. "I gained their trust. I pushed them hard, but they knew we could still be friends off the court. I told them they couldn't be satisfied with where they were. Kids who won't be pushed or don't want to get better will tear up your program."

Van Scyoc ran a tight ship and a tighter organization. He preached fundamentals and didn't let ego get in the way of his coaching. He surrounded himself with outstanding assistants, including Ed Brooks, Wayne McClain, Westendorf, Chuck Buescher, and Gary Stowell, who taught his system and made certain there were no glitches.

"He was very much a control freak with kids," Wayne McClain said. "Things had to be done exactly the way he wanted. He paid attention to detail. Anyone who walked in the gym knew that was his territory. He was the boss. You had to respond to everything he said in a timely manner and in a respectful way. He never got into the personal lives of his players but made you realize you were representing Manual and things you did off the court said something about the school."

David Booth, an All-Stater on a 29–5 team that finished third in Class AA in 1988, remembers that Van Scyoc never cracked a smile. Everyone was scared of him. But if it weren't for the coach, he wouldn't have gone to DePaul.

"Now I see other programs where if kids can test a coach and know they can put something over on him, they will," Booth said. "We never questioned him. He was the law. We all believed in him and his system. He was consumed by his job, but he cared about his players."

Sergio McClain, Wayne's son and a four-year starter on the championship teams of the 1990s, recalled how Van Scyoc talked about life beyond basketball. "My dad played for him. He had to like him to be with him for eighteen years," he said.

The Van Scyoc/McClain/Westendorf coaching trinity began to reap benefits in the 1980s. The 1981–82 team lost to Chicago's Mendel Catholic 53–51 in the quarterfinals. The 1983–84 team, which was ranked second in the state, lost to Rock Island 51–49 in the supersectional. The 1987 team, which was ranked number one in the state, lost to Quincy 61–59 in overtime in the quarterfinals. Manual finished third in 1986 and 1988 and lost to Proviso East and Sherrell Ford, Michael Finley, and Donnie Boyce for the 1991 state championship.

"We were knocking on the door and on the verge of knocking the door down, but we couldn't get it done," McClain said. "We ran into great teams. . . . We were always around but never got it done, not until 1994 when no one expected us to do anything."

In 1993–94, Chicago King and Joliet Township were unbeaten and ranked first and second at the end of the regular season. Peoria Central was ranked ninth, and Peoria Manual, with six losses, was number thirteen. Then Westinghouse upset King 59–58 in the Chicago Public League, and Joliet lost to Carbondale in the quarterfinals.

Manual saw a crack in the doorway and barged through. Led by Brandun Hughes, Willie Coleman, Darrell Ivory, Ivan Watson, Sergio McClain, and Marcus Griffin, the Rams edged Springfield 55–52 and Quincy 58–56, overcame an early sixteen-point deficit to smash Galesburg 80–53, then beat Westinghouse 81–76 in the quarterfinals and Rockford Boylan 80–67 in the semifinals.

In the final, Hughes scored twenty-seven points, including the game-winning free throws with four seconds to play, as Manual overcame a twenty-one-point deficit to beat Carbondale and Troy Hudson 61–60. Hughes, with four fouls, preserved a one-point lead by blocking a layup by 6' 7" Rashad Tucker with a minute left. Hughes also converted all six of his three-point shots in the second half, a state final record. The game wasn't settled until Hudson's last shot bounced off the rim.

"It was the finest five-game state tournament run I've ever seen," Wayne McClain said of Hughes's closing performances.

"What I liked about the team is they played so well together," Van Scyoc said. "In a three-on-two or four-on-three situation, the guy who had the best shot or had better position would get the ball. They were very unselfish, a good passing team. They all knew their roles. And we were lucky, too. You have to be lucky and good to win a state title."

Hughes was the leader. A gifted all-around athlete, he played football as a senior and took awhile to get his basketball legs. McClain and Griffin were outstanding freshmen. McClain became a starter at midseason, but Van Scyoc had to persuade Griffin's mother to let her son play on the varsity. As the sixth man, he gave the team a big lift as a rebounder.

The Rams weren't intimidated by anyone. Van Scyoc had scheduled tough opponents in tournaments in Missouri and Arkansas. "A few years earlier, we were in awe of Chicago teams. But these kids didn't back away from anyone," he said.

"High school basketball put Peoria on the map in a positive way," said Van Scyoc, who retired after the 1994 season and handed his playbook to McClain. "It used to be a negative connotation on late-night talk shows on television, as in, 'How does it play in Peoria?' Our town was referred to as the Mayberry of the Midwest. Now colleges from all over the country come here to recruit our players."

Peoria Manual: Four State Titles in a Row

As young players at Peoria Manual in the 1970s and 1980s, Wayne McClain and David Booth were always on the fringe, always on the outside looking in. They played on good teams that were long on potential but short on production. In other words, they never won a state championship.

McClain started on Manual's 1972 team that finished fourth in the first Class AA tournament. Later, he assisted Dick Van Scyoc on Manual teams that finished second in 1991 and third in 1986 and 1988.

"We were knocking on the door and on the verge of knocking the door down, but we couldn't get it done," McClain said. "We ran into great teams from Chicago and East St. Louis Lincoln. We were always around but never got it done."

In 1960–61, Eddie Jackson led Manual to the Elite Eight. After scoring twenty-seven points in a supersectional victory over Ottawa, however, he was declared ineligible because he was nineteen years old. Manual lost to Collinsville in the semifinals and finished fourth.

In 1986–87, Booth starred on a 31–0 team that was ranked number one in the state and number five in the nation before losing in the state quarterfinals to Quincy 61–59 in overtime on James Bailey's half-court shot that banked off the glass.

In 1987–88, Booth returned to the Assembly Hall only to be disappointed again. Manual lost to East St. Louis Lincoln by seventeen points in the semifinals. "Later, I felt we could have won two state titles in a row," Booth said. "We should have won in 1987. My era was the last era when we were knocking on the door but never got through."

The breakthrough finally came in 1994, almost thirty years after Van Scyoc took over the program. While the media was touting unbeaten Joliet and Westinghouse, which had upset top-ranked and unbeaten King for the Chicago Public League championship, few people outside Peoria noticed as Manual, a six-time loser without a starter taller than 6' 3", rode guards Brandun Hughes, Willie Coleman, and Ivan Watson to the state title.

The Rams beat Danville by nine, Westinghouse by five, and Rockford Boylan by thirteen, then edged Carbondale and Troy Hudson 61–60 in the final. Hughes, a sixfooter, blocked a layup by Carbondale's 6' 7" Rashad Tucker with a minute to play and then converted two free throws with 4.2 seconds left to account for the winning margin.

"It was the best thing that ever happened to us, becoming a champion," McClain said. "You always think you are doing good when you finish second, third, or fourth. But there is nothing like the feeling when you finish first. Once our kids experienced it, they wanted to experience it again."

When Van Scyoc decided to retire after the season, McClain was ready to step up. He was indebted to Van Scyoc, who had helped to prepare him for the job. It was a smooth transition because Van Scyoc was secure in his position and never felt threatened by his younger, ambitious assistant.

As a youngster, McClain lettered in football, basketball, and baseball in high school. He thought that baseball was his best sport, but he earned an academic scholarship to Bradley University and played basketball for three years.

He idolized Al Smith, perhaps the best athlete ever developed in Peoria. He was an All-Stater in 1965 and later played at Bradley. He took McClain to his first Bradley game.

McClain lived on the South Side, but he knew that the place for all aspiring basketball players to be in the summer was State Park, located near the downtown area.

"Everyone played there. If you could play, you played there. That's where everyone got their reputation. If you could play, you had to play at State Park," he said.

In an era when there were no AAU or traveling teams, no Nike or Adidas camps, McClain played at State Park, then at Carver Center and Proctor Center.

He took the game as far as he could, then used his degree in education to begin teaching and coaching in the Peoria public school system. He joined the staff at Peoria Manual in 1984 and served as Van Scyoc's assistant until he retired after the 1994 season. Then it was his time.

"I always felt I was ready for the job," McClain said. "I knew the system so well, but I changed some things. Van used to be a walk-it-down-the-court coach but became up-tempo at the end of his career. I always wanted to run fast, be quick, press, apply defensive pressure from the beginning. I wanted to be an entertaining type of coach."

He also was knowledgeable, flexible, and a disciplinarian, and he knew a good thing when he saw it. Coleman and Watson returned in 1994–95 to key another championship. Then Sergio McClain, the coach's son, and Marcus Griffin were the headliners on the 1996 and 1997 state champions. The 1997 club, which also included junior sensation Frank Williams and sophomore whiz Marlon Brooks, was ranked number one in the nation by *USA Today*.

"When we opened the door, we got a swagger, an attitude you get that tells everybody that you are the best," Wayne McClain said. "If you have talent, you put that swagger to use. You hope no one can knock that chip off your shoulder."

Along the way, Manual had to defeat three outstanding Thornton teams that lost only four games in three years. The Rams beat a Thornton team led by Tai Streets, Chauncey Jones, and James Johnson 65–53 for the 1995 state title, then clipped Thornton powerhouses led by Melvin Ely, Erik Herring, and Napoleon Harris 57–51 for the 1996 crown and 65–62 in the 1997 semifinals. In the 1997 final, Manual rallied to edge West Aurora 47–43 to claim its fourth title in a row.

"Four state titles . . . what was most fun and most satisfying was knowing we could go on the court and win," said Sergio McClain, who played on all four championship teams. "When you go to college, you deal with different personalities and guys who didn't grow up in the streets. Some players have heart, and some don't. I learned that, no matter how much talent you have, you can't beat someone who has a bigger heart, is better coached, works harder, and plays like a team."

Wayne McClain was a player's coach. He treated his players like Van Scyoc had once treated him, like family: he provided clothes and groceries for those in need. But the coach/player relationship created a schism between the father and his son.

"At first it was tough to play for him because he would use me to set an example," Sergio said. "We didn't get along sometimes because I felt things weren't fair. Things got cool between us. He expected a lot out of me—and I was just a sophomore in high school. He expected me to do things that a senior could do."

For a while, basketball ceased to be fun. Wayne McClain was in a tough position, succeeding Van Scyoc, the winningest coach in state history, and there was a lot of pressure on him to win another state championship. He was a hard worker, and he always wanted to be in the gym. Sergio wanted to be a kid.

"It came to the point where I wanted to quit basketball," Sergio said. "It wasn't fun anymore. The more we won, the worse the pressure got. We couldn't be ourselves because everyone was looking at us. Kids looked at us as role models."

Finally, midway during Sergio's sophomore season, father/coach and son/player sat down to clear the air. Sergio told his father how he felt, that the game wasn't fun and he felt like quitting. The coach understood, but he made Sergio realize that to reach his potential, he had to accept challenges.

Sergio and Marcus Griffin felt even more pressure as seniors. Manual was heavily favored to win an unprecedented fourth state title in a row, and the two All-Staters were neck-and-neck for the Mr. Basketball prize as the state's top player.

"It wasn't the best of times," Wayne McClain admitted. "It was a case of senioritis. It was my toughest coaching job. I had to keep checks and balances, keep them humble, keep a carrot out there in terms of goals. I had to make sure they worked as hard as ever."

One day during practice, father told son, "Sergio, if you don't want it, be a student."

"I didn't want any conflict," the coach said. "They were all feeling the heat of trying to win four state titles in a row. They also were in the race for the national championship. It got crazy. Expectations were high. Every game was sold out. It was so competitive."

Sergio observed how his father handled the pressure, how he kept the team together, how he handled personal conflicts, how he deflated egos, and how he dealt with the media, parents, and fans. Someday, he said, after he stops chasing his dreams, he might want to be a coach. If so, he has a wealth of personal experiences to draw from.

"To be great at any level, you have to have the trust of your players, and they have to want to play for you and win for you," Sergio said. "There must be a two-way street. A coach must sacrifice for his team, and the team must sacrifice for him.

"You can't let ego problems get in the way. You can't have a dominant role. When a player sees something isn't working and he tells the coach and the coach doesn't listen because he doesn't respect you or is too set in his ways . . . well, you can't win like that. Leadership isn't something that you can put on a statistics sheet."

Quad Cities: "The Greatest High School Arena"

It was a hot summer day, and Whitey Verstraete and George Gnatovich were standing in Wharton Fieldhouse in Moline, recalling its proud history and admiring the many banners hanging from the ceiling and the pure majesty of the cavernous interior.

The sixty-five-hundred-seat barnlike structure, with a balcony overlooking the playing floor, was built in 1927. It is Moline's home court and home to the Moline/Rock Island series, the oldest rivalry in the state. Moline once sold over five thousand season tickets and realized a hundred thousand dollars per game in revenue.

"It is the greatest high school arena in the state," said Verstraete, who was an All-Stater at Moline in 1954 and 1955 and later coached at Rock Island and Moline. "It was better when the old floor was raised. It had a spring to it, like the Boston Celtics' old arena and New York's Madison Square Garden."

Wharton has been a showcase for high school basketball. Gnatovich recalls when Lyons Township and Ted Caiazza played before a standing-room-only crowd in 1953. "You had to have a season ticket to be sure of getting a seat," he said.

Everyone wanted to experience the electric atmosphere. Moline snapped Paris's thirty-nine-game winning streak in 1943. Verstraete's team snapped Lyons's forty-four-game winning streak in 1954. Chicago Du Sable played there in the 1950s, Chicago King in the 1980s. Proviso East's Glenn Rivers played at Wharton for four years in a row. Moline also hosted great teams from Quincy, Proviso East, Collinsville, Bloom, Lockport, and Decatur.

"When you played there, you thought you had died and gone to heaven," said Sharm Scheuerman, a 1952 Rock Island graduate who later teamed with Moline's Bill Seaberg to win two Big Ten championships at Iowa. "Most high school gyms are wide open, but Wharton looked like a professional facility. When we played Moline, it was like playing for a world championship."

Herb Thompson, who coached at Moline for thirteen years, concedes that Quincy and Galesburg have great traditions, "but I would put Moline ahead of them in a lot of ways," and Wharton is most of them.

"There was an aura about it," Thompson said. "It has a particular flavor about it that makes it such a good place to coach. The school owns the building. Nobody bothers you. We had the floor all the time, no girls, no gym classes. There is no other place like it."

Thompson was on the bench for one of the most memorable games ever played at Wharton. In 1968, Galesburg, with Ruben Triplett and Zach Thiel, was rated number one in the nation. A local television station persuaded Moline to switch the game to Thursday night for a live telecast. Moline won in overtime.

"It was the stuff that dreams are made of," said Scott Thompson, Herb's son. "I was an eighth grader, sitting in the front row of the student section. It was like NBC coming to town to do a game with Dick Enberg and Billy Packer."

Later, Scott played on his father's 1969–72 teams, played at Iowa, and coached at Iowa, Arizona, Rice, Wichita State, and Cornell. But he never forgot the excitement of a Friday night at Wharton. "I never played before an empty seat," he said.

"Back before ESPN, before college games were on television, that's where people went on Friday night," Scott said. "Watching the great teams in that atmosphere was the same feeling as when you went to Wrigley Field. It was a college atmosphere, like Williams Arena in Minneapolis or Cameron Indoor Stadium at Duke or Robertson Field House at Bradley."

Something is missing, however. Despite the great teams (Moline, Rock Island, East Moline, Rock Island Alleman), the great coaches (Don Morris, Herb Thompson, Duncan Reid, Cliff Talley), and the great players (Verstraete, Don Nelson, Steve Kuberski, Steve Spanich, Steve Hunter, Pete Mickeal), the Quad Cities have never produced a state champion.

All of them have finished second in the state tournament. Some were ranked number one in the state at one time or other. Moline "should have won" in 1965 but lost to Chicago Marshall and Rich Bradshaw in the quarterfinals. East Moline "had the best team" in 1979 but blew a nine-point lead in the fourth quarter and lost to the eventual champion, Maine South, 77–76 in overtime in the semifinals.

Rock Island was 27–4 but lost to the eventual champion, Chicago Simeon, by four in the 1984 quarterfinals. The Rocks were 27–6 but lost to St. Francis de Sales and Eric Anderson 58–56 in overtime in the 1988 semifinals. And they were 28–5, led Thornton by thirteen, and lost by one in the 1995 semifinals.

"We have been close, but some good teams lost to good Rockford or Chicago or Collinsville teams," said Reid, who won more than six hundred games before retiring in 2001. "For years, the regional was the thing that mattered most. We played at Rock Island or East Moline or Wharton. We'd play three times in one year. There were a lot of upsets. Sometimes we were victimized by the luck of the draw or just bad luck."

Reid recalls a 72–69 loss to Moline in the 1980 regional final. It was such a gut-wrenching emotional setback that one distraught player, Leon Baker, quit school the following Monday, and Reid never saw him again.

"People still remind me of that game. I still remember the game and the final score," Reid said. "It's like asking me where I was when President Kennedy was assassinated. The players said the loss hurt so much, that the game was their whole life."

"We all have reasons why we didn't win," Verstraete said. "There are certain years you coach and you know you're not as good as someone or not good enough to win the state. You played all over the state and had a good idea where you stood."

Spanich, who led Alleman to fourth in 1964, said that until recently he never realized that the Quad Cities had never won a state title. "It wasn't because of competition. We still play Chicago schools and play in the Western Big Six, one of the best conferences in the state," he said. "Unless you have two or three dominating players on a team, you can't win the state title. Maybe we haven't had dominating players like other teams. We also beat each other to death. But wouldn't you think the law of averages would catch up?"

Scott Thompson pointed out that the Quad Cities have never produced a Mr. Basketball in Illinois. As a college recruiter, he recalled that he rarely returned to the Quad Cities to seek talent. Aside from Nelson and Kuberski, how many went on to have great college careers and play in the NBA?

"Not a lot of great players have come out of the Quad Cities," Thompson said. "I have recruited everywhere, and the talent level and teams in Chicago get better and better, starting in the 1960s. In the Quad Cities, there is culture and tradition and competition. But how many Division I prospects have gone on to play well in college?"

Mickeal might be best of all, better than Nelson or Kuberski. The 6' 6", 235-pounder led Rock Island to 28–5 and 29–2 records in 1995 and 1996. He averaged twenty-four points per game. At Indian Hills Junior College in Ottumwa, Iowa, he was national junior college player of the year and led his team to two national championships. At Cincinnati he was a standout on two nationally ranked teams. He was the fifty-eighth selection in the NBA draft by the Dallas Mavericks, was traded to the New York Knicks, and then released. He played in Poland and the ABA. He hopes to land a spot on an NBA roster next season.

He credits Reid for jump-starting his career. "Not too many people cared about me when I was growing up in Rock Island. He grabbed me out of bed one day. I was so lazy. He dragged me to a summer school session. Without that day, I wouldn't have played as a junior and senior. That's when I realized I had a future. It was one of the turning points of my life. He is the guy who started my career and taught me how to play basketball and to be responsible," he said.

But neither of them could win a state title. Both remember that 1996 loss to Thornton. "It was our best chance. Josh Elston had a wide open three at the buzzer. It hit the backboard and went in and out. Sometimes breaks don't go for you. In junior college, we won seventy-two games in a row. Three times we hit threes at the buzzer to send games into overtime. If breaks don't happen, it's a whole different season," Mickeal said.

Old-timers insist that Moline's 1965 team was best of all. Herb Thompson's Maroons, led by the 6' 7" Kuberski, guard Geoff Smithers, and 6' 9" center Terry Carlson, started 12–0 and were ranked number one in the state. In the supersectional, they trounced Freeport by seventeen. Kuberski had thirty points and eighteen rebounds.

In the quarterfinals, it was Moline versus Chicago Marshall, Kuberski versus Bradshaw. Moline led by three with less than a minute to play. Don Price was fouled and made his first free throw for a four-point edge, but an official ruled that a Moline player had stepped over the line, took the point away, and gave Marshall the ball. Bradshaw scored, Clyde Oatis stole the ball and scored, and Marshall won 75–72.

"It was the most disappointing loss of my career, college or pro," Kuberski said. "We lost to the Knicks in the seventh game of the NBA playoff, but that loss to Marshall was even more disappointing. I scored thirty-four points in that game. We should have been the first Quad Cities champion."

East Aurora/West Aurora: Rivalry Heats Up

The East Aurora/West Aurora basketball rivalry is the second oldest in Illinois. It began in 1912, about a dozen years after Moline and Rock Island began their intercity feud.

But folks in the Kane County communities that straddle the Fox River insist that the series didn't really begin to heat up until the 1960s, when John McDougal became head coach at West and Ernie Kivisto became head coach at East. "Until then, it was a friendly rivalry because we knew each other from the playgrounds," said Neal Ormond, who played with Bill Small and Grayal Gilkey on West Aurora's 1958 team that finished fourth in state. "But it intensified when Kivisto showed up."

"Until McDougal/Kivisto, football was a bigger rivalry than basketball," Gilkey said. "When I played, it wasn't friendly as it is now. It was more intense before, because kids didn't play against each other in the spring and summer. It was special."

Growing up, Ormond stayed home from school to listen to WMRO's Chick Hearn do play-by-play for the 1949 state tournament, when West's John Biever beat Tilden's Johnny Kerr in the quarterfinals and went on to finish fourth. As a student at Yale, he spotted for college football games covered by Curt Gowdy and Paul Christman. He has covered East/West basketball games on radio for forty years.

"I realized the East/West rivalry really meant something," he said. "Kids talked about the East game all the time, what it meant to them. In high school, my main goal was to make the varsity basketball team. I'd like to think I would have started if Bill Small hadn't transferred from Roanoke-Benson."

Small became one of the most celebrated players in East/West history. He was the leading scorer in the 1959 state tournament, leading West to second place. Ormond ranks him with Biever (West), Kenny Battle (West), John Bryant (West), and Tom Kivisto (East) on his All-Aurora team.

McDougal and Kivisto were complete opposites, like sparklers and hand grenades. McDougal, who was hired at West in 1965 and retired after his 1976 team finished second at state, was 15–14 against East in eleven years. Kivisto, who came from East Moline in 1967 and coached until 1982, was 19–20 against West in fifteen years.

In his first season, Kivisto won 61–59, 65–62, and 66–65. He won his first eight games against West. In 1973 he fired his longtime scorekeeper Art Court, who worked the clock during the regional at West. East lost to West 50–48 on a tip-in at the buzzer, and Kivisto blamed Court for being slow to press the button.

"It was the most unique rivalry," said former West coach Dick Dorsey, who was 12–0 in five years against East. "I've seen East/West games for forty years, and, as intense as the rivalry is, I've never seen an incident occur. I think East Aurora is the best high school gym to see a game . . . Four thousand seats, very intimate setting. The crowd is electric, like the players."

McDougal was very low-key; he was John Wooden to Kivisto's Dick Vitale. He shunned the spotlight. He was a disciplinarian but never profane. His hallmarks were pattern offense, high-percentage shots, and defense. He restored pride and commitment to a program that had faded after Dorsey's retirement.

"What made the East/West rivalry interesting were the differences in our style of coaching and our contrasting personalities," McDougal said. "One [East] picked you up when you got off the bus. West played a very disciplined game on offense, Ernie didn't. And Ernie had a persona that people loved or despised.

"No matter which side of the river you lived on, you knew when East/West was coming. We prepared for them even though we wouldn't play for two or three weeks. We had to combat Ernie's pressure defense. Ernie had to prepare for our picks and patience. We always knew we would play three times in a season, and a berth in state might be at stake."

McDougal was third in 1973 with Matt Hicks and John Bryant and runner-up in 1976 with Jay Bryant and Ron Hicks, losing to Morgan Park 45–44 on Laird Smith's shot at the buzzer. After the game, he retired and was succeeded by his assistant, Gordon Kerkman.

Kivisto was a tempest in a teapot: perpetually in motion, very enthusiastic, a showman. He wanted to score a hundred points whenever he could. He copied the Harlem Globetrotters' pregame warm-up with his son Tom orchestrating the behind-the-back, between-the-legs drills. He was criticized for being too flamboyant, overhyping his players, trying to recruit players from West Aurora and other areas, and talking too much.

But kids loved to play for him, and East fans were very supportive. He emphasized offense, putting up a lot of shots and scoring a lot of points. He was exciting, never boring. His 1969 team, led by Tom Kivisto and Algie Neal, finished fourth in state, and his 1972 team, led by tournament scoring leader Greg Smith, finished third.

"He was tough as a boot but fair," said Tom Kivisto. "He loved kids who came from disadvantaged backgrounds because he could influence them. He needed them, and they needed him. He was there to succeed. Winning was a measure of success and achievement, and we would pay whatever the price to get there."

Ernie's best team, his first, didn't qualify for the state finals. His 1967–68 squad, with Tom and Bob Kivisto, 6' 8" Tom Hoover, Charlie McGhee, and Rich Lowery, won the conference championship. But Lowery was sidelined with a knee injury. The Tomcats beat West Aurora by one in the regional but lost to DeKalb in the sectional. DeKalb finished third in the state.

"Those were the best of times," Tom Kivisto said. "You realized what you were made of. You'd get up at five o'clock in the morning during a Chicago winter to get to the gym by six. East/West was the emotional game of the year. Kids couldn't wait for the game, to decorate their cars and ride up and down the streets."

Bob Kivisto was a two-time All-Stater at East Moline in 1967 and at East Aurora in 1968. Later, he coached at East Aurora for four years. He also coached under Sherrill Hanks at Quincy and Steve Goers at Rockford Boylan, but he still recalls the impact that his father had on the game.

"He built basketball in the Fox Valley area," Bob said. "He made every school pick up its emphasis on basketball. McDougal didn't become a great coach until he put in work to beat my dad. After my dad's first three years, if you were going to be competitive, you had to work as hard as he did."

McDougal worked hard enough to get to the state final, something Kivisto never did. Along the way, the Blackhawks' toughest test was a 50–48 victory over East Aurora in the regional final.

In the final against Morgan Park, West Aurora led by seven after the third quarter. Sparked by Levi Cobb, the Chicago Public League champion rallied. West Aurora lost momentum when Jay Bryant fouled out but still led until the last shot.

With a few ticks left, Cobb tied up Larry Hatchett on an in-bounds pass to set up a jump ball. Cobb tipped to Smith, who scored the game winner. Sitting next to his coach, Jay Bryant collapsed on the floor in despair.

"I can still see it," said McDougal, who later coached at Northern Illinois University for ten years. "My heart was where Jay was. I never thought we would lose it. I never had a more devastating loss. It still has a tendency to haunt me."

The rivalry continued to sizzle in the 1980s and 1990s as Kerkman and East coach Scott Martens produced several state qualifiers. Martens won 231 games in twelve years, including state quarterfinalists in 1988, 1989, and 1992 that featured Thomas Wyatt and Durrell Williams.

"Coach Martens doesn't get as much credit as he should," said Wyatt, a three-time All-Stater who scored 2,575 career points and played in more East/West games than anyone else. "It was Kivisto's town because he put it on the map. But I owe a lot of my success to [Martens]. He taught me moves to take advantage of my quickness and leaping ability."

Kerkman, who has won more than five hundred games since 1976 and holds a 35–26 edge in the East/West rivalry, finished third in 1984 with Kenny Battle and second in 1997 with Jason Passley, Greg Miller, Vince Green, Travis Williams, and Andre Newsom.

"That group set the tempo for what we have done in the last seven years," said Kerkman about the team that lost to Peoria Manual 47–43 in the state final. "We led by five in the fourth quarter. But our kids tightened up at the end. For the last seven years, we have averaged twenty-seven victories per year."

The 2000 squad was reminiscent of 1997 but with great leadership and great poise in crucial situations. Led by All-Stater Louis Smith, Austin Real, Derik Hollyfield, Jamall Thompson, and Mike Fowler, the Blackhawks finished 32–1, beating Darius Miles and East St. Louis in the semifinals and Cedrick Banks, Martell Bailey, and Westinghouse 60–57 for the title.

"You usually can identify a team leader like Battle or Bryant, but it was hard to do with this group," Kerkman said. "Everyone showed leadership when things were going badly. Even though they didn't have a star, they had what it took to win state."

Westinghouse: The White Shadow's Legacy

Eddie Johnson didn't want to attend Austin, which was located across the street from his house on Chicago's West Side, because swimming was a requirement in physical education; he couldn't swim and didn't want to learn. So he enrolled at Westinghouse because his brother didn't and the school didn't have a pool.

At the same time, Mark Aguirre chose to attend Austin. He preferred baseball and football to basketball, but the Ernie Banks wannabe began to concentrate on basketball when he noticed college recruiters wooing Bo Ellis and Mo Cheeks on the playgrounds. Two years later, after coach Gary Peckler was fired, Aguirre transferred to Westinghouse.

Westinghouse was a converted candy factory. It opened in 1968. The neighborhood joke was that athletes who couldn't make it at Marshall or Crane ended up at Westinghouse. The gym was on the fourth floor. The basketball coach had played football at the University of Illinois with Dick Butkus.

But the coach, Frank Lollino, orchestrated the program. He described himself as the "White Shadow," a reference to a popular television drama that portrayed a white basketball coach who related to the problems of an all-black team at an inner-city high school.

"He put Westinghouse on the map," said former Taft coach Frank Hood. "He put a spirit into the school that has carried on to today. Because of what he built in the late 1970s, Westinghouse is known all over the country."

"I took a program that was ragweed and turned it into a greenhouse," Lollino said. "When I took over the program, no one had ever heard of Westinghouse, and now it is one of the most respected programs in the country."

Lollino won 325 games in fifteen years. He won Public League championships in 1979 and 1981. His 1981 squad, led by Wayne Montgomery, Melvin Bradley, and William Mixon, finished third in the Class AA tournament. His teams qualified for the city final four times in five years. He produced six All-Staters, including three future NBA stars—Aguirre, Johnson, and Hersey Hawkins.

"Lollino was the White Shadow," Johnson said. "He was my father figure. Anything he said, I took as gospel. He did so much for us. What he taught me was worth more than a championship. It defined how I carried on in my life."

Aguirre said that Lollino was "one of the straightest guys you could imagine. There was no fooling him. He wouldn't lie to you. He cared about the kids, and he was always there for you. He looked at every game like it was for a championship."

Hawkins flunked three courses as a freshman and quit the frosh-soph basketball team because he didn't want to commit to two-a-day practices. But his counselor, Lona Bibbs, now Westinghouse's principal, urged him to use basketball to get out of the city. He took her advice, and Lollino pointed him in the right direction.

"I owe him so much," Hawkins said. "I recall sitting in a meeting with him after I quit as a freshman. He cursed me out. He told me how I had a great opportunity and I was screwing it up. You need someone to tell you the truth, and he did."

When Lollino left Westinghouse in 1986, he left a legacy and a sturdy foundation that succeeding coaches Roy Condotti, Frank Griseto, Chris Head, and Quitman Dillard could build on.

Condotti took five teams to the Sweet Sixteen in nine seasons and then moved to Homewood-Flossmoor. His 1992 team, led by David Greer and three-time All-Stater Kiwane Garris, finished third. Griseto finished third in 1996. Head was second in 2000, won the school's first state championship in 2002, and then was wooed to Proviso West.

The basketball program wouldn't have grown if Lollino hadn't planted the seeds. "He was P.T. Barnum. He loved the spotlight, he embraced it, he was magnetic," said Condotti, who was twenty-three when he became Lollino's assistant in 1973. "The kids loved him. They were drawn to him. He would have been successful in anything he coached."

Lollino was an All–Big Ten football player. He became a basketball coach because he couldn't get a coaching job in football. When he got to Westinghouse, he didn't know a pick-and-roll from a quarterback sneak. But he attended clinics, read textbooks, and picked the brains of such knowledgeable coaches as St. Joseph's Gene Pingatore, St. Patrick's Max Kurland, and East Aurora's Ernie Kivisto.

"The time was right for him," said Condotti, who formed a team with George Cappizano, Lollino's boyhood friend. "Basketball had been popular in the city in the 1950s and 1960s, but it exploded when he was there. I don't know if too many guys could have pulled it off. But he did."

Condotti said that Westinghouse's game with Phillips for the 1977 Public League championship "capped the golden era in the city," coming on the heels of state championships by Hirsch (1973), Phillips (1975), and Morgan Park (1976). Phillips and Westinghouse were unbeaten and ranked first and second in the state. Phillips, with Darius Clemons, beat Westinghouse, with Aguirre and Johnson, 77–65 before twelve thousand at the Amphitheater.

"It was one of the most hurtful losses in my career," said Aguirre, who was a two-time All-America at DePaul and played in the NBA for fourteen years. "But when I look back on it, it was the most incredible experience I could have in high school. Two high school teams on the front page of the newspaper. And how many kids play in front of twelve thousand people?"

Johnson, who was an All-American at Illinois and played in the NBA for seventeen years, said that he appreciates the 1977 game more today. At the time, he felt that Westinghouse had the most talent, that he could have done more to change the outcome, even though he scored twenty-three points. "We put a buzz in the city," he said.

In 1978 Johnson had graduated, but Aguirre returned with Skip Dillard and Michael Jenkins. They won the school's first Public League championship but lost to Isiah Thomas and St. Joseph 63–60 in the state quarterfinals.

In 1979, the Johnson/Aguirre era was over. Despite losing ten games in the regular season, Westinghouse returned to the city final, losing to Manley 88–83 in double overtime. Jenkins, Melvin Bradley, Bernard Randolph, and Larry Roby stood out.

In 1981, Lollino made his last trip to Champaign. Westinghouse lost eleven games during the regular season and wasn't rated among the top four teams in the city, but the Warriors finished third in the state.

Condotti was an X's and O's man. What he learned from Lollino was how to treat athletes like family. Like Lollino, he picked the brains of other coaches, such as Phillips's Herb Brown and Marshall's Luther Bedford. But he most admired Kivisto.

"Kivisto had the program we wanted to be like," Condotti said. "He ran and pressed. It was an exciting brand of basketball. He wanted to score a hundred points per game. We patterned ourselves after him. If we scored a hundred points, we bought pizza. That was the kids' goal in every game."

Condotti lost in the city final to King and Marshall in 1990 and 1991 but beat King 76–68 for the city title in 1992 and went on to finish third in the Class AA tournament. He lost to King in the 1993 city final but beat King 59–58 for the city crown in 1994 with Mark Miller and Damion Dantzler, then lost to Peoria Manual in the state quarterfinals. In five years, they won 84 percent (130–25) of their games.

Condotti handpicked his successors. Griseto, a boyhood friend, had coached at St. Ignatius and Notre Dame of Niles. Griseto's 1996 team, led by 5' 6" guard Jimmy Sanders, was 29–5 and finished third in state.

Head, who had been frosh-soph coach at Farragut, was hired in 1987 to coach the frosh-soph. "He was intense. I liked the way he ran his team. I saw a lot of potential in him. He always seems to have a chip on his shoulder, but his intensity makes him successful," Condotti said.

In four years as Westinghouse's head coach, Head produced teams that finished 29–1, 31–2, 16–12, and 30–5. His 2000 team, led by Cedrick Banks and Martell Bailey, finished second in state. His 2002 squad, sparked by Darius Glover and Jamaal Brown, upset Springfield Lanphier 76–72 for the state title.

"Roy Condotti was like Mike Krzyzewski, Chris Head was like Bob Knight," said David Bailey, who starred on Head's first team. "Head taught us the seven B's—books before basketball because broads bring babies. He made sure I went to class and set an example for the younger players."

Head says that he owes everything to Condotti. "None of this would be possible without Condotti. He is the man who gave me a chance, and it is something I can never repay. I got to participate in one of the great programs in the state and learned the game of basketball," he said.

But it all started with Frank Lollino. He died in 1999 at age fifty-eight. His big heart finally gave out.

"He was the life of the party," Frank Hood said. "He had fun in coaching, and his kids picked up on it. Most important, he cared about his kids. He was concerned about them as individuals and what they did in the future. He treated them well, and they produced for him."

Overtime

All-Time Best Players

(Top ten players by decades)

1940s: Dike Eddleman, Centralia; John Orr, Ron Bontemps, Taylorville; Andy Phillip, Granite City; Ted Beach, Champaign; Bob Doster, Decatur; Fred Green, Urbana; Irv Bemoras, Chicago Marshall; Jake Fendley, Chicago South Shore; Max Hooper, Mount Vernon.

1950s: McKinley Davis, Freeport; Ted Caiazza, La Grange; Archie Dees, Mount Carmel; Nolden Gentry, West Rockford; Harv Schmidt, Kankakee; Art Hicks, Chicago St. Elizabeth; Tom Hawkins, Chicago Parker; Bobby Joe Mason, Centralia; Paxton Lumpkin, Chicago Du Sable; Terry Bethel, Collinsville.

1960s: Cazzie Russell, Chicago Carver; George Wilson, Chicago Marshall; Bogie Redmon, Rodger Bohnenstiehl, Tom Parker, Collinsville; Jerry Sloan, McLeansboro; Dave Robisch, Springfield; Jim Brewer, Proviso East (Maywood); Billy Harris, Chicago Dunbar; Greg Starrick, Marion.

1970s: Class A: Jay Shidler, Rick Leighty, Lawrenceville; Jim Crews, Normal University High; Don Noort, Chicago Christian (Palos Heights); Jack Sikma, St. Anne; Mike Duff, Eldorado; Perry Range, South Beloit; Darryl Winston, Lovejoy; Bob Guyette, Ottawa Marquette; Rick Suttle, Assumption (East St. Louis).

Class AA: Lloyd Batts, Thornton (Harvey); Isiah Thomas, St. Joseph (Westchester); Quinn Buckner, Thornridge (Dolton); Rickey Green, Chicago Hirsch; Glen Grunwald, East Leyden (Franklin Park); Mark Aguirre, Chicago Westinghouse; Terry Cummings, Chicago Carver; Owen Brown, La Grange; Darius Clemons, Chicago Phillips; Roger Powell, Joliet Central.

1980s: Class A: Marty Simmons, Doug Novsek, Lawrenceville; Walter Downing, Providence (New Lenox); Anthony Webster, Cairo; Lowell Hamilton, Chicago Providence–St. Mel; Jesse Hall, Venice; Brian Sloan, McLeansboro; Barry Sumpter, Lovejoy; Bill Braksick, Flanagan; Rennie Clemmons, Springfield Calvary.

Class AA: Glenn "Doc" Rivers, Proviso East (Maywood); Russell Cross, Chicago Manley; Bruce Douglas, Quincy; Nelison "Nick" Anderson, Deon Thomas, Chicago Simeon;

Marcus Liberty, Chicago King; Joe Stiffend, Chicago Marshall; Thomas Wyatt, East Aurora; Andy Kaufmann, Jacksonville; Ed Horton, Springfield Lanphier.

1990s: Class A: Jerry Gee, Tyron Triplett, Chicago St. Martin de Porres; Marc Davidson, Aurora Christian; Tyrone Nesby, Cairo; JoJo Johnson, Benton; Shane Hawkins, Pinckneyville; Tony Baker, Pittsfield; Shawn Jeppson, Spring Valley Hall; Rich Beyers, Shelbyville; T. J. Wheeler, Christopher.

Class AA: Jamie Brandon, Rashard Griffith, Chicago King; Sergio McClain, Peoria Manual; Kevin Garnett, Ronnie Fields, Chicago Farragut; Mike Robinson, Peoria Richwoods; Antoine Walker, Chicago Mount Carmel; Kiwane Garris, Chicago Westinghouse; Juwan Howard, Chicago Vocational; Troy Hudson, Carbondale.

Top Five Players:

Dike Eddleman, Centralia; Isiah Thomas, St. Joseph (Westchester); Cazzie Russell, Chicago Carver; Quinn Buckner, Thornridge (Dolton); George Wilson, Chicago Marshall.

Taylor Bell's Favorite Five:

Quinn Buckner, Thornridge (Dolton); Isiah Thomas, St. Joseph (Westchester); Glen Grunwald, East Leyden (Franklin Park); Tom Parker, Collinsville; Lloyd Batts, Thornton (Harvey).

Top Five Teams:

Thornridge 1972; Quincy 1981; Chicago Marshall 1958; Collinsville 1961; Taylorville 1944.

Top Five Coaches:

Vergil Fletcher, Collinsville; Arthur Trout, Centralia; Dolph Stanley, Equality, Mount Pulaski, Taylorville, Rockford Auburn, Rockford Boylan; Ernie Eveland, Paris; Gay Kintner, Decatur.

Top Five Championship Games:

1989: East St. Louis Lincoln 59, Peoria Central 57, 3 OT
1963: Chicago Carver 53, Centralia 52
1976: Chicago Morgan Park 45, West Aurora 44
1952: Hebron 64, Quincy 59, OT
1985: Chicago Mount Carmel 46, Springfield Lanphier 44, 2 OT

All-Time Winningest Programs:

(Four consecutive years or more)

East Leyden (Franklin Park), 1974–78 Coach Norman Goodman	104–4	.963
King (Chicago), 1989–94 Coach Landon Cox	177–7	.962
Quincy, 1978–82 Coach Jerry Leggett	123–5	.961
Lawrenceville, 1979–83 Coach Ron Felling	123–7	.946
Peoria Manual, 1994–98 Coach Wayne McClain	121–8	.938
Bunker Hill, 1980–84 Coach Jim Hlafka	101–7	.935
Simeon (Chicago), 1983–89 Coach Bob Hambric	163–12	.931
Centralia, 1960–64 Coaches Bill Davies, Bob Jones	118–9	.929
Proviso East (Maywood), 1989–93 Coach Bill Hitt	116–9	.928
Lockport, 1976–80 Coach Bob Basarich	110–9	.924
Mount Vernon, 1948–52 Coach Stan Changnon	120–11	.916
Collinsville, 1962–67 Coach Vergil Fletcher	161–15	.915
Champaign, 1943–47 Coach Harry Combes	136–13	.913
Pekin, 1963–67 Coach Dawson Hawkins	115–11	.913
Marshall (Chicago), 1957–61 Coaches Isadore (Spin) Salario, Harvey Hartenstein	115–11	.913
Paris, 1937–43 Coach Ernie Eveland	208–20	.912
Rockford Boylan, 1983–87 Coach Steve Goers	113–11	.911
Pinckneyville, 1951–56 Coach Merrill (Duster) Thomas	155–17	.901

Thornton (Harvey), 1992–97 Coaches Sam Cameli, Rocky Hill	137–15	.901
Taylorville, 1941–45 Coach Dolph Stanley	155–18	.896

All-Time Winningest Coaches:

(Based on winning percentage)

Landon Cox, Chicago King, 1980–2001	503–89	.850
Harry Combes, Champaign, 1938–47	254–46	.847
Wayne McClain, Peoria Manual, 1995–2001	177–35	.835
Bob Basarich, Lockport, 1967–1987	496–99	.834
Ron Felling, Lawrenceville, 1967–1983	388–77	.834
Ernie Eveland, Paris, 1935–1949, 1952–1958	779–175	.817
Glenn Whittenberg, Proviso East (Maywood), 1969–1983	301–68	.816
John Thiel, Galesburg, 1956–1973	396–90	.815
Merrill (Duster) Thomas, Pinckneyville, 1938–1957	495–118	.808
Bob Hambric, Chicago Simeon, 1980–2003	528–129	.804
Tony Maffia, Chicago South Shore, Dunbar, 1941–1957	438–107	.804
Eugene DeLacey, Dundee, 1928–1959	691–172	.801

Top Five Teams That Didn't Win a State Title:

Chicago Du Sable, 1954; Centralia, 1941; Chicago Farragut, 1995; Collinsville, 1957; Paris, 1942.

Top Five Players Who Didn't Compete in the State Finals:

Glenn "Doc" Rivers, Proviso East (Maywood); Dan Issel, Batavia; Glen Grunwald, East Leyden (Franklin Park); Bobby Joe Mason, Centralia; Jerry Sloan, McLeansboro.

Three-Time All-Staters:

Lou Boudreau, Thornton (Harvey), 1933–35; Dike Eddleman, Centralia, 1940–42; Walt Moore, Mount Vernon, 1949–51; George Wilson, Chicago Marshall, 1958–60; Glen Grunwald, East Leyden (Franklin Park), 1974–76; Glenn "Doc" Rivers, Proviso East (Maywood), 1978–80; Marcus Liberty, Chicago King, 1985–87; Jamie Brandon, Chicago King, 1988–90; Thomas Wyatt, East Aurora, 1988–90; Kiwane Garris, Chicago Westinghouse, 1991–93; Rashard Griffith, Chicago King, 1991–93; Ronnie Fields, Chicago Farragut, 1994–96; Corey Maggette, Fenwick (Oak Park), 1996–98; Andre Brown, Chicago Leo, 1998–2000.

Top Five Games:

(Excluding the State Finals)

1. Collinsville 66, Centralia 64, 1961 supersectional at Salem
2. West Rockford 66, Galesburg 64, 2 OT, 1956 supersectional at Moline
3. Lockport 42, Burbank St. Laurence 41, 1978 sectional semifinal at Downers Grove North
4. La Grange 83, Kankakee 74, 1953 sectional semifinal at Joliet
5. East Leyden (Franklin Park) 64, Maine South (Park Ridge) 62, OT, 1974 East Aurora Holiday Tournament semifinal

Did You Know?

According to *Student Sports* magazine, based in Torrance, California, six Illinois players have earned National Player of the Year recognition since 1955—Cazzie Russell of Chicago Carver in 1962, Quinn Buckner of Thornridge (Dolton) in 1972, Mark Aguirre of Chicago Westinghouse in 1978, Glenn "Doc" Rivers of Proviso East (Maywood) in 1980, Kevin Garnett of Chicago Farragut in 1995, and Darius Miles of East St. Louis in 2000.

In 1979, Isiah Thomas of St. Joseph (Westchester) lost a close vote to Clark Kellogg of Cleveland, Ohio, preventing a three-year sweep by Chicago-area players. In 1987, Marcus Liberty of Chicago King was runner-up to Larry Johnson of Dallas, Texas.

Sources

Interviews:

Acker, Isreal (Izzy). Former Chicago Marshall basketball player. Now retired and living in Chicago. Interviewed via telephone on October 31, 2002.

Aden, Joe. Former Dongola basketball player. Now mayor of East Cape Girardeau, Illinois. Interviewed at his home in East Cape Girardeau on August 22, 2002.

Adkins, Jim. Former Benton basketball player. Currently safety director for the Tuscaloosa, Alabama, city schools. Interviewed via telephone on August 2, 2002.

Aguirre, Mark. Former Chicago Westinghouse basketball player, former NBA player, formerly assistant coach with the Indiana Pacers, current assistant coach with the New York Knicks. Interviewed via telephone on November 15, 2002.

Allen, Sterling (Dunnie). Bunker Hill basketball fan since the late 1950s. Interviewed via telephone on October 7, 2002.

Anderson, Bob. Former Thornton (Harvey) Township basketball coach. Now retired and living in Michigan. Interviewed via telephone on April 11, 2002.

Ator, Wayne. A graduate of Pittsfield in 1934, a long-time Pittsfield basketball fan and radio sports broadcaster (known as the "Voice of the Saukees"). Interviewed at Pittsfield High School on September 4, 2002.

Avant, Al. Former Mount Vernon basketball player. Athletic director at Chicago State University since 1988. He lives in Chicago. Interviewed via telephone on October 22, 2002.

Bailey, David. Former Chicago Westinghouse basketball player. Recently graduated from Loyola University in Chicago. Interviewed via telephone on November 13, 2002.

Baker, Jeff. Former Maine South (Park Ridge) basketball player. Now an executive with Terminix, a termite and pest control company, in Toledo, Ohio. Interviewed via telephone on April 23, 2002.

Baker, Harold "Curly." Former Decatur basketball player. Now retired and living in Decatur. Interviewed at the Holiday Inn in Decatur on August 28, 2002.

Baker, Tony. Former Pittsfield basketball player. Currently employed as information technology support for Archer Daniels Midland and living in Decatur. He also owns his own online web company that advertises homes for sale. Interviewed at the Holiday Inn in Decatur on August 27, 2002.

Banks, Renault (Ray). Former Thornton (Harvey) Township basketball player. Formerly employed by United Airlines. Now retired and living in Corona, California. Interviewed via telephone on June 2, 2002.

Bankston, Tim. Former Chicago Simeon basketball player. Currently head basketball coach at Thornton Fractional North High School in Calumet City. Interviewed via telephone on November 2, 2002.

Barnes, Ken. Former Decatur basketball player. Now a teacher at Rockford Auburn High School. Head basketball coach at Auburn from 1977 to 1982. In 2002, he was the school's head football coach. Interviewed via telephone on June 5, 2002.

Battle, Kenny. Former West Aurora basketball player. A member of the NBA Retired Players Association, now living in Scottsdale, Arizona. He is studying to obtain a master's degree in sports business at the University of Illinois. He wants to be a sports agent. Interviewed via telephone on April 30, 2002.

Batts, Boyd. Former Thornridge (Dolton) basketball player. Currently employed by the U.S. Postal Service in Madison, Wisconsin. Interviewed via telephone on March 1, 2002.

Batts, Lloyd. Former Thornton (Harvey) Township basketball player. Currently head basketball coach at South Shore High School in Chicago. Interviewed via telephone on November 8, 2002.

Beach, Ted. Former Champaign basketball player. Now retired and living in Champaign. Interviewed at his home in Champaign on September 23, 2002.

Becker, Dick. Former Elgin basketball player. Now retired after working for Chicago Rawhide, an oil seal manufacturing company in Elgin, for forty-two years. He lives in Elgin. Interviewed via telephone on November 1, 2002.

Bedford, Luther. Former Chicago Marshall basketball coach. Retired from coaching in 1999. Now the school's athletic director. He lives in Bellwood. Interviewed via telephone on May 28, 2002.

Bell, Bobby. Former Bloom basketball player. Retired from teaching in 1994 after thirty-two years. He lives in Chicago Heights. Interviewed via telephone on June 5, 2002.

Bemoras, Irv. Former Chicago Marshall basketball player. Currently a general broker for Mass Mutual insurance company. He lives in Chicago. Interviewed via telephone on June 6, 2002.

Bennett, Dave. Former Pittsfield basketball coach. Retired from coaching basketball in 1999 but continues to teach and coach golf at Pittsfield. Interviewed at his home in Pittsfield on September 4, 2002.

Berkow, Ira. A Sullivan graduate of 1957. Currently a sports columnist and senior writer for the *New York Times*. Interviewed via telephone on April 22, 2002.

Bethel, Terry. Former Collinsville basketball player. Now retired and living in Greer, South Carolina. Interviewed via telephone on August 16, 2002.

Bohnenstiehl, Rodger. Former Collinsville basketball player. Former basketball coach at Kankakee, Rich East, Bradley, and Rich South. Now retired and living in Park Forest. Interviewed via telephone on July 29, 2002.

Bonczyk, Mike. Former Thornridge (Dolton) basketball player. Former head coach at Wichita (West), Kansas, Brimfield, Illinois, and Peoria (Illinois) Notre Dame. Currently head coach at Newton (Kansas) High School. Interviewed via telephone on March 2, 2002.

Bone, Bob. Collinsville basketball coach. Interviewed at Collinsville High School on August 5, 2002.

Booker, Abe. Former Chicago Wells basketball player. Now retired and living in Chicago. Interviewed via telephone on November 23, 2002.

Booth, David. Former Peoria Manual basketball player. Currently playing professional basketball in Japan. Interviewed via telephone on October 18, 2002.

Bontemps, Carl. Former Taylorville basketball player. Now retired and living in Naples, Florida. Interviewed at his home on July 8, 2002.

Bontemps, Ron. Former Taylorville basketball player. Now retired and living in Morton. Interviewed at his home on September 17, 2002.

Border, Butch. President of the Centralia all-sports booster club and past president of the Centralia Hall of Fame. Interviewed at the Green Grill Restaurant in Centralia on September 9, 2002.

Boyle, Bruce. Former Peoria Central basketball coach. Now retired and living in Peoria. Interviewed at Jim's Steakhouse in Peoria on September 16, 2002, and via telephone on October 14, 2002.

Bradshaw, Rich. Former Chicago Marshall basketball player. Currently employed by the State of Illinois as a consultant and living in Chicago. Interviewed via telephone on May 30, 2002.

Brandt, Chuck. Former Elgin basketball player. Currently working for Monroe Calculating Machine Co. in Fort Wayne, Indiana. He lives in Fort Wayne. Interviewed via telephone on April 5, 2002.

Brewer, Jim. Former Proviso East (Maywood) basketball player. Currently an assistant coach for the Toronto Raptors in the NBA. He lives in Toronto, Canada. Interviewed via telephone on June 2, 2002.

Brewer, Tyrone. Former St. Joseph (Westchester) basketball player. Currently section coordinator for RQA Inc., a retail quality assurance company. He lives in Chicago. Interviewed via telephone on November 1, 2002.

Brooks, David. Former Lawrenceville basketball player. Currently a plant manager in North Vernon, Indiana. He lives in North Vernon. Interviewed via telephone on May 13, 2002.

Brown, Charlie. Former Chicago Du Sable basketball player. Retired in 1984 after officiating in the Chicago Public League for more than thirty years. Founded the Windy City Senior Basketball League in 1995. He lives in Chicago. Interviewed via telephone on November 18, 2002.

Brown, Jim. Former Chicago Du Sable basketball coach. Retired from coaching in 1968. Worked as a supervisor for the Chicago Board of Education for sixteen years. Now retired and living in Chicago. Interviewed via telephone on October 29, 2002.

Browning, Brent. Former Ridgway basketball player. Currently president of IFS Inc., which provides investment services to community banks. He lives in Batavia. Interviewed via telephone on May 1, 2002.

Buckner, Quinn. Former Thornridge (Dolton) basketball player. One-time owner of a consulting firm in Milwaukee and Dallas. Now color commentator for college basketball games on ESPN and Indiana Pacers basketball games. Interviewed via telephone on March 3, 2002.

Buhs, Terry. Former Bunker Hill basketball player. Currently president of Wegman Electric in East Alton. He lives in Brighton. Interviewed at the home of former Bunker Hill coach Jim Hlafka in Bunker Hill on August 8, 2002.

Buescher, Chuck. Peoria Central basketball coach. Interviewed at his home in Peoria on March 13, 2002. He provided a videotape of the Peoria Central/East St. Louis Lincoln 1989 state Class AA championship game.

Byassee, Jim. Former Mounds City and Meridian basketball coach. Also coached at Shawnee College. Now retired and living in Florida. Interviewed via telephone on May 29, 2002.

Cabutti, Lee. Former Herrin and Champaign (Central) basketball coach. Now retired and living in Champaign. Interviewed at his home on September 23, 2002.

Caiazza, Ted. Former Lyons (La Grange) Township basketball player and former track and cross-country coach and athletic director at Reavis High School in Oak Lawn. Now retired. Interviewed via telephone on April 19, 2002. He also provided newspaper articles relating to the La Grange/Kankakee sectional game in 1953.

Calloway, Chris. Former Mount Carmel basketball player. A former wide receiver in the NFL, he currently lives in Atlanta and is CEO of his own company, Global Vision Investment. Interviewed via telephone on November 18, 2002. He also provided his scrapbook of the 1984–85 season and a copy of Mount Carmel's 1985 yearbook.

Cameli, Sam. Former Thornton (Harvey) Township basketball coach. Now retired. Interviewed via telephone on October 29, 2002.

Campbell, Mike. Former Galesburg basketball player. Now a partner in a Chicago law firm that focuses on corporate securities and public offerings. Interviewed via telephone on October 10, 2002.

Caress, Bob. Former Thornton (Harvey) Township basketball player. He lives in Toledo, Ohio. Interviewed via telephone on April 11, 2002.

Carlson, Ruby Thomas. Sister of former St. Joseph (Westchester) basketball player Isiah Thomas. She lives in Clarendon Hills. Interviewed via telephone on November 25, 2002.

Carnahan, Bud. Former Chicago South Shore basketball player. Retired in 1990, he lives in Philadelphia. Interviewed via telephone on November 8, 2002.

Carr, Jimmy. Former Galesburg basketball player and long-time color commentator on radio broadcasts of Galesburg basketball games. Retired after the 1998–99 season. Interviewed via telephone on July 31, 2002.

Carrodine, Coleman. Former Mount Vernon basketball player. Head basketball coach at Champaign Centennial for twenty-two years. Now retired and living in Champaign. Interviewed via telephone on May 13, 2002.

Castleman, Bill. Former Centralia basketball player. Now retired. Interviewed at the Green Grill Restaurant in Centralia on September 9, 2002.

Chesbrough, Bill. Former Elgin basketball coach. Started coaching at Elgin in 1951 and retired in 1985. He lives in Elgin. Interviewed via telephone on November 1, 2002.

Coffman, Rod. Former West Rockford basketball player. Former owner of a food processing company. He sold the business in 1987 and is now a private investor. He lives in California. Interviewed via telephone on May 31, 2002.

Colangelo, Jerry. Former Bloom basketball player. Chairman of the board and CEO of the Phoenix Suns of the NBA and managing general partner, CEO, and chairman of the board of the Arizona Diamondbacks of Major League Baseball. Interviewed via telephone on December 11, 2002.

Cole, Tom. Former Springfield basketball player. Owns a manufacturing representative agency that sells to the automotive industry. He lives in Ann Arbor, Michigan. Interviewed via telephone on May 20, 2002.

Collier, Warren. Former Paris basketball player. Former high school basketball coach and high school administrator, he is retired and living in Kansas, Illinois. Interviewed via telephone on October 14, 2002.

Condotti, Roy. Former Chicago Westinghouse basketball coach. Currently head basketball coach at Homewood-Flossmoor High School in Flossmoor. Interviewed via telephone on October 31, 2002.

Corn, Dick. Pinckneyville basketball coach. Interviewed at Pinckneyville High School on September 10, 2002.

Cox, Landon "Sonny." Former Chicago King basketball coach. Currently director of elementary school sports for the Chicago Board of Education. Interviewed via telephone on November 11, 2002.

Cox, Tony. Former Ridgway basketball player. Now operates a funeral home in Ridgway. Interviewed at the farm of former Ridgway basketball coach Bob Dallas near Harrisburg on August 18, 2002.

Cross, Gene. Former Mounds Douglass player and basketball coach. Interviewed at his home in Villa Ridge on August 21, 2002. He died of cancer in September 2002 at age seventy-five.

Cunningham, Darius (Pete). Former Chicago Carver basketball coach. Retired and living in Lansing, Michigan. Interviewed via telephone on April 4, 2002.

Dallas, Bob. Former Ridgway basketball coach. Now retired and living on his farm near Harrisburg. Interviewed at home on August 18, 2002.

Decker, Tom. Former Pinckneyville basketball player. Now retired and living in Pinckneyville. Interviewed in Pinckneyville on September 10, 2002.

Dehnert, Al. Former Thornton (Harvey) Township basketball player. Currently owns his own industrial furniture business based in Barrington. Interviewed via telephone on June 10, 2002.

Dennis, Karl. Former Chicago Du Sable basketball player. Ran Kaliedoscope, an agency for child welfare and mental health, for twenty-seven years. Currently operates his own consulting company and lives in Chicago. Interviewed via telephone on October 30, 2002.

Dildy, Tracy. Former Chicago King basketball player. Currently an assistant basketball coach at Auburn University in Auburn, Alabama. Interviewed via telephone on December 7, 2002.

Dillard, Norman "Skip." Former Chicago Westinghouse basketball player. Currently works in a warehouse at O'Hare Airport in Chicago. Interviewed via telephone on November 17, 2002.

Dore, Tom. Former East Leyden basketball player. Covers the Chicago Bulls as the television play-by-play announcer for Fox Sports Net in Chicago. He lives in Chicago. Interviewed via telephone on November 15, 2002.

Dorsey, Dick. Former West Aurora basketball coach. Worked at West Aurora as a teacher, coach, counselor, and administrator from 1953 to 1982. Now retired and living in Aurora. Interviewed via telephone on November 6, 2002.

Doster, Robert "Chick." Former Decatur basketball player. Currently an independent life insurance agent and living in Flossmoor. Interviewed via telephone on July 24, 2002.

Douglas, Bruce. Former Quincy basketball player. Currently employed as a center manager for Commonwealth Edison and living in Woodridge. He also is associate minister of the Broadview Baptist Church. Interviewed via telephone on October 26, 2002.

Douglas, Keith. Former Quincy basketball player. Currently service manager for a BMW dealership in Peoria. Interviewed via telephone on May 23, 2002.

Downey, Mike. *Chicago Tribune* sports columnist. A graduate of Bloom Township in Chicago Heights. As a sportswriter for *Star Publications* in Chicago Heights, he covered former Bloom basketball coach Wes Mason. He provided a memo on his recollections of Mason via e-mail on May 7, 2002.

Doyle, Dennis. Former assistant basketball coach at St. Joseph (Westchester). Currently a guidance counselor and head basketball coach at Willowbrook High School in Villa Park. He lives in Westchester. Interviewed via telephone on December 10, 2002.

Drone, Heath. Former Ridgway basketball player. Currently attends Southeast Illinois College in Harrisburg. Interviewed at the farm of former Ridgway basketball coach Bob Dallas near Harrisburg on August 18, 2002.

Duffy, Marty. Former Ridgway basketball player. Currently employed as an insurance agent and living in Harrisburg. Interviewed at the farm of former Ridgway basketball coach Bob Dallas near Harrisburg on August 18, 2002.

Dunbar, Rob. Former Benton basketball player. Currently employed in the Illinois State Police's crime laboratory in Benton. Interviewed at the Days Inn in Benton on August 19, 2002.

Eddleman, Teddy Townsley. Widow of former Centralia basketball player Dike Eddleman. Interviewed at her home in Champaign on September 23, 2002.

Eddleman, Thomas Dwight "Dike." Tapes courtesy of Teddy Eddleman and Diana Eddleman Lenzi. Newspaper clippings and memorabilia courtesy of Butch Border, Centralia.

Esposito, Tom. Former Chicago South Shore basketball player. Retired in 1989. Now lives in McHenry. Interviewed via telephone on November 18, 2002.

Evans, Jimmy. Former Winchester basketball player. Currently works and lives in Bluffs. Interviewed via telephone on October 19, 2002.

Eveland, Mary. Widow of former Paris basketball coach Ernie Eveland. Now living in a nursing home in Paris. Interviewed at the nursing home on September 24, 2002.

Fallstrom, Bob. Former sports editor of the *Decatur Herald and Review.* After covering sports for thirty-six years, he currently is the *Herald and Review's* community news editor and writes a weekly column on community affairs. Interviewed at the *Herald and Review* offices in Decatur on August 27, 2002.

Farr, James. Former Mount Carmel basketball player. Currently an assistant basketball coach at Loyola University in Chicago. Interviewed via telephone on November 15, 2002.

Feezel, Brian. Former Pittsfield basketball player. Currently practicing general corporate law at a law firm in St. Louis. Interviewed via telephone on September 7, 2002.

Felling, Ron. Former Lawrenceville basketball coach (1967 to 1983) and an assistant basketball coach at Indiana for fourteen and a half years. He is retired and living in Hot Springs, Arkansas. Interviewed via telephone on May 14, 2002.

Ferguson, Ron. Former Thornridge (Dolton) basketball coach. Former athletic director and director of special events at Bradley University. He is retired and living in Naples, Florida. Interviewed at Jim's Steakhouse in Peoria on September 16, 2002.

Fiddler, Dan. Former Maine South (Park Ridge) basketball player. Now an anesthesiologist in Medford, Oregon. Interviewed via telephone on May 20, 2002.

Finley, Michael. Former Proviso East (Maywood) basketball player. Currently plays for the Dallas Mavericks. Interviewed via telephone on July 25, 2002.

Fitzhugh, Harry. Former executive director of the IHSA. In a *Chicago Sun-Times* poll, he was singled out as the most influential figure in the history of high school sports in Illinois. He retired in 1978 after forty-four years in education. Interviewed via telephone on October 30, 2002. He died on June 29, 2003, at age ninety.

Fletcher, Marc. Former Collinsville basketball player and son of former Collinsville basketball coach Vergil Fletcher. Currently lives in Naples, Florida, and works in the real estate business and owns an antique and design store. Interviewed via telephone on November 6, 2002.

Fletcher, Mike. Former Collinsville basketball player and son of former Collinsville basketball coach Vergil Fletcher. Currently an assistant city attorney in Memphis, Tennessee, and a partner in the law firm of Norfleet and Fletcher. Interviewed via telephone on October 12, 2002.

Fletcher, Vergil. Former Collinsville basketball coach. Now retired and living in Collinsville. Interviewed at his home in Collinsville on August 5, 2002. He also provided memorabilia from his career.

Flick, Ken. Former Cobden basketball player. Now a warehouseman for an explosives company in Wolf Lake. He lives in Cobden. Interviewed via telephone on October 17, 2002.

Flynn, Jim. Assistant executive director of the IHSA. He will retire in 2004. He lives in Bloomington. Interviewed via telephone on April 15, 2002. He provided documentation pertaining to the IHSA's decision to move the site of the Class A and Class AA boys state basketball tournaments from Champaign to Peoria.

Foley, Dick. Former Paris basketball player. Former president of Felmley-Dickerson Construction Co. in Urbana. He retired after forty-one years in 1990. He was project manager of construction of the University of Illinois's Assembly Hall, which was opened in 1963. Now retired and living in Champaign. Interviewed via telephone on September 11, 2002. He also provided information on former Paris teammate Nate Middleton.

Foreman, Jim. Former Chicago Dunbar basketball coach. Currently a physical education teacher and director of the driver's education program at Dunbar. Interviewed via telephone on November 13, 2002.

Frailey, Hugh. Former Benton basketball player. Now works for State Farm Insurance in Benton. Interviewed at the Days Inn in Benton on August 19, 2002.

Freidinger, Mark. Former Pekin basketball player. Currently a scout for the San Antonio Spurs and the Philadelphia 76ers and a radio color commentator covering Wake Forest University basketball games in Winston-Salem, North Carolina. Interviewed via telephone on October 15, 2002.

Fry, David. Former executive director of the IHSA. He lives in Bloomington. Interviewed via telephone on April 3, 2002.

Gamber, Terry. Former Mount Vernon basketball player. Now a Circuit Court judge in the Second Judicial Circuit. He lives in Mount Vernon. Interviewed via telephone on October 21, 2002.

Gamble, Kevin. Former Springfield Lanphier basketball player. A former player in the NBA, he currently is head basketball coach at the University of Illinois at Springfield. Interviewed at the Renaissance Hotel in Springfield on August 26, 2002.

Garris, Kiwane. Former Chicago Westinghouse basketball player. Currently a professional basketball player in Europe. Interviewed via telephone on November 15, 2002.

Gentry, Nolden. Former West Rockford basketball player. Now cofounding partner in the Brick Gentry law firm in Des Moines, Iowa. Interviewed via telephone on May 8, 2002.

Giannetti, Glen. Former Bloom basketball coach. Former assistant to Bloom basketball coach Wes Mason. Currently assistant principal at Bloom Trail High School. He lives in Chicago Heights. Interviewed via telephone on May 7, 2002.

Gilkey, Grayal. Former West Aurora basketball player. A teacher and coach at East Aurora from 1964 to 1993. He lives in Aurora. Interviewed via telephone on November 7, 2002.

Gill, Scott. Former Mount Vernon basketball coach. A teacher and coach at Mount Vernon for thirty-eight years. He retired in 1973. He lives in Mount Vernon. Interviewed via telephone on June 4, 2002.

Gladson, Frank. Former Pinckneyville basketball player. Now retired and living in Pine Bluff, Arkansas. Interviewed via telephone on April 8, 2002.

Glenn, Charles. Former Chicago Carver basketball player. Currently works for a Chicago-based private agency, Trucare for Children, that works with disadvantaged boys in the nine-to-seventeen age group. Interviewed via telephone on November 20, 2002.

Gnatovich, George. Quad Cities basketball fan. Interviewed at Wharton Fieldhouse in Moline on August 12, 2002.

Goodman, Norm. Former East Leyden basketball coach. He coached at East Leyden from 1961 to 1990. He currently is a part-time scout for the Toronto Raptors. He lives in Northlake. Interviewed via telephone on May 29, 2002.

Goers, Steve. Rockford Boylan basketball coach. Interviewed at his home in Rockford on August 13, 2002. He also provided memorabilia from his career.

Golden, Dave. Former Pekin basketball coach. An insurance broker for twenty-seven years. Currently employed by the U.S. Postal Service and living in Parlin, New Jersey. Interviewed via telephone on April 11, 2002.

Gonzalez, Hector. Former St. Joseph (Westchester) basketball player. Works for a Chicago-based company that designs, builds, and installs air pollution control systems for power plants and steel mills. Also flies helicopters for the Army National Guard. He lives in Chicago. Interviewed via telephone on November 17, 2002.

Goolsby, Lawrence. Former Chicago St. Elizabeth basketball player. Now retired and living in Chicago. Interviewed via telephone on February 3, 2003.

Grasewicz, Wade. Former Pinckneyville basketball player. Operates a dog food company in Ohio. Interviewed in Pinckneyville on September 10, 2002.

Green, Rickey. Former Chicago Hirsch basketball player. Former NBA player. Now working as an assistant superintendent of recreation for the Cook County Forest Preserve. Interviewed via telephone on October 30, 2002.

Gregg, Jack. A Leyden graduate of 1954. A scorekeeper and record keeper for East Leyden football and basketball teams for more than fifty years. He has written a book on the history of East Leyden football. He plans to write books on the history of East Leyden basketball. He lives in Franklin Park. Interviewed via telephone on October 28, 2002. He provided documentation on the history of East Leyden basketball.

Grunwald, Glen. Former East Leyden basketball player. Former general manager of the Toronto Raptors. He lives in Toronto. Interviewed at the Four Seasons restaurant in Chicago on June 3, 2002, and via telephone on June 4, 2002.

Hall, Harry. Former Thornton (Harvey) Township basketball player. Currently president of World Merchants, Inc., an international trading company based in Chicago. Interviewed via telephone on May 30, 2002.

Hallihan, Jim. Former Decatur basketball player. Former assistant basketball coach at Virginia Tech, East Tennessee State, and Iowa State. Currently the executive director of the Iowa Games, an amateur Olympic competition for Iowans from ages five through ninety-five. He lives in Ames, Iowa. Interviewed via telephone on May 31, 2002.

Hambric, Bob. Head basketball coach at Chicago Simeon. Interviewed via telephone on October 29, 2002.

Hammerton, Wayne. Former Peoria Richwoods basketball coach. Now retired and living in Peoria. Interviewed at Jim's Steakhouse in Peoria on September 16, 2002, and via telephone on October 7, 2002.

Hanks, Sherrill. Former Quincy basketball coach. Now retired and living in Quincy. Interviewed at his home on September 5, 2002. He also provided memorabilia from his career.

Hardaway, Tim. Former Chicago Carver basketball player. Currently playing in the NBA. He lives in Miami, Florida. Interviewed via telephone on January 17, 2003.

Hardy, Emir. Former Bloom basketball player. Currently executive director of Future, which sponsors youth after-school enrichment programs. He lives in Chicago Heights. Interviewed via telephone on December 18, 2002.

Harmon, Pat. Born in East St. Louis and graduated from Freeport High School in 1932. Former sports editor of the *Champaign News-Gazette*. Founded the first all-state basketball selections in 1933 while living in Freeport. After covering sports in Champaign-Urbana, Cedar Rapids, Iowa, and Cincinnati, Ohio, for more than fifty years, he retired in 1985. He lives in Cincinnati. Interviewed via telephone on April 23, 2002.

Harr, Jack. Former Chicago South Shore basketball player. Retired in 1993 after serving as vice president for public affairs for ABC in New York. He lives in New York. Interviewed via telephone on May 17, 2002.

Harrington, Jim. Former Chicago Weber and Elgin basketball coach. He coached at Elgin from 1986 to 2000. He lives in Elgin. Interviewed via telephone on October 30, 2002.

Harris, Billy. Former Chicago Dunbar basketball player. Currently a car salesman at a Toyota dealership in Chicago. Interviewed via telephone on November 12, 2002.

Harrison, Earl. Former Champaign basketball player. Now retired and living in Champaign. Interviewed via telephone on October 10, 2002.

Hawkins, Hersey. Former Chicago Westinghouse basketball player. Former NBA player. Currently living in Charlotte, North Carolina, and a color commentator for the Memphis Grizzlies. Interviewed via telephone on December 16, 2002.

Hawkins, Larry. Former Chicago Carver basketball coach. Currently director of the Office of Special Programs at the University of Chicago and founder and director of the Institute for Athletics and Education. He lives in Chicago. Interviewed via telephone on November 11, 2002.

Hawkins, Rich. Former Pekin basketball player and son of former Pekin basketball coach Dawson Hawkins. Now working as a salesman at Dennison Chevrolet in Pekin. Interviewed at the dealership on September 16, 2002.

Hawkins, Shane. Former Pinckneyville basketball player. Currently completing work toward a master's degree in sports studies at Southern Illinois University in Carbondale. Interviewed via telephone on October 21, 2002.

Hawkins, Tom. Former Pinckneyville basketball player and former assistant basketball coach at Pinckneyville. He works construction in Pinckneyville. Interviewed via telephone on October 10, 2002.

Head, Chris. Former Chicago Westinghouse and Proviso West (Hillside) basketball coach. Currently employed as head of security at Proviso West. Interviewed by *Chicago Sun-Times* high school sports editor Steve Tucker on November 8, 2002.

Heinzelman, Steve. Former Lyons (La Grange) Township basketball player. Currently employed by American Airlines and living in Chicago. Interviewed via telephone on November 19, 2002.

Hellenthal, Mike. Former assistant basketball coach at Quincy from 1972 through 1987. Currently assistant principal at McDowell High School in Marion, North Carolina. Interviewed via telephone on April 16, 2002.

Hendler, John. Former East Leyden basketball player. Currently director of local sales for Worldcom in Vienna, Virginia. Interviewed via telephone on May 14, 2002.

Herrin, Rich. Former Benton basketball coach. Currently the basketball coach at Marion High School. He lives in Benton. Interviewed at the Days Inn in Benton on August 19, 2002.

Herrin, Dr. Roger. Attended Ridgway's 1973 state championship team. A longtime friend of former Ridgway basketball coach Bob Dallas. Now retired and living in Harrisburg. Interviewed at Dallas's farm near Harrisburg on August 18, 2002.

Hicks, Art. Former Chicago St. Elizabeth basketball player. Now retired and living in Chicago. Interviewed at Army and Lou's Restaurant in Chicago on February 6, 2003.

Hill, Jerry. Former Decatur basketball player. Now working as an analyst for Caterpillar in Decatur. Interviewed at the Holiday Inn in Decatur on August 28, 2002.

Hill, Rocky. Former Thornton (Harvey) Township basketball coach. Interviewed via telephone on November 8, 2002.

Hitt, Bill. Former Proviso East (Maywood) basketball coach. Currently assistant principal for student services at Glenbard West High School in Glen Ellyn. Interviewed via telephone on November 5, 2002.

Hlafka, Jim. Former Bunker Hill basketball coach. Now retired and living in Bunker Hill. Interviewed at his home on August 8, 2002. He also provided memorabilia from his career.

Hooper, Max. Former Mount Vernon basketball player. Retired in 1994. He lives in Birmingham, Alabama. Interviewed via telephone on May 12 and July 30, 2002.

Horton, Ed. Former Springfield Lanphier basketball player. Former professional basketball player. Currently assistant basketball coach at the University of Illinois at Springfield. Interviewed at the Renaissance Hotel in Springfield on August 26, 2002.

House, Randy. Former Benton basketball player. Currently owns his own insurance brokerage company, based in West Frankfort. Interviewed via telephone on October 11, 2002.

Hughes, Mike. Former Peoria Central basketball player. Currently living in Peoria. After being injured in a motorcycle accident, he is on disability leave. Interviewed via telephone on June 1, 2002.

Hughes, Robert "Cotton." Former West Frankfort basketball player. Worked at Acme Steel for nearly forty years. Now retired and living in Westchester, Pennsylvania. Interviewed via telephone on October 24, 2002.

Hull, Rodney. Former Chicago Simeon basketball player. Currently principal of Nicholson Elementary School in Chicago. Interviewed via telephone on November 14, 2002.

Humerickhouse, Dave. Former Paris basketball player. Former construction company employee. Retired in 1989. He lives in Bartonville. Interviewed via telephone on October 23, 2002.

Huyler, Jay. Former Maine South (Park Ridge) basketball player. Former television sportscaster, currently living in San Francisco. Interviewed via telephone on April 30, 2002.

Irvin, Ken. Former Benton basketball player. Now a coal miner and living in Benton. Interviewed at the Days Inn in Benton on August 20, 2002.

Jackson, Don. Former Chicago Marshall basketball player. Chairman and CEO of Central City Productions, Inc., based in Chicago. Interviewed via telephone on June 3, 2002.

Jackson, Thom. Former Collinsville basketball player. Now retired and living in Baton Rouge, Louisiana. Interviewed via telephone on October 8, 2002.

Jackson, Tyrone. Former East St. Louis Lincoln basketball player. Currently territorial sales manager for Pepsi Cola, in Jacksonville, Florida. Interviewed via telephone on October 17, 2002.

James, David. Former Bunker Hill basketball player and former assistant basketball coach at Bunker Hill. Currently a psychosocial rehabilitation counselor in Alton. Interviewed at the home of former Bunker Hill coach Jim Hlafka in Bunker Hill on August 8, 2002.

Joesting, Fritz. Former member of the Pekin school board and chairman of the board's athletic committee. Now retired. Interviewed via telephone on October 12, 2002.

Johnson, Danny. Former Benton basketball player. Now operates a stress and crisis intervention hotline in Benton. Interviewed at the Days Inn in Benton on August 20, 2002.

Johnson, Eddie. Former Chicago Westinghouse basketball player. Former NBA player. Currently a television commentator for the Phoenix Suns. Interviewed via telephone on April 19, 2002.

Johnson, James "Bulldog." Former Decatur basketball player. Currently owns his own company, Cultural Arts, which promotes motivational speaking. He lives in Atlanta. Interviewed via telephone on December 6, 2002.

Johnson, Scott. Assistant executive director of the IHSA. He lives in Bloomington. He provided documentation on the history of Elgin High School basketball. Interviewed via telephone on December 6, 2002.

Jones, Bob. Former Centralia basketball coach and athletic director. Now retired. Interviewed at the Green Grill Restaurant in Centralia on September 9, 2002.

Jones, Charlie. Former Chicago Marshall basketball player. A plumber and plumbing contractor in Chicago and pastor of the Rose of Light Missionary Baptist church. Interviewed via telephone on May 7, 2002.

Joor, Bob. Former Chicago South Shore basketball player. Former basketball coach at Waukegan. Retired from teaching in 1986. He lives in Lake Forest. Interviewed via telephone on November 14, 2002.

Judson, Paul. Former Hebron basketball player. Former basketball coach at Mattoon and Dundee and former basketball coach and athletic director at Hampshire. Now retired. He lives in Spring Hill, Florida. Interviewed via telephone on April 16, 2002.

Judson, Phil. Former Hebron basketball player. Former basketball coach at North Chicago, Adrian College, and Zion-Benton. Father of Northern Illinois University coach Rob Judson. Now retired, he lives in Gurnee. Interviewed via telephone on October 31, 2002.

Jones, Tim. Former Elgin basketball player. Now is a teacher at the Tefft Middle School in Streamwood. He lives in Streamwood. Interviewed via telephone on November 2, 2002.

Kaufmann, Andy. Former Jacksonville basketball player. Currently employed as a residential care worker for blind children at the Illinois School for the Visually Impaired in Jacksonville. Interviewed at his home in Winchester on September 3, 2002.

Kelley, Dale. Former Galesburg basketball player. Currently chief financial officer for a small automobile-hauling company in Chicago. Also an ordained minister. He lives in Chicago. Interviewed via telephone on October 29, 2002.

Kenny, Jack. Former Decatur basketball coach and principal of Decatur Lakeview and Decatur High Schools from 1970 to 1992. Now retired, he serves on the Decatur Park Board. Interviewed at the Holiday Inn in Decatur on August 27, 2002.

Kerkman, Gordon. West Aurora basketball coach. Interviewed via telephone on November 13, 2002.

King, Eddie. Former Mount Vernon basketball player. After a thirty-eight-year career in education, he retired in 1996. He lives in Peoria. Interviewed via telephone on May 22, 2002.

Kivisto, Bob. Former East Moline and East Aurora basketball player and son of former East Moline and East Aurora coach Ernie Kivisto. A former coach at East Aurora, he currently is a teacher at East Aurora. He lives in Aurora. Interviewed via telephone on November 21, 2002.

Kivisto, Tom. Former East Aurora basketball player and son of former East Aurora coach Ernie Kivisto. He is president and CEO of Seminole Transportation and Gathering Co., a pipeline, transportation, and marketing oil company based in Tulsa, Oklahoma. He lives in Tulsa. Interviewed via telephone on July 22, 2002.

Kouri, Steve. Judge of the Circuit Court, based in Peoria. As a member of the Peoria City Council, he was instrumental in forming an organizing committee that proposed a plan to persuade the IHSA to move the boys state basketball tournaments from Champaign to Peoria. He lives in Peoria. Interviewed via telephone on November 7, 2002.

Krupica, Glen. 1978 graduate of East Leyden and former manager of the East Leyden basketball team. Currently executive director of the Independence Bowl football game in Shreveport, Louisiana. He lives in Shreveport. Interviewed via telephone on May 9, 2002.

Kuba, Andy. Former Staunton basketball player. Currently a chemical engineer with Bridgestone/Firestone in Akron, Ohio. Interviewed via telephone on April 10, 2002.

Kuberski, Steve. Former Moline basketball player. Former player in the NBA. Currently founder and president of Pro-Quip Co., an industrial supply company based in Boston, Massachusetts. Interviewed via telephone on July 26, 2002.

Lamore, Dave. Former Staunton basketball coach. Retired from coaching after the 1994 season and now serves as athletic director of the junior high school in Staunton. Interviewed at Staunton High School on August 7, 2002.

Lazenby, Jim. Former Pinckneyville basketball player. Former coach at Rockford Guilford. Retired from teaching in 1993. Interviewed in Pinckneyville on September 10, 2002.

Legendre, Randy. Former Staunton basketball coach. Retired from coaching after the 1995 season, then returned in 1998 and continues to serve as an assistant basketball coach at Staunton. Interviewed at Staunton High School on August 7, 2002.

Leggett, Jane. Widow of former Quincy basketball coach Jerry Leggett. Interviewed via telephone on October 17, 2002.

Lenzi, Diana Eddleman. Daughter of former Centralia basketball player Dike Eddleman. Interviewed at her mother's home in Champaign on September 23, 2002.

Lewis, Bennie. Former East St. Louis Lincoln and East St. Louis basketball coach. Now retired and living in East St. Louis. Interviewed at his home in East St. Louis on August 6, 2002.

Liberty, Marcus. Former Chicago King basketball player. Currently assistant basketball coach at Cheyenne High School in Las Vegas, Nevada. Interviewed via telephone on December 9, 2002.

Lober, Arlyn. Former Springfield Lanphier basketball coach. Head coach from 1953 to 1974, and then athletic director for eleven years before retiring in 1985. Interviewed at the Renaissance Hotel in Springfield on August 26, 2002.

Lose, Glen. Former Elgin basketball player. After serving as a teacher and administrator in Elgin's U-46 for thirty-eight years, he retired in 1996. He lives in Naples, Florida. Interviewed via telephone on April 16, 2002.

Lotzer, Mark. Former Rockford Boylan basketball player. An insurance and investment planner, he works for the Waterside Financial Group in Rockford. Interviewed at his office in Rockford on August 13, 2002.

Major, Fred. Former Champaign basketball player. Now retired and living in Houston, Texas. Interviewed via telephone on October 15, 2002.

Martens, Scott. Former East Aurora basketball coach (1985 to 1997). He continues to teach at East Aurora. He lives in Aurora. Interviewed via telephone on January 6, 2003.

Martin, Cuonzo. Former East St. Louis Lincoln basketball player. Now assistant basketball coach at Purdue. Interviewed via telephone on May 5, 2002.

Mason, Bobby Joe. Former Centralia basketball player. Currently employed by the Springfield Housing Authority Community Center. Interviewed at the Springfield Youth Center on August 26, 2002.

Massa, Amel. Former Pekin basketball player. Currently a divorce attorney in Long Island. Interviewed via telephone on August 3, 2002.

Mathis, Jack. Owner of Jack Mathis Advertising in Chicago. Created the Jamaco Saints AAU basketball team, which played in Chicago from 1957 to 1967. Interviewed via telephone on May 10, 2002.

Matthews, Audie. Former Bloom basketball player. Former professional basketball player in Australia. Now owns his own basketball program, Audie Matthews Youth Development Training. He lives in Brisbane, Australia. Interviewed via telephone on August 29, 2002.

Maxey, Ken. Former Chicago Carver basketball player. Currently a teacher and assistant athletic director at Crenshaw High School in Los Angeles. Interviewed via telephone on April 24, 2002.

McBride, Ken "Preacher." Former Centralia basketball player. Now retired. Interviewed at the Green Grill Restaurant in Centralia on September 9, 2002.

McCants, Melvin. Former Mount Carmel basketball player. Currently playing for a professional basketball team in Autreppe, Belgium. Interviewed via telephone on November 19, 2002.

McClain, Sergio. Former Peoria Manual basketball player. Now playing professional basketball overseas and also coaching and living in Peoria. Interviewed via telephone on May 31, 2002.

McClain, Wayne. Former Peoria Manual basketball player and coach. Currently an assistant basketball coach at the University of Illinois. Interviewed via telephone on October 16, 2002.

McCoy, Larry. Former Bloom basketball player. Now operates a computer graphics company and McCoy's Sports and Entertainment Pub in Richton Park. He lives in Richton Park. Interviewed via telephone on November 6, 2002.

McCoy, Raymond. Former Bloom basketball player. Now transportation manager for World Kitchen. He lives in Harvey. Interviewed via telephone on September 19, 2002.

McCoy, Robert. Former Bloom basketball player. Larry McCoy's younger brother; not related to Raymond McCoy. Now operates a small home improvement business in Chicago Heights. He lives in Chicago Heights. Interviewed via telephone on January 7, 2003.

McCrary, Leighton. Former Chicago Dunbar basketball player. Currently head basketball coach at Grand Canyon University in Phoenix, Arizona. Interviewed via telephone on November 15, 2002.

McDermott, John. Former Champaign basketball player. Now retired and living in Bloomington. Interviewed via telephone on October 15, 2002.

McDougal, John. Former West Aurora basketball coach. Also coached at Palestine, Carmi, Prospect, Northern Illinois University, Western Michigan University, Rockford Lutheran, and Rock Valley Community College. He retired in 1997. He lives in Oswego. Interviewed via telephone on November 11, 2002.

McMullin, Dan "Moon." A 1976 graduate of East Leyden and a boyhood friend of former East Leyden basketball player Glen Grunwald. Also a former manager of the East Leyden basketball team. Now public safety officer for the village of Rosemont, a Chicago suburb. He lives in Franklin Park. Interviewed via telephone on May 21, 2002.

McQuillan, Ed. Former Mount Carmel basketball coach. Currently head basketball coach at the Illinois Institute of Technology in Chicago. Interviewed via telephone on November 13, 2002.

Meyer, Kevin. Former Staunton basketball player. Currently works for an architectural firm in Belleville and lives in Collinsville. Interviewed at Staunton High School on August 7, 2002.

Mickeal, Pete. Former Rock Island basketball player. Currently playing professional basketball overseas. Interviewed via telephone on April 16, 2002.

Miller, Fred. Former Pekin basketball player. Former sales manager for a real estate company. Currently a seventh- and eighth-grade teacher at Calvin Coolidge Middle School in Peoria. Interviewed via telephone on September 12, 2002.

Mims, Fred. Former Galesburg basketball player. Now associate athletic director at the University of Iowa. Interviewed via telephone on November 8, 2002.

Miranda, Sam. Former Collinsville basketball player. Former coach at Galatia, Vandalia, Kankakee, the University of New Mexico, and the University of Kansas. Now retired and living in Lawrence, Kansas. Interviewed via telephone on April 3, 2002.

Moore, Bert. Former Bloom basketball coach. Retired in 1958. After serving as a guidance counselor at Homewood-Flossmoor for twenty-three years, he retired in 1986. He lives in Flossmoor. Interviewed via telephone on April 17, 2002.

Moore, Larry. Former Quincy basketball player. Currently employed by JK Creative Printing in Quincy. Interviewed at the home of former Quincy coach Sherrill Hanks in Quincy on September 5, 2002.

Moore, Walt. Former Mount Vernon basketball player. Coached at Macomb, Carbondale Attucks, Carbondale, and Western Illinois University, then worked in the university's admissions and records office before retiring in 1995. He lives in Macomb. Interviewed via telephone on May 15, 2002.

Morgan, Bob. A 1954 graduate of Galesburg and a former elementary school basketball coach in Galesburg. Retired from teaching after thirty-two years in 1994. He lives in Galesburg. Interviewed via telephone on October 20, 2002.

Moss, Rick. Former Centralia basketball coach. Currently vice principal at Centralia. Interviewed via telephone on October 23, 2002.

Mott, Dave. Former assistant basketball coach at Pekin. Currently head basketball coach at Bartonville (Illinois) Limestone High School. Interviewed via telephone on October 16, 2002.

Mottlow, Martin "Red." A Chicago Marshall graduate in 1945. A radio sports broadcaster in Chicago for forty-five years. He died in 2003. Interviewed via telephone on October 31, 2002.

Nardi, Frank. Former Bloom basketball coach. Retired from coaching in 1990, then served four years as Bloom's principal. He continues to work as a part-time counselor at Beecher. He lives in Crete. Interviewed via telephone on December 4, 2002.

Neal, Chuck. Former Cobden basketball player. Now a pilot for Northwest Airlines. Interviewed at his home in Anna on August 22, 2002. He also provided memorabilia from the 1963–64 season.

Neal, Jim. Former Cobden basketball player. A former minister. Currently an insurance agent in Bakersfield, California. Interviewed via telephone on June 6, 2002.

Niepoetter, Bill. Former sports editor of the *Centralia New Sentinel* and radio sportscaster. Now retired. Interviewed at the Green Grill Restaurant in Centralia on September 9, 2002.

Nika, Bob. Springfield Lanphier basketball coach from 1975 to 1993. Interviewed at the Renaissance Hotel in Springfield on August 26, 2002.

Nikcevich, Ron. Former Lyons (La Grange) Township basketball coach. Currently serves as a consultant for USA Basketball and college and professional teams in the United States and overseas. Interviewed via telephone on November 4, 2002.

Norman, Max. Former Paris basketball player. Former missionary and high school teacher and coach. Retired in 1990. He lives in Fisher. Interviewed at the Holiday Inn in Champaign on September 23, 2002. He also provided memorabilia from the 1942–43 season.

Novsek, Doug. Former Lawrenceville basketball player. Assistant basketball coach at Southern Illinois, Indiana State, Southwest Texas State, Illinois State, and Nebraska. He lives in Lincoln, Nebraska. Interviewed on May 9, 2002.

Ormond, Neal. A 1962 graduate of West Aurora, he has covered East Aurora and West Aurora basketball games via radio broadcasts for forty years. Interviewed via telephone on November 8, 2002. He also provided documentation on the East Aurora/West Aurora basketball rivalry.

Orr, John. Former Taylorville basketball player. Former head basketball coach at Michigan and Iowa State. Now retired and living in Naples, Florida, and Ames, Iowa. Interviewed via telephone on May 24, 2002.

Owen, Ray. Sports editor of the *Missourian* in Cape Girardeau, Missouri. A 1952 graduate of Mounds High School, he also covered high school basketball in southern Illinois for several years while working for the Cairo, Illinois, newspaper. Interviewed via telephone on December 3, 2002.

Owens, Mike. Former Galesburg basketball player and coach. Also former principal at Galesburg and former athletic director at Moline. He retired in 2000. He lives in Moline. Interviewed via telephone on October 22, 2002.

Owens, Ted. Former Kansas University basketball coach (1964–83). Recruited several Illinois products, including Rodger Bohnenstiehl, Dave Robisch, and Tom Kivisto. Now retired and living in Tulsa, Oklahoma. Interviewed via telephone on July 7, 2003.

Pace, Dennis. Former Collinsville basketball player. Former coach at Joliet, Carl Sandburg, and O'Fallon. Now retired and living in Collinsville, Illinois, and Lake of the Ozarks, Missouri. Interviewed via telephone on October 22, 2002.

Page, Ray. Former Springfield basketball coach. Served for eight years as Illinois's superintendent of public instruction. Executive director of the Tucson Trade Bureau until 1976. Now retired and living in Tucson, Arizona. Interviewed via telephone on June 5, 2002.

Park, Ken. Former Decatur basketball player. At eighty-four, he still teaches girls tumbling at Argenta-Oreana High School. Interviewed at the Holiday Inn in Decatur on August 28, 2002.

Parker, Rex. Former West Rockford basketball player. Former vice president and general manager of the Best Western Clock Tower Resort in Rockford. Now retired and living in Rockford. Interviewed via telephone on October 11, 2002.

Parker, Robert "Sonny." Former Chicago Farragut basketball player. Former NBA player. Retired from basketball in 1983. He founded the Sonny Parker Youth Foundation in 1990. He lives in Chicago. Interviewed via telephone on October 30, 2002.

Parker, Tom. Former Collinsville basketball player. Former insurance executive. Currently the owner of the Parkette Drive-In in Lexington, Kentucky. Interviewed via telephone on April 25, 2002.

Parrish, Harold. Former Taylorville basketball player. He has been taking pictures and filming Taylorville football and basketball games since 1948. Interviewed at his business in Taylorville on August 27, 2002. He also provided memorabilia relating to Taylorville's 1943–44 basketball team.

Payne, Michael. Former Quincy basketball player. Currently a sales representative for Allegiance Health Care Corporation in Ashburn, Virginia. Interviewed via telephone on June 1, 2002.

Pingatore, Gene. Head basketball coach at St. Joseph (Westchester). He was hired as a freshman basketball coach and history teacher when the school opened in 1960. He became head basketball coach in 1969. He also is the school's director of building and grounds, special events, and alumni. He lives in Westchester. Interviewed via telephone on November 4, 2002.

Pitts, Jim. Former Chicago Marshall basketball player. Now a professor of sociology at the University of North Carolina at Asheville. Interviewed via telephone on May 30, 2002.

Ponsetto, Joe. Former Proviso East (Maywood) basketball player. Currently chief of special prosecutions in the Illinois Attorney General's office in Chicago. Interviewed via telephone on October 28, 2002.

Porter, Todd. Former East St. Louis Lincoln basketball player. Currently a bartender on the Casino Queen riverboat in East St. Louis. Interviewed at former coach Bennie Lewis's home in East St. Louis on August 6, 2002.

Purden, Bill. Former Thornton (Harvey) Township basketball coach. Retired and living in Phoenix, Arizona. Interviewed via telephone on April 25, 2002.

Quinn, Dave. Illinois high school basketball historian. He lives in Naperville, Illinois. He provided memorabilia and records on the history of high school basketball in Illinois. Interviewed via telephone on September 30, 2002.

Rapp, Rich. Former Centralia basketball player. Now stadium director and sports coordinator for girls basketball with the Chicago Board of Education. He lives in Alsip. Interviewed via telephone on October 16, 2002.

Redmon, Bogie. Former Collinsville basketball player. Now heads his own insurance agency in Collinsville. Interviewed at his office in Collinsville on August 5, 2002.

Reid, Duncan. Former Lincoln and Rock Island basketball coach. Now retired and living in Rock Island. Interviewed at his home on August 12, 2002. He also provided newspaper articles and other memorabilia from his career.

Reynolds, Chris. Former Peoria Central basketball player. Currently assistant athletic director at Notre Dame. Interviewed via telephone on May 16, 2002.

Reynolds, Eddie. Former Decatur basketball player. Now retired after working for Nabisco for forty-two years. Interviewed at the Holiday Inn in Decatur on August 28, 2002.

Richardson, Bill. Sports editor of the *Daily Record* in Lawrenceville, Illinois. He provided a souvenir edition of *68–0: Recording History,* an account of Lawrenceville's 1982 and 1983 state championship basketball teams. Interviewed via telephone on May 16, 2002.

Riddle, Fred. Former Collinsville basketball player. Currently a dentist in Iowa City. Interviewed via telephone on May 21, 2002.

Ridley, Billy. Former Taylorville basketball player. Former president of a consulting firm and an insurance salesman. Now retired and living in Springfield. Interviewed via telephone on April 18, 2002.

Rigdon, Eldon. Longtime Pinckneyville basketball fan. Retired and living in Pinckneyville. Interviewed in Pinckneyville on September 10, 2002.

Riley, John. Former Mount Vernon basketball player. After working for Alcoa for more than thirty years, he retired in 1994. He lives in Scottsdale, Arizona. Interviewed via telephone on April 22, 2002.

Rivers, Glenn. Former Proviso East (Maywood) basketball player. Former NBA player. Former head coach of the Orlando Magic. New head coach of the Boston Celtics. Interviewed via telephone on January 9, 2003.

Rivers, Grady. Father of Glenn Rivers. Formerly employed by the Maywood Police Department. Now retired. Interviewed via telephone on November 10, 2002.

Robinson, Flynn. Former Elgin basketball player. After a career in the NBA and ABA, he worked for the Abe Saperstein Foundation in Chicago, then moved to Los Angeles in

1990. He plays in a senior Olympic basketball league and conducts basketball clinics. He lives in Los Angeles. Interviewed via telephone on December 20, 2002.

Robinson, Levertis. Former Chicago King basketball player. Currently director of security and an assistant basketball coach at Chicago Bogan. Interviewed via telephone on November 5, 2002.

Robisch, Dave. Former Springfield basketball player. Former player in the NBA. Currently works for the Department of Human Services in Springfield in its after-school program, Teen Reach. Interviewed at Outback Steakhouse in Springfield on August 26, 2002.

Roeder, Bill. Superintendent of the riverfront division for the Peoria Park District. He was a member of the organizing committee that proposed a plan to persuade the IHSA to move the boys state basketball tournament from Champaign to Peoria. He lives in Peoria. Interviewed via telephone on November 12, 2002.

Rolinski, Chuck. Former Toluca basketball coach. Now retired from coaching. Executive director and treasurer of the Illinois Basketball Coaches Association, an organization he helped to found in 1971–72. Interviewed via telephone on May 29, 2002.

Rose, Greg. Former Thornridge (Dolton) basketball player. Now a professional singer and musician living in Hawthorne, California. Interviewed via telephone on March 3, 2002.

Rudoy, Herb. Chicago attorney who represents many European professional basketball players and once represented Chicago Dunbar basketball player Billy Harris. Interviewed via telephone on April 12, 2002.

Ruggles, Dick. Former Cobden basketball coach. Retired from coaching and teaching in 1993. Interviewed at his home in Nashville, Illinois, on September 9, 2002.

Roustio, Mel. Former head basketball coach at Washington (Illinois), Edwardsville, Jacksonville, and Decatur Eisenhower. Now retired and living in Decatur. Author of *Courtside Memories* (1998), a collection of stories about Illinois basketball, and *Ninety-Nine Answers for the Sport Parent* (2002), answers to frequently asked questions about the college recruiting process. Interviewed via telephone on August 24, 2002.

Russell, Cazzie. Former Chicago Carver basketball player. Currently basketball coach at Savannah (Georgia) College of Art and Design. Also associate pastor of the Happy Home Missionary Baptist church in Savannah. Interviewed via telephone on May 15, 2002.

Sanders, Don. A graduate of Ridgway in 1959 and the owner of the *Vienna (Ill.) Times,* a weekly newspaper. Interviewed at the farm of former Ridgway basketball coach Bob Dallas on August 19, 2002.

Saudargas, Alice. Widow of former West Rockford basketball coach Alex Saudargas. Interviewed at her home in Rockford and at old West Rockford High School on August 13, 2002. She also provided newspaper clippings and memorabilia from her husband's career.

Scheuerman, Sharm. Former Rock Island basketball player. Former head coach at Iowa. He was in the real estate business in Iowa City for thirty years. Currently employed as general manager for Athletes in Action and living in Denver. Interviewed via telephone on May 14, 2002.

Schmidt, Harv. Former Kankakee basketball player. Former head basketball coach at the University of Illinois. Now retired and living in Denver. Interviewed via telephone on April 29, 2002.

Schmitt, John. Former assistant basketball coach at Ridgway. Continues to teach and lives in Harrisburg. Interviewed at the farm of former Ridgway coach Bob Dallas on August 19, 2002.

Schnake, Don. Former Centralia basketball player and former head football coach at Elk Grove (Illinois) High School. Now retired. Interviewed via telephone on October 12, 2002.

Schneiter, John. Former Decatur and New Trier basketball coach. Now retired. Interviewed via telephone on April 10, 2002.

Scholz, Dave. Former Decatur basketball player. Currently works for a steel fabricator in Nashville. Interviewed via telephone on October 8, 2002.

Schreiter, Louis. Former superintendent of schools at Carrollton, Carlineville, and Mendon Unity. Now retired and living in Carrollton. Interviewed via telephone on June 6, 2002.

Schuckman, Matt. Sportswriter for the *Quincy (Ill.) Herald-Whig*. He provided copies of stories he had written on the Centralia, Collinsville, and Quincy basketball programs, Quincy coaches Sherrill Hanks and Jerry Leggett, and Quincy players Bruce Douglas and Michael Payne. Interviewed via telephone on October 28, 2002.

Schulz, Bill. Former Hebron basketball player. Owner of a hardware store in Waukegan. He lives in Northbrook. Interviewed via telephone on November 20, 2002.

Seaberg, Bill. Former Moline basketball player. Currently in the real estate business and living in Evergreen, Colorado. Interviewed via telephone on May 9, 2002.

Sedgwick, Chuck. Former Lyons (La Grange) Township basketball player. Former coach at Rich (East) Township in Park Forest. Now retired and living in Marco Island, Florida, and Hayward, Wisconsin. Interviewed via telephone on May 7, 2002.

Sell, Verl. Former football coach at Bloom Township in Chicago Heights. Also former Big Ten basketball official. Longtime friend of former Bloom basketball coach Wes Mason. Currently technical adviser to the supervisor of football officials for the Big Ten. He lives in Orland Park. Interviewed via telephone on May 17, 2002.

Selvie, Johnny. Former Chicago King basketball player. Currently head basketball coach at Chicago Bogan High School. Interviewed via telephone on November 6, 2002.

Shaw, Scott. Former Lyons (La Grange) Township basketball player. Currently the owner of Veritas Strategies, a financial planning company based in Doylestown, Pennsylvania. Interviewed via telephone on November 21, 2002.

Shidler, Dennis. Former Lawrenceville basketball player and brother of Jay Shidler. Now a broker with LPL Financial Services in Boston, Massachusetts. He lives in Winston-Salem, North Carolina. Interviewed via telephone on April 24, 2002.

Shidler, Jay. Former Lawrenceville basketball player. Currently bar and beverage manager at the Maker's Mark Club in Applebee's Park in Lexington, Kentucky. Interviewed via telephone at April 26, 2002.

Shirar, Linda Eveland. Daughter of former Paris basketball coach Ernie Eveland. Interviewed at her home in Paris on September 24, 2002. She also provided memorabilia on her father and Paris's state championship basketball teams of 1943 and 1947.

Simmons, Marty. Former Lawrenceville basketball player. Currently the head basketball coach at Southern Illinois University at Edwardsville. He lives in Edwardsville. Interviewed via telephone on May 16, 2002.

Sir, Brian. Former Maine South (Park Ridge) basketball player. Currently CEO of a financial services company based in Chicago. Interviewed via telephone on December 23, 2002.

Skertich, Brad. Former Staunton basketball player. Currently principal of Meissner Elementary School in Bunker Hill. Interviewed at Staunton High School on August 7, 2002.

Small, Bill. Former West Aurora basketball player. Former vice president of personnel and industrial relations for Lauhoff Grain Co. in Danville. He retired in 2002. He lives in Danville. Interviewed via telephone on April 4, 2002.

Smedley, Anthony (Tony). Former Chicago Carver basketball player. Currently lives in Madison, Wisconsin. Interviewed via telephone on May 6, 2002. He also provided a videotape copy of the Centralia/Carver 1963 state championship game.

Smith, Billy. Former Benton basketball player. Now a software consultant living in Benton. Interviewed at the Days Inn in Benton on August 19, 2002.

Smith, Dennis. Former Benton basketball player. He is a retired coal miner and lives in Benton. Interviewed at the Days Inn in Benton on August 19, 2002.

Smith, Grant. Former Pittsfield basketball player. Currently assistant football coach and varsity girls basketball coach at Oregon (Illinois) High School. Interviewed via telephone on September 6, 2002.

Smith, Ken. Former Cobden basketball player. Former correctional counselor at Marion, Illinois, federal prison. Now retired and living in Cobden. Interviewed via telephone on November 22, 2002.

Sommer, Jim. Former Pekin basketball player. Currently president of Sommer Brothers Seed Company in Pekin. Interviewed via telephone on September 12, 2002.

Spanich, Steve. Former Rock Island Alleman basketball player. Currently the administrator of Isaac Newton Christian Academy in Cedar Rapids, Iowa. Interviewed via telephone on May 1, 2002.

Spear, Bob. Former Quincy basketball player. Currently specializes in pediatric intensive care and pediatric anesthesia at Children's Hospital in San Diego. Interviewed via telephone on October 25, 2002.

Spurgeon, Lowell. Former Centralia basketball player. Now retired. Interviewed at the Green Grill Restaurant in Centralia on September 9, 2002.

Stallings, Ron. Former Ridgway basketball player. Former security guard for the Illinois Department of Corrections. Now retired and living in New Haven, Illinois. Interviewed on the farm of former Ridgway coach Bob Dallas near Harrisburg on August 18, 2002.

Stanton, Don. Former Pinckneyville basketball coach. Retired from school administration in 1994. He lives in Centralia. Interviewed via telephone on October 14, 2002.

Stevens, Danny. Former Ridgway basketball player. Currently principal of Massac County High School in Metropolis. Interviewed via telephone on October 16, 2002.

Stewart, Steve. Former Benton basketball player. Currently a teacher and coach in Murphysboro. Interviewed at the Days Inn in Benton on August 19, 2002.

Stiffend, Joe. Former Chicago Marshall basketball player. Now employed by the University of Cincinnati. Interviewed via telephone on June 8, 2002.

Stimpson, Charles. Former Chicago Hirsch basketball coach. Retired from coaching basketball in 1992. Now a part-time truck driver. He lives in Las Vegas, Nevada. Interviewed via telephone on May 1, 2002.

Stark, Shelly. A 1954 graduate of South Shore. A longtime fan of South Shore and Chicago Public League basketball. In 2002, he retired after thirty years in public relations marketing. Interviewed via telephone on November 11, 2002.

Stotlar, Gene. Former Pinckneyville basketball player. Retired from his general medical practice in 1991. Interviewed in Pinckneyville on September 10, 2002.

Stowell, Joe. Former Bradley University basketball coach. Now retired and living in Peoria. Interviewed via telephone on October 17, 2002.

Sullins, Quitman. Former Maine South (Park Ridge) basketball coach. Now retired. Interviewed via telephone on April 17, 2002, from his home in Booneville, Mississippi.

Sund, Rick. Former Elgin basketball player. Currently general manager of the Seattle SuperSonics. Interviewed via telephone on November 20, 2002.

Suttner, Roger. Former Ridgway basketball player. Currently a truck driver for a company in Harrisburg. Interviewed on the farm of former Ridgway coach Bob Dallas near Harrisburg on August 18, 2002.

Swanson, Barry. Former Galesburg basketball player and coach. Retired from coaching in 1996. He was chair of the language arts department at Lyons Township in La Grange until he retired from teaching in 2003. He lives in Galesburg. Interviewed via telephone on October 17, 2002.

Sweeting, Jamie. Former Pittsfield basketball player. Currently employed by the U.S. Postal Service and living in Jacksonville, Illinois. Interviewed via telephone on September 6, 2002.

Taylor, Bill "Pops." Centralia basketball fan. Interviewed at the Green Grill Restaurant in Centralia on September 9, 2002.

Thiel, Marilyn. Widow of former Galesburg coach John Thiel. She lives in Bloomington. Interviewed via telephone on October 9, 2002.

Thiel, Zach. Former Galesburg basketball player and son of former Galesburg coach John Thiel. Now sales branch manager for Royal Publishing Co. in Moline. He lives in Galesburg. Interviewed via telephone on October 9, 2002.

Thomas, Isiah. Former St. Joseph (Westchester) basketball player. A member of the NBA Hall of Fame. Former head coach of the Indiana Pacers. Currently head of basketball operations for the New York Knicks. Interviewed via telephone on December 16, 2002.

Thomas, LaMarr. Former Thornton (Harvey) Township basketball player. Currently employed by the Equal Employment Opportunity Commission in Chicago. Interviewed via telephone on June 5, 2002.

Thomas, Noble. Former Mount Vernon coach. Assisted former basketball coach Stan Changnon for six years. Now retired and living in Mount Vernon. Interviewed via telephone on June 6, 2002.

Thomas, Terry. Former Benton basketball player. Now retired and living in Benton. Interviewed at the Days Inn in Benton on August 19, 2002.

Thompson, Goff. Former Mount Vernon basketball player. He has spent nearly forty years in a family medical practice, running a medical rehabilitation and geriatrics unit. He lives in Mount Vernon. Interviewed via telephone on October 10, 2002.

Thompson, Herb. Former Moline basketball coach. His son, Scott, played on his teams from 1969 to 1972. Retired from coaching in 1977 to sell real estate. He lives in Moline. Interviewed via telephone on August 1, 2002.

Thompson, M. C. Former Chicago Marshall basketball player. Now retired and living in Atlanta. Interviewed via telephone on May 10, 2002.

Thompson, Prentiss. Former Chicago St. Elizabeth basketball player. Now retired and living in Glenwood. Interviewed via telephone on January 13, 2003.

Thompson, Scott. Former Moline basketball player. Former college basketball coach at Iowa, Arizona, Rice, Wichita State, and Cornell. Currently special assistant to the athletic director at Cornell. Interviewed via telephone on August 2, 2002.

Tokars, Jerry. Former Chicago De La Salle basketball coach. Now retired and living in Worth. Interviewed via telephone on November 19, 2002.

Toomey, Bill. Former Chicago South Shore basketball player. Now retired and living in Madison, Wisconsin. Interviewed via telephone on November 18, 2002.

Trahey, Dan. Former Chicago South Shore basketball player. Retired in 1993 after serving as a teacher and administrator for more than forty years. Interviewed via telephone on November 8, 2002. He also provided memorabilia on the South Shore team of 1944.

Tribble, Bobby. Former Chicago Simeon basketball player. Currently a physical education instructor at Beethoven Elementary School in Chicago. He lives in Chicago. Interviewed via telephone on October 31, 2002.

Trumpy, Bob. Former Springfield basketball player. Former player in the NFL. Currently a radio sports broadcaster in Cincinnati. Interviewed via telephone on May 3, 2002.

Umbles, Lee. Former Chicago Harlan basketball coach. Retired from coaching basketball in 1985. Retired from teaching in 1995. He lives in Chicago. Interviewed via telephone on December 20, 2002.

Van Scyoc, Dick. Former Peoria Manual basketball coach. After coaching for forty-five years, he is retired and living in Peoria. Interviewed at the Holiday Inn in Peoria on September 16, 2002.

Van Skike, Dave. Former Lyons (La Grange) Township basketball player. Currently a high school teacher in Durham, North Carolina. Interviewed via telephone on December 16, 2002.

Vaughn, Charles "Chico." Former Tamms basketball player. Now a security guard at Meridian High School. Lives in Cairo. Interviewed at Meridian High School on August 20, 2002.

Verber, George. Former assistant basketball coach at Maine South (Park Ridge). Now retired. Interviewed via telephone on June 3, 2002.

Verstraete, Whitey. Former Moline basketball player and former basketball coach at Rock Island at Moline. He retired from coaching in 1985 and went into private business. He currently lives in Moline and is a member of the county board and also serves as a township commissioner. Interviewed at Wharton Fieldhouse in Moline on August 12, 2002.

Wallace, Loren. Former Nokomis, Lincoln, Bloomington, and Quincy basketball coach. Now retired and living in Quincy. Interviewed at the Pier Restaurant in Quincy on September 4, 2002.

Walton, Lloyd. Former Mount Carmel, Marquette, and NBA basketball player. Currently works in Chicago. Interviewed via telephone on April 13, 2002.

Washington, Marcus. Former Lyons (La Grange) Township basketball player. Currently employed by Lucent Technologies and pastor of the St. Luke Missionary Baptist church in Maywood. Interviewed via telephone on November 22, 2002.

Watson, Jim. A graduate of Peoria Manual in 1955. A longtime friend of former Peoria Manual basketball coach Dick Van Scyoc. Now retired and living in Peoria. Interviewed via telephone on October 22, 2002.

Weber, Bert. Former assistant basketball coach at Collinsville and former principal at Glenbard East High School in Lombard. Now retired and living in Effingham. Interviewed via telephone on April 3, 2002.

Wentura, Dick. Former scoreboard operator and timekeeper for Quincy basketball games. Currently a member of the Adams County Merit Commission. He lives in Quincy. Interviewed via telephone on October 25, 2002.

Westendorf, Chuck. Former assistant basketball coach at Peoria Manual. Currently athletic director and assistant basketball coach at Peoria Central. He is former Peoria Manual basketball coach Dick Van Scyoc's son-in-law. Interviewed via telephone on October 18, 2002.

White, Charles. Former Peoria Central basketball player. Currently a national catastrophe claims specialist based in Peoria. Interviewed via telephone on May 30, 2002.

Williams, Herb. Former Centralia basketball player. Currently assistant chief administrator for East St. Louis Community College. He lives in Centralia. Interviewed via telephone on October 22, 2002.

Williams, Kent. Former Mount Vernon basketball player. Graduated from Southern Illinois University in Carbondale in 2003 and hopes for a career in coaching and professional basketball. He lives in Mount Vernon. Interviewed via telephone on October 26, 2002.

Williams, Walt. Former Proviso East (Maywood) basketball player. Currently assistant principal for student services at Glenbard South High School in Glen Ellyn. Interviewed via telephone on November 7, 2002.

Wilson, George. Former Chicago Marshall basketball player. Now retired and living in Cincinnati. Interviewed via telephone on May 4, 2002.

Wineburgh, Bud. Former Chicago South Shore basketball player. Currently president and CEO of Dwinn-Shaffer, a national mortgage company based in Chicago. He lives in Chicago. Interviewed via telephone on November 20, 2002.

Wisman, Jim. Former Quincy basketball player. Currently an executive vice president at the Leo Burnett advertising company in Chicago. Interviewed via telephone on October 9, 2002.

Wyatt, Thomas. Former East Aurora basketball player. Currently an assistant basketball coach at East Aurora. He also works with troubled teens at Linden Oaks, a DCFS holding facility based in Naperville. He lives in Aurora. Interviewed via telephone on December 19, 2002.

Yunkus, Rich. Former Benton basketball player. Currently an investment representative for the Edward Jones brokerage company in Benton. Interviewed at the Days Inn in Benton on August 19, 2002.

Print Sources:

Badgley, Matt. "The Integration of the Black Athlete." Undergraduate term paper, Southern Illinois University, 1996.

Batterson, Steve. "Reid Loses His Fire." *Quad-City Times,* February 13, 2001.

Bell, Taylor. "Aguirre: He's Nobody's Fool." *Chicago Daily News,* February 13, 1978.

———. "Carver's Victory Still No. 1 Stunner" and "Smedley Finds Fame Is Fleeting." *Chicago Sun-Times,* February 15, 1988.

———. "E. Aurora Movie Had Bad Ending." *Chicago Sun-Times,* March 22, 1989.

———. "Grunwald Makes It to the NBA." *Chicago Sun-Times,* May 10, 1999.

———. "Hitt Worthy of Recognition." *Chicago Sun-Times,* March 18, 1991.

———. "King's Cox Abdicates His Throne." *Chicago Sun-Times,* June 26, 2001.

———. "Memories Still Fond Even after Forty Years." *Chicago Sun-Times,* March 8, 1998.

———. "The Most Celebrated Undefeated Teams in the History of the Illinois High School Basketball Tournament." *Chicago Sun-Times,* February 25, 1991.

———. "Nikcevich's 'D' Remembered." *Chicago Sun-Times,* March 20, 2000.

———. "Panthers, Mosley Chill Hot Harris, Dunbar." *Chicago Daily News,* January 8, 1969.

———. "Proviso Champions Revisit Their Roots." *Chicago Sun-Times,* March 21, 1999.

———. "Rough Past Helps Hicks Enlighten Kids' Future." *Chicago Sun-Times,* September 15, 1986.

———. "Salario Spinning Basketball Yarns." *Chicago Sun-Times,* December 4, 1989.

———. "They Need to Know the Ghosts." *Chicago Sun-Times,* March 6–7, 1988.

Berkow, Ira. *The Du Sable Panthers: The Greatest, Blackest, Saddest Team from the Meanest Street in Chicago.* New York: Atheneum, 1978.

Champaign News-Gazette coverage of the 1955 state championship game, March 20, 1955.

Champaign News-Gazette coverage of the 1956 state championship game, March 18, 1956.

Champaign-Urbana Courier coverage of the 1956 state championship game, March 18, 1956.

Champaign-Urbana Courier coverage of the 1963 state championship game, March 24, 1963.

Champaign-Urbana Courier coverage of the 1965 state championship game, March 21, 1965.

Chicago Sun-Times coverage of the 1944 state semifinals, March 18, 1944.

Chicago Sun-Times coverage of the 1944 state consolation game, March 19, 1944.

Chicago Sun-Times coverage of the 1952 state championship game, March 23, 1952.

Chicago Sun-Times coverage of the 1954 state championship game, March 21, 1954.

Chicago Sun-Times coverage of the 1956 Chicago city championship game, April 4, 1956.

Chicago Sun-Times coverage of the 1958 state championship game, March 23, 1958.

Chicago Sun-Times coverage of the 1960 state championship game, March 20, 1960.

Chicago Tribune coverage of 1956 state championship game, March 18, 1956.

Doyle, Mike. "A Legend Is Dead." *Rockford Register-Republic,* July 11, 1990.

"Elgin High School Celebrating 100 Years of Boys Basketball." *(Arlington Heights, Ill.) Daily Herald,* special section, February 27, 2002.

Enright, Jim. *March Madness: The Story of High School Basketball in Illinois.* Bloomington: Illinois High School Association, 1977.

"Forever Giants." *Peoria Journal-Star,* special section, March 15, 2002.

"Four Closure." *Peoria Journal-Star,* special section, March 24, 1997.

French, Dave. "Stanley an Innovator, Gentleman." *Rockford Register-Republic,* July 11, 1990.

Goddard, Joe. "What's Up with Billy Harris?" *Chicago Sun-Times,* March 3, 2002.

Heston, Patrick C. *The Millennium Picks.* Maryville, Ill.: N.p., 2001.

Holtzman, Jerome. "La Grange Ousts Kays." *Chicago Sun-Times,* March 13, 1953.

Johnson, Scott, and Julie Kistler. *Once There Were Giants: How Tiny Hebron Won the Illinois High School Basketball Championship and the Hearts of Fans Forever.* Bloomington: Illinois High School Association, 2002.

Lenzi, Diana Eddleman. *Dike Eddleman: Illinois' Greatest Athlete.* Champaign, Ill.: Sports Publishing, Inc., 1997.

March Madness Encyclopedia, 1995–96 Edition. Bloomington: Illinois High School Association, 1995.

Merwin, Don. "La Grange Topples Kankakee, 83 to 74." *Kankakee Journal,* March 13, 1953.

Mottlow, Red. *Fast Break to Glory: Marshall High School's Ninety-Eight-Game Basketball Winning Streak.* Chicago: N.p., 2002.

Myslenski, Skip. "Joe Stiffend's Best Shot." *Chicago Tribune,* March 13, 1983.

———. "That Championship Season." *Chicago Tribune,* March 14, 1982.

Nesseler, Marc. "Reid Resigns as R.I. Coach." *Moline Dispatch,* February 13, 2001.

"Paris Hails First State Champion." *Paris Daily Beacon-News,* March 22, 1943.

Pinckneyville Democrat coverage of the 1988 state Class A supersectional game at Carbondale, March 9, 1988.

Pinckneyville Panther Booster Club. *Go Panthers: An Historical Tribute to Boys Basketball at Pinckneyville High School.* Pinckneyville, Ill.: Pinckneyville Panther Booster Club, 1998.

Pitol, Frank R. *The Wonderful World of Collinsville Basketball.* Collinsville, Ill.: Collinsville Herald Publishing Co., 1976.

Rockford Register-Republic coverage of the 1956 state championship game, March 18–19, 1956.

Schnake, Don. *Trout: The Old Man and the Orphans.* Elk Grove Village, Ill.: Richview Press, 1992.

Schmidt, George N. "The Cover-Up at King High." *The Chicago Reader,* October 1, 1982.

Sellett Michael. "In the Town of Benton, They Have a Dream." *Chicago Tribune,* May 2, 1971.

Talley, Rick. "Dolph Always Found Ways to Win." *Rockford Register-Republic,* July 11, 1990.

Weigel, Tim. "Billy the Kid: Will Dream Die?" *Chicago Daily News,* February 16, 1974.

Wilson, Mary. *To Benji with Love.* N.p.: African American Book Distributors, 1987.

Wittick, Bud. "Paris Dedicates Gym Tonight to Honor PHS Coach Ernie Eveland." *Paris Daily Beacon-News,* December 16, 1977.

Wolff, Alexander. *Big Game, Small World: A Basketball Adventure.* New York: Warner Books, 2002.

Wolff, Alexander, and Armen Keteyian. *Raw Recruits.* New York: Pocket Books, 1990.

Index

Taylor H. A. Bell covered high school basketball during a long career as a sports journalist, reporting for the *Champaign-Urbana* (Ill.) *Courier,* the *St. Louis Globe Democrat,* and the *Chicago Daily News* and *Sun-Times.* The recipient of several awards, including the Illinois Basketball Coaches Association's Buzzy O'Connor Award for contributions to basketball and the United Press International's Sportswriter of the Year, Bell has been inducted into the Chicago Journalism Hall of Fame, the Chicagoland Sports Hall of Fame, and the Illinois Basketball Coaches Association's Hall of Fame. He is now retired.

The University of Illinois Press
is a founding member of the
Association of American University Presses.

———————————————————

Composed in 9.5/13 Cheltenham
with Meta display
by Jim Proefrock
at the University of Illinois Press
Designed by Dennis Roberts
Manufactured by Sheridan Books, Inc.

University of Illinois Press
1325 South Oak Street
Champaign, IL 61820-6903
www.press.uillinois.edu